CENSORED

"Project Censored is one of the organizations that we should listen to, to be assured that our newspapers and our broadcasting outlets are practicing thorough and ethical journalism."—Walter Cronkite

"[*Censored*] should be affixed to the bulletin boards in every newsroom in America. And, perhaps read aloud to a few publishers and television executives."—Ralph Nader

"[*Censored*] offers devastating evidence of the dumbing-down of mainstream news in America. . . . Required reading for broadcasters, journalists and well-informed citizens."—*Los Angeles Times*

"A distant early warning system for society's problems."
—*American Journalism Review*

"One of the most significant media research projects in the country."
—I. F. Stone

"A terrific resource, especially for its directory of alternative media and organizations. . . . Recommended for media collections."
—*Library Journal*

"Project Censored shines a spotlight on news that an informed public must have . . . a vital contribution to our democratic process."
—Rhoda H. Karpatkin, President, Consumer's Union

"Buy it, read it, act on it. Our future depends on the knowledge this collection of suppressed stories allows us."—*San Diego Review*

"This volume chronicles 25 news stories about events that could affect all of us, but which we most likely did not hear or read about in the popular news media."—*Bloomsbury Review*

"*Censored* serves as a reminder that there is certainly more to the news than is easily available or willingly disclosed. To those of us who work in the newsrooms, it's an inspiration, an indictment, and an admonition to look deeper, ask more questions, then search for the truth in the answers we get."—*Creative Loafings*

"This invaluable resource deserves to be more widely known."
—*Wilson Library Bulletin*

CENSORED2009

The Top 25 Censored Stories

Edited by PETER PHILLIPS, ANDREW ROTH, and PROJECT CENSORED

INTRODUCTION BY CYNTHIA MCKINNEY
CARTOONS BY KHALIL BENDIB

Seven Stories Press

New York / London / Melbourne / Toronto

A Seven Stories Press First Edition

Seven Stories Press
140 Watts Street
New York, NY 10013
www.sevenstories.com

In Canada: Publishers Group Canada, 559 College Street, Suite 402, Toronto,
ON M6G 1A9

In the U.K.: Turnaround Publisher Services Ltd., Unit 3, Olympia Trading
Estate, Coburg Road, Wood Green, London N22 6TZ

In Australia: Palgrave Macmillan, 15–19 Claremont Street, South Yarra, VIC 3141

College professors may order examination copies of Seven Stories Press titles for
a free six-month trial period. To order, visit www.sevenstories.com/textbook/ or
fax on school letterhead to 212.226.1411.

ISSN 1074-5998

9 8 7 6 5 4 3 2 1

Book design by Jon Gilbert

Printed in the U.S.A.

Contents

Dedication

BARBARA SEAMAN

(September 11, 1935 – February 27, 2008)

Author, Friend, Feminist Health Activist

and

Project Censored National Judge

Preface

by Peter Phillips and Project Censored

Will the November 2008 election bring a meaningful change to America? Will getting rid of George W. Bush and Richard Cheney without impeachment or indictment really make a difference? Will a $600 billion war and defense budget be cut in half and used for desperately needed domestic spending? Will the $38 billion dollar profits of the top nine private health insurance companies—those parasitic intermediates between you and your doctor—be used instead for full healthcare coverage for all? Will habeas corpus be restored to the people? Will torture stop and the US withdraw from Iraq immediately? Will the US national security agencies stop mass spying on our personal communications? Will the neoconservative agenda of total military domination of the world be reversed?

The answer to these questions in the context of the current billion dollar presidential campaign is "probably not." The final candidates for the top two political parties are so deeply embedded with the military-industrial complex, the health insurance companies, Wall Street, and corporate media that it is difficult to determine where the boardrooms separate from the state rooms.

Fortunately, people are coming to understand that the US government's primary mission has become the protection of the wealthy and the continuing insurance of capital expansion worldwide. The US military—spending more than the rest of the militaries of the world combined—is the muscle behind this protect-capital-at-all-costs agenda, and will be used against the American people if deemed necessary to support the mission.

Americans are faced with a truth emergency (a media/news situation so dire that no other terminology fits—See chapter 11). This is not just a few activists calling the situation a truth emergency, but rather a nationwide network of human rights activists, impeachment advocates, election fraud researchers, 9/11 truthers, civil libertarians, environmentalists, and just plain upset Americans.

As such, the "Top 25 Censored Stories" in Chapter 1, stewarded again this year by Project Censored research coordinator Trish

Boreta, are the real news stories that fill in the gaps left by corporate media.

Chapter 2 follows with updates on censored stories from our 2008 volume, as well as key under-covered stories from prior years. Chapter 3, "Junk Food News and News Abuse," is our in-depth review of the most frivolous news stories contrasted with important real news from the same time periods. Kate Sims, Project Censored support staff, coordinated the research effort on Chapter 3 again this year.

Chapter 4 is a collaboration with *Yes! Magazine* edited by Kate Sims that details stories of hope and change we don't hear about in the mainstream corporate media.

Chapter 5, a research study by Sonoma State University professor Andrew Roth with researchers Sarah Maddox and Kaitlyn Pinson, includes a content analysis of how corporate media failed to cover the *Censored 2008* number one story on habeas corpus.

Chapter 6, "Universal Healthcare, Media, and the 2008 Presidential Campaign," was researched by Kat Pat Crespán, Carmela Rocha, Corey Sharp Sabatino, Bridget Thornton, and Peter Phillips.

Chapter 7 covers US television news bias in the Middle East regarding the Israel-Hamas conflict in Gaza. Research was conducted by Janeen Rashmawi, Nelson Calderon, Sarah Maddox, Christina Long, Andrew Hobbs, and Peter Phillips.

Chapter 8, always a welcome addition from the Center for Media and Democracy & PR Watch, was written by associate director Judith Siers-Poisson covering Merck pharmaceutical company's marketing of Gardasil.

Chapter 9, our annual "Fear and Favor" report from our friends at Fairness and Accuracy in Reporting (FAIR), is written this year by Janine Jackson and Peter Hart.

We again welcome the Index on Censorship's annual global review on press freedom as Chapter 10. Research this year was by Index news editor Padraig Reidy.

Chapter 11, "Truth Emergency Meets Media Reform," by Peter Phillips, Mickey S. Huff, Carmela Rocha, Andrew Hobbs, April Pearce, Kat Pat Crespán, Nelson Calderon, and David Kubiak, documents the first annual Truth Emergency Conference in Santa Cruz California in January 2008. The Santa Cruz organizing team conducted a sociological survey of the attendees at the Media Reform Conference in Minneapolis in June 2008 further documenting growing support for a response to the truth emergency in the US.

Chapter 12 is directly related to our censored story in Chapter 1 on the Winter Soldier hearings in Silver Spring, Maryland, in March 2008. These hearings were so important that we were compelled to more extensively document the testimonies of the Afghanistan and Iraq war veterans. Elizabeth Stinson from the Sonoma Peace and Justice Center attended the hearings and organized the chapter.

Practicing pediatrician and Sonoma County peace activist Gary Evans researched and wrote Chapter 13 on the Pentagon's child recruiting strategies.

Chapter 14, by college professors Mickey S. Huff and Paul W. Rea, addresses corporate media myth building as deliberate cultural deceit in American society.

Chapter 15, by SSU graduate student Nelson Calderon, addresses the US's disruptive involvement in Central and South America using thirty years of Project Censored news stories.

Project Censored's students, faculty, staff, and national judges welcome you to *Censored 2009*.

Project Censored Addresses Truth in America

by Cynthia McKinney

On Saturday, June 7, 2008, Hillary Clinton announced that her 2008 presidential bid is over, making Barack Obama the first-ever Black presidential nominee of a major party in the history of the United States.

Congratulations to Senator Obama for achieving such a feat!

Many of us never thought we would see in our lifetime a Black person with a real possibility of becoming president of the United States.

The fact that this is now possible is a sign of the deep discontent among the American people, and particularly among African Americans, with the corporate-dominated, business-as-usual politics that has prevailed in Washington for too many years.

While congratulating Senator Obama for a feat well done, I would also like to bring home the very real need for change and a few of the issues from Project Censored's annual report that must be addressed for the change needed in this country to be real.

Did you know that President Bush's first education advisor is now an education profiteer? Yes, that's right! It seems that a Bush protégée has found a way to present legislation to Congress, have it promoted in the press through questionable journalism tactics, and then assemble a well-connected cabal to profit from it, too! This year's Project Censored offering, "Bush Profiteers Collect Billions from No Child Left Behind," gives us all the "sad, but true" scoop on how things are done in Washington, with impunity, and in this case, the children and the taxpayers are left worse off and holding the bag. In the years since President Bush signed the No Child Left Behind Act, none of his budgets has come close to meeting the levels of funding authorized. Pentagon spending is at around $700 billion, can you imagine? And K-12 education is at about $38 billion. There's something wrong with that.

You probably knew about money misspent in Iraq, but did you know how some of those billions were lost? Nine billion dollars, to be exact, was misplaced when the Federal Reserve shipped $12 billion in cash bricks weighing a total of 363 tons. Our authors tell us that there was no auditing arm established by the Pentagon to track the money. Incredibly, and certainly not broadcast widely, was the fact that the Coalition Provisional Authority cash distribution arm had no formal documents establishing it and was run out of a home in La Jolla, California. Our authors tell us that it was a shell corporation with no certified public accountants on staff; its address of record was a post office box in the Bahamas where it was legally incorporated. Remember, that's Paul Bremer's former outfit. And although Bremer's father was president of the Christian Dior Perfumes Corporation in New York, something surely doesn't smell right about his role in Iraq at the time of the "loss" of that money!

And, you'd better not have any ideas about protesting the occupation of Iraq, because if you do, you're subject to have your assets seized by the United States government! The White House itself gives us this offering, along with Michel Chossudovsky at *Global Research*. Very quietly, George Bush signed an executive order entitled "Blocking Property of Certain Persons Who Threaten Stabilization Efforts in Iraq" that provides the president with the authority to confiscate the assets of US citizens and organizations who oppose US operations in Iraq.

A friend of mine recently announced her decision to leave the United States and relocate to Canada. Canada was a refuge for anti-war protesters during the Vietnam War era. And with our President viewing the US Constitution as just an inconvenient piece of paper, and the decrease in tolerance for dissent here in the United States, many are "Canada Dreamin'" once again. Well, they'd better think again. Because the US Department of Homeland Security will have even more suzerainty over Canada and Mexico as a result of the Security and Prosperity Partnership (SPP)—the militarization of the North American Free Trade Agreement (NAFTA). Story # 2 tells us that the SPP—headquartered in Washington—aims to integrate Canada, the United States, and Mexico into a single political, economic, and security bloc.

And finally, if there were ever any reason to immediately withdraw US troops from Iraq, the testimonies at Winter Soldier this year document the case. How poignant are the real-life experiences as told to us by Iraq veterans themselves. Their testimonies shed light on the complicity of high-ranking officials in the Bush administration and the Pentagon in violation of international law. The soldiers' testimony clearly establishes that Abu Ghraib and Haditha were not isolated incidents, but rather were part of a pattern of a bloody occupation.

As shocking as these stories are, the submissions to Project Censored included even more shocking new realities that we all must understand and counter. From slavery and human trafficking, to the gulag of jails, prisons, and juvenile detention centers, now being established inside the United States. And then there's the new FBI program called InfraGard, with over 25,000 members, which establishes a network of corporations from agribusiness to the chemical industry, to research and technology firms, working with the Department of Homeland Security and the Secret Service to prevent crime and provide expertise to the FBI. Yeah right!

When considered along with the language of Congresswoman Jane Harman's Homegrown Terrorism Prevention Act, the nature of executive orders, and an unprecedented number of arrests for marijuana, this is exactly the kind of public-private partnership that people in this country should be concerned about.

And thanks to Project Censored, we know about them all! From NATO, to 9/11, to the issue of Right of Return for Iraqis and the conditions inside that country, to indigenous rights and the treatment of the indigenous peoples in United Nations proceedings, to US efforts to attack the peaceful ballot-box revolutions that have taken place in Latin America, we are all richer because of the journalists who wrote these stories and the ability of Project Censored to highlight them and bring them to our attention.

Much of what is now happening in the world can be laid at the public policy doorstep of Washington, DC. Citizens can act to defend themselves and the integrity of our country only when they know what it is that our country is doing. When organizations take laudatory steps to protect that integrity, they, too, should be recognized—as is the case with CARE and its rejection of US food subsidies. From torture to food, the stories are here for our consideration in this year's Project Censored entries.

I welcome a real discussion of all the issues that face our country today and the real public policy options that exist to resolve them. For many Americans, this important discussion has been too vague or completely non-existent. Now is the time to talk about the concrete measures that will move our country forward: on race, war, climate change, the economy, healthcare, and education. Our votes and our political engagement must be about ensuring that fairness truly for all is embodied in "liberty and justice for all."

You would not have read about these issues if you relied solely on the US television news for your information. It is clear, however, that those who read and support Project Censored are in the know. They also are aware that the media in this country obviously do not want the people to be informed about the truths presented by Project Censored. And in the end, Project Censored is about the truth. Thank you for supporting Project Censored. And thank you, Project Censored, for not being afraid of telling us the truth.

———————————

CYNTHIA ANN MCKINNEY is an American politician from the US state of Georgia. McKinney served as a Democrat in the US House of Representatives from 1993 to 2003, and from 2005 to 2007, representing Georgia's eleventh and fourth congressional districts. McKinney was defeated in the 2002 Democratic primary, in part due to Republican crossover voting in Georgia's open primary election, which permits anyone from any party to vote in any party primary. Later returning to the House following her successor's run for Senate, she was defeated again in the same manner in the 2006 Democratic primary. She left the Democratic Party in September 2007 and joined the Green Party in order to continue her political issues in a more public forum.

CHAPTER I

The Top Censored Stories of 2007 and 2008

by Tricia Boreta and Project Censored

The final year of the Bush administration has peaked with a concentration of absolute executive power. The Constitution has been replaced with draconian (often secret) executive orders. There is a barrage of assaults on human rights, both at home and abroad. But who in polite company is talking about it? Reality has, by design, become a fringe topic.

Corporate media was too busy keeping the general public consumed with endless and empty blow-by-blow coverage of the entertaining 2008 presidential campaign, and Congress has either stepped aside, or is vigilantly working alongside the administration to allow the final ransacking of the federal budget and of the Constitution.

Project Censored and independent journalists from around the world have been busily tracking the actions of an unchecked and overly ripe empire. The undercovered news stories in *Censored 2009* reveal an increasingly desperate demand on the part of US corporations for conquest of international resources, as well as the increased reliance on military means to silence and eliminate dissent and achieve compliance. Our list this year shows more clearly than ever that the People's Will is the main enemy to be violently reckoned with by corporate America. The term "terrorism" is quickly expanding to include even thoughts that run contrary to US agenda of conquest.

Each of this year's Top 25 is a story of corptocracy—of life under a government of, for, and by large multinational corporations that increasingly diminish the value of life in the quest of profit. This system has turned our American pledge of allegiance to "liberty and justice for all" not only into a sad travesty, but importantly also into a reminder of our responsibility as Americans. A simple change in the faces of Empire in November 2008 will likely result in little more than another media orchestrated ruse. We need change that comes from more deeply knowing, spreading the truth about, and taking responsibility for the social and environmental realities that feed our consumptive American way of life.

Please share the following stories. Support independent media and a free Internet. Become active in *real* change.

1
—
Over One Million Iraqi Deaths Caused by US Occupation

Sources:
After Downing Street, July 6, 2007
Title: "Is the United States Killing 10,000 Iraqis Every Month? Or Is It More?"
Author: Michael Schwartz

AlterNet, September 17, 2007
Title: "Iraq death toll rivals Rwanda genocide, Cambodian killing fields"
Author: Joshua Holland

AlterNet, January 7, 2008
Title: "Iraq conflict has killed a million, says survey"
Author: Luke Baker

Inter Press Service, March 3, 2008
Title: "Iraq: Not our country to Return to"
Authors: Maki al-Nazzal and Dahr Jamail

Student Researchers: Danielle Stanton, Tim LeDonne, and Kat Pat Crespán
Faculty Evaluator: Heidi LaMoreaux, PhD

Over one million Iraqis have met violent deaths as a result of the 2003 invasion, according to a study conducted by the prestigious British polling group, Opinion Research Business (ORB). These numbers suggest that the invasion and occupation of Iraq rivals the mass killings of the last century—the human toll exceeds the 800,000 to 900,000 believed killed in the Rwandan genocide in 1994, and is approaching the number (1.7 million) who died in Cambodia's infamous "Killing Fields" during the Khmer Rouge era of the 1970s.

ORB's research covered fifteen of Iraq's eighteen provinces. Those not covered include two of Iraq's more volatile regions—Kerbala and Anbar—and the northern province of Arbil, where local authorities refused them a permit to work. In face-to-face interviews with 2,414 adults, the poll found that more than one in five respondents had had at least one death in their household as a result of the conflict, as opposed to natural cause.

Authors Joshua Holland and Michael Schwartz point out that the dominant narrative on Iraq—that most of the violence against Iraqis is being perpetrated by Iraqis themselves and is not our responsibility—is ill conceived. Interviewers from the *Lancet* report of October 2006 (*Censored 2006*, #2) asked Iraqi respondents how their loved ones died. Of deaths for which families were certain of the perpetrator, 56 percent were attributable to US forces or their allies. Schwartz suggests that if a low pro rata share of half the unattributed deaths were caused by US forces, a total of approximately 80 percent of Iraqi deaths are directly US perpetrated.

Even with the lower confirmed figures, by the end of 2006, an average of 5,000 Iraqis had been killed every month by US forces since the beginning of the occupation. However, the rate of fatalities in 2006 was twice as high as the overall average, meaning that the American average in 2006 was well over 10,000 per month, or over 300 Iraqis every day. With the surge that began in 2007, the current figure is likely even higher.

Schwartz points out that the logic to this carnage lies in a statistic released by the US military and reported by the Brookings Institute: for the first four years of the occupation the American military sent over 1,000 patrols each day into hostile neighborhoods, looking to capture or kill "insurgents" and "terrorists." (Since February 2007, the number has increased to nearly 5,000 patrols a day, if we include the Iraqi troops participating in the American surge.) Each patrol invades an average of thirty Iraqi homes a day, with the mission to interrogate, arrest, or kill suspects. In this context, any fighting age man is not just a suspect, but a potentially lethal adversary. Our soldiers are told not to take any chances (see Story #9).

According to US military statistics, again reported by the Brookings Institute, these patrols currently result in just under 3,000 firefights every month, or just under an average of one hundred per day (not counting the additional twenty-five or so involving our Iraqi allies). Thousands of patrols result in thousands of innocent Iraqi deaths and unconscionably brutal detentions.

Iraqis' attempts to escape the violence have resulted in a refugee crisis of mammoth proportion. According to the United Nations Refugee

Agency and the International Organization for Migration, in 2007 almost 5 million Iraqis had been displaced by violence in their country, the vast majority of which had fled since 2003. Over 2.4 million vacated their homes for safer areas within Iraq, up to 1.5 million were living in Syria, and over 1 million refugees were inhabiting Jordan, Iran, Egypt, Lebanon, Turkey, and Gulf States. Iraq's refugees, increasing by an average of almost 100,000 every month, have no legal work options in most host states and provinces and are increasingly desperate.[1]

Yet more Iraqis continue to flee their homes than the numbers returning, despite official claims to the contrary. Thousands fleeing say security is as bad as ever, and that to return would be to accept death. Most of those who return are subsequently displaced again.

Maki al-Nazzal and Dahr Jamail quote an Iraqi engineer now working at a restaurant in Damascus, "Return to Iraq? There is no Iraq to return to, my friend. Iraq only exists in our dreams and memories."

Another interviewee told the authors, "The US military say Fallujah is safe now while over 800 men are detained there under the worst conditions. . . . At least 750 out of the 800 detainees are not resistance fighters, but people who refused to collaborate with occupation forces and their tails." (Iraqis who collaborate with occupation forces are commonly referred to as "tails of the Americans.")

Another refugee from Baghdad said, "I took my family back home in January. The first night we arrived, Americans raided our house and kept us all in one room while their snipers used our rooftop to shoot at people. I decided to come back here [Damascus] the next morning after a horrifying night that we will never forget."

Citation

1. "The Iraqi Displacement Crisis," *Refugees International*, March 3, 2008.

UPDATE BY MICHAEL SCHWARTZ

The mortality statistics cited in "Is the United States Killing 10,000 Iraqis Every Month?" were based on another article suitable for Project Censored recognition, a scientific investigation of deaths caused by the war in Iraq. The original article, published in *Lancet* in 2006, received some dismissive coverage when it was released, and then disappeared from view as the mainstream media returned to reporting biased estimates that placed Iraqi casualties at about one-tenth the *Lancet* estimates. The corporate media blackout of the original study extended to my article as well, and has continued unabated, though the *Lancet* article has withstood several waves of criticism, while being confirmed and updated by other studies (*Censored 2006*, #2).

By early 2008, the best estimate, based on extrapolations and replications of the *Lancet* study, was that 1.2 million Iraqis had died as a consequence of the war. This figure has not, to my knowledge, been reported in any mass media outlet in the United States.

The blackout of the casualty figures was matched by a similar blackout of other main evidence in my article: that the Bush administration military strategy in Iraq assures vast property destruction and lethality on a daily basis. Rules of engagement that require the approximately one thousand US patrols each day to respond to any hostile act with overwhelming firepower—small arms, artillery, and air power—guarantee that large numbers of civilians will suffer and die. But the mainstream media refuses to cover this mayhem, even after the Winter Soldier meetings in March 2008 featured over one hundred Iraq veterans who testified to their own participation in what they call "atrocity producing situations." (see Story #9)

The effectiveness of the media blackout is vividly illustrated by an Associated Press poll conducted in February 2007, which asked a representative sample of US residents how many Iraqis had died as a result of the war. The average respondent thought the number was under 10,000, about 2 percent of the actual total at that time. This remarkable mass ignorance, like so many other elements of the Iraq War story, received no coverage in the mass media, not even by the Associated Press, which commissioned the study.

The Iraq Veterans Against the War has made the brutality of the occupation their special activist province. The slaughter of the Iraqi people is the foundation of their demand for immediate and full withdrawal of US troops, and the subject of their historic Winter Soldier meetings in Baltimore. Though there was no mainstream US media coverage of this event, the live streaming on Pacifica Radio and on the IVAW website reached a huge audience—including a vast number of active duty soldiers—with vivid descriptions of atrocities committed by the US war machine. A growing number of independent news sites now feature regular coverage of this aspect of the war, including *Democracy Now!*, Tom Dispatch, Dahr Jamail's MidEast Dispatches, Informed Comment, Antiwar.com, and ZNet.

UPDATE BY MAKI AL-NAZZAL AND DAHR JAMAIL

The promotion of US general David Petraeus to head CENTCOM, and General Raymond Odierno to replace Petraeus as commanding general of the Multi-National Force in Iraq, provoked a lot of anger amongst Iraqis in both Syria and Jordan. The two generals who convinced US and international society of improvement in Iraq do not seem to have succeeded in convincing Iraqi refugees of their success.

"Just like the Bush Administration decorated Paul Bremer (former head of the Coalition Provisional Authority), they are rewarding others who participated in the destruction to Iraq," stated Muhammad Shamil, an Iraqi journalist who fled Iraq to Syria in 2006. "What they call violence was concentrated in some parts of Iraq, but now spread to be all over the country, thanks to US war heroes. People are getting killed, evicted or detained by the thousands, from Basra (South) to Mosul (North)."

Other Iraqi refugees seem to have changed attitudes regarding their hopes to return. Compared to when this story was published in March 2008, the refugee crisis continues to deepen. This is exacerbated by the fact that most Iraqis have no intention of returning home. Instead, they are looking for permanent residence in other countries.

"I decided to stop dreaming of going back home and find myself a new home anywhere in the world if I could," said thirty-two-year-old Maha Numan in Syria, "I have been a refugee for three years now living on the dream of return, but I decided to stop dreaming. I have lost faith in all leaders of the world after the surges of Basra, Sadr City and now Mosul. This seems to be endless and one has to work harder on finding a safe haven for one's family."

Iraqis in Syria know a lot more of the news about their country than most journalists. At an Internet café in Damascus, each of them calls his hometown and reports the happenings of the day to other Iraqi refugees. News of ongoing violence across much of Iraq convinces them to remain abroad.

"There were four various explosions in Fallujah today," said Salam Adel, who worked as a translator for US forces in Fallujah in 2005. "And they say it is safe to go back! Damn them, go back for what? For roadside bombs or car bombs?"

It has been important, politically, for the Bush administration to claim that the situation in Iraq is improving. This claim has been assisted by a complicit corporate media. However, the 1.5 million Iraqis in Syria, and over 750,000 in Jordan, will tell you differently. Otherwise, they would not remain outside of Iraq.

To obtain updated information on the refugee crisis, see http://www.irinnews.org/IRIN-ME.aspx, http://www.iraqredcrescent .org/, http://www.refugeesinternational.org/section/waystohelp, http://www.unhcr.org/iraq.html, and http://www.dahrjamailiraq.com/.

2

Security and Prosperity Partnership: Militarized NAFTA

Sources:
Center for International Policy, May 30, 2007
Title: "'Deep Integration'—the Anti-Democratic Expansion of NAFTA"
Author: Laura Carlsen

Global Research, July 19, 2007
Title: "The Militarization and Annexation of North America"
Author: Stephen Lendman

Global Research, August 2, 2007
Title: "North American Union: The SPP is a 'hostile takeover' of democratic government and an end to the Rule of Law"
Author: Constance Fogal

Student Researchers: Rebecca Newsome and Andrea Lochtefeld
Faculty Evaluator: Ron Lopez, PhD

Leaders of Canada, the US, and Mexico have been meeting to secretly expand the North American Free Trade Agreement (NAFTA) with "deep integration" of a more militarized tri-national Homeland Security force. Taking shape under the radar of the respective governments and without public knowledge or consideration, the Security and Prosperity Partnership (SPP)—headquartered in Washington—aims to integrate the three nations into a single political, economic, and security bloc.

The SPP was launched at a meeting of Presidents George W. Bush and Vicente Fox, and Prime Minister Paul Martin, in Waco, Texas, on March 31, 2005. The official US web page describes the SPP as ". . . a

White House-led initiative among the United States and Canada and Mexico to increase security and to enhance prosperity . . ." The SPP is not a law, or a treaty, or even a signed agreement. All these would require public debate and participation of Congress.

The SPP was born in the "war on terror" era and reflects an inordinate emphasis on US security as interpreted by the Department of Homeland Security. Its accords mandate border actions, military and police training, modernization of equipment, and adoption of new technologies, all under the logic of the US counter-terrorism campaign. Head of Homeland Security Michael Chertoff, along with Secretary of State Condoleezza Rice and Secretary of Finance Carlos Gutierrez, are the three officials charged with attending SPP ministerial conferences.

Measures to coordinate security have pressured Mexico to militarize its southern border. US military elements already operate inside Mexico and the DEA and the FBI have initiated training programs for the Mexican Army (now involved in the drug war), federal and state police, and intelligence units. Stephen Lendman states that a Pentagon briefing paper hinted at a US invasion if the country became destabilized or the government faced the threat of being overthrown because of "widespread economic and social chaos" that would jeopardize US investments, access to oil, overall trade, and would create great numbers of immigrants heading north.

Canada's influential Department of National Defence; its new Chief of Defence Staff, General Rick Hillier; and Defense Minister Gordon O'Connor are on board as well. They're committed to ramping up the nation's military spending and linking with America's "war on terror."

The SPP created the North American Competitiveness Council (NACC) that serves as an official tri-national SPP working group. The group is composed of representatives of thirty giant North American companies, including General Electric, Ford Motors, General Motors, Wal-Mart, Lockheed-Martin, Merck, and Chevron.

NACC's recommendations centered on "private sector involvement" being "a key step to enhancing North America's competitive position in global markets and is the driving force behind innovation and growth." The NACC stressed the importance of establishing policies for maximum profits.

The US-guided agenda prioritizes corporate-friendly access to resources, especially Canadian and Mexican oil and water. The NACC's policy states that "the prosperity of the United States relies heavily on a secure supply of imported energy." US energy security is seen as a top priority encouraging Canada and Mexico to allow privatization of state-run enterprises like Mexico's nationalized oil company, PEMEX. In January 2008, Halliburton signed a $683 million contract with PEMEX to drill fifty-eight new test holes in Chiapas and Tabasco and take over maintenance of pipelines. This is the latest of $2 billion in contracts Halliburton has received from PEMEX during Fox's and current Mexican president Felipe Calderone's administrations, which the opposition warns has become the public front for US monopoly capital privatization.[1] US policy seeks to insure America gets unlimited access to Canada water as well.

Connie Fogal of Canadian Action Party says, "The SPP is the hostile takeover of the apparatus of democratic government . . . a coup d'etat over the government operations of Canada, US and Mexico."

Citation
1. "Mexican Farmers Protest NAFTA Hardships," *People's Weekly World*, February 7, 2008.

UPDATE BY STEPHEN LENDMAN
A fourth SPP summit was held in New Orleans from April 22 to 24, 2008. George Bush, Canada's Prime Minister Stephen Harper, and Mexico's President Felipe Calderon attended. Protesters held what they called a "people's summit." They were in the streets and held workshops to inform people how destructive SPP is, strengthen networking and organizational ties against it, maintain online information about their activities, promote efforts and build added support, and affirm their determination to continue resisting a hugely repressive corporate-sponsored agenda.

Opponents call the "Partnership" NAFTA on steroids. Business-friendly opposition also exists. The prominent Coalition to Block the North American Union (NAU) is backed by the Conservative Caucus, which has a "NAU War Room," a "headquarters of the national campaign to expose and halt America's absorption into a North American Union with Canada and Mexico." It opposes building "a massive, continental 'NAFTA Superhighway.'"

This coalition has congressional allies, and on January 2007, Rep. Virgil Goode and six co-sponsors introduced House Concurrent Resolution 40, which expresses "the sense of Congress that the United

States should not engage in (building a NAFTA) Superhighway System or enter into a NAU with Mexico and Canada."

The April summit reaffirmed SPP's intentions—to create a borderless North America, dissolve national sovereignty, put corporate giants in control, and assure big US companies most of it. It's also to create fortress-North America by militarizing the continent under US command.

SPP maintains a website. Its "key accomplishments" since August 2007 are updated as of April 22, 2008. The information is too detailed for this update, but can be accessed from the following link: http://www.spp.gov/pdf/key_accomplishments_since_august_2007.pdf.

The website lists principles agreed to; bilateral deals struck; negotiations concluded; study assessments released; agreements on the "Free Flow of Information"; law enforcement activities; efforts related to intellectual property, border and long-haul trucking enforcement; import licensing procedures; food and product safety issues; energy issues (with special focus on oil); infrastructure development; emergency management; and much more. It's all laid out in deceptively understated tones to hide its continental aim—to enable enhanced corporate exploitation with as little public knowledge as possible.

Militarization includes the US Northern Command (NORTHCOM), established in October 2002, which has air, land, and sea responsibility for the continent regardless of Posse Comitatus limitations that no longer apply or sovereign borders that are easily erased. The Department of Homeland Security (DHS) and its Immigration and Customs Enforcement (ICE) also have large roles. So does the FBI, CIA, all US spy agencies, militarized state and local police, National Guard forces, and paramilitary mercenaries like Blackwater USA.

They're headed anywhere on the continent with license to operate as freely as in Iraq and New Orleans post-Katrina. They'll be able to turn hemispheric streets into versions of Baghdad and make them unfit to live on if things come to that.

Consider other militarizing developments as well. On February 14, 2008, the US and Canada agreed to allow American troops inside Canada. Canadians were told nothing of this agreement, which was drafted in 2002. Neither was it discussed in Congress or in the Canadian House of Commons. The agreement establishes "bilateral integration" of military command structures in areas of immigration, law enforcement, intelligence, or whatever else the Pentagon or Washington wishes. Overall, it's part of the "war on terror" and militarizing the continent to make it "safer" for business and being prepared for any civilian opposition.

Mexico is also being targeted, with a "Plan Mexico" that was announced in October 2007. It's a Mexican and Central American security plan called the Merida Initiative, supported by $1.4 billion in allocated aid. Congress will soon vote on this initiative, likely well before this is published. It's a "regional security cooperation initiative" similar to Plan Colombia and presented as an effort to fight drug trafficking.

In fact, the Merida Initiative is part of SPP's militarization of Mexico and gives Washington more control of the country. Most of the aid goes to Mexico's military and police forces, with a major portion earmarked for US defense contractors for equipment, training, and maintenance. The touchy issue of deploying US troops will be avoided by instead employing private US security forces, i.e., Blackwater and DynCorp.

STEPHEN LENDMAN lives in Chicago and can be reached at lendmanstephen@sbcglobal.net. Also visit his blog at sjlendman.blogspot.com and listen to *The Global Research News Hour* on RepublicBroadcasting.org, Mondays from 11 AM to 1 PM CT.

3

InfraGard: The FBI Deputizes Business

Source:
The Progressive, February 7, 2008
Title: "Exclusive! The FBI Deputizes Business"
Author: Matthew Rothschild

Student Researchers: Chris Armanino and Sarah Maddox
Faculty Evaluator: Josh Meisel, PhD

More than 23,000 representatives of private industry are working quietly with the FBI and the Department of Homeland Security (DHS) to collect and provide information on fellow Americans. In return, members of this rapidly growing group, called InfraGard, receive secret warnings of terrorist threats before the public, and at times before elected officials. "There is evidence that InfraGard may be closer to a corporate Total Information Awareness program (TIPS), turning private-sector corporations—some of which may be in a position to observe the activities of millions of individual customers—into surrogate eyes and ears for the FBI," according to an ACLU report titled "The Surveillance-Industrial Complex: How the American Government Is Conscripting Businesses and Individuals in the Construction of a Surveillance Society."

InfraGard, with members from 350 companies of the Fortune 500, started in Cleveland back in 1996, when the private sector there cooperated with the FBI to investigate cyber threats. "Then the FBI cloned it," says Phyllis Schneck, chairman of the board of directors of the Infra-Gard National Members Alliance, and the prime mover behind the growth of InfraGard over the last several years.

FBI Director Robert Mueller addressed an InfraGard convention on August 9, 2005. "To date, there are more than 11,000 members of InfraGard . . . from our perspective, that amounts to 11,000 contacts . . . and 11,000 partners in our mission to protect America." He added a little later, "Those of you in the private sector are the first line of defense."

On May 9, 2007, George Bush issued National Security Presidential Directive 51 entitled "National Continuity Policy." In it, he instructed the Secretary of Homeland Security to coordinate with "private sector owners and operators of critical infrastructure, as appropriate, in order to provide for the delivery of essential services during an emergency."

"They're very much looped into our readiness capability," says Amy Kudwa, spokeswoman for the DHS. "We provide speakers, as well as joint presentations [with the FBI]. We also train alongside them, and they have participated, sometimes hundreds at a time, in national preparation drills." According to more than one interviewed member, an additional benefit to InfraGard membership is permission to shoot to kill in the event of martial law, without fear of prosecution.

"We get very easy access to secure information that only goes to InfraGard members," Schneck says. "If you had to call 1-800-FBI, you probably wouldn't bother," she says. "But if you knew Joe from the local meeting you had with him over a donut, you might call. Either to give or to get [information]. We want everyone to have a little black book."

Jay Stanley, public education director of the ACLU's technology and liberty program, warns that, "The FBI should not be creating a privileged class of Americans who get special treatment. There's no 'business class' in law enforcement. If there's information the FBI can share with 22,000 corporate bigwigs, why don't they just share it with the public? That's who their real 'special relationship' is supposed to be with. Secrecy is not a party favor to be given out to friends. . . . This bears a disturbing resemblance to the FBI's handing out 'goodies' to corporations in return for folding them into its domestic surveillance machinery."

InfraGard is not readily accessible to the general public. Its communications with the FBI and DHS are beyond the reach of the Freedom of Information Act under the "trade secrets" exemption, its website says. And any conversation with the public or the media is to be carefully rehearsed.

UPDATE BY MATT ROTHSCHILD

The Progressive sent out a press release on the InfraGard story, and I was interviewed on *Air America, Democracy Now!* and lots of other alternative radio shows. But the mainstream media have ignored this story, with the exception of one small wire service report. The FBI hasn't ignored it, though.

On February 15, the FBI issued a press release denouncing our article.

"The article's claims are patently false," said the FBI's Cyber Division Assistant Director Shawn Henry. "InfraGard members have no extraordinary powers and have no greater right to 'shoot to kill' than other civilians."

"No greater right"? That's odd language, isn't it? It reminded me of a quote in my article from Curt Haugen, CEO of S'Curo Group, and a proud InfraGard member. When I asked him about whether the FBI or Homeland Security agents had told InfraGard members they could use lethal force in an emergency, he said: "That much I cannot comment on. But as a private citizen, you have the right to use force if you feel threatened."

Note that the FBI did not deny that it ever told InfraGard members that they could "shoot to kill." All that Henry said was that InfraGard members "have no greater right." That doesn't exactly blow a hole in my story.

The FBI seemed put out that I did not give enough information about the meeting the whistleblower attended. "Unfortunately, the author of the *Progressive* article refused even to identify when or where the claimed 'small meeting' occurred in which issues of martial law were discussed," Henry said in the press release. "If we get that information, the FBI certainly will follow up and clarify any possible misunderstandings."

The reason I didn't identify where or when the meeting took place is obvious: I didn't want to reveal anything that would expose my whistleblower.

Incidentally, the press release fails to mention that I received confirmation about discussions of "lethal force" from another member of InfraGard, whom I did name.

I stick by every single word of my story. And I call on Congress to investigate InfraGard and to inspect the plans that the FBI may have in store, not only for InfraGard, but for all of us in times of an emergency.

One final note: since the story appeared, I've received several new leads, including one confirming that a private company has been given "lethal powers."

4

ILEA: Is the US Restarting Dirty Wars in Latin America?

Sources:

Upside Down World, June 14, 2007
Title: "Exporting US 'Criminal Justice' to Latin America"
Author: Community in Solidarity with the People of El Salvador

NACLA Report on the Americas, March/April 2008
Title: "Another SOA?: A Police Academy in El Salvador Worries Critics"
Author: Wes Enzinna

CISPES, March 15, 2007
Title: "ILEA Funding Approved by Salvadoran Right Wing Legislators"
Author: Community in Solidarity with the People of El Salvador

AlterNet, August 31, 2007
Title: "Is George Bush Restarting Latin America's 'Dirty Wars'?"
Author: Benjamin Dangl

Student Researchers: Courtney Snow, Erica Elkinton, and April Pearce
Faculty Evaluator: Jessica Taft, PhD, and Jeffrey Reeder, PhD

A resurgence of US-backed militarism threatens peace and democracy in Latin America. By 2005, US military aid to Latin America had increased by thirty-four times the amount spent in 2000. In a marked shift in US military strategy, secretive training of Latin American military and police personnel that used to just take place at the notorious School of the Americas, in Fort Benning, Georgia—including torture and execution techniques—is now decentralized. The 2008 US federal budget includes $16.5 million to fund an International Law Enforcement Academy (ILEA) in El Salvador, with satellite operations in Peru. With provision of immunity from charges of crimes against humanity, each academy will train an average of 1,500 police officers, judges, prosecutors, and other law enforcement officials throughout Latin America per year in "counterterrorism techniques."

The academy in El Salvador is part of a network of ILEAs created in 1995 under President Bill Clinton, who touted the training facilities as a series of US schools "throughout the world to combat international drug trafficking, criminality, and terrorism through strengthened international cooperation." There are ILEAs in Budapest, Hungary; Bangkok, Thailand; Gaborone, Botswana; and Roswell, New Mexico.

According to ILEA directors, the facility in El Salvador is designed to make Latin America "safe for foreign investment" by "providing regional security and economic stability and combating crime." Most instructors come from US agencies such as the Drug Enforcement Agency (DEA), Immigration and Customs Enforcement (ICE), and the FBI, the latter of which has had a remarkably large presence in El Salvador since opening its own office there in 2005. Most of the school's expenses are paid with US tax payers' dollars.

Salvadorans refer to the ILEA as a new School of the Americas (SOA) for police. Suspicions are exacerbated by comparable policies of secrecy. As with SOA, the ILEA list of attendees and graduates is classified, as is course content. Many observers are troubled by this secrecy, considering how SOA atrocities came to light with *Washington Post* reporter Dana Priest's discovery, in September 1996, of SOA torture training manuals, and later with the acquisition by the founder of SOA Watch, Father Roy Bourgeois, of a previously classified list of SOA graduates, many of whom were recognized as leaders of death squads and notorious counterinsurgency groups.

After Condoleezza Rice announced plans for the ILEA in San Salvador at a June 2005 Organization of American States meeting in Miami, Father Roy wrote, "The legacy of US training of security forces at the SOA and throughout Latin America is one of bloodshed, of torture, of the targeting of civilian populations, of desaparecidos . . . Rice's recent announcement about plans for the creation of an international law enforcement academy in El Salvador should raise serious concerns for anyone who cares about human rights."

Suspicions are further aggravated by the US-mandated immunity clause that exempts ILEA personnel from crimes against humanity.

Though lack of transparency makes it impossible to know the content of courses, the conduct of the Salvadoran police—who compose 25 percent of the academy's graduates—has shown an alarming turn for the worse since the ILEA was inaugurated. In early May 2007, the Archbishop's Legal Aid and Human Rights Defense Office (Tutela Legal) released a report implicating the Salvadoran National Police (PNC) in eight death squad–style assassinations in 2006 alone. Meanwhile, the Salvadoran Human Rights Defense Office has also published reports connecting the

PNC to death squads and repeated cases of corruption and misconduct.

While US interest in ILEAs is to ensure an environment that protects free trade and US economic interests, the PNC has played an active role in a crackdown against civil liberties, aimed at curbing both crime and social protest. Free trade agreements like CAFTA have been highly contentious, and President Saca's administration has gone to significant lengths to ensure that they succeed—including passing an anti-terror law in September 2006, modeled on the USA PATRIOT Act, that has been used to arrest everyone from anti-water-privatization activists to street venders who violate CAFTA's intellectual property rules (see Story #11).

As ILEA graduates are employed throughout Latin America, the US military is establishing similar mechanisms of cooperation throughout the region as well. The ILEA joins a host of other police and military training facilities that are run by US agencies such as the FBI, ICE, and the DEA, as well as programs run by private US security companies like DynCorp International and Blackwater.

Ben Dangl notes that in carrying on the legacy of Latin America's "Dirty Wars" of the 1970s and 1980s, in which kidnapping, torture, and murder were used to squash dissent and political opponents, Colombia and Paraguay also illustrate four characteristics of right-wing militarism in South America: joint exercises with the US military in counterinsurgency training; monitoring potential dissidents and social organizations; the use of private mercenaries for security; and the criminalization of social protest through "anti-terrorism" tactics and legislation.

UPDATE BY WES ENZINNA

On May 22, the US Congress approved the "Merida Initiative," which, as part of a $450 million package for anti-gang and anti-crime programs in Mexico and Central America, provides $2 million for the ILEA San Salvador's 2009 budget. With these new funds the academy will step up its efforts, training police from throughout the hemisphere, without public oversight or transparency as to the academy's operations or curriculum. What exactly is taught at the school remains a secret, and the involvement of the National Civilian Police (PNC) at the academy continues unabated, as does alleged PNC abuse.

While Instituto de Derechos Humanos de la Universidad Centroamericana (IDHUCA) director Benjamin Cuellar's presence at the school has been the source of scorn and criticism in El Salvador—a topic I focused on in my article—a US human rights organization, the Washington Office on Latin America (WOLA), has publicly come to Cuellar's defense. At the same time, WOLA is currently negotiating with the State Department to work jointly with Cuellar and IDHUCA to monitor the ILEA. While WOLA's logic is that they hope "to press for greater transparency and accountability within the institution," they have not articulated a plan for how exactly they are going to accomplish what Cuellar has been unable to achieve (making the school more transparent, making the curriculum public), nor have they addressed the way in which their presence at the school, like Cuellar's, might offer legitimacy to the ILEA's activities without actually producing any changes in the way the academy operates. As Lesley Gill pointed out in my original piece, the use of human rights discourse and the co-optation of human rights advocates by US military and police institutions in Latin America is a tried-and-true public relations strategy pioneered at the infamous School of the Americas, and it is *not*, Gill reminds us, "indicative of any effort by the US to reform the military or police forces they are involved with."

Only time will tell whether or not WOLA's planned partnership with the State Department to monitor the ILEA will help make the school more transparent, or whether it will lend legitimacy to an academy that continues to be linked to copious human rights abuses.

The signs, however, are not promising. In March, the Freedom of Information Act (FOIA) request made by this writer for ILEA course materials was rejected because, as the rejection letter states, "disclosure of these training materials could reasonably be expected to risk circumvention of the law. Additionally, the techniques and procedures at issue are not well known to the public."

Since publication of my article, PNC abuse and political assassinations in El Salvador have continued, and ILEA secrecy appears only to have become more entrenched, despite Cuellar and IDHUCA's involvement and despite increased international protest. It is still unclear whether or not the ILEA will turn out to be "another School of Assassins," as critics call the academy. If the present situation is any indication, however, these critics may prove to be correct.

UPDATE BY BENJAMIN DANGL

A number of recent developments have dramatically changed the military and political landscape of Latin America. While some electoral victories in

Latin America signal a regional shift to the left, Washington continues to expand its military and navy presence throughout the hemisphere.

On April 20, 2008, left-leaning Fernando Lugo was elected president of Paraguay. His victory broke the right-wing Colorado Party's sixty-one-year rule. Lugo, a former bishop who endorses Liberation Theology, joins a growing list of left-of-center leaders throughout the region and has pledged to crack down on Paraguay's human rights violations linked to US–Paraguayan military relations. Shortly after his victory, Lugo told reporters that Washington must acknowledge the new regional environment in which Latin American governments "won't accept any type of intervention from any country, no matter how big it is."

In neighboring Bolivia, leftist indigenous president Evo Morales has faced increased resistance from the right-wing opposition. US government documents and interviews on the ground in Bolivia prove that Washington has been spending millions of dollars to empower the Bolivian right through the US Agency for International Development and the National Endowment for Democracy. (For more on this topic, see "Undermining Bolivia," *The Progressive*, February 2008, www.progressive.org/mag_danglo208.)

On March 1, 2008, the Colombian military bombed an encampment of the Revolutionary Armed Forces of Colombia (FARC) on Ecuadorian soil, sparking a regional crisis. This attack was part of a decades-long conflict fueled by US military training and funding of the Colombian military.

The following month, on April 24, the Pentagon announced that the US Navy's Fourth Fleet would be repositioned to monitor activity in the Caribbean and Central and South America. The Fourth Fleet hadn't been operating in the area since 1950. Analysts in the region suggest that the Fourth Fleet's reactivation is a warning to Latin American leaders, such as Venezuela's Hugo Chávez, that are working to build a progressive regional bloc outside of Washington's influence.

Though Washington continues to expand its reach throughout an increasingly leftist Latin America, regional alliances such as the Bolivarian Alternative for the Americas are growing between progressive Latin American leaders. Such political, economic, and military cooperation is effectively countering US hegemony. At the same time, the future of US–Latin American relations will depend largely on how the next US president interacts with this radically transformed region.

While most corporate media ignores Latin America, their reporting on the region is usually biased against the region's leftist leaders and social movements. Two online publications that provide ongoing reporting and analysis on the region are UpsideDownWorld.org, a website covering activism and politics in Latin America, and TowardFreedom.com, a progressive perspective on world events. Activists interested in confronting US military aggression in Latin America could visit the School of the Americas Watch website: soaw.org. For information on US military operations in the region and the hopeful response among progressive governments and social movements, see my book, *The Price of Fire: Resource Wars and Social Movements in Bolivia* (AK Press).

5

Seizing War Protesters' Assets

Sources:
Global Research, July 2007
Title: "Bush Executive Order: Criminalizing the Antiwar Movement"
Author: Michel Chossudovsky

The Progressive, August 2007
Title: "Bush's Executive Order Even Worse Than the One on Iraq"
Author: Matthew Rothschild

Student Researchers: Chris Navarre and Jennifer Routh
Faculty Evaluator: Amy Kittlestrom, PhD

President Bush has signed two executive orders that would allow the US Treasury Department to seize the property of any person perceived to, directly or indirectly, pose a threat to US operations in the Middle East.

The first of these executive orders, titled "Blocking Property of Certain Persons Who Threaten Stabilization Efforts in Iraq," signed by Bush on July 17, 2007, authorizes the Secretary of Treasury, in consultation with the Secretary of State and the Secretary of Defense, to confiscate the assets of US citizens and organizations who "directly or indirectly" pose a risk to US operations in Iraq. Bush's order states:

> I have issued an Executive Order blocking property of persons determined 1) to have committed, *or pose a significant risk of* committing, an act or acts of violence that have the purpose *or effect* of threatening the peace or stability of Iraq or the Government

of Iraq or undermining efforts to promote economic reconstruction and political reform in Iraq . . . or 2) to have materially assisted, sponsored, or provided financial, material, logistical, or technical support for, or goods or services in support of, such an act or acts of violence *or* any person whose property and interests in property are blocked pursuant to this order . . .

Section five of this order announces that, "because of the ability to transfer funds or other assets instantaneously, prior notice to such persons of measures to be taken pursuant to this order would render these measures ineffectual. I therefore determine . . . there need be no prior notice of listing or determination [of seizure] . . ."

On August 1, Bush issued a similar executive order, titled "Blocking Property of Persons Undermining the Sovereignty of Lebanon or Its Democratic Processes and Institutions." While the text in this order is, for the most part, identical to the first, the order regarding Lebanon is more severe.

While both orders bypass the Constitutional right to due process of law in giving the Secretary of Treasury authority to seize properties of those persons *posing a risk of* violence, or in any vague way assisting opposition to US agenda, the August 1 order targets any person determined to have taken, or to pose a significant risk of taking, *actions*—violent or nonviolent—that undermine operations in Lebanon. The act further authorizes freezing the assets of "a spouse or dependent child" of any person whose property is frozen. The executive order on Lebanon also bans providing food, shelter, medicine, or any humanitarian aid to those whose assets have been seized—including the "dependent children" referred to above.

Vaguely written and dangerously open to broad interpretation, this unconstitutional order allows for the arbitrary targeting of any American for dispossession of all belongings and demands ostracism from society. Bruce Fein, a constitutional lawyer and former Justice Department official in the Reagan administration says of the order, "This is so sweeping it's staggering. I have never seen anything so broad. It expands beyond terrorism, beyond seeking to use violence or the threat of violence to cower or intimidate a population."

In an editorial for the *Washington Times*, Fein states, "The person subject to an asset freeze is reduced to a leper. The secretary's financial death sentences are imposed without notice or an opportunity to respond, the core of due process. They hit like a bolt of lightning. Any person whose assets are frozen immediately confronts a comprehensive quarantine. He may not receive and benefactors may not provide funds, goods, or services of any sort. A lawyer cannot provide legal services to challenge the secretary's blocking order. A doctor cannot provide medical services in response to a cardiac arrest." Fein adds, "The Justice Department is customarily entrusted with vetting executive orders for consistency with the Constitution. Is the Attorney General sleeping?"[1] (see Story #8).

Citation
1. Bruce Fein, "Our Orphaned Constitution," *Washington Times*, August 7, 2007.

UPDATE BY MATT ROTHSCHILD
This is a story that went virtually nowhere that I know of in the main-stream press. When I traveled around the country giving speeches last summer and brought up the subject of this executive order, people couldn't believe it and wondered why they hadn't heard about it. I'm still wondering that myself.

Here are a couple of good places to check for issues related to this story:

The American Civil Liberties Union, aclu.org.

The Center for Constitutional Rights, ccrjustice.org.

6

The Homegrown Terrorism Prevention Act

Sources:
Indypendent, November 16, 2007
Title: "Bringing the War on Terrorism Home"
Author: Jessica Lee

In These Times, November 2007
Title: "Examining the Homegrown Terrorism Prevention Act"
Author: Lindsay Beyerstein

Truthout, November 29, 2007
Title: "The Violent Radicalization Homegrown Terrorism Prevention Act of 2007"
Author: Matt Renner

Student Researchers: Dan Bluthardt and Cedric Therene
Faculty Evaluator: Robert Proctor, PhD

In a startling affront to American freedoms of expression, privacy, and ·association, the Violent Radicalization and Homegrown Terrorism Prevention Act (H.R. 1955) passed the House on October 23, 2007, by a vote of 404–6. The Senate is currently considering a companion bill, S. 1959. The act would establish a national commission and a university-based "Center for Excellence" to study and propose legislation to prevent the threat of "radicalization" of Americans.

Author of the bill Jane Harman (D-CA) explains, "We're studying the phenomenon of people with radical beliefs who turn into people who would use violence."

The act states, "While the United States must continue its vigilant efforts to combat international terrorism, it must also strengthen efforts to combat the threat posed by homegrown terrorists based and operating within the United States. Understanding the motivational factors that lead to violent radicalization, homegrown terrorism, and ideologically based violence is a vital step toward eradicating these threats in the United States."

The act's purpose goes beyond academic inquiry, however. In a press release Harman stated, "The National Commission will propose to both Congress and [Department of Homeland Security Secretary Michael] Chertoff initiatives to intercede before radicalized individuals turn violent."

The act states, "Preventing the potential rise of self radicalized, unaffiliated terrorists domestically cannot be easily accomplished solely through traditional Federal intelligence or law enforcement efforts, and can benefit from the incorporation of State and local efforts."

Harman, who chairs the House Subcommittee on Intelligence, Information Sharing, and Terrorism Risk Assessment, also has close ties to the RAND Corporation, a right-wing think tank, which appears to have influenced the bill. Two weeks prior to the introduction of H.R. 1955 on April 19, 2007, Brian Michael Jenkins of RAND delivered testimony on "Jihadist Radicalization and Recruitment" to Harman's subcommittee.

In June, Jenkins was back before Harman's subcommittee discussing the role of the National Commission. "Homegrown terrorism is the principal threat that we face as a country and it will likely be the principal threat that we face for decades. . . . Unless a way of intervening in the radicalization process can be found, we are condemned to stepping on cockroaches one at a time," he stated. In a 2005 RAND report titled "Trends in Terrorism," one chapter is devoted entirely to a non-Muslim "homegrown terrorist" threat—the threat of anti-globalists.

In an effort to prevent people from becoming "prone to" radicalization, this preemptive measure of policing thought specifically identifies the Internet as a tool of radicalization: "The Internet has aided in facilitating violent radicalization, ideologically based violence, and the homegrown terrorism process in the United States by providing access to broad and constant streams of terrorist-related propaganda to United States citizens," says Harman.

The legislation authorizes a ten-member National Commission (the Senate bill calls for twelve members) appointed by the President, the Secretary of Homeland Security, congressional leaders, and the chairpersons of both the Senate and House committees on Homeland Security and Governmental Affairs.

After convening, the Commission is to submit reports at six-month intervals for eighteen months to the President and Congress, stating its findings, conclusions, and legislative recommendations "for immediate and long-term countermeasures . . . to prevent violent radicalization, homegrown terrorism and ideologically based violence."

This commission has disturbing similarities to the Counterintelligence Program (COINTELPRO), which was investigated by a US Senate select committee on intelligence activities (the Church Committee), in 1975. The Church Committee found that from 1956 to 1971, "The Bureau [FBI] conducted a sophisticated vigilante operation aimed squarely at preventing the exercise of First Amendment rights of speech and association, on the theory that preventing the growth of dangerous groups and the propagation of dangerous ideas would protect the national security and deter violence."

H.R. 1955 would give the DHS secretary power to establish a "Center of Excellence," a university-based research program to "bring together leading experts and researchers to conduct multidisciplinary research and education for homeland security solutions." the DHS currently has eight Centers at academic institutions across the country, strengthening what many see as a growing military-security-academic complex. Harman, in an October 23 press release, stated that the Center would "examine the social, criminal, political, psychological and economic roots of domestic terrorism."

Hope Marston, regional organizer with the Bill of Rights Defense Committee (BORDC) warns against the danger of vaguely defined terms in this legislation, which, open to very broad interpretation, mirrors a historical pattern of sweeping government repression.

Jules Boykoff, author and professor of politics and government at Pacific University, is alarmed by the circular definition, for example, of "ideologically based violence," which itself fails to define the terms "threat," "force," or "violence." Boykoff commented that the bill used the terms "extremism" and "radicalism" interchangeably. "The word 'radical' shares the etymological root to the word 'radish,' which means to get to the root of the problem," he says. "So, if the government wants to get at the actual root of terrorism, then let's really talk about it. We need to talk about the economic roots, the vast inequalities in wealth between the rich and poor."

Caroline Fredrickson, director of the Washington Legislative Office of the American Civil Liberties Union, says of the Act, "Law enforcement should focus on action, not thought. We need to worry about the people who are committing crimes rather than those who harbor beliefs that the government may consider to be 'extreme.'"

UPDATE BY JESSICA LEE

While civil liberties and religious freedom groups credit independent journalists and grassroots activists with helping to stall the passage of the Violent Radicalization and Homegrown Terrorism Prevention Act of 2007, some members of Congress continue to push for Internet censorship and racial profiling as necessary to prevent "homegrown terrorism."

The House of Representatives approved the Violent Radicalization and Homegrown Terrorism Prevention Act in October 2007 by a 404-6 vote, but widespread opposition forced the Senate to shelve the bill. As of June 1, 2008, no vote was scheduled or expected during the current legislative year.

I became aware of the Act in early November 2007. Other than an article by Lindsay Beyerstein, "Examining the Homegrown Terrorism Prevention Act," (*In These Times*, November 1, 2007), no major media outlet had reported on the bill despite the dangers it posed to civil liberties, privacy, and Muslim and Arab communities in the United States. Nonetheless, I did discover active online discussion about the bill, mainly on blogs and videos posted to YouTube.com.

Isabel Macdonald, communications director for Fairness and Accuracy in Reporting, commented: "Perhaps due to the symbiotic relationship between corporate media outlets and government officials, the corporate media has shown a consistent aversion to offering critical coverage of the erosion of civil liberties. The independent media—and specifically *The Indypendent*—played a critical role in breaking the story of this bill, and, through coverage in blogs and on *Democracy Now!*, keeping the story alive."

Within a month of *The Indypendent* article, rallies were held from Maine to California, and numerous civil liberties, religious freedom and American Muslim and Arab organizations issued action alerts encouraging people to contact their congressional representatives in an effort to stop the US Senate companion bill, S. 1959.

According to civil rights lobbyists, the public outcry forced Senate committee chair Sen. Joseph Lieberman (I-CT) to put the bill on the backburner. However, Lieberman and committee ranking minority leader Sen. Susan Collins (R-ME) continue to claim "homegrown terrorism" by Islamists is a grave menace, and on May 8, 2008, issued their own report, without public backing by other committee members, that warned "the threat of homegrown terrorism is on the rise, aided by the Internet's capacity to spread the core recruitment and training message of violent Islamist terrorist groups."

In response, more than thirty civil liberties and religious freedom groups sent a letter to the Senate committee on May 30, expressing concern that the report could impinge on freedom of expression, unjustly target Muslims, and define the Internet as a "weapon."

A group of organizations representing American Muslim and Arab communities also submitted a letter in response to the report and the Senate hearings charging that they have been largely excluded from the legislative process and that the report relies on a discredited 2007 New York Police Department report that attempts to explain the process of "violent radicalization" of Muslim individuals.

Shortly after issuing the report, Lieberman demanded that Google remove YouTube videos produced by "terrorist organizations such as al-Qaeda." Google responded May 19 by removing eighty videos that the company agreed violated YouTube's Community Guidelines, which depict gratuitous violence, advocated violence or used hate speech. Google, however, refused to meet all of Lieberman's demands, which included censoring all videos mentioning or featuring groups listed by the US State Department as foreign terrorist organizations, such as al-Qaeda.

"Senator Lieberman stated his belief . . . that all videos mentioning or featuring these groups should be removed from YouTube—even legal nonviolent or non-hate speech videos," Google said. "YouTube encourages free speech and defends everyone's right to express unpopular points of view."

Chip Berlet, senior analyst at the Boston-based Political Research Associates, said that he believes Lieberman's actions are a "political dirty trick" with the motive of trying to push the presidential candidates towards accepting a more aggressive stance in the Middle East.

Organizations leading the effort to oppose the legislation include Defending Dissent Foundation (www.defendingdissent.org), the Bill of Rights Defense Committee (www.bordc.org), the Center for Constitutional Rights (www.ccrjustice.org), the American Civil Liberties Union (www.aclu.org), and the Council on American-Islamic Relations (www.cair.com).

UPDATE BY LINDSAY BEYERSTEIN

The Homegrown Terrorism bill has been bogged down in the Senate since last October. The bill sailed through the House with little public comment but subsequently encountered stiff opposition from across the political spectrum. Until recently, it appeared that civil liberties groups and Muslim civic organizations had successfully blocked the Senate version of the bill.

The bill seemed destined to die in committee—that is, until Sen. Joe Lieberman, the chair of the Senate Committee on Homeland Security, signaled his eagerness to revisit the issue by releasing a new report and picking a fight with YouTube.

On May 8, Chairman Lieberman and ranking member Susan Collins (R-ME) released "Violent Islamist Extremism, The Internet, and the Homegrown Terrorist Threat," a bipartisan report based on hearings before the Senate Committee on Homeland Security.

Even before it was released to the public, the report drew fire from a coalition of civil liberties organizations spearheaded by the ACLU. The coalition outlined its concerns about the report in a May 7 memo to committee members.

"Our concern is that this focus on the Internet could be a precursor to proposals to censor and regulate speech on the Internet. Indeed, some policy makers have advocated shutting down objectionable websites," the memo said.

Lieberman reinforced those misgivings on May 19 when he wrote to the CEO of Google (YouTube's parent company) demanding that an unspecified number of Islamic propaganda videos be removed from the popular video-sharing site. Lieberman alleged in the letter that the clips were the work of a sophisticated Islamic propaganda network discussed in his committee's recent report. He also claimed that these videos violated YouTube's community guidelines.

YouTube rules expressly forbid gratuitous violence, hate speech, threats, harassment, and depictions of crimes such as bomb-making. Hundreds of thousands of videos are uploaded to the site daily. Rather than prescreening the content, YouTube relies on users to flag material that violates community standards. Content that breaks the rules is routinely removed.

After reviewing the clips, YouTube refused to remove the bulk of the material flagged by Lieberman's staff. A handful of clips that violated community standards were taken down, but the rest stayed up.

"Most of the videos, which did not contain violent or hate speech content, were not removed because they do not violate our Community Guidelines," read a statement issued by the YouTube Team. The statement went on to affirm the right of YouTube users to express unpopular points of view.

Lieberman was not satisfied with the response.

"No matter what their content, videos produced by terrorist organizations like al-Qaeda that are committed to attacking America and killing Americans should not be tolerated. Google must reconsider its policy," Lieberman stated on May 20.

No vote has been scheduled, but Lieberman's fight with Google has pushed the Homegrown Terrorism bill back into the spotlight. After months of silence, the established media are finally beginning to ask questions about the government's increasing enthusiasm for monitoring "radical" speech online. The *New York Times* sharply criticized Lieberman and the bill in a May 25 editorial. The op/ed called Lieberman a "would-be censor" whose efforts to restrict constitutionally protected speech on YouTube "contradict fundamental American values."

Readers can make their views on the Homegrown Terrorism bill known by contacting their senators and the members of the Senate Committee on Homeland Security. The two frontrunners in the 2008 presidential race are senators. Now is a good time for voters to pressure the presidential candidates to take clear positions on the Homegrown Terrorism bill. Sen. Barack Obama (D-IL) sits on the Homeland Security Committee, but did not contribute to the report. Sen. John McCain (R-AZ) is closely allied with Sen. Lieberman, especially on issues pertaining to terrorism.

UPDATE BY MATT RENNER

A controversial plan to study and profile domestic terrorism was scrapped after popular push back, but the spirit of the legislation lives on in Senator Joe Lieberman's office.

H.R. 1955, "The Violent Radicalization and Homegrown Terrorism Prevention Act of 2007" passed the House in October 2007 with almost unanimous support. The bill immediately came under fire from civil liberties watchdogs because of what many saw as a deliberate targeting of Muslims and Arabs and the possible chilling effect it might have on free speech.

The original bill intended to set up a government commission to investigate the supposed threat of domestically produced terrorists and the ideologies that underpin their radicalization. The ten-member commission was to be empowered to "hold hearings and sit and act at such times and places, take such testimony, receive such evidence, and administer such oaths as the Commission considers advisable to carry out its duties." The bill also singled out the Internet as a vehicle for terrorists to spread their ideology with the intention of recruiting and training new terrorists.

After significant public pressure, the bill stalled in the Senate. However, Senator Joe Lieberman (D-CT), the current chairman of the Senate Homeland Security and Governmental Affairs Committee, embraced the thrust of the legislation and has been working to push forward some of the goals of the original bill, including an attempt to weed out terrorist propaganda from the Internet.

On May 19, Lieberman sent a letter to Google's CEO Eric Schmidt demanding that YouTube's parent company Google "immediately remove content produced by Islamist terrorist organizations from YouTube."

"By taking action to curtail the use of YouTube to disseminate the goals and methods of those who wish to kill innocent civilians, Google will make a singularly important contribution to this important national effort," Lieberman wrote.

Google fired back, refusing to take off material that did not violate the site's code of conduct. "While we respect and understand his views, YouTube encourages free speech and defends everyone's right to express unpopular points of view," Schmidt said in response, adding, "we believe that YouTube is a richer and more relevant platform for users precisely because it hosts a diverse range of views, and rather than stifle debate, we allow our users to view all acceptable content and make up their own minds."

Google removed some of the videos that violated their rules against posting violence and hate speech, but made a point to write, "most of the videos, which did not contain violent or hate speech content, were not removed because they do not violate our Community Guidelines."

According to civil liberties activists, Chairman Lieberman has been spearheading an effort to censor speech on the Internet. His committee recently released a report titled "Violent Islamist Extremism, The Internet, and the Homegrown Terrorist Threat," a report detailing the use of web sites and Internet tools to spread pro-terrorism propaganda.

The report repeatedly blames websites and chat rooms for "radicalization," calling the websites "portals" through which potential terrorists can "participate in the global violent Islamist movement and recruit others to their cause." As civil liberties groups have pointed out, the report focuses solely on terrorism seen as associated with Islam.

Caroline Fredrickson, director of the ACLU Washington, DC, legislative office, said that Lieberman "is trying to decide what he thinks should go on the Internet," which, she said, "reeks of an interest in censoring all sorts of different dialogs."

"If someone criticizes Israel's treatment of Palestinians and favors Hamas, should that be censored?" Fredrickson asked.

Links:

"Violent Islamist Extremism, The Internet, and the Homegrown Terrorist Threat": http://hsgac.senate .gov/public/_files/ IslamistReport.pdf.

New York Times editorial on Lieberman's attempt to censor YouTube: http://www.nytimes.com/ 2008/05/25/opinion/25sun1.html?_r=1&ref=opinion&oref=slogin.

Lieberman's response to the *New York Times* editorial: http://www.nytimes.com/2008/05/25/opinion/ 25sun1.html?_r=1&ref=opinion &oref=slogin.

COMMENT BY MICKEY S. HUFF, author of Chapter 14

The coverage of this story by these journalists is highly commendable. However, another element that appears to have been censored regarding the possible application of H.R. 1955 and S. 1959, even in the independent and progressive press coverage, is the specificity of possible domestic activists mentioned in the hearings Representative Jane

Harman held in Washington, DC. While the aforementioned authors allude to animal rights activists and anti-globalists as potential targets of these bills, none mention 9/11 Truth activists and scholars even though they were mentioned by name in the Harman hearings at the Capitol. (For possible explanations, see *Censored 2008*, Chapter 7, for more on the propaganda model inside left progressive press.)

Among the claims of those testifying to Congress about the "need" for H.R. 1955 was that anyone who questions the official government line on 9/11 is akin to a terrorist or a material supporter to terrorism. One speaker, Mark Weitzman of the Wiesenthal Center (ironically founded by Holocaust survivor Simon Wiesenthal to educate the public about war crimes), claimed that architects, engineers, and scientists that question the official 9/11 narrative are the same as alleged violent jihadist groups. This was further implied in a Powerpoint presentation in which Weitzman showed architect Richard Gage's website, http://AE911Truth.org, alongside alleged violent jihadist sites. Gage has criticized the 9/11 official story about the destruction of the Twin Towers and WTC7. On the basis of his professional expertise of steel frame buildings, Gage contends the buildings could not have been brought down the way the government has explained and offers alternative theories supported by evidence. Regardless of whether one believes the counterarguments about the events of 9/11, free speech and questioning of the government on such crucial issues should not be criminalized.

This is the latest round of official conflation between terrorists and activists in the US. Is there a proven link between these aforementioned groups? No, there is not. But that didn't stop people from simply saying so on the public record while providing no evidence. And Jane Harman, Democratic cosponsor of the bill, didn't ask for any, nor did she invite rebuttal. This is reminiscent of McCarthyism of the Red Scare period of the 1950s.

I originally wrote about this issue here:

http://mythinfo.blogspot.com/2007/11/state-terror-hr-1955-weapon-of-mass.html

http://www.911truth.org/article.php?story=2007112285903892.

For C-Span video footage of the hearing (just after thirty-nine minutes), see: http://www.c-spanarchives.org/library/index.php?main_page=product_video_info&products_id=202123-1.

7

Guest Workers Inc.: Fraud and Human Trafficking

Sources:
Southern Poverty Law Center, March 2007
Title: "Close to Slavery: Guestworker Programs in the United States"
Authors: Mary Bauer and Sarah Reynolds

The Nation, June 25, 2007
Title: "Coming to America"
Author: Felicia Mello

Times of India, March 10, 2008
Title: "Trafficking racket: Indian workers file case against US employer"
Author: Chidanand Rajghatta

Student Researchers: Cedric Therene, Sam Burchard, April Pearce, and Marley Miller
Faculty Evaluator: Francisco Vazquez, PhD

While the guest worker program in the United States has been praised and recommended for expansion by President Bush, and is likely to be considered by Congress as a template for future immigration reform, human rights advocates warn that the system seriously victimizes immigrant workers. Workers, labor organizers, lawyers, and policy makers say that the program, designed to open up the legal labor market and provide a piece of the American dream to immigrants, has instead locked thousands into a modern-day form of indentured servitude. Congressman Charles Rangel has called the guest worker program "the closest thing I've ever seen to slavery."

In the process of attaining a H-2 guest worker visa, workers typically fall victim to bait-and-switch schemes that force them to borrow huge sums of money at high interest rates (often leveraging family homes) in order to land short-term, low-wage jobs that all too often end up shorter-term and lower-waged than promised. Under crushing debt, and legally bound to work only for the employer who filed petition for them, these workers often face the most dangerous and harsh of working conditions in places like shipyards, the forestry department, or construction, with no medical benefits for on-the-job injuries or access to legal services. Bosses often hold workers' documents to make sure they don't "jump jobs."

There are two levels of the current guest worker program—H-2A for agricultural work, and H-2B for non-agricultural work. Though the H-2A program provides legal protections for foreign farm workers—such as a guarantee of at least three quarters of the total employment hours promised, free housing, transportation compensation, medical benefits, and legal representation—many of these protections exist only on paper. H-2B workers, on the other hand, have no rights or protections.

The exploitation of guest workers begins with the initial recruitment in their home country—a process that often leaves them in a precarious economic state and therefore extremely vulnerable to abuse by unscrupulous employers in this country. US employers almost universally rely on private agencies to find and recruit guest workers in their home countries.

These labor recruiters usually charge fees to the worker—sometimes many thousands of dollars to cover travel, visas, and other costs, including profit for the recruiters. The workers, most of whom live in poverty, frequently obtain high-interest loans to come up with the money to pay the fees. In addition, recruiters sometimes require them to leave collateral, such as the deed to their house or car, to ensure that they fulfill the terms of their individual labor contract.

The entirely unregulated recruiting business is quite lucrative. With more than 121,000 workers recruited in 2005 alone, tens of millions of dollars in recruiting fees are at stake. This financial bonanza provides a powerful incentive for recruiters and agencies to import as many workers as possible, with little or no regard to the impact on individual workers and their families.

Though Southern Poverty Law Center reports that the H-2 program brought about 121,000 guest workers into the US in 2005, with approximately two thirds of those in the H-2B section, the *Nation's* Felicia Mello reports that the number rose to more than 150,000 by June 2007. And while participation in the H-2A program, with its housing requirements and wage guarantees, has remained almost flat in recent years, the more laissez-faire H-2B system has flourished, with the government adjusting the cap several times to cope with skyrocketing employer demand.

"The tendency has been for the H-2 program . . . to devolve into a system that approximates the exploitative, illegal, underground labor market it was (in part) designed to replace," writes anthropologist David Griffith in his 2006 book *American Guestworkers*. "Indeed, there is some evidence that without this downward trend in conditions . . . legal guestworkers become less attractive to US employers."

In March 2008, more than 500 shipyard workers from India filed a class action suit against the Northrop Grumman subsidiary Signal International in Louisiana and Mississippi, and against recruiters in India and the US, on charges of forced labor, human trafficking, fraud, and civil rights violations. The workers claim they were caught up in a trafficking racket within the federal government's H-2B guest worker program. In a typical bait and switch scheme that occurred in 2006, over 600 Indians paid up to $25,000 each for a promise of green cards and permanent US residency. They instead found themselves trapped in squalid and dangerous conditions, bonded through the H-2B guest worker program to an employer under what is being called "twenty-first century slavery." In one incident of protest, Signal sent in armed guards to apprehend protesters in a pre-dawn raid. Plaintiffs, as they press their class action lawsuit, have asked the Indian government to protect their families in India from vengeful recruiters.

When Mello asked an African-American Katrina survivor who supported the guest workers' grievance how he justified comparing guest work to slavery, he responded, "Do you know the story of the Middle Passage? . . . In slavery, you send a slave catcher, they go to the chiefs and make a deal. They say, We're going to take your people to heaven, and they show them a few pretty things from heaven. You load them onto the ships and only when they get out to sea do they know they're slaves. You take them to one owner, and if they leave they're a runaway. Well, with guest workers . . ." He trails off, says Mello, his meaning clear.

UPDATE BY MARY BAUER

In the year since "Close to Slavery" was published, conditions for guest workers in the US have not improved. A case recently filed by the Southern Poverty Law Center illustrates this in compelling terms.

Hundreds of guest workers from India, lured by false promises of permanent US residency, paid tens of thousands of dollars each to obtain temporary jobs at Gulf Coast shipyards only to find themselves forced into involuntary servitude and living in overcrowded, guarded labor camps, according to the class action lawsuit filed in March of 2008.

Signal International LLC and a network of recruiters and labor brokers engineered a scheme to defraud the workers and force them to work against their will in Signal facilities. Signal is a marine and fabrication company with shipyards in Mississippi and Texas. It is a subcontractor for global defense company Northrop Grumman Corp.

Several of the workers were illegally detained by company security guards during a pre-dawn raid of their quarters after some began organizing other workers to complain about abuses they faced.

After Hurricane Katrina scattered its workforce, Signal used the federal H-2B guest worker program to import employees to work as welders, pipefitters, shipfitters, and in other positions. Hundreds of Indian men mortgaged their futures in late 2006 to pay recruiters as much as $20,000 or more for travel, visa, recruitment, and other fees after they were told it would lead to good jobs, green cards, and permanent US residency.

Many of the workers gave up other jobs and sold their houses, family farms, jewelry, and other valuables to come up with the money. Many were also told that for an extra $1,500-per person fee, they could bring their families to live in the United States.

When the men arrived in early 2007, they discovered they wouldn't receive the green cards as promised, but only ten-month, H-2B guest-worker visas. They were forced to pay $1,050 a month to live in crowded company housing in isolated, fenced labor camps where as many as twenty-four men shared a trailer with only two toilets. When they tried to find their own housing, Signal officials told them they would still have the rent deducted from their paychecks. With the exception of rare occasions, such as Christmas, visitors were not allowed into the camps, which were enclosed by fences. Company employees regularly searched the workers' belongings.

Workers who complained about the conditions they faced were threatened with deportation. By March 9, 2007, the workers had started organizing. Signal responded with an early morning raid by armed guards on the labor camp in Pascagoula, Mississipi. Three of the organizers were locked in a room for hours. They were told they would be fired and deported. One of the workers, Sabulal Vijayan, who had sold his wife's jewelry and borrowed from friends to build a better life in America, slit his wrist in desperation. He recovered after being hospitalized. The incident prompted hundreds of workers to strike. Signal fired the organizers.

UPDATE BY FELICIA MELLO

A year after "Coming to America" detailed the plight of guest workers in the H-2A and H-2B programs, Congress has failed to enact any expansion of the programs, despite urging from business groups and the Bush administration. Yet the immigration issue continues to occupy the national stage.

In a nationwide crackdown, Immigrations and Customs Enforcement (ICE) arrested over 30,000 allegedly undocumented immigrants last year, double the number for 2006. While ICE agents say they are simply enforcing the law, some immigrant advocates believe the raids are designed to increase support for a new guest worker plan.

In February, President Bush proposed changes to the H-2A program that would make it quicker and easier for growers to import farm workers, but do little to protect the workers' rights. Under Bush's plan, farmers could offer housing vouchers instead of directly providing shelter to workers—a method unlikely to work in areas with housing shortages—and would no longer be required to prove that they tried to hire US workers first. The formula used to calculate H-2A visa holders' wages would also change to one advocates believe would result in lower salaries.

The two-pronged approach of stricter enforcement and support for guest worker programs is also gaining ground at the state level. Arizona, which has enacted some of the strictest sanctions in the country against hiring undocumented immigrants, is now considering starting its own independent guest worker scheme to ease a shortage of farm labor in the state.

Meanwhile, guest workers and their allies are stepping up their organizing. The Indian workers who paid recruiters up to $20,000 for jobs at ship builder Signal International sued the company in March, saying it committed fraud by promising them permanent residency and deducted exorbitant rent from their paychecks while housing them in cramped trailers.

Two months later, twenty of the workers went on a month-long hunger strike, camping out near the Indian embassy in Washington, DC. They demanded the right to remain in the country while they pursue their case, Congressional hearings into abuse of guest workers, and bilateral negotiations between the US and India on the rights of Indian guest workers. The Justice Department has since launched an investigation into their claims.

#304   06-09-2009 5:18PM
Item(s) checked out to 27814000364060.

TITLE: Censored 2009 : the top 25 censor
BARCODE: 35410000132076
DUE: 06-30-2009

Baker County Public Library
541 523-6419

The murder of union organizer Santiago Rafael Cruz, who helped Mexican guest workers challenge exploitation by recruitment firms, remains unsolved.

8

Executive Orders Can Be Changed Secretly

Sources:
Senator Sheldon Whitehouse website, December 7, 2007
Title: "In FISA Speech, Whitehouse Sharply Criticizes Bush Administration's Assertion of Executive Power"
Author: Senator Sheldon Whitehouse

The Guardian, December 26, 2007
Title: "The Rabbit Hole"
Author: Marcy Wheeler

Student Researchers: Dana Vaz and Bill Gibbons
Faculty Evaluator: Noel Byrne, PhD

On December 7, 2007, Senator Sheldon Whitehouse, as a member of the Senate Intelligence Committee, disclosed on the floor of the US Senate that he had declassified three legal documents of the Office of Legal Counsel (OLC) within the Department of Justice that state:

1. An executive order cannot limit a president. There is no constitutional requirement for a president to issue a new executive order whenever he wishes to depart from the terms of a previous executive order. Rather than violate an executive order, the president has instead modified or waived it.

2. The President, exercising his constitutional authority under Article II, can determine whether an action is a lawful exercise of the President's authority under Article II.

3. The Department of Justice is bound by the President's legal determinations.

Whitehouse discovered the OLC's classified legal opinions while researching the Protect America Act legislation passed in August 2007, which Whitehouse warns will allow the administration to bypass Congress and the Courts in order to facilitate unchecked spying on Americans. He noted that for years under the Bush administration, the Office of Legal Council has been issuing highly classified secret legal opinions related to surveillance.

The senator warned of the danger of the poorly written Protect America Act legislation, which provides no statutory restrictions on government wiretapping of Americans and eliminates checks and balances from the legislative and judicial branches. The only restriction on government eavesdropping on Americans is an executive order that limits surveillance to those who the attorney general determines to be agents of a foreign power. However, in light of the first declassified OLC proclamation that the president can secretly change his signing statements at will, we are left exposed to the whims of a secret, unchecked executive agenda.

Of the second OLC legal determination, Whitehouse reminded Senate that *Marbury v. Madison*, written by Chief Justice John Marshall in 1803, established the proposition that it is "emphatically the province and duty of the judicial department to say what the law is." Yet the OLC, operating out of the judicial department, has declared that it is now the president who decides the legal limits of his own power.

Lastly, Whitehouse repeated the third of these legal declarations several times as if in disbelief, asking members of Senate to allow the assertion to sink in: *"The Department of Justice is bound by the President's legal determinations."*

Whitehouse said, "These three Bush administration legal propositions boil down to this: one, 'I don't have to follow my own rules, and I don't have to tell you when I'm breaking them'; two, 'I get to determine what my own powers are'; and three, 'The Department of Justice doesn't tell me what the law is, I tell the Department of Justice what the law is.'"

Whitehouse closed his address to Senate with the statement, "When the Congress of the United States is willing to roll over for an unprincipled president, this is where you end up. We should not even be having this discussion. But here we are. I implore my colleagues: reject these feverish legal theories. I understand political loyalty, trust me, I do. But let us also be loyal to this great institution we serve in the legislative branch of our government. Let us also be loyal to the Constitution we took an oath to defend, from enemies foreign and domestic. And let us be loyal to the American people who live each day under our Constitution's principles and protections. . . . The principles of congressional legislation and oversight, and of judicial approval and review, are simple and longstanding. Americans deserve this protection . . ."

UPDATE BY MARCY WHEELER

The president's claimed authority to be able to ignore his own executive orders without revising the orders themselves—reported in "The Rabbit Hole"—was one of several issues discussed in an April 29, 2008, Senate Judiciary Hearing on "Secret Laws and the Threat to Democratic and Accountable Government."

In that hearing, the Office of Legal Counsel Deputy Assistant Attorney General John Elwood confirmed the proposition that "The activities authorized by the President cannot violate an executive order in any legally meaningful sense." Effectively, the Department of Justice's key advisory lawyers confirmed they believe the President can act contrary to his own executive orders without formally changing those executive orders.

The hearing attracted some new media attention to this story. In the *New York Times'* reporting of the hearing, Scott Shane and David Johnston referred to the "previously unpublicized method to cloak government activities," for example. In addition, commentator Nat Hentoff wrote a column on the hearing as a whole.

The hearing did not answer one question raised in "The Rabbit Hole": whether the President had altered the executive order on classification (12958, as amended by 13292) as well as the executive order on intelligence activities (12333) that Senator Whitehouse cited in his first comments on the OLC opinion. But Bill Leonard, the former head of the Information Security Oversight Office who testified at the hearing, did reveal that top administration lawyers were seemingly violating that executive order with regards to a key opinion on torture even as they were revising the order itself.

What is most disturbing is that at the exact time these officials were writing, reviewing, and being briefed on the classified nature of this memorandum [on enhanced interrogation], they were also concurring with the president's reaffirmation of the standards for proper classification, which was formalized the week after the OLC memo was issued when the president signed his amended version of the executive order governing classification.

In other words, it remains unclear whether the administration has "altered" this executive order, or whether it is simply ignoring it when convenient.

And that remains the significance of this story. The Yoo Memo on torture, by all accounts, should have been released to the public in 2003. Had it been, the US's policy on torture—and the dubious opinions on which that policy is based—would have been exposed five years earlier. But for some reason, it wasn't. In the arbitrary world where the president can ignore his own executive orders, we have no way of knowing what to expect.

For information on Senator Whitehouse, see http://whitehouse.senate.gov/.

For the Senate Hearing (including the statements of witnesses), see http://judiciary.senate.gov/hearing.cfm?id=3305.

For Leonard's statement, see http://judiciary.senate.gov/testimony.cfm?id =3305&wit_id=7148.

For Nat Hentoff's article, see http://washingtontimes.com/news/2008/ may/12/let-the-sunshine-in/.

For the *New York Times* coverage, see http://www.nytimes.com/2008/ 05/01/washington/01justice.html?_r=1&oref=slogin.

9

Iraq and Afghanistan Vets Testify

Sources:
Iraq Vets Against the War, March 13–16, 2008
Title: "Winter Soldier: Iraq & Afghanistan Eyewitness Accounts of the Occupations"

War Comes Home, Pacifica Radio, March 14–16, 2008
Title: "Winter Soldier 2008 Eyewitness Accounts of the Occupations"
Co-hosts: Aaron Glantz, Aimee Allison, and Esther Manilla

One World, March 19, 2008
Title: "US Soldiers 'Testify' About War Crimes"
Author: Aaron Glantz

The Nation, July 30, 2007
Title: "The Other War: Iraq Vets Bear Witness"
Authors: Chris Hedges and Laila Al-Arian

Student Researchers: April Pearce, Erica Elkington, and Kat Pat Crespán
Community Evaluator: Bob Alpern

Iraq and Afghanistan war veterans are coming forward to recount the brutal impact of the ongoing occupations. An investigation by the

Nation (July 2007) and the Winter Soldier hearings in Silver Spring, Maryland, in March 2008, which was organized by Iraq Veterans Against the War and brought together over 300 veterans, have made their experiences public. Soldiers' harrowing testimony of atrocities they witnessed or participated in directly indicate a structural problem in the US military that has created an environment of lawlessness. Some international law experts say the soldiers' statements show the need for investigations into potential violations of international law by high-ranking officials in the Bush administration and the Pentagon. Though BBC predicted that the Winter Soldier event would dominate headlines around the world that week, there was a near total back-out on this historic news event by the US corporate media.[1]

Dozens of veterans of the Iraq and Afghanistan occupation publicly testified at the four-day Winter Soldier gathering about crimes they committed during the course of battle—many of which were prompted by the orders or policies laid down by superior officers. Such crimes include targeting innocent, unarmed civilians for murder and detention, destroying property, desecrating corpses, severely abusing detainees (often torturing to death), and using corpses for medical practice.

Winter Soldier 2008 was organized to demonstrate that well-publicized incidents of US brutality, including the Abu Ghraib prison scandal and the massacre of an entire family of Iraqis in the town of Haditha, were not isolated incidents perpetrated by "a few bad apples," as many politicians and military leaders have claimed. They are part of a pattern, the organizers said, of "an increasingly bloody occupation." The veterans also stressed the similarities between the occupations in Iraq and Afghanistan, ". . . units that are getting the exact same training and the exact same orders are being sent to both Iraq and Afghanistan," explains a former US Army Medic.

The *Nation* investigation vividly documents the experiences of fifty combat veterans of the Iraq occupation. Their testimonies reveal that American troops lack the training and support to communicate with or even understand Iraqi civilians. They were offered little to no cultural or historical education about the country they control. Translators are in short supply and often unqualified. Interviewed vets said stereotypes about Islam and Arabs that soldiers and marines arrive with tend to solidify rapidly in the close confines of the military and the risky streets of Iraqi cities into a crude racism. Veterans said the culture of this counterinsurgency war, in which most Iraqi civilians were assumed to be hostile, made it difficult for soldiers to sympathize with their victims—at least until they returned home and had a chance to reflect. Former US Army Sergeant Logan Laituri argues, "The problem that we face in Iraq is that policymakers in leadership have set a precedent of lawlessness where we don't abide by the rule of law, we don't respect international treaties, so when that atmosphere exists it lends itself to criminal activity."

International law expert Benjamin Ferencz, who served as chief prosecutor of Nazi War Crimes at Nuremberg after World War II, told *OneWorld* that none of the veterans who testified at Winter Soldier should be prosecuted for war crimes. Instead, he said, President Bush should be sent to the dock for starting an "aggressive" war. "Nuremberg declared that aggressive war is the supreme international crime." He said the United Nations charter, which was written after the carnage of World War II, contains a provision that no nation can use armed force without the permission of the UN Security Council.

Many Iraq and Afghanistan veterans return home deeply disturbed by the disparity between the reality of the occupations and the way they are portrayed by the US government and American media. The occupation the vets describe is a dark and even depraved enterprise, one that bears a powerful resemblance to other misguided and brutal colonial wars and occupations, from the French occupation of Algeria to the American war in Vietnam and the Israeli occupation of Palestinian territory. Although international and independent US media covered Winter Soldier ubiquitously, there was an almost complete media blackout on this event by US mainstream media (see Chapter 12).

Citation

1. "Why Are Winter Soldiers Not News?" *Fairness & Accuracy In Reporting,* March 19, 2008.

UPDATE BY AARON GLANTZ, AIMEE ALLISON, AND ESTHER MANILLA

The veterans who spoke at Winter Soldier could have stayed silent. They could have accepted parades and accolades of heroism and blended back into society, and the world would have never known about the terrible atrocities they committed or witnessed in Iraq or Afghanistan. By coming forward to share their stories at considerable risk to their honor, however, these veterans have done a great service, permanently changing the historical record of "what happened" in the war zones.

While their testimony continues to be largely ignored by the mainstream media (to date the *New York Times*, CNN, ABC, NBC, and CBS have failed to cover it), their words were not in vain. Our three-day broadcast lead to a Capitol Hill hearing in front of the Congressional Progressive Caucus. During our March broadcast, we brought on the Caucus's co-chair, Congresswoman Barbara Lee, as a guest by phone from California and allowed two veterans to join us in conducting the interview. In opening remarks at Winter Soldier on the Hill, Lee referenced that interview.

"I remember one of the persons I talked with wanted to know why there weren't any members of Congress there," she said. "And someone asked me over the interview 'Well, what about having a hearing in Washington, DC?' And I said 'Right.'"

On May 15, 2008, nine Iraq and Afghanistan Veterans stood before the Congressional Progressive Caucus, which is co-chaired by Lee and Congresswomen Lynne Woolsey. A half dozen other Congress members also participated and or listened to the three-hour testimony. Many of the representatives in attendance were visibly moved by it and Congresswoman Maxine Waters applauded the veterans for their bravery. KPFA and Pacifica Radio broadcast the hearing live.

Just as importantly, our three-day live broadcast showed many veterans they were not alone. During the course of both broadcasts, we were deluged with phone calls, e-mails, and blog posts from service members, veterans, and military families thanking us for breaking a cultural norm of silence about the reality of war. Since then, we have heard from many veterans about the importance our broadcast and how it impacted them personally. One soldier, Sergeant Matthis Chiroux, said learning about Winter Soldier caused him to refuse his orders to deploy to Iraq.

Before Winter Soldier, Chiroux said he was suicidal. "I just sat in my room reading news about Iraq and feeling completely hopeless, like I would be forced to go and no one would ever know how I felt," he said. "I was getting looped into participating in a crime against humanity and all with the realization that I never wanted to be there in the first place."

The turning point, Chiroux said, came when one of his professors at Brooklyn College in New York suggested he listen to a broadcast of March's Winter Soldier hearings. "Here's an organization of soldiers and veterans who feel like me," he said. "All this alienation and depression that I feel started to ease. I found them, and I've been speaking out with them ever since."

Since Silver Spring in March, regional Winter Soldier hearings have been organized across the country. New veterans are stepping forward to tell their stories and those who spoke in Maryland are revealing more about the reality of their service. To date, regional hearings have been held in Los Angeles, Chicago, and Gainesville, Florida. In Seattle, 800 people gathered to hear veterans' testimonies. Many more are expected to be organized in the future. With their continued testimony, veterans' stories have become their most powerful weapon.

For more information and to listen to the testimonies from March and May 2008, please visit www.warcomeshome.org or www.ivaw.org.

10

APA Complicit in CIA Torture

Sources:

Salon, June 21, 2007
Title: "The CIA's torture teachers"
Author: Mark Benjamin

Vanity Fair, July 17, 2007
Title: "Rorschach and Awe"
Author: Katherine Eban

Democracy Now!, August 20, 2007
Titles: "American Psychological Association Rejects Blanket Ban on Participation in Interrogation of US Detainees," "APA Interrogation Task Force Member Dr. Jean Maria Arrigo Exposes Group's Ties to Military," "Dissident Voices: Ex-Task Force Member Dr. Michael Wessells Speaks Out on Psychologists and Torture," and "APA Members Hold Fiery Town Hall Meeting on Interrogation, Torture"

Student Researchers: Dan Anderson, Corey Sharp-Sabatino, Lindsey Lucia, and Andrea Lochtefeld
Faculty Evaluator: David Van Nuys, PhD

When in 2005 news reports exposed the fact that psychologists were working with the US military and the CIA to develop brutal interrogation methods, American Psychological Association (APA) leaders assembled a task force to examine the issue. After just two days of deliberations, the ten-member task force concluded that psychologists were playing a "valuable and ethical role" in assisting the military. A high level of secrecy surrounding the task force prohibited disclosure of the pro-

ceedings and of members and attendees. It wasn't until a year later that the membership was finally published on Salon.com, revealing that six of nine voting members were from the military and intelligence agencies with direct connections to interrogations at Guantánamo and CIA black sites that operate outside of Geneva Conventions.

The Psychological Ethics and National Security (PENS) task force was assembled in response to growing evidence that psychologists were not only taking part in procedures that have shocked the senses of humanity around the world, but were in fact in charge of designing those brutal tactics and training interrogators in those techniques.

Two psychologists in particular played a central role: James Elmer Mitchell, who was contracted to the CIA, and his colleague Bruce Jessen. Both worked in the classified military training program for Survival, Evasion, Resistance, and Escape (SERE)—which conditions soldiers to endure captivity in enemy hands. In a very quasi-scientific manner, according to psychologists and others with direct knowledge of their activities, Mitchell and Jessen reverse-engineered the tactics inflicted on SERE trainees for use on detainees in the "global war on terror."

With complete adoption of SERE interrogative techniques by the US Military, the CIA put Mitchell and Jessen in charge of training interrogators in the brutal techniques, including waterboarding, in its network of black sites. Meanwhile it is increasingly clear that the US has sacrificed its conscience and its global image for tactics that are at best ineffective.

With close to 150,000 members, the APA is the largest body of psychologists in the world. Unlike the American Medical Association and the American Psychiatric Association who, since 2006, have completely barred doctors from participation, the APA continues to allow its members to participate in detainee interrogations, arguing that their presence keeps interrogations safe and prevents abuse.

Dr. Jean Maria Arrigo, one of the three civilian members of the 2005 PENS task force, whose task was to consider the appropriateness of psychologists' involvement in harsh methods of interrogations, claims that the highest levels in the Department of Defense (DOD) preordained the task force's conclusions.

Citing a series of irregularities, including haste, intimidation, and secrecy, Arrigo contends that the task force was far from balanced or independent. She discloses that APA President Gerald Koocher exerted strong control over task force decisions and censured dissidents. Six of the ten members were highly placed in the DOD, clearly in attendance to represent decisions that had already been made. Those were a) the adoption of the permissive definition of torture in US law as opposed to the strict definition in international law, and b) the participation of military psychologists in interrogation settings.

Many angry psychologists insist that the APA policy has made the organization an enabler of torture.

At the annual APA convention in August 2007, members presented the APA Council of Representatives with a moratorium amendment to the APA resolution, stating,

> Be it resolved that the objectives of the APA shall be to advance psychology as a science and profession and as a means of promoting health, education and welfare. And therefore the roles of psychologists in settings in which detainees are deprived of adequate protection of their human rights should be limited as health personnel to the provision of psychological treatment.

The Council voted overwhelmingly to reject this measure that would have banned its members from participating in abusive interrogation of detainees.

In a fiery town hall meeting that followed the convention, dozens of infuriated psychologists testified. Among them, Dr. Steven Reisner, a member of the Coalition for an Ethical APA, asked why the Council of Representatives voted to reject the moratorium in such clear contradiction to the convictions of a vast majority of APA membership.

Reisner reflected on the lack of ethical standards essential to such an association and its members, "This goes to the essence of who we are as ethical psychologists. If we cannot say, 'No, we will not participate in enhanced interrogations at CIA black sites,' I think we have to seriously question what we are as an organization and, for me, what my allegiance is to this organization, or whether we might have to criticize it from outside at this point."

UPDATE BY MARK BENJAMIN

A month after *Salon* published "The CIA's Torture Teachers," *Vanity Fair* followed in July 2007 with an in-depth article revealing more details about the same small cabal of psychologists who helped create the CIA's brutal interrogation program: a model that would metastasize at Guantánamo Bay, Afghanistan, and in Iraq at places like Abu Ghraib.

By December, I was taking readers on an insider's tour of the CIA's secret "black sites," when *Salon* published the first in-depth interview with a former prisoner of the agency, Mohamed Farag Ahmad Bashmilah. Bashmilah even provided chilling drawings of his barren cells. Apparently the Yemeni man was guilty of nothing more than being in the wrong place at the wrong time: the CIA released him after nineteen months of grueling imprisonment. "Whenever I saw a fly in my cell, I was filled with joy," he told me about the crushing sensory deprivation and isolation. "Although I would wish for it to slip from under the door so it would not be imprisoned itself."

On April 22, 2008, the *Washington Post* published an article suggesting that the US government had gone beyond abusing detainees with stress positions, sleep deprivation, and sexual humiliation and may have resorted to mind-altering drugs to further disorient prisoners. Somehow, it seemed, the agency believed this would result in squeezing out reliable information. At the end of that month, Senators Joe

Biden, Jr. (D-DE), Carl Levin (D-MI), and Chuck Hagel (R-NE), asked the inspectors general at the Pentagon and CIA to look into the story.

In May 2008, the Department of Justice inspector general released a separate report showing that for years, FBI agents had complained about the rough interrogation tactics employed by the CIA and the Pentagon. That concern fell on deaf ears at the National Security Council.

It would be great to say that justice will prevail in the end. When it comes to torture, however, most of the efforts by Congress to look into the behavior of the CIA and the military have been anemic at best.

On paper at least, at the time of this writing the Senate Armed Services Committee was still looking into the activities of James Mitchell and Bruce Jessen, the two psychologists first identified by *Salon* who allegedly helped the government reverse-engineer tactics devised to help elite soldiers resist torture into interrogation techniques. The House Judiciary Committee is probing into this as well.

But few expect anyone in the administration to be frog marched in front of any kind of a tribunal. And with a White House utterly convinced that abuse is an effective interrogation tactic—and equally committed to protecting those who traffic in it—few experts think justice will be served. That goes for the psychologists who set up the diabolical program, and those who gave them the authority to carry it out.

Physician for Human Rights has consistently chased this story. You can learn more about that organization and how you can get involved at http://physiciansforhumanrights.org/.

11

El Salvador's Water Privatization and the Global War on Terror

Sources:

NACLA–*Upside Down World*, August 24, 2007
Title: "El Salvador: Water Inc. and the Criminalization of Protest"
Author: Jason Wallach

The Nation, December 31, 2007
Title: "GWOT: El Salvador"
Author: Wes Enzinna

Peacework, September 2007
Title: "Salvadoran Activists Targeted with US-Style Repression"
Author: Chris Damon

In These Times, November 13, 2007
Title: "El Salvador's Patriot Act"
Author: Jacob Wheeler

Inter Press Service, August 19, 2007
Title: "El Salvador: Spectre of War Looms After 15 Years of Peace"
Author: Raul Gutierrez

Student Researchers: Juana Som and Andrea Lochtefeld
Faculty Evaluator: Jeffrey Reeder, PhD

Salvadoran police violently captured community leaders and residents at a July 2007 demonstration against the privatization of El Salvador's water supply and distribution systems. Close range shooting of rubber bullets and tear gas was used against community members for protesting the rising cost, and diminishing access and quality, of local water under privatization. Fourteen were arrested and charged with terrorism, a charge that can hold a sixty-year prison sentence, under El Salvador's new "Anti-terrorism Law," which is based on the USA PATRIOT Act. While criminalization of political expression and social protest signals an alarming danger to the peace and human rights secured by Salvadorans since its brutal twelve-year civil war, the US government publicly supports the Salvadoran government and the passage of the draconian anti-terrorism law that took effect October 2006.

Salvadorans, however, maintain that fighting for water is a right, not a crime.

The conflict that confronted the small community of Santa Eduviges over their demand that their water system be de-privatized and put under the National Water and Sewage Administration's (ANDA) control stands to be repeated now that right-wing deputies in El Salvador's Legislative Assembly are threatening to pass a controversial General Water Law. The legislation calls for water administration to shift from the national to the municipal level and requires local governments to sign over water management through "concessions"—or contracts with private firms—for up to fifty years. The proposed law has become a lightning rod for opposition from community groups and social organizations who say it amounts to a privatization of the country's water system.

El Salvador's water workers union (SETA) accuses the government of engaging in a plan to discredit the state agency in order to justify privatization. ANDA's budget was slashed by 15 percent in 2005, falling to its lowest level in a decade, a perplexing reduction in a country where 40 percent of rural Salvadorans have no access to potable water.

SETA took out half-page ads in the nation's two biggest daily newspapers opposing the General Water Law, which according to the ad "would privatize water and condemn thousands of our compatriots to suffer thirst for the inability to pay."

SETA members point to the devastating results of the recent privatizations of the country's telecommunications and electricity sectors, which led to the firing of thousands of workers. Many of these workers were forced to re-apply for the same jobs at half the pay with none of the state-provided benefits.

Privately run water concessions in Latin America have a terrible track record. The most notorious example occurred with a project imposed by the World Bank in Cochabamba, Bolivia. The Bank made delivery of a loan conditional on the privatization of the country's largest water systems. When the Cochabamba water services concession ran by the US-based Bechtel Corporation raised household water bills by 200 percent, it sparked a civil uprising that forced the company to leave the country and the water system to be put under public control (*Censored 2001*, #1).

After Cochabamba, the World Bank retired the word "privatization" and replaced it with terms like "concessions" and "decentralization," or "private sector participation." But critics say whatever the euphemism, the end result is the same: higher rates, lower quality, and less access.

Outcry from international human rights organizations led to the release of the Santa Eduviges activists, after nearly a month of imprisonment. But instead of loosening their grip, in August of 2007, President Saca and his ultra right-wing Nationalist Republican Alliance Party (ARENA) pushed through penal code reforms that changed disorderly conduct from a misdemeanor to a felony. Three weeks later, the government arrested eight leaders of a nurses' trade union for striking against the privatization of healthcare services and lack of medicine. If convicted, the union leaders could face eight years in prison under El Salvador's new "Patriot Act."

"The objective of these anti-terrorist laws isn't to fight terrorism, because there haven't been acts of terrorism here in many years," says

Pedro Juan Hernandez, a professor of economics at the University of El Salvador and an activist. He says the new law's objective is to "criminalize the social movement and imprison community leaders."

The Salvadoran social activists fighting for water access, healthcare and education, and now the right to protest, have seen enough war, says Hernandez. "But the origins of the violence are in the politics, the unemployment, and the government's policies against the population," he explains. "We are back to the level we were when the armed conflict began."

Washington's support for these repressive measures comes at a time when El Salvador is the only Latin American country with troops still in Iraq and was the first to sign the Central American Free Trade Agreement. Adoption of a US-based Patriot Act and the housing of the controversial US-run International Law Enforcement Academy (see Story #4) establish Saca as a strong US ally in the increasingly militarized neo-liberal agenda in Latin America—sometimes understandably confused with the Global War on Terror.

UPDATE BY JACOB WHEELER
So much of the destruction wrought upon the people of El Salvador during the second half of the twentieth century originated in Washington—corporate land grabs, environmental destruction, abuse of workers, death squads and counterinsurgency, harmful trade pacts and stunted democratic movements—and yet, a positive new chapter to El Salvador's history may be written in early 2009. For the first time since the Peace Accords were signed in 1992, ending El Salvador's brutal, twelve-year civil war, the progressive Farabundo Martí National Liberation Front (FMLN) party has a reasonable shot at winning power in national elections (the parliamentary election will take place in January 2009, followed by the presidential election in March). As of late spring 2008, the FMLN held a comfortable lead over the incumbent, right-wing ARENA party, which has perpetuated the same harmful policies that led to civil war in 1980.

If it gains power, FMLN is expected to stop the disastrous privatization of healthcare and water access, restore workers' rights, fight to amend trade deals so that they benefit more than just wealthy corporations, end El Salvador's participation in the occupation of Iraq, and, in general, follow the path paved by pragmatically progressive Latin American governments—such as those of Lula in Brazil and Correa in Ecuador, instead of the fiery, combative style of Chávez in Venezuela. FMLN presidential candidate Mauricio Funes has made one thing clear:

Washington is not going anywhere, and despite the scars of the past, he's willing to work with George W. Bush's successor.

I'll be penning a series of stories in late 2008 and early 2009 about El Salvador's upcoming elections for *In These Times*. In them I hope to broadcast the voices of those who are rarely heard, chronicle the evolution of the Salvadoran progressive movement—from *guerilla* rebels, to grassroots organizers, to politicians ready to seize San Salvador—and influence the way both independent and mainstream media in the United States cover these important elections. Please look for future coverage of El Salvador in our magazine and at www.InTheseTimes.com.

UPDATE BY WES ENZINNA

Since the publication of my article, and following an international outcry by human rights observers, the charges against the thirteen protestors arrested in Suchitoto have been dropped. The judge presiding over the case, Ana Lucila Fuentes de Paz—who I later discovered had been trained at the US-run International Law Enforcement Academy (ILEA) in San Salvador—ruled that there was not enough evidence to convict the protestors. Under the "Special Law Against Acts of Terrorism," the protestors faced up to eighty years in prison.

Despite this positive ruling, however, the story of the Suchitoto 13 does not end happily. On May 3, nineteen-year-old Hector Antonio Ventura—one of the thirteen arrested and charged in the Suchitoto case—was murdered in the town of Villa Verde. Ventura was beaten in the head and fatally stabbed in the heart by unknown assailants.

There is considerable suspicion that the killing was politically motivated, and Ventura's murder followed a spate of political assassinations against leftist activists in El Salvador, among them the January slaying of FMLN mayor Wilber Funes. Further, the killing occurred just two days after Ventura had agreed to give testimony of his experience at a public 'Day Against Impunity,' planned for July 2, 2008, by the mayor of Suchitoto. "Given his role as one of the accused in the high-profile anti-terrorism case," writes a member of the Committee in Solidarity with the People of El Salvador (CIS-PES), "Ventura's death could likely be politically motivated."

Members of the Salvadoran human rights community are demanding a full investigation of Ventura's death, yet the government has not been forthcoming about such an investigation. Political crimes often go uninvestigated in El Salvador, and many critics say that ARENA has contributed to the climate of impunity by prosecuting leftist activists, such as the vendors and Suchitoto 13, while ignoring cases of alleged political violence.

The 2009 presidential election represents the biggest possibility for the Salvadoran public to reject by electoral means ARENA's "iron fist" policies. Indeed, many analysts predict an FMLN victory in March. However, while many observers look hopefully toward the March elections, other critics claim ARENA has been engaged in electoral fraud. In particular, the ruling party has been accused of manipulating census numbers in FMLN strongholds such as Santa Tecla, Soyapango, and Las Vueltas, in order to deny FMLN candidates of government funds. Further, on May 9, 2008, Walter Aruajo, ARENA representative and head of El Salvador's Supreme Electoral Tribunal, announced new restrictions for international election observers. The new restrictions, Aruajo explained, "intend to regulate that no group of observers come and take part in political activity in the country." "Meddling in the electoral process," he continued, will result in expulsion from the country.

Critics worry the absence of a clear definition of "meddling" could leave the door open for the arbitrary application of these new restrictions, and more generally, they worry that these moves foreshadow an effort by ARENA to protect its electoral power through the creation and enforcement of self-serving and constitutionally questionable laws.

UPDATE BY CHRIS DAMON

In the year following the arrest of fourteen social movement activists in Suchitoto, there have been gains for the Salvadoran social movement, which launched unified, concerted actions to overturn the law and to achieve the unconditional liberty of the detainees; however, there have also been significant losses.

Thirteen of the original fourteen activists arrested spent twenty-six days under detention in the main men's and women's prisons. As a result of prison overcrowding, for some this meant going without a bed and having to purchase water for bathing and drinking. The thirteen were released July 27, 2007, under conditional terms that prevented them from traveling outside the country pending the presentation of further evidence against them by the state.

This waiting period extended for seven months, finally ending on February 8, 2008, at which point the state attempted to quietly change the charges from "Acts of Terrorism" to "Public Disorder and Aggravated Damages." Given this change, the Special Tribune appointed to handle terrorism charges transferred the case to the regular judicial system. An audience was held February 19 for which the States Attorney's office failed to show up to present their case leading the presiding judge to grant definitive liberty to all fourteen defendants due to the lack of charges or evidence presented. Despite an appeal by the States Attorney, the ruling was upheld on April 4.

Jubilation over these victories was short lived, given that on the night of May 2 one of the former defendants, Hector Antonio Ventura, was murdered as he slept in his small village of Valle Verde, Suchitoto.

While no one has been arrested or charged in the murder, both the media and authorities have characterized the death as related to the epidemic of gang crime which plagues the country, the most violent in Latin America.

However, the murders of activists like Ventura have caused human rights organizations to take notice. On May 12, the Foundation for the Study of Law Application (FESPAD), together with other social movement organizations, presented the case as the central element of a formal request to the States Attorney's office to investigate this and fourteen other murders that they argue may represent the use of gang elements to commit political assassinations. They cite the "Combined Group for the Investigation of Illegal Armed Groups with Political Motivations" (1994), which established criteria for determining the probability of political motivation in a given crime: modus operandi, characteristics of the victim, and level of impunity achieved by the authors. Since the initial release of FESPAD's list of fifteen suspicious murders, the list has been expanded to nineteen.

As of yet there has been no official response to these demands. And the controversial Anti-Terrorism Legislation remains in effect.

UPDATE BY RAUL GUTIERREZ

I strongly believe that it is important for Salvadoran society to be informed adequately on developments such as those that happened in Suchitoto on July 2, 2007, since that confrontation represented a strong risk for the country's political stability and democratic coexistence—particularly after the achievement of 1992 peace accords that left behind twelve years of war, 75,000 deaths, and 8,000 disappeared.

From my perspective, independent journalism should provide Salvadorans in-depth information and analysis on the national reality based above all on ethics, giving voice to those mostly unheard.

Meanwhile, the assassination of Héctor Ventura—one of those arrested during the protest in Suchitoto—on May 2 has added more fear among those detained in Suchitoto, according to David Morales, one of the accused defendants, who then worked for Tutela Legal (Legal Guardians), a human rights agency of the Roman Catholic Church, and now is member of the Foundation for the Study of Law Application (FESPAD).

The fourteen detainees who were arrested during the demonstration spent twenty-seven days in jail under charges of "acts of terrorism."

Lorena Martínez, president of the Association for Development in El Salvador (CRIPDES) and one of those jailed, reported that Ventura was stabbed in his heart while visiting a friend near Suchitoto. Ventura's friend was also injured during the attack but now is recuperating.

"We believe this was a political attack; first of all, we were accused of being terrorists and during detention our human rights were cynically violated," stated Martínez. When asked if the crime could be part of the country's circle of violence, she replied: "It could be."

The community leader said that the charges against the fourteen protesters went on for nine months and finally on April 16, a court dropped the charges against all the accused.

"It was a very tough experience; I could never have imagined being in jail in time of peace without committing any crime whatsoever," Martínez explained, and added that mass detention "was part of the Salvadoran Government plan to criminalize social unrest which seeks to intimidate people."

On the other hand, it seems there was no direct response to the article published on Inter Press Service. Nevertheless, I have to point out that most mainstream media coverage was biased, and in most cases only used government accounts of the confrontation. Further, some media did not cover police aggressions against protesters, journalists, and town residents not participating in the demonstration. The detention of Haydé Chicas, press officer of CRIPDES, while documenting the arrest of three coworkers, was aired by some media implying that she had been part of a protest that had blocked the road minutes before.

Anyone wanting further information regarding Suchitoto developments may contact the following persons:

Lorena Martínez, president of the Association for the Development of El Salvador; (503) 226-3717; www.cripdes.org

David Morales, defendant of those arrested in Suchitoto; (503) 236-1888; davidmorales@fespad.org.sv

12

Bush Profiteers Collect Billions From No Child Left Behind

Source:
Diatribune and Daily Kos, March, 30, 2007
Title: "Bush Profiteers Collect Billions From NCLB"
Author: Mandevilla

Researchers: Alan Scher and Sam Burchard
Faculty Evaluator: Karen Grady, PhD

The architect of No Child Left Behind (NCLB), President Bush's first senior education advisor, Sandy Kress, has turned the program, which has consistently proven disastrous in the realm of education, into a huge success in the realm of corporate profiteering. After ushering NCLB through the US House of Representatives in 2001 with no public hearings, Kress went from lawmaker—turning on spigots of federal funds—to lobbyist, tapping into those billions of dollars in federal funds for private investors well connected to the Bush administration.

A statute that once promised equal access to public education to millions of American children now instead promises billions of dollars in profits to corporate clients through dubious processes of testing and assessment and "supplemental educational services." NCLB—the Business Roundtable's revision of Lyndon Johnson's Education and Secondary Education Act (ESEA)—created a "high stakes testing" system through which the private sector could siphon federal education funds. The result has been windfall corporate profit. What was once a cottage industry has become a corporate giant. "Millions of dollars are being spent," says Jack Jennings, director of the Center on Education Policy, "and nobody knows what's happening."

The wedding of big business and education benefits not only the interests of the Business Roundtable, a consortium of over 300 CEOs, but countless Bush family loyalists. Sandy Kress, chief architect of NCLB; Harold McGraw III, textbook publisher; Bill Bennett, former

Reagan education secretary; and Neil Bush, the president's youngest brother, have all cashed in on the Roundtable's successful national implementation of "outcome-based education." NCLB's mandated system of state standards, state tests, and school sanctions has together transformed our public school system into a for-profit frenzy.

Kress, former president of the Dallas School Board, began "A Draft Position for George W. Bush on K-12 Education" as early as 1999. Working successfully with then-Governor Bush in Texas for years, the Democrat bolstered bipartisan support behind the compassionate marketing promise to "leave no child behind" through the adoption of high state standards measuring school performance. Signed into law in early 2002, NCLB dramatically extended the federal role in public education, mandating annual testing of children in Grades 3 to 8, providing tutoring for children in persistently failing schools, and setting a twelve-year timetable for closing chronic gaps in student achievement. Having then crafted the legislation, Kress transitioned from public servant to corporate lobbyist, guiding clients to the troth of federal funds. By 2005 he had made upwards of $4 million from lobbying contracts.

While the Business Roundtable maintains that the high-stakes tests administered nationwide hold schools accountable to "Adequate Yearly Progress," NCLB has instead benefited the testing industry in the amount of between $1.9 and $5.3 billion a year. NCLB requires states to produce "interpretive, descriptive, and diagnostic reports," all of which are provided at a price by members of the industry. Among these are the top four or five players in the textbook market, including the Big Three—McGraw-Hill, Houghton-Mifflin, and Harcourt General—who have, since the passage of NCLB, come to dominate the testing market. Identified by Wall Street analysts in the wake of the 2000 election as "Bush stocks," all three represent owners like Harold McGraw III, who has longstanding ties to the Bush administration and the lobbying efforts of Sandy Kress.

Other Kress clients, including Ignite! Learning, a company headed by Neil Bush, and K12 Inc., a for-profit enterprise owned by Bill Bennett, tailored themselves to vie for NCLB dollars.

Under NCLB, as school districts receive federal funding they are required by law to hold 20 percent of those funds aside, anticipating that its schools will fail to meet its Annual Yearly Progress formula. When that "failure" is certified by test scores, the district is required to use those set-aside federal funds to pay supplemental education service

(SES) providers. Ignite! has placed products in forty US school districts, and K12 offers a menu of services "as an option to traditional brick-and-mortar schools," including computer-based "virtual academies," that have qualified for over $4 million in federal grants. Under NCLB, supplemental educational services, whose results are being increasingly challenged, reap $2 billion annually.

Nationally, there are over 1,800 approved providers of supplemental educational services, but little in the way of regulation. To the contrary, Michael Petrilli, former member of the Department of Education, purports, "We want as little regulation as possible so the market can be as vibrant as possible." To that end, Kress is currently lobbying on behalf of another bipartisan coalition to win reauthorization of NCLB for another six years.

13

Tracking Billions of Dollars Lost in Iraq

Sources:
Vanity Fair, October 2007
Title: "Billions over Baghdad"
Authors: Donald Barlett and James Steele

Rolling Stone, August 23, 2007
Title: "The Great American Swindle"
Author: Matt Taibbi

Student Researchers: Brian Gellman, Dan Bluthardt, and Bill Gibbons
Faculty Evaluator: John Kramer, PhD

Beginning in April 2003, one month after the invasion of Iraq, and continuing for little more than a year, the United States Federal Reserve shipped $12 billion in US currency to Iraq. The US military delivered the bank notes to the Coalition Provisional Authority, to be dispensed for Iraqi reconstruction. At least $9 billion is unaccounted for due to a complete lack of oversight.

The initial $20 million came exclusively from Iraqi assets that had been frozen in US banks since the first Gulf War in 1990. Subsequent airlifts of cash included billions from Iraqi oil revenues formerly controlled by the United Nations. After the creation of the Development

Fund for Iraq—a kind of holding pit of money to be spent for "purposes benefiting the people of Iraq"—the UN turned over control of Iraq's billions of dollars from oil revenue to the United States.

When the US military delivered the cash to Baghdad, the money passed into the hands of an entirely new set of players—the Coalition Provisional Authority (CPA). The CPA had been hastily created by the Pentagon to serve as the interim government in Iraq. On May 9, 2003, President Bush appointed L. Paul Bremer III as CPA administrator. Over the next year, a compliant Congress gave $1.6 billion to Bremer to administer the CPA. This was over and above the $12 billion in cash that the CPA had been given to disburse from Iraqi oil revenues and unfrozen Iraqi assets.

Few in Congress had any idea about the true nature of the CPA as an institution. Lawmakers had never discussed the establishment of the CPA, much less authorized it—odd, given that the agency would be receiving taxpayer dollars. Confused members of Congress believed that the CPA was a US government agency, which it was not, or that at the very least it had been authorized by the United Nations, which it had not.

The Authority was in effect established by edict outside the traditional framework of American government. Because it was a rogue operation, no one was responsible for what happened to that money. Accountable to no one, its finances "off the books" for US government purposes, the CPA provided an unprecedented opportunity for fraud, waste, and corruption involving American government officials, American contractors, renegade Iraqis, and many others. In its short life more than $23 billion would pass through its hands. And that didn't include potentially billions of dollars more in oil shipments the CPA neglected to meter.

Incidents of flagrant abuse were rampant. Of 8,206 "guards" drawing CPA paychecks, only 602 actually existed; the other 7,604 were ghost employees. Halliburton charged the CPA for 42,000 meals for soldiers while in fact serving only 14,000. Contractors played football with bricks of $100,000 shrink-wrapped $100 bills.

Yet the precedent for legal impunity was established when whistle-blowers brought to light the case of Custer Battles, considered to be one of the worst cases of fraud in US history. The Bush administration not only refused to prosecute, it actually tried to stop a lawsuit filed against the contractors by whistle-blowers hoping to recover stolen CPA money. The administration argued that Custer Battles could not be found guilty of defrauding the US government because the CPA was not part of the US government. When the lawsuit went forward despite the administration's objections, Custer Battles mounted a defense arguing that they could not be guilty of theft since it was done with the government's approval.

At the core of this government-sanctioned free-for-all was the award of a CPA contract to NorthStar for services of accounting and auditing. The odd thing about this accounting service was that there was no certified public accountant on staff. A businessman, Thomas Howell, ran NorthStar out of his home in La Jolla, California, along with three other unrelated businesses, including home remodeling and furnishing. The company did have the advantage of a post office box in the Bahamas as its legal address of record.

NorthStar is incorporated in the Bahamas as an international business company (IBC). Despite their impressive name, IBCs are little more than paper operations. As a rule, they don't perform any business; they are empty vessels that can be used for anything. They have no chief executive officer or board of directors, and they don't publish financial statements. And IBC's books, if there are any, can be kept anywhere in the world, but no one can inspect them. IBCs aren't required to file annual reports or disclose the identity of their owners. They are shells, operating in total secrecy.

The Pentagon put this company in charge of monitoring billions of dollars of Iraqi and US citizens' money and of making sure it was spent honestly.

In one of his last official acts before leaving Baghdad, Bremer issued an order prepared by the Pentagon, declaring that all coalition-force members "shall be immune from any form of arrest or detention other than by persons acting on behalf of their Sending States." Contractors also got the same get-out-of-jail-free card. According to Bremer's order, "contractors shall be immune from Iraqi legal process with respect to acts performed by them pursuant to the terms and conditions of a contract or any sub-contract thereto." The Iraqi people would have no say over illegal conduct by Americans in their new democracy.

Matt Taibbi says, "What the Bush administration has created in Iraq is a sort of paradise of perverted capitalism, where revenues are forcibly extracted from the customer by the state, and obscene profits are handed out not by the market but by an unaccountable government bureaucracy."

He concludes, "What happened in Iraq went beyond inefficiency, beyond fraud even. This was about the business of government being corrupted by the profit motive to such an extraordinary degree that now we all have to wonder how we will ever be able to depend on the state to do its job in the future. If catastrophic failure is worth billions, where's the incentive to deliver success?"

UPDATE BY DONALD BARLETT AND JAMES STEELE

It's possible to sum up in two words what has happened since *Vanity Fair* published "Billions over Baghdad" in October 2007: Not much. Despite the ongoing theft, misappropriation, bribery, gratuities, profiteering, and waste of billions of taxpayer dollars, only a few low-level military people and civilians have been prosecuted. To be sure, the Defense Department has announced with great fanfare that it has launched scores of criminal investigations. But the end results are meager.

What's more, many in Washington believe that such investigations are unwarranted. In the heat of war, they say, it isn't possible to abide by the niceties of generally accepted accounting principles. But that doesn't explain why the Pentagon cuts checks for millions of dollars and mails them to anonymous post office boxes in tax havens. Nor does it explain the secrecy accorded its contractors. But it does help explain why the Pentagon is unable to reconcile more than $1 trillion in spending—that's *trillion*, not billion.

The Bush Justice Department has made clear by its actions that it has no intention of vigorously looking for or prosecuting those who rip off taxpayers. Similarly, Congress has failed to wage the kind of relentless probe that helped catapult a young senator from Missouri into the vice presidency and eventually the White House during World War II. In the heat of that war, the Truman committee conducted hundreds of hearings and issued scores of reports. The number of comparable hearings and reports coming out of Congress today can be counted on the fingers of one hand. Maybe.

One possible explanation is that running for election today has become so expensive that companies that help finance campaigns receive an informal immunity for their contracting fraud. Another is that Congress and the White House, whether occupied by Republicans or Democrats, have long taken the position that some corporations and financial institutions are too big to allow them to fail. Think Bear Stearns, most recently.

Now Congress and the federal government in general have seemingly applied that same principle to government contractors, who are deemed too important to indict, their top officers too essential to send to jail.

Finally, don't expect any extended probes by the news media. Newspapers and magazines are in such turmoil as a result of their changing economic fortunes that they are incapable of mounting any meaningful or sustained examination of government operations. They are much too busy worrying about falling profit margins. As a result, their journalistic commitments go no further than the next weekly poll.

14

Mainstreaming Nuclear Waste

Sources:

Nuclear Information and Resource Service, May 14, 2007
Title: "Nuclear Waste in Landfills"
Author: Diane D'Arrigo

Environment News Service, May 14, 2007
Title: "US Allows Radioactive Materials in Ordinary Landfills"
Author: Sunny Lewis

Environment News Service, February 4, 2008
Title: "US Company Seeks Permit to Import Nuclear Waste"
Author: Sunny Lewis

Student Researchers: Derek Harms and Cedric Therene
Faculty Evaluator: Noel Byrne, PhD

Radioactive materials from nuclear weapons production sites are being dumped into regular landfills, and are available for recycling and resale. The Nuclear Information and Resource Service (NIRS) has tracked the Department of Energy's (DOE) release of radioactive scrap, concrete, equipment, asphalt, chemicals, soil, and more, to unaware and unprepared recipients such as landfills, commercial businesses, and recreation areas. Under the current system, the DOE releases contaminated materials directly, sells them at auctions or through exchanges, or sends the materials to processors who can release them from radioactive controls. The recycling of these materials—for reuse in the production of everyday household and personal items such as zippers, toys, furniture, and automobiles, or to build roads, schools, and play-grounds—is increasingly common.

The NIRS report, "Out of Control on Purpose: DOE's Dispersal of Radioactive Waste into Landfills and Consumer Products," tracks the laws, methods, and justifications used by the DOE to expedite the mandatory cleanup of the environmental legacy being created by the nation's nuclear weapons program and government-sponsored nuclear energy research. One of the largest and most technically complex environmental cleanup programs in the world, the effort includes cleanup of 114 sites across the country to be completed by the end of 2008.

The DOE has unilaterally chosen allowable radioactive contamination and public exposure levels to facilitate "clean-up" of these sites. Pressure is increasing to allow clearing radioactivity from control in order to legalize the dispensing and disbursing of nuclear waste.

In 2000, the Secretary of Energy banned the commercial recycling of potentially radioactive metal. However, the ban does not apply to the disposal, reuse, or recycling of metal equipment, components, and pipes, or of other materials.

Seven sites of importance were investigated for the NIRS report: Oak Ridge, Tennessee; Rocky Flats, Colorado; Los Alamos, New Mexico; Mound and Fernald, Ohio; West Valley, New York; and Paducah, Kentucky. Of these, Tennessee is said to be the main funnel that pours nuclear weapon and power waste from around the country into landfills and recycling facilities without public knowledge. "People around regular trash landfills will be shocked to learn that radioactive contamination from nuclear weapons production is ending up there, either directly released by DOE or via brokers and processors," says author Diane D'Arrigo, NIRS's Radioactive Waste Project director.

EnergySolutions, the company that operates the only private low-level radioactive waste disposal business in the US, disposes of more than 90 percent of the low-level radioactive waste generated in the US. It operates waste processing and disposition facilities in Tennessee, South Carolina, and Utah. The company also operates low-level radioactive waste disposal facilities, vaults, and landfills on the DOE Oak Ridge Reservation in Tennessee.

Amazingly, as the DOE struggles through desperate and irresponsible measures to "disappear" this nation's nuclear waste by the end of 2008, EnergySolutions has applied for a license in Tennessee to process nuclear waste from Italy.

This application marks the first time in the history of the Nuclear Regulatory Commission that a company has asked to dispose of large amounts of foreign-generated low-level radioactive waste in the United States.

In February 2008, Bart Gordon, the Tennessee Democrat who chairs the House Committee on Science and Technology, asked the Northwest Interstate Compact of Low-Level Radioactive Waste Management to withhold licensing that he says would put the US on a path to becoming "the world's nuclear garbage waste dump."

In an understatement, Gordon argued, "The US already faces capacity issues and other challenges in treating and disposing of radioactive waste produced domestically. We should be working on solving this problem at home before taking dangerous waste from around the world."

UPDATE BY DIANE D'ARRIGO

The nuclear power and weapons industry and the government agencies that promote, oversee, and regulate nuclear activities are trying to save money by allowing large amounts of man-made, radioactively contaminated materials and property to be redefined as not radioactive. They don't want to pay to try to isolate nuclear waste, including metal, concrete, asphalt, plastic, soil, equipment, and buildings, so they have developed ways to send the waste to regular landfills or even into commercial recycling that could end up in daily-use items the public makes contact with regularly.

This story is increasingly important as old nuclear weapons sites and power reactors close and the companies seek relief from responsibility and liability for the long-lasting nuclear waste they generated. It is especially dangerous as new nuclear power and weapons facilities are proposed, which will dramatically increase the amount of waste generated that could get into the public realm.

Although the US federal agencies have not generally allowed nuclear waste to be released from controls, they are still working on it. The Environmental Protection Agency and the Nuclear Regulatory Commission (NRC) have proposed rules in the wings, likely to emerge at any time. NRC is encouraging case by case releases of nuclear waste. The DOE has procedures to allow some radioactive waste out of controls but claims to be preventing radioactive metal from getting into the commercial metal market. A programmatic environmental review could overturn that prohibition, and internally DOE has many loopholes to let nuclear wastes out.

The story wasn't covered much in the mainstream news. One notable exception was the investigative team led by Demetria Kalodimos on Channel 4 WSMV, Nashville's NBC affiliate, who reported on the story and did over twenty follow-ups in the Nashville area (see www.nirs.org for links). Public awareness led to legislative attention and a commitment by the landfill operator who was taking nuclear waste to stop taking it. Kalodimos received three journalism awards for reporting and following up on the story herself.

The community is not satisfied with this voluntary commitment, because the Tennessee State Department of Environment and Conservation (TDEC) still allows nuclear waste to be released from controls. TDEC licenses companies to import nuclear waste from around the country and world for "processing," including incineration and metal melting and reuse.

The report identified TDEC and Tennessee as leaders in releasing nuclear waste out of control.

The situation has worsened since last year. One of the processors is proposing to import a huge portion of Italy's nuclear power waste to burn, process, melt and dump in the US (Tennessee and Utah).

Action against this can be taken by contacting your state governors to oppose it and by supporting federal legislation that would prohibit the US from importing foreign nuclear waste.

Citizens can also contact their state officials to find out if their state is allowing nuclear waste into the solid waste streams in their communities.

Contact dianed@nirs.org for more information.

15

Worldwide Slavery

Sources:

Sojourners, March 15, 2007
Title: "From Sex Workers to Restaurant Workers, the Global Slave Trade Is Growing"
Author: David Batstone

Foreign Policy, March/April 2008
Title: "A World Enslaved"
Author: E. Benjamin Skinner

Student Researcher: Brandon Leahy
Faculty Evaluator: David McCuan, PhD

Twenty-seven million slaves exist in the world today, more than at any time in human history. Globalization, poverty, violence, and greed facilitate the growth of slavery, not only in the Third World, but in the most developed countries as well. Behind the façade in any major town or city in the world today, one is likely to find a thriving commerce in human beings.

As many as 800,000 are trafficked across international borders annually, and up to 17,500 new victims are trafficked across US borders each year, according to the US Department of Justice (DOJ). More than 30,000 additional slaves are transported through the US on their ways to other international destinations. Attorneys from the DOJ have prosecuted ninety-one slave trade cases in cities across the United States and in nearly every state of the nation.

Commerce in human beings today rivals drug trafficking and the illegal arms trade for top criminal activity on the planet. The slave trade sits at number three on the list, but the gap is closing. According to the US State Department's 2004 Trafficking in Persons Report, the FBI projects that the slave trade generates $9.5 billion in revenue each year. A report put out by the International Labor Office in 2005, titled "Global Alliance Against Forced Labor," estimates that figure to be closer to $32 billion annually.

Like the slaves who came to America's shores over 200 years ago, today's slaves are not free to pursue their own destinies. They are coerced to perform work for the personal gain of those who subjugate them. If they try to escape the clutches of their masters, modern slaves risk personal violence or reprisals to their families.

Increasingly severe and widespread poverty and social inequality ensure a growing pool of recruits. Parents in desperate straits may sell their children or at least be susceptible to scams that will allow the slave trader to take control over the lives of their sons and daughters. Young women in poverty-ridden communities are more likely to take risks on job offers in faraway locations. The poor are apt to accept loans that slave traders can later manipulate to steal their freedom. Thousands of traffickers lure children from impoverished rural parents with promises of scholarships, free schooling, and a better life. All of these paths carry unsuspecting recruits into the supply chains of slavery.

Though modern day forms of slavery are emerging to suit global markets, bonded labor continues to be the most common form of slavery in the world. In a typical scenario, an individual falls under the control of a wealthy patron after taking a small loan. The patron adds egregious rates of interest and inflated expenses to the original principal so that the laborer finds it impossible to repay. Debt slaves may spend their entire lives in service to a single slaveholder, and their "obligation" may be passed on to their children. Bondage, with no legal standing, is typically established through fraud and maintained through violence.

The United Nations, whose founding principles call for it to fight bondage in all its forms, has done little to combat modern slavery. And though since 1817 nations have signed more than a dozen international antislavery resolutions, very little effect has been realized.

Authors David Batstone and E. Benjamin Skinner are, however, impressed and heartened by the effectiveness of nongovernmental abolitionists around the world involved not only in brave acts of liberating slaves, but in launching transitional schools and training facilities for those recently freed.

UPDATE BY BENJAMIN SKINNER

When *Foreign Policy* published "A World Enslaved" in March 2008, they dropped a rock in a pool. There were few ripples. The mainstream media seems to have trouble grasping and presenting the concept that there are more slaves today than at any point in human history. And for understandable reasons: legal slavery was buried in most countries a long time ago. On a positive note, in its June 4 Trafficking in Persons Report the US State Department began to seriously address forms of slavery other than sex slavery. But the media seems to find little of interest in the bondage of millions who are enslaved in industries other than commercial sex. And such a narrow presentation means that the struggle against slavery in all its forms remains hidden and underfunded.

Despite the media abandonment, a handful of American citizens who had never been exposed to the issue before got involved after reading *A Crime So Monstrous: Face-to-Face with Modern Day Slavery*, the book that the *Foreign Policy* piece excerpted. A plastic surgeon in Missouri offered his services pro bono to those survivors who had scars as a result of their slavery; a woman from North Carolina lobbied her elected officials to stop slavery in Romania; a famous visual artist is working on a series of pieces about modern-day slavery, and has offered to give the proceeds from the sales to Free The Slaves, the most effective organization working to combat slavery worldwide; other readers made their own contributions to Free The Slaves or to domestically-focused antislavery organizations like the DC-based Polaris Project. Those few Americans have made commitments that will help turn the tide against modern-day slavery—and carry on the struggle of our ancestors who were slaves and abolitionists.

16

Annual Survey on Trade Union Rights

Source:

International Trade Union Confederation website, September 2007
Title: "2007 Annual Survey of Violations of Trade Union Rights"

Student Researchers: Carmela Rocha and Elizabeth Allen
Faculty Evaluator: Robert Girling, PhD

The first Annual Survey of Violations of Trade Union Rights to be published by the year-old International Trade Union Confederation (ITUC) documents enormous challenges to workers rights around the world. The 2007 edition of the survey, covering 138 countries, shows an alarming rise in the number of people killed as a result of their trade union activities, from 115 in 2005 to 144 in 2006. Many more trade unionists around the world were abducted or "disappeared." Thousands were arrested during the year for their parts in strike action and protests, while thousands of others were fired in retaliation for organizing. Growing numbers of trade union activists in Africa, the Americas, Europe, Asia, and the Pacific are facing police brutality and murder as unions are viewed as opponents of corporatist governments.

Colombia is still the deadliest country in the world for trade unionists. In 2006, seventy-eight people were murdered because of their union activities, an increase of eight from the previous year. There is strong and disturbing evidence of government involvement in these killings. Of 1,165 recorded crimes against trade unionists in Colombia, just fifty-six went before the courts, and only ten resulted in sentences.

In Mexico, two miners died and forty-one were injured when 800 police officers were sent to confront 500 striking miners and began a brutal evacuation of the mining company's premises. Violent scenes erupted in Ecuador when police and the army aggressively repressed a union-organized protest against the negotiation of a free trade agreement with the US, leaving fifteen seriously injured.

Employers in the Export Processing Zones (EPZ) of Central America have managed thus far to thwart workers' efforts to organize.

In the United States, a National Labor Relations Board ruling deprived millions of the right to organize by expanding the definition of the term "supervisor."

Across Africa, the use of disproportionate force and mass dismissals in retaliation for strike action were a frequent occurrence in 2007. In Kenya, over 1,000 workers on a flower plantation were dismissed after going on strike over workplace injuries and discrimination. Mass dismissals were also reported at a diamond mine in Botswana and at a road-construction site in Cameroon. In Egypt, Libya, and Sudan, the single trade union system prohibits effective bargaining or representation, while in Equatorial Guinea the dictatorship is too absolute to allow organizing.

In the Middle East, some governments took steps towards the recognition of trade union rights, but overall, workers in the region still have fewer rights than anywhere in the world. For example, in Jordan, Kuwait, Yemen, and Syria, laws impose an ineffective single trade union system. In Palestine, hostilities with Israel have made the organizing of trade unions virtually impossible. Migrant workers still make up the most vulnerable group in the region. At least twenty migrant workers at two factories in Jordan were arrested and deported for demanding improved wages and working conditions. In Saudi Arabia, the total lack of workers' rights and protection means that migrant workers, particularly women, are frequently subjected to blatant abuse, such as nonpayment of wages, forced confinement, rape, and other physical violence.

There were more mass dismissals and arrests in response to collective action in Asia than in any other region in the world in 2007. In Bangladesh, the phased introduction of (limited) trade union rights in EPZs got off to a poor start, as employers routinely harassed, suspended, and fired leaders of Workers' Representation and Welfare Committees during the year. In one incident, police opened fire on strikers at an EPZ garment factory, killing one worker and injuring others. In Malaysia police used batons, dogs, and water cannons to disperse a workers' protest. The Philippines stand out as the most violent country in the region. In an attempt to crush popular protests against the president's rule, labor leaders were among those targeted as "enemies of the state."

There was no change in China where the law does not allow for any independent trade union activity. Over one hundred workers were arrested and detained for involvement in collective protest, while the official "trade union" did nothing to protect them.

A recent report published by the social audit company Vigeo, based on a study of 511 enterprises in seventeen European countries, shows that less then 10 percent of European companies are committed to freedom of association and the promotion of collective bargaining. Changes in labor legislation in several countries added to existing restrictions on trade union rights. The most serious change was announced in Belarus, where a draft trade union law would make it virtually impossible to establish trade unions outside the state-controlled Federation of Trade Unions of Belarus.

Despite all these difficulties, millions of women and men remain firm in their commitment to, or are discovering the benefits of, trade union action.

17
UN's Empty Declaration of Indigenous Rights

Sources:
One World, September 14, 2007
Title: "UN Adopts Historic Statement on Native Rights"
Author: Haider Rizvi

BSNorrell.blogspot.com, December 11, 2007
Title: "Indigenous Peoples Protest World Bank Carbon Scam in Bali"
Author: Brenda Norrell

Common Dreams, December 12, 2007
Title: "Indigenous Peoples Shut Out of Climate Talks, Plans"
Author: Haider Rizvi

Forest Peoples Programme, November 30, 2007
Title: "NGO Statement on the World Bank's Proposed Forest Carbon Partnership Facility"
Author: Tom Griffiths

Student Researchers: Jessica Read, Andrea Lochtefeld, and Christina Long
Faculty Evaluator: John Wingard, PhD

In September 2007, the United Nations General Assembly adopted the Universal Declaration on the Rights of Indigenous Peoples. The resolution called for recognition of the world's 370 million indigenous peoples' right to self-determination and control over their lands and resources. The adoption of this resolution comes after twenty-two years of diplomatic negotiations at the United Nations (UN) involving its member states, international civil society groups, and representatives of the world's aboriginal communities.

The declaration emphasizes the rights of indigenous peoples to maintain and strengthen their institutions, cultures, and traditions, and to pursue their development in keeping with their own needs and aspirations. The declaration was passed by an overwhelming majority vote of 143–4. Only the United States, Canada, Australia, and New Zealand voted against the resolution, expressing the view that strong emphasis on rights to indigenous self-determination and control over lands and resources would hinder economic development and undermine "established democratic norms."

Three months following the passage of the Universal Declaration on the Rights of Indigenous Peoples, however, a delegation of indigenous peoples were forcibly barred from entering the United Nations Framework Convention on Climate Change (UNFCCC) in Bali, despite the fact that the delegation was invited to attend. Indigenous peoples from around the world protested the exclusion from the climate negotiations.

The indigenous delegates went to Bali to denounce what they contend are false solutions to climate change proposed by the UN—such as carbon trading, agrofuels, and so-called "avoided deforestation."

The World Bank initiative, Forest Carbon Partnership Facility (FCPF), was launched in Bali as part of the discussions on Reducing Emissions Through Deforestation in Developing Countries (REDD), despite indigenous disapproval and the fact that 18–20 percent of annual global carbon emissions are caused by deforestation. The initiative, which allows tropical forests to be included in carbon offsetting schemes, fails to combat climate change, the groups say, because it allows industrialized countries and companies to buy their way out of emission reduction. The bank, which has a vested interest in carbon trading, has a particularly appalling track record in relation to funding deforestation and carbon emission projects.

The nongovermental organization (NGO) Statement on the World Bank's proposed FCPF, endorsed by eighty-four organizations on November 30, 2007, pointed to shortcomings in the World Bank's proposal: "As the World Bank Group positions itself to become a lead agency on climate change mitigation and the central administrative body of the proposed FCPF, we are concerned that the Bank risks losing sight of its central mission of reducing poverty as it adopts a narrow focus on carbon accounting. We note also that the Bank continues to undermine its own climate change mitigation efforts by persisting in funding fossil fuel industries on a global scale and enabling deforestation."

The statement continues, "We are alarmed that to date the FCPF plans have been developed in a rushed way with little public discussion. Only weeks before it proposes to launch the FCPF at the 13th COP [Conference of Parties] of the UNFCCC in Bali, potentially affected forest peoples in tropical and sub-tropical countries have not been properly consulted about the design and objectives of the FCPF. It remains unclear who benefits from this accelerated timeline . . . The proposed governance mechanisms confine decision-making to governmental and commercial participants. They do not allow opportunities for civil society and affected forest peoples to take part in decision-making regarding readiness plans, packages and implementation, eligibility, and REDD strategies and transactions."

Jihan Gearon, of the indigenous Environmental Network, responded to the ban on Indigenous participation by stating, "Our communities and livelihoods are the first affected by climate change. We are also the most affected by the unsustainable solutions being proposed to solve climate change. . . . This past September 13, the UN General Assembly adopted the UN Declaration on the Rights of Indigenous Peoples, which protects the rights of Indigenous Peoples to their lands, territories, and environment. Yet through the faulty process and false climate change solutions of the UNFCCC, these fundamental human rights are being violated."

Sandy Gauntlett of the Global Forest Coalition and chairman of the Pacific Indigenous Peoples Environment Coalition said, "With this proposal, the World Bank is violating the principle of Prior Informed Consent, which is enshrined in the UN Declaration on the Rights of

Indigenous Peoples. Indigenous peoples should not just be consulted on this facility. Without their full and prior informed consent this facility should be disbanded."

UPDATE BY BRENDA NORRELL

Indigenous peoples continue to expose carbon credits as a scam for profiteering corporations and the World Bank, fueled by the easily manipulated news media. While carbon brokers become millionaires, the reality of the carbon credit scheme hits indigenous peoples around the world with full force, particularly in South America, India, and Africa.

While the carbon credit scam is designed to be vague and lack accountability, Tom Goldtooth, Navajo and executive director of the Indigenous Environmental Network (IEN), said the carbon scheme serves as a means of relieving guilt for the rich, but is a fictional concept.

"It allows the polluter to continue to pollute and actually pays them to pollute," said Goldtooth, while continuing IEN's education campaign on carbon credits in 2008.

While the goal of carbon credits is reduction of greenhouse gasses, Goldtooth said there is no assurance that the schemes ever become reality. For example, Goldtooth said there is no guarantee that a tree planted today will live until maturity, without being chopped down, and then offset deforestation and fossil fuel gasses.

The promotion of carbon trading was a focus of caucuses of the 7th Session of the United Nations Permanent Forum on Indigenous Issues in April 2008.

At the United Nations in New York, many indigenous peoples voiced outrage when the Permanent Forum's final report praised the World Bank funded carbon trading, including the Clean Development Mechanism, without exposing human rights violations and environmental destruction.

Florina Lopez, coordinator of the Indigenous Women's Biodiversity Network of Abya Yala, urged the forum to affirm the rejection of carbon trading mechanisms and concerns over specific implementations. Over thirty organizations called for the final report to include a section outlining their concerns.

The grave problems with carbon trading include violations of the UN Declaration on the Rights of Indigenous Peoples. For example, those objecting to carbon trade promotion said the Wayuu people in

Colombia did not give free, prior, and informed consent for construction of the Jepirachi Wind Project in their sacred territory. In fact, they were unaware of the project.

More than 200 Wayuu were assassinated prior to clearing the land for implementation of wind projects in the area, according to indigenous peoples at the forum. Further, the energy generated from the wind farm is used to power the mega coalmine, Cerrejon mine.

Goldtooth said the carbon market is a huge contradiction, which ultimately funds the nuclear power and fossil fuel industries. Citing human rights violations, Goldtooth said indigenous peoples do not want to be "seduced by the World Bank's money."

"In promoting the clean development mechanism projects and carbon trading, the Permanent Forum is allowing oil companies, who are the biggest emitters for greenhouse gases, to continue to pollute," Goldtooth said. "Promoting the commodification of the air is a corruption of our traditional teachings and violates the original instructions of Indigenous Peoples. We have to make the transition to alternative energy solutions."

For more information, see the Indigenous Environmental Network (http://www.ienearth.org), Censored News (http://www.bsnorrell.blogspot.com), and Earthcycles (http://www.earthcycles.net).

UPDATE BY TOM GRIFFITHS

Since the NGO statement expressing serious concerns about the World Bank's Forest Carbon Partnership Facility (FCPF) presented to the World Bank forest carbon team and several governments in a World Bank meeting in Washington, DC, in November 2005, things have gone from bad to worse.

First, the bank ignored the plea to withhold activation of the facility until public concerns were addressed. The bank plowed ahead with the public launch of the facility at the 13th Conference of the Parties to the UN Framework Convention on Climate Change held in Bali in December 2007, generating a storm of loud protest by indigenous peoples and civil society representatives outside the meeting room. Inside the meeting room, Vicky Corpuz, chair of the UN Permanent Forum on Indigenous Issues, made a strong statement condemning the bank's failure to consult properly with indigenous peoples about global climate and forest initiatives that may affect their communities and lands directly.

In response to these intense criticisms, the bank announced that it would conduct "retroactive consultation" with indigenous peoples on its FCPF plans. Bank meetings with indigenous peoples' representatives went ahead in February and March 2008 through three meetings in Asia (Katmandu), Africa (Bujumbura) and Latin America (La Paz).

In Asia, indigenous participants presented a series of concerns about rights and accountability problems in the FCPF charter and proposed governance structure that bank staff could not address and only agreed to take away to study further. Some replies given to the participants were arguably misleading, suggesting that the bank's safeguards would apply to the FCPF when the bank's legal department in November had already confirmed that the safeguards do *not* apply in any binding way to FCPF activities unless monies are to be disbursed to specific projects through the facility (while much of its work will not be based on bank-funded projects, but rather policy making and strategy formulation).

In Africa, the same potentially confusing information on the bank's safeguard policies was presented to meeting participants, and many answers to concerns raised were vague or very general.

In Latin America, some national indigenous organizations have complained that they were not invited to the bank meeting, and those that did attend on the first day rejected the meeting as a non-consultation and obliged the bank to acknowledge that the meeting was only an "information sharing" activity (as dissemination of complete information prior to the meeting, to properly prepare participants, had not taken place). In the same meeting, a statement by indigenous leaders was read aloud, condemning top-down climate change mitigation policies that have not been developed with indigenous peoples, like REDD and the FCPF.

Forest People's Programme asked for clarification on the vital safeguards issue in May 2008, and was advised by the bank's FCPF team that this issue is "still being discussed internally within the Bank." The draft FCPF charter likewise remains inside a black box in the bank, and it is not clear if FPP and civil society concerns about the draft charter have been taken up in any revised legal instrument establishing this controversial forest carbon fund.

In short, the whole question of proper safeguards and accountability of the FCPF to affected citizens and communities and whether or not there will be guarantees for full FCPF conformity with international human rights and environmental law remains unresolved.

At the same time, the bank has pushed forward with even bigger plans on forest and climate change and now proposes to establish a mega forest funds called the Forest Investment Fund (FIF) with a possible budget of $2 billion USD.

It seems that the World Bank just cannot learn lessons: this new FIF is being developed in 2008 without meaningful consultation with forest peoples in developing countries and is coming under increasing public criticism for the lack of transparency in its formulation.

For further information on this news topic in briefings issued by FPP in February 2008, see www.forestpeoples.org/documents/forest_issues/bases/forest_issues.shtml. Check this website for more news and ongoing controversy over the bank's forest carbon funds.

Also contact tom@forestpeoples.org and amarantha@forestpeoples.org, or call 44 1608 652893, for more information.

Other useful sources for information include www.un.org/esa/socdev/unpfii/, www.brettonwoodsproject.org/, www.ifiwatchnet.org/, www.sinkswatch.org/, www.foei.org/en/campaigns/climate, and www.globalforestcoalition.org/paginas/view/32.

18

Cruelty and Death in Juvenile Detention Centers

Source:
Associated Press, March 2, 2008
Title: "13,000 Abuse Claims in Juvie Centers"
Author: Holbrook Mohr

Student Researcher: Sarah Maddox
Faculty Evaluator: Barbara Bloom, PhD

In states across the country, child advocates have harshly condemned the conditions under which young offenders are housed—conditions that involve sexual abuse, physical abuse, and even death. The US Justice Department (DOJ) has filed lawsuits against facilities in eleven states for supervision that is either abusive or harmfully negligent. While the DOJ lacks the power to shut down juvenile correction facilities, through litigation it can force a state to improve its detention centers and protect the civil rights of jailed youth.

Lack of oversight and nationally accepted standards of tracking abuse make it difficult to know exactly how many youngsters have been assaulted or neglected.

In a nationally conducted survey, the Associated Press contacted each state agency that oversees juvenile correction centers and asked for information on the numbers of deaths as well as the numbers of allegations and confirmed cases of physical, sexual, and emotional abuse by staff members since January 1, 2004. According to the survey, more than 13,000 claims of abuse were identified in juvenile correction centers around the country from 2004 through 2007—a remarkable total given that the total population of detainees was about 46,000 at the time the states were surveyed in 2007.

The worst physical confrontations have ended in death. At least five juveniles died after being forcibly placed in restraints in facilities run by state agencies or private facilities with government contracts since January 1, 2004.

The use of restraint techniques and devices and their too-aggressive application have long been controversial and came under intense scrutiny last year after the death of fourteen-year-old Martin Lee Anderson. A grainy video taken at a Florida boot camp in January 2006 showed several guards striking the teen while restraining him. On October 12, 2006, six guards and a nurse were acquitted of manslaughter charges after defense attorneys argued that the guards used acceptable tactics.

In Maryland, seventeen-year-old Isaiah Simmons lost consciousness and died after he was held to the floor face down at a privately owned facility that was contracted by the state. Prosecutors say the staff waited forty-one minutes after the boy was unresponsive to call for help. An attorney for one of the counselors said the men were only trying to prevent Simmons from hurting himself or someone else. A judge dismissed misdemeanor charges against five counselors. The state has appealed.

Other restraint-related deaths involve three boys—seventeen, fifteen, and thirteen years of age—in facilities in Tennessee, New York, and Georgia, respectively. At least twenty-four other juveniles died in correction centers between 2004 and 2007 from suicide and natural causes or preexisting medical conditions.

A drive to reform California's juvenile justice system follows successful landmark litigation against the California Youth Authority (CYA) in April 2006. During litigation, advocates learned that conditions in many California county juvenile halls were as bad as those in the state CYA facilities. Yet as the appalling conditions in the CYA were revealed, officials shifted much of the population from the CYA facilities to the county juvenile halls.

In 2006, reported conditions in California juvenile halls included severe overcrowding, with teenagers sleeping floors; nonexistent educational opportunity; nonexistent mental healthcare or rehabilitative programs; isolation for over twenty-three hours a day for months straight; use of excessive force, including beatings and pepper sprayings; and inappropriate administration of medications.

Attorney Richard Ulmer states, "California law expressly requires that a juvenile hall not be regarded as a penal institution, but rather be a safe and supportive homelike environment. But many juvenile halls in the state are more like penitentiaries than homes."[1]

Similar crises of institutional abuse against troubled youth are occurring in states across the nation.

Citation:
1. Richard Ulmar, "California Juvenile Justice System in Crisis; Lawsuits to End Abuses Against Children," *PR Newswire*, April 19, 2006.

19

Indigenous Herders and Small Farmers Fight Livestock Extinction

Sources:
Trade BioRes, September 21, 2007
Title: "Conference Agrees Steps to Safeguard Farm Animal Diversity"
Author: The International Centre for Trade and Sustainable Development

La Via Campesina, September 11, 2007
Title: "Wilderswil Declaration on Livestock Diversity"
Authors: Representatives of pastoralists, indigenous peoples, and smallholder farmers

Student Researchers: Maureen Santos, Andrew Kochevar, and Stephanie Smith
Faculty Evaluator: Nick Geist, PhD

The industrial model of livestock production is causing the worldwide destruction of animal diversity. At least one indigenous livestock breed becomes extinct each month as a result of overreliance on select breeds imported from the United States and Europe, according to the study, "The State of the World's Animal Genetic Resources," conducted by the UN Food and Agriculture Organization (FAO). Since research for the report began in 1999, 2,000 local breeds have been identified as at risk.

The industrial livestock breeding and production system that is being imposed on the world requires high levels of investment in technology and receives subsidies and other resources that have distorted the market.

Consequences of the livestock industry's globalization include the threat to sustainable development and global food security, destruction of the livelihoods of over one billion people worldwide, smallholder bankruptcies and suicides, and the extinction of some of the world's hardiest breeds of animals.

The FAO report, which the International Livestock Research Institute (ILRI) contributed to, surveyed farm animals in 169 countries, and found that nearly 70 percent of the world's entire remaining unique livestock are bred in developing countries. The findings were presented to over 300 policy makers, scientists, breeders, and industrialized livestock keepers at the First International Technical Conference on Animal Genetic Resources, held in Interlaken, Switzerland, from September 3 to 7, 2007.

In response to these findings, scientists from the Consultative Group on International Agricultural Research, ILRI's supporting organization, have called for the rapid establishment of gene banks to conserve the sperm and ovaries of key animals critical for the survival of global animal populations. Over the past six years, ILRI has built a detailed database, called the Domestic Animal Genetic Resoures Information System, containing research-based information on the distribution, characteristics, and statuses of 669 breeds of cattle, sheep, goats, pigs, and chickens indigenous to Africa and Asia.

Meanwhile, concurrent with the Interlaken summit, around 300 representatives from thirty organizations of pastoralists, indigenous peoples, smallholder farmers, and NGOs from twenty-six countries met in a parallel conference, to establish opposition to globalized industrial livestock production. The Livestock Diversity Forum to Defend Food Sovereignty and Livestock Keepers' Rights met in Wilderswil, Switzerland, and presented an alternative Declaration on Livestock Diversity on September 6, 2007.

The Wilderswil Declaration maintains that while the FAO report contains good analysis and squarely points to the industrial livestock system as one of the main forces behind destruction of diversity, the FAO Global Plan of Action contains nothing that addresses these causes. The Declaration states:

> It is totally unacceptable that governments agree on a plan that does not challenge the policies that cause the loss of diversity . . .
>
> Defending livestock diversity is not a matter of [privatized] genes but of collective rights.
>
> The social organizations of pastoralists, herders, and farmers have no interest in participating in a plan which does not address the central causes behind the destruction of livestock diversity, but rather provides crutches and weak support for a collapsing global livestock production system. Because the Global Plan of Action does not challenge industrial livestock production, we reinforce our commitment to organize ourselves to save livestock diversity and to counter the negative forces bearing on us.

This peoples' proposal asserts that it is not possible to conserve animal diversity without protecting and strengthening the local communities that currently maintain and nurture such diversity. These livestock keepers maintain that governments should accept and guarantee collective rights and community control over natural resources, including communal grazing lands and migration routes, water, and livestock breeds.

The Declaration further states:

> Local knowledge and biodiversity can only be protected and promoted through collective rights. Collective knowledge is intimately linked to cultural diversity, particular ecosystems, and biodiversity, and cannot be dissociated from any of these other three aspects. Any definition and implementation of the rights of livestock keepers should take this fully into account. It is clear that the rights of livestock keepers are not compatible with intellectual property rights systems [i.e., gene banks] because these systems enable exclusive and private monopoly

control. There must be no patents or other forms of intellectual property rights on biodiversity and the knowledge related to it.

The organization maintains that they want livestock keeping that is on a human scale, based on the health and wellbeing of humankind not industrial profit. They point out that the dominant model of production is based on a dangerously narrow genetic base of livestock that is propped up by the widespread use of veterinary drugs. Yet this risky and high-cost system is providing more and more of our food: globally, one third of pigs, one half of eggs, two thirds of milk, and three quarters of the world's chickens are produced from industrial breeding lines.

20

Marijuana Arrests Set New Record

Sources:
Marijuana Policy Project, September 27, 2007
Title: "Marijuana Arrests Set New Record for Fourth Year in a Row"
Author: Bruce Mirken

National Organization for Reform of Marijuana Laws, September 24, 2007
Title: "Marijuana Arrests for Year 2006—829,625 Tops Record High"
Author: Paul Armentano

Student Researchers: Ben Herzfeldt and Caitlyn Ioli
Faculty Advisor: Pat Jackson, PhD

For the fourth year in a row, US marijuana arrests set an all-time record, according to 2006 FBI Uniform Crime Reports. Marijuana arrests in 2006 totaled 829,627, an increase from 786,545 in 2005. At current rates, a marijuana smoker is arrested every thirty-eight seconds, with marijuana arrests comprising nearly 44 percent of all drug arrests in the United States. According to Allen St. Pierre, executive director of the National Organization for Reform of Marijuana Laws (NORML), over 8 million Americans have been arrested on marijuana charges during the past decade, while arrests for cocaine and heroine have declined sharply.

The number of arrests in 2006 increased more than 5.5 percent from 2005. Of the 829,627 arrests, 89 percent were for possession, not sale or manufacture. Possession arrests exceeded arrests for all violent crimes combined, as they have for years. The remaining offenders, including those growing for personal or medical use, were charged with sale and/or manufacturing.

A study of New York City marijuana arrests conducted by Queens College, released in April 2008, reports that between 1998 and 2007 the New York police arrested 374,900 people whose most serious crime was the lowest-level misdemeanor marijuana offense. That number is eight times higher than the number of arrests (45,300) from 1988 to 1997. Nearly 90 percent arrested between 1998 and 2007 were male, despite the fact that national studies show marijuana use roughly equal between men and women. And while national surveys show Whites are more likely to use marijuana than Blacks and Latinos, the New York study reported that 83 percent of those arrested were Black or Latino. Blacks accounted for 52 percent of the arrests, Latinos and other people of color accounted for 33 percent, while Whites accounted for only 15 percent.[1]

Over the years, roughly 30 percent of those arrested nationally have been under the age of twenty. The Midwest accounts for 57 percent of all marijuana-related arrests, while the region with the fewest arrests is the West, with 30 percent. This is possibly a result of the decriminalization of marijuana in western states, such as California, on the state and local level over the past several years.

"Enforcing marijuana prohibition . . . has led to the arrests of nearly 20 million Americans, regardless of the fact that some 94 million Americans acknowledge having used marijuana during their lives," says St. Pierre.

In the last fifteen years, marijuana arrests have increased 188 percent, while public opinion is increasingly one of tolerance, and self-reported usage is basically unchanged. "The steady escalation of marijuana arrests is happening in direct defiance of public opinion," according to Rob Kampia, executive director of the Marijuana Policy Project in Washington, DC, "Voters in communities all over the country—from Denver to Seattle, from Eureka Springs, Arkansas to Missoula County, Montana—have passed measures saying they don't want marijuana arrests to be priority. Yet marijuana arrests have set an all-time record for four years running . . ."

Meanwhile, enforcing marijuana laws costs between $10 and $12 billion a year.

Citation

1. Jim Dwyer, "On Arrests, Demographics, and Marijuana," *New York Times*, April 30, 2008.

UPDATE BY BRUCE MIRKEN

This story was essentially a subset of a larger annual story, the FBI's yearly Uniform Crime Reports (UCR), and the 2006 report, released in September 2007, marked the fourth year in a row that marijuana arrests set a new record. While the UCR, as usual, got wide mainstream coverage, the only major mainstream outlet to note the marijuana arrest record was the Reuters wire service. Marijuana Policy Project staffers also did two or three local radio interviews, and the story was picked up in one form or another by a handful of other outlets—most notably Bill Steigerwald's column in the conservative *Pittsburgh Tribune-Review*, an article on AlterNet, and Andrew Sullivan's blog, The Daily Dish.

This is typical of the mass media tendency to view marijuana policy through the lens of Cheech-and-Chong stereotypes—as a trivial story of minor importance, more a curiosity than serious news. But the sheer numbers suggest it deserves more attention. Nearly 830,000 marijuana arrests are made annually, about 89 percent of them for simple possession, not sales or trafficking. That's one marijuana arrest every thirty-eight seconds, and more arrests for marijuana possession than for all violent crimes combined. Put another way, it's the equivalent of arresting every man, woman, and child in the state of North Dakota plus every man, woman, and child in Des Moines, Iowa, in one year—and doing the same thing every year, year after year. All of this comes at a total cost to taxpayers estimated at anywhere from $14 billion to $42 billion per year.

New national arrest statistics won't be out until about the time this book is published, but scientific data continue to emerge that demolish the intellectual underpinnings of marijuana prohibition. Studies continue to find marijuana far less toxic or addictive than such legal drugs as alcohol and tobacco, while in Britain, where most marijuana possession arrests were discontinued in January 2004, marijuana use has steadily declined since arrests stopped, according to official government surveys. Sadly, even though the British government's scientific advisors urge continuation of the no-arrest policy, as of this writing in May 2008, Prime Minister Gordon Brown appears determined to launch a new crackdown.

In the US, the clearest signs of progress have come from efforts to permit medical use of marijuana. Twelve states now have medical marijuana laws, and a medical marijuana initiative on Michigan's November 2008 ballot was ahead by nearly two to one in the only public poll released so far. Democratic presidential candidate Barack Obama has indicated he would end the federal war on these state medical marijuana laws, and fellow Democrat Hillary Clinton has also indicated some willingness to rethink federal policy. Republican John McCain has expressed support for current federal law.

Extensive information about marijuana policy and efforts to change our current laws is available from the Marijuana Policy Project, www.mpp.org or (202) 462-5747. A more wide-ranging newsletter on drug policy issues is the *Drug War Chronicle*, at stopthedrugwar.org.

UPDATE BY PAUL ARMENTANO

Since beginning my tenure at NORML in the mid-1990s, I've observed the growth of the annual number of Americans arrested for minor marijuana violations from a low of 288,000 in 1991 to a record 830,000 in 2006. Yet despite this nearly 300 percent increase in minor pot busts (nearly 90 percent of all marijuana arrests are for possession offenses), mainstream media coverage of these skyrocketing arrest rates remains nominal.

The media's disinterest in this subject is uniquely troubling, given that the arrest data is derived from the FBI's Uniform Crime Report, and that other aspects of this report (for example: has the violent crime rate risen or fallen?) traditionally generate hundreds of major news stories each year. Equally troubling is the media's habit of improperly attributing these marijuana arrest figures to NORML rather than to the FBI, the law enforcement organization that actually tracks and reports said data.

Arguably, the most disturbing result of these rising arrests is that record numbers of Americans are now being ordered by the courts to attend 'drug treatment' programs for marijuana—regardless of whether they require treatment (most don't) or not.

According to the most recent state and national statistics, up to 70 percent of all individuals in drug treatment for pot are now placed there by the criminal justice system. Of those enrolled in treatment, more than one in three hadn't even used marijuana in the thirty days prior to their admission. Yet, disingenuously, the White House argues that these rising admission rates justify the need to continue arresting cannabis users—despite the fact that it is the policy, not the drug itself—that is actually fueling the spike in drug treatment.

Finally, it must be emphasized that criminal marijuana enforcement disproportionately impacts citizens by age—an all too often overlooked fact that has serious implications for those of us who work in drug policy reform. According to a 2005 study commissioned by the NORML Foundation, 74 percent of all Americans busted for pot are under age thirty, and one out of four are age eighteen or younger. Though these young people suffer the most under our current laws, they lack the financial means and political capital to effectively influence politicians to challenge them. Young people also lack the money to adequately fund the drug law reform movement at a level necessary to adequately represent and protect their interests. As a result, marijuana arrests continue to climb unabated, and few in the press—and even fewer lawmakers—feel any need or sufficient political pressure to address it.

(Paul Armentano is the deputy director of NORML and the NORML Foundation in Washington, DC.)

21

NATO Considers "First Strike" Nuclear Option

Source:
The Guardian, January 22, 2008
Title: "Pre-emptive nuclear strike a key option, NATO told"
Author: Ian Traynor

Student Researchers: Stephanie Smith and Sarah Maddox
Faculty Evaluator: Robert McNamara, PhD

North Atlantic Treaty Organization (NATO) officials are considering a first strike nuclear option to be used anywhere in the world a threat may arise. Former armed force chiefs from the US, Britain, Germany, France, and the Netherlands authored a 150-page blueprint calling for urgent reform of NATO, and a new pact drawing the US, NATO, and the European Union (EU) together in a "grand strategy" to tackle the challenges of an "increasingly brutal world." The authors of the plan insist that "the first use of nuclear weapons must remain in the quiver of escalation as the ultimate instrument to prevent the use of weapons of mass destruction." The manifesto was presented to the Pentagon in Washington and to NATO's secretary general in mid-January 2008. The proposals are likely to be discussed at a NATO summit in Bucharest in April 2008.

The authors—General John Shalikashvili, former chairman of the US joint chiefs of staff and NATO's ex-supreme commander in Europe; General Klaus Naumann, Germany's former top soldier and ex-chairman of NATO's military committee; General Henk van den Breemen, a former Dutch chief of staff; Admiral Jacques Lanxade, a former French chief of staff; and Lord Inge, field marshal and ex-chief of the general staff and the defense staff in the UK—paint an alarming picture of the threats and challenges confronting the West in the post-9/11 world and deliver a withering verdict on the ability to cope. The five commanders argue that the West's values and way of life are under threat, while the West is struggling to summon the will to defend them.

They claim that the following are key threats:

➤ Political fanaticism and religious fundamentalism

➤ The "dark side" of globalization, meaning international terrorism, organized crime and the spread of weapons of mass destruction

➤ Climate change and energy insecurity, entailing a contest for resources and potential "environmental" migration on a mass scale

➤ The weakening of the nation state as well as of organizations such as the UN, NATO and the EU.

To prevail, the generals call for an overhaul of NATO decision-making methods, a new "directorate" of US, European, and NATO leaders to respond rapidly to crises, and an end to EU "obstruction" of, and rivalry with, NATO. Among the most radical changes demanded are the following:

➤ A shift from consensus decision-making in NATO bodies to majority voting, resulting in faster action through an end to national vetoes

➤ The abolition of national caveats in NATO operations of the kind that plague the Afghan campaign

➤ No role in decision-making on NATO operations for alliance members who are not taking part in the operations

➤ Use of force without UN Security Council authorization when "immediate action is needed to protect large numbers of human beings."

Reserving the right to initiate nuclear attack was a central element of the West's Cold War strategy against the Soviet Union. Critics argue that what was once a method used to face down a nuclear superpower is no longer appropriate.

UPDATE BY IAN TRAYNOR

I was the only person to write about this and nothing much has really happened since.

22

CARE Rejects US Food Aid

Sources:

Inter Press Service, July 23, 2007
Title: "Mutiny Shakes US Food Aid Industry"
Author: Ellen Massey

Revolution Magazine, October 1, 2007
Title: "Starvation, Aid Agencies and the Benevolence of the Imperialists"
Author: Revolution Cooperative

Student Researchers: Susanna Gibson, Cedric Therene, and Chris Armanino
Faculty Evaluator: Keith Gouveia, JD

In August 2007, one of the biggest and best-known American charity organizations, CARE, announced that it was turning down $45 million a year in food aid from the United States government. CARE claims that the way US aid is structured causes rather than reduces hunger in the countries where it is received. The US budgets $2 billion a year for food aid, which buys US crops to feed populations facing starvation amidst crisis or enduring chronic hunger.

The organization's announcement prompted argument about the forms and objectives of the aid given by the US and other big powers to third world countries and the role that most charity organizations are playing. The reasoning behind CARE's decision is part of a years-long debate that has influenced everything from US trade and domestic legislation to the Doha Round of the World Trade Organization talks.

CARE's 2006 report, "White Paper on Food Aid Policy," points out that the current food aid program is motivated by profit rather than altruism. The policy, which dictates that donated money be used to purchase food in the home country, results in a program driven by "the export and surplus disposal objectives of the exporting country" and not the needs of people in hunger.

The US policy implements the practice of monetization, a food aid policy in which the US government buys surplus food from American agribusinesses that have already been heavily subsidized, and ships it via US shipping lines (generating transport costs that eat up much of the $2 billion annual food aid provided by the US government) to aid organizations working around the world. The aid organizations then sell the US-grown crops to local populations, at a dramatically reduced cost. The aid organizations use proceeds from these sales to fund their development and anti-poverty programs. But several groups, with CARE at the forefront, have pointed out that this policy has the effect of undermining local farmers and destabilizing the very food production systems that aid organizations are working to strengthen.

A policy that puts local farmers out of commission and undermines agriculture in developing countries becomes part of a process by which those countries lose the means to develop—and thus grow more dependent on the stronger and more dominant nations. These countries become more vulnerable in every sphere, not only economically but politically as well. The result is likely to be more hunger and less sovereignty as countries are tied ever more tightly to the world market.

"We are not against emergency food aid for things like drought and famine," CARE spokeswoman Alina Labrada said, "but local farmers are being hurt instead of helped by this mechanism."

The European Union has also been critical of the US food aid program. European countries all but phased out the practice of monetization in the 1990s. Only 10 percent of their budgeted food aid is reserved for crops grown in Europe. Suspicions remain that the US uses monitized food aid programs to avoid limits on its universally contested farm subsidies.

The UN World Food Programme, the largest distributor of food aid in the world, has rejected the practice of monetization and does not allow its grain to be sold by NGOs.

The past two US congressional farm bills presented proposals to shift portions of the food aid budget from grain to cash donations, to be made available for people in need to buy locally grown crops. Both attempts were voted down.

23

FDA Complicit in Pushing Pharmaceutical Drugs

Source:
NewStandard, April 20, 2007
Title: "FDA Complicit in Pushing Prescription Drugs, Ad Critics Say"
Author: Shreema Mehta

Student Researchers: Lauren Anderson, Corey Sharp-Sabatino, and Marie Daghlian
Faculty Evaluator: Noel Byrne, PhD

While the US Food and Drug Administration (FDA) turns a blind eye, drug companies are making false, unsubstantiated, and misleading claims in their advertising, often withholding mandated disclosure of dangerous side effects. Though companies are required to submit their advertisements to the FDA, the agency does not review them before they are released to the public. A Government Accountability Office report released November 2006 found that the FDA reviews only a small portion of the advertisements it receives, and does not review them using consistent criteria.

Claiming lack of funds and resources necessary to impose effective regulations on drug marketing, the FDA is asking Congress to charge drug companies fees in order to fund FDA review of advertisements before they go public as part of renewing the Prescription Drug User Fee Act (PDUFA). PDUFA has come under fire from consumer advocates who say it gives the pharmaceutical industry too much leverage over the FDA and has resulted in rushing drugs to market. But the FDA hopes that if Congress approves the plan, it will raise more than $6 million annually through "user fees" to review advertisements.

Although Congress may approve the plan, author Shreema Mehta says a range of public-interest groups, from ad critics at Commercial Alert to senior advocates at Gray Panthers, want an outright ban on all prescription drug advertisements. Public Citizen and Consumers Union warn that the FDA review of drug advertisements will likewise be tainted if funded by the very companies the FDA is charged with scrutinizing. Critics are calling for stricter regulations over drug companies and they say eliminating the financial ties between the FDA and the pharmaceutical industry should be the first step.

But the pharmaceutical industry is not the only industry that benefits from inconsistent FDA reviews and inadequate investigations of advertising claims. One of the nation's biggest infant bottled water companies, Nursery Water, is misleading parents with erroneous information and false health claims on its website and in advertising materials, touting the safety and benefits of fluoride in infant bottled water, in clear violation of Federal Trade Commission (FTC) and FDA rules.

A letter sent from scientists at the Environmental Working Group (EWG) to officials at the FDA and FTC uncovers EWG's extensive review of Nursery Water's claims that both misrepresent the position of the American Academy of Pediatrics, which states, "supplementary fluoride should not be provided during the first six months of life" (AAP 2005), and contradict the official position of the FDA, which states, "the health claim [for fluoride] is not intended for use on bottled water products specifically marketed for use by infants" (FDA 2006).[1]

Mehta reports that representatives from the food and pharmaceutical industries say banning ads would violate the First Amendment. "In our system of jurisprudence we have a very high threshold that protects the right to free speech, whether it's political or commercial," Jim Davidson, attorney for the drug-company-funded Advertising Coalition, told the Associated Press.

Mehta warns of the increased leverage food and drug companies may have over the FDA should Congress approve the fee plan. She reports that in 2005, pharmaceutical companies spent about $4.2 billion in advertisements aimed at the public, known as "direct-to-consumer" ads, up from about $2.5 billion in 2000 and $1.1 billion in 1997. And the promoting of drugs to physicians, with almost $7.2 billion spent in 2005, dwarfs advertising to the public. At the same time, public spending on prescription drugs has steadily increased, reaching about $140 billion in 2001, more than tripling since 1990.

Meanwhile, Mehta reports that it's not clear whether the FDA reviews most advertisements at all. The agency can direct drug companies to change their advertisements after they are released to the public if it finds they violate regulations, but does no screening before the release of ads that may be dangerously deceptive.

Citation

1. Anila Jacob, M.D., M.P.H. and Jane Houlihan, "EWG calls for Investigation of Nursery Water," Environmental Working Group, February 1, 2008.

UPDATE BY SHREEMA MEHTA

Americans are taking more prescription drugs than ever before, leading the world in drug consumption and reaping huge profits for pharmaceutical companies. America is also one of the few countries that allow public advertising of prescription drugs. This is not a coincidence. Many doctors and consumer advocates have criticized advertisements featuring beaming people explaining how Valtrex changed their lives as deceptive, inaccurate, and invasive to the doctor-patient relationship. Many activists favor an outright ban on prescription drug ads; others call for strict regulation. This article dealt with the FDA's ties to the pharmaceutical industry and its proposal to regulate what critics feel is dangerously deceptive advertising by charging drug companies to review their commercials.

A few months after this article ran, President Bush renewed the Prescription Drug User Fee, which includes the industry-funded review process of drug advertisements, putting into effect what critics argue is yet another conflict of interest in the agency.

Though the *Washington Post* ran several articles on PDUFA, few explored the importance of the new proposal for company-funded advertisement regulation. Though press coverage of the problems of drug advertising is slim, advocacy groups remain active on the issue.

Commercial Alert runs a prescription drug ad campaign that is currently working to raise support for the Public Health Protection Act, which would ban drug ads designed for the public. They are on the web at http://www.commercialalert.org/. The Consumers Union also supports this bill. Learn more about their campaign at https://secure.consumersunion.org/site/Advocacy?JServSessionIdr 009=vjqvqork51.app44a&cmd=display&page=UserAction&id=1889.

24

Japan Questions 9/11 and the Global War on Terror

Source:
Rense.com and *Rock Creek Free Press*, January 14, 2008
Title: "Transcript Of Japanese Parliament's 911 Testimony"
Author: Benjamin Fulford

Student Researchers: Kyle Corcoran, Alan Scher, Bill Gibbons, and Elizabeth Rathbun
Faculty Evaluator: Mickey S. Huff, MA

Testimony in the Japanese parliament, broadcast live on Japanese television in January 2008, challenged the premise and validity of the Global War on Terror. Parliament member Yukihisa Fujita insisted that an investigation be conducted into the war's origin: the events of 9/11.

In a parliament Defense and Foreign Affairs Committee session held to debate the ethics of renewing Japan's "anti-terror law," which commits Japan to providing logistical support for coalition forces operating in Afghanistan, Fujita opened the session by stating, "I would like to talk about the origin of this war on terrorism, which was the attacks of 9/11, . . . When discussing these anti-terror laws we should ask ourselves, what was 9/11? And what is terrorism?"

Fujita pointed out that, "So far the only thing the government has said is that we think it was caused by al-Qaeda because President Bush told us so. We have not seen any real proof that it was al-Qaeda." He reminded parliament that twenty-four Japanese citizens were killed on 9/11, yet the mandate of a criminal investigation by the Japanese government never followed. "This is a crime so surely an investigation needs to be carried out," said Fujita (*Censored 2008*, #16).

Fujita went on extensively to ask "about the suspicious information being uncovered and the doubts people worldwide are having about the events of 9/11."

The Japanese parliament viewed several slides from the Pentagon and World Trade Center (WTC) sites as Fujita explained each. The slides showed evidence inconsistent with official explanation: damage in and around the Pentagon was not consistent with the damage a 757 airplane would cause. Fujita noted, "Also, there were more than eighty security cameras at the Pentagon, but officials have refused to release the footage. In any case, as you have just seen, there is no picture of the airplane or of its wreckage in any of these photographs. It is very strange that no such pictures have been shown to us." A US Air Force official corroborated the fact that the plane executed a U-turn and avoided the Defense Secretary's office, a feat that would be impossible for an unskilled first-time pilot to maneuver; and no air defense was made in the ninety-minute interval between the initial impact of the planes at the WTC and the Pentagon. Fujita added, "It is baffling that no flight records were found at any of four sites." On the ground at the WTC sites, both sounds and visual evidence from explosions were verified. Flying debris shot out as far as 150 meters consistent with buildings exploding. A New York fireman during rescue operations confirmed that a series of explosions resembled a professional demolition, and a Japanese survivor heard explosions while fleeing the site. The World Trade Center Building 7 (WTC 7), forty-seven stories high and located one block away, collapsed into its footprint, seven hours after the main WTC buildings were attacked, in five or six seconds, although no plane struck it and it had minimal fire damage. Not only did the 9/11 Commission fail to mention WTC 7, but the US Federal Emergency Management Agency (FEMA and National Institute of Standards and Technology (NIST) made no mention of it in their reports.

Fujita went on to detail proof of insider trading from September 6 through 8, when investors executed "put options" to sell stock in United and American Airlines at a fixed price. Finance specialist Keiichiro Asao responded with confirmation that such complex transaction would be the work of insiders rather than al-Qaeda.

Fujita then addressed Prime Minister Yasuo Fukuda, "I would like to know why the Prime Minister thinks it was the Taliban who was responsible for 9/11." He continued, "We need to go back to the beginning and not just simply and blindly trust the US government explanation and indirect information provided by them. . . . We need to look at this evidence and ask ourselves what the war on terrorism really is. . . . We need to ask who the real victims of this war on terrorism are. I think the citizens of the world are its victims."

"Prime Minister," Fujita continued, "what about the origin of the War on Terror and the idea of whether it is right or wrong to participate in it? Is there really a reason to participate in this War on Terror?"

Fujita received support for concluding that the reason for participating in the US War on Terror needs to be investigated and analyzed.

Opposition blocked the extension of Japan's anti-terror law and colleagues acknowledged his bravery with congratulatory phone calls.

This came to an end in mid-January when, after months of parliamentary debates and the opposition of at least 50 percent of the Japanese public, Fukuda rammed the anti-terror bill through parliament. After the bill was voted down by opposition in the Upper House plenary session on January 12, the government resubmitted it later that same day to the Lower House, where the ruling conservative party holds the majority, and turned a bill into a law. Thus, they overturned a veto in the Upper House.

This is the first time in half a century that a Japanese government has resorted to such tactics—deemed a drastic measure by Japanese standards.[1]

According to Christopher W. Hughes, professor of politics and international studies at University of Warwick, "Fukuda's government was under a lot of US pressure to re-deploy ships, and even if he was always somewhat doubtful about the importance of the mission in military terms and the whole US War on Terror, he perceived passing the bill as very important to US-Japan relations. This was also impressed upon him by a personal meeting with US President Bush."

Citation

1. Axel Berkofsky, "Japan: The Deployment Dilemma," International Relations and Security Network, January 24, 2008.

UPDATE BY BENJAMIN FULFORD

If you still believe that the English language corporate media is free, take a look behind the scenes at the Foreign Correspondents Club of Japan (FCCJ) and think again.

I was a member of that club for over two decades, but I had no clue about what it really represented until I tried to stage a press conference about 9/11. From that point on all sorts of nasty things started to happen and I suddenly realized the place seemed more like a nest of spies than a club for journalists.

For example, people I did not know tried to have me evicted from the club, e-mails vanished from my inbox before I got to read them, and people started to spread the word that I had mental issues.

The list of insults to press freedom at the club since that initial conference is too long to write about in detail here, so I will merely cite the most recent example.

Yukihisa Fujita, a member of parliament for the opposition Democratic Party, in a parliamentary debate broadcast nationwide on NHK, asked Prime Minister Yasuo Fukuda about many of the glaring discrepancies in the official US government explanation of what happened on 9/11. A member of parliament in Japan, a US ally, showed powerful evidence on national TV that the US government murdered 3,000 of its own citizens as well as people from Japan and many other nations. I suggested we call him for a press conference, and nine working journalists—representing a potential audience of billions—agreed. Usually, only three or more yes votes from working journalists is enough for an event to go ahead. Despite this, the *Wall Street Journal*'s James Sims, head of the Professional Activities Committee (PAC), in confederation with FCCJ President Martyn Williams, vetoed the event even though it was subject matter that they, as technical journalists, do not cover. They vetoed it in violation of Article 3 of the club bylaws that call for press freedom. Not only that, they kicked me off the PAC in a blatant attempt to shut me up.

Fujita has since been invited to speak to the EU parliament and many other venues. Fujita has been given a chance to ask more questions in parliament, and many Japanese news magazines have written about his activities. Books about 9/11 are also selling well in Japan. A growing group of Japanese politicians has become aware of what really happened on that day. The Japanese government itself actually knows the truth and is starting to affect the US–Japan alliance in fundamental ways. The Japanese government's formal replies to Fujita's questions show it is becoming increasingly suspicious that the US government murdered over twenty Japanese citizens. The long-term repercussions for US security could be huge.

25

Bush's Real Problem with Eliot Spitzer

Sources:
Truthout, February 2008
Title: "Predatory Lenders' Partner in Crime"

Global Research, March 17, 2008
Title: "Why the Bush Administration 'Watergated' Eliot Spitzer"
Author: F. William Engdahl

Student Researchers: Rob Hunter, Elizabeth Rathbun, and Rebecca Newsome
Faculty Evaluator: Mickey S. Huff, MA

The exposure of New York State Governor Eliot Spitzer's tryst with a luxury call girl had little to do with the Bush administration's high moral standards for public servants. Author F. William Engdahl advises that, "in evaluating spectacular scandals around prominent public figures, it is important to ask what and who might want to eliminate that person." Timing suggests that Spitzer was likely a target of a White House and Wall Street operation to silence one of its most dangerous and vocal critics of their handling of the current financial market crisis.

Spitzer had become increasingly public in blaming the Bush administration for the subprime crisis. He testified in mid-February before the US House of Representatives Financial Services subcommittee and later that day, in a national CNBC interview, laid blame squarely on the administration for creating an environment ripe for predatory lenders.

On February 14, the *Washington Post* published an editorial by Spitzer titled, "Predatory Lenders' Partner in Crime: How the Bush Administration Stopped the States From Stepping In to Help Consumers," which charged, "Not only did the Bush administration do nothing to protect consumers, it embarked on an aggressive and unprecedented campaign to prevent states from protecting their residents from the very problems to which the federal government was turning a blind eye."

In this editorial, Spitzer explained:

> The administration accomplished this feat through an obscure federal agency called the Office of the Comptroller of the Currency (OCC). The OCC has been in existence since the Civil War. Its mission is to ensure the fiscal soundness of national banks. For 140 years, the OCC examined the books of national banks to make sure they were balanced, an important but uncontroversial function. But a few years ago, for the first time in its history, the OCC was used as a tool against consumers.
>
> In 2003, during the height of the predatory lending crisis, the OCC invoked a clause from the 1863 National Bank Act to issue formal opinions preempting all state predatory lending laws, thereby rendering them inoperative. The OCC also promulgated new rules that prevented states from enforcing any

of their own consumer protection laws against national banks. The federal government's actions were so egregious and so unprecedented that all 50 state attorneys general, and all 50 state banking superintendents, actively fought the new rules.

But the unanimous opposition of the 50 states did not deter, or even slow, the Bush administration in its goal of protecting the banks. In fact, when my office opened an investigation of possible discrimination in mortgage lending by a number of banks, the OCC filed a federal lawsuit to stop the investigation."

The editorial appeared the day after Spitzer's ill-fated rendezvous with the prostitute at the Mayflower Hotel. With that article, some Washington insiders believe, Spitzer signed his own political death warrant.

On March 4, 2008, Spitzer furthermore proposed legislation that would have imposed penalties for mortgage fraud and predatory lending.[1]

Curiously, Spitzer, who had been elected governor in 2006, defeating a Republican by winning nearly 70 percent of the vote, has been not charged with any crime. His case went into the hands of Washington and not those of New York State authorities, underscoring the clear political nature of Spitzer's "offense." New York Assembly Republicans immediately announced plans to impeach Spitzer or put him on public trial if he were to refuse resignation. Although prostitution is illegal in most US states, clients of prostitutes are almost never charged, nor are their names typically released while a case is in process.

Spitzer's editorial concluded, "When history tells the story of the subprime lending crisis and recounts its devastating effects on the lives of so many innocent homeowners, the Bush administration will not be judged favorably . . . it will be judged as a willing accomplice to the lenders who went to any lengths in their quest for profits. The administration was so willing, in fact, that it used the power of the federal government in an unprecedented assault on state legislatures, as well as on state attorneys general and anyone else on the side of consumers."

Citation

1. "Governor Spitzer Proposes Legislation to Address Sub-prime Mortgage Crisis," New York State website, March 4, 2008.

CENSORED 2009 HONORABLE MENTIONS

US Attempted Coup of Hamas

Source:
Vanity Fair, April 2008
Title: "The Gaza Bombshell"
Author: David Rose

After failing to anticipate Hamas's victory over Fatah in the 2006 Palestinian election, the Bush administration backed an armed force under Fatah strongman Muhammad Dahlan, touching off a bloody civil war in Gaza. Confidential documents, corroborated by sources in the US and Palestine, reveal a White House plan for forces, led by Dahlan and armed with weapons supplied at America's behest, to give Fatah the muscle it needed to remove the democratically elected Hamas-led government from power. But the secret plan backfired, resulting in a further setback for American foreign policy under Bush. Instead of driving its enemies out of power, the US-backed Fatah fighters inadvertently provoked Hamas to seize control of Gaza.

US Colonizes Kosovo

Sources:
Foreign Policy In Focus, March 7, 2008
Title: "Kosovo: A New Versailles?"
Author: Tomaz Mastnak

Global Research, February 28, 2008
Title: "Washington gets a new colony in the Balkans"
Author: Sara Flounders

Global Research, February 19, 2008
Title: "Large Potential Albanian Oil and Gas Discovery Underscores Kosovo's Importance"
Author: Stephen Lendman

Kosovo's unilateral declaration of independence from Serbia will gain it neither independence nor even minimal self-government. In violation of UN resolutions, the replacement of the UN mandate over Kosovo with a EU mandate will allow the US more freedom to shape its presence. Author Tomaz Mastnak notes that there is strong parody in the coordinated action by which a state declares its independence and other states send in missions to create that state. The EU is sending in 1,800 lawyers, judges, police, and administrators who are replacing the UN mission and whose task is to set up Kosovo's "institutions, legal authorities and agencies for law enforcement as well as other executive responsibilities." KFOR, the NATO-led Kosovo force, will stay, which means that 16,000 foreign soldiers will be stationed in Kosovo. The Ahtisaari plan, which was zealously advocated by the United States, gives NATO military supremacy over Kosovo. The only major construction in Kosovo is Camp Bondsteel, the largest US base built in Europe in over a generation. The new colonial structure in Kosovo grants absolute power similar to that held by Paul Bremer in the first two years of the US occupation of Iraq.

Farmers vs. Seed Vault

Sources:
Inter Press Service, March 4, 2008
Title: "NGOs Wary of Doomsday Seed Vault"
Author: Keya Acharya

GRAIN, February 26, 2008
Title: "Svalbard seed vault: not everyone is celebrating"

Agricultural NGOs in India and elsewhere are criticizing the newly opened Global Seed Vault (GSV) at Svalbard in Norway as fundamentally unjust in its objectives. GRAIN, with branches in major developing nations in Africa, Asia, and Latin America, says a serious deficiency of GSV is that it deals only with state and private-body depositors. The system of seed banks (of which GSV is one of hundreds) is controlled by an international research agency that has totally excluded farmers from its trusteeship and has granted itself almost exclusive access to the seed vault's deposits. The storage system takes seeds of unique plant varieties away from the farmers and communities that originally propagated, protected, and shared the seeds, and makes them inaccessible to them. The logic is that while newer seeds from research labs replace people's traditional varieties, those traditional seeds will be vaulted as "raw material" for laboratory breeding. "This vault is more the need of the life-sciences industry, known for its 'pirating' of farmers' material and traditional knowledge," says a GRAIN representative. "The ultimate beneficiaries will thus be the very same corporations that are at the roots of crop-diversity destruction."

Researching Livestock Disease for Germ Warfare?

Source:
GRAIN, January 2008
Title: "Germ warfare: Livestock disease, public health and the military-industrial complex"

The US, largely through its military-industrial complex, is busy locating livestock disease, getting control of virus samples from around the world, and building a network of laboratories—all under the guise of combating bioterrorism. Developing countries are, however, becoming increasingly resistant to US and UK coercion in securing material transfer agreements and patenting rights that ignore national sovereignty over biological resources. Of serious concern is the lack of transparency around scientific research dealing with animal diseases and the human health implications. The privatization of viruses, vaccines and related materials and technologies for commercial purposes is seen to violate public interest. Finally, the growing connection between scientific research and development and its military use provides for powerful argument in favor of much stricter oversight and governance over research, ownership, and control of animal-borne disease pathogens.

Holes in the Border Wall

Source:
Texas Observer, February 18, 2008
Title: "Holes in the Wall"
Author: Melissa del Bosque

The Department of Homeland Security is not answering questions of why the US-Mexico fence is bypassing properties of the wealthy and politically connected. As the DHS files eminent domain lawsuits to evict homeowners and public entities (such as city and state parks and universities), local residents are questioning the justification for their sacrifice, and just how secure this fence can be, given all the "gaps" for the affluent. One condemned property borders that of billionaire Ray L. Hunt, of one of the wealthiest oil and gas dynasties in the world, and a major donor to some of Bush's pet projects. The wall stops at Hunt's 6,000-acre property of exclusive gated communities and a 1,800-acre business park. At another point the wall stops at the edge of a popular retreat and golf course, and starts up again at its other side. The Secure Border Initiative contract awarded to Boeing (one of Washington's biggest political contributors to both parties) is an "indefinite delivery" contract with little oversight and no maximum on how much they can spend. Residents argue that the fence's construction has everything to do with politics and private profit, and nothing to do with stopping illegal immigration.

Suppressed Report on Great Lakes Toxins

Source:
Center for Public Integrity, March 2008
Title: "Great Lakes: Danger Zones?"
Author: Sheila Kaplan

A top U.S. public health agency, the Agency for Toxic Substances and Disease Registry, has blocked the publication of a 400-plus page federal study, *Public Health Implications of Hazardous Substances in the Twenty-Six US Great Lakes Areas of Concern*, regarding environmental hazards in the eight Great Lakes states, reportedly because it contains such potentially "alarming information" as evidence of elevated infant mortality and cancer rates. The study that was to have been released in July of 2007 was undertaken by the Centers for Disease Control and Prevention. Researchers found low birth weights, elevated rates of infant mortality and premature births, and elevated death rates from breast cancer, colon cancer, and lung cancer. The Center for Public Integrity has obtained the study, which warns that more than 9 million people who live in the more than two dozen "areas of concern"—including such major metropolitan areas as Chicago, Cleveland, Detroit, and Milwaukee—may face elevated health risks from being exposed to dioxin, PCBs, pesticides, lead, mercury, or six other hazardous pollutants.

Gaza's £2 Billion Gas Field

Sources:
The Telegraph (UK), June 11, 2007
Title: "Gaza Doesn't Need Aid: It Has a £2bn Gas Field"
Author: Tim Butcher

The Electronic Intifada, January 23, 2008
Title: "Gaza Siege Intensified After Collapse of Natural Gas Deal"
Author: Mark Turner

Israel and the United States are blocking Palestine from profiting from a gas field located twenty miles off its coast that is worth an estimated £2 billion. The Palestinian Investment Fund was negotiating for the sale of the natural gas to Egypt but redirected its efforts toward Israel after receiving pressure from then–British Prime Minister Tony Blair. But after the Hamas election victory, concerns of Hamas profiting from the agreement led to a long impasse. In January 2008, British Gas announced it was pulling the plug on negotiations with Israel and was again considering Egypt as a buyer. Since the announcement, Israel has radically expanded its sanctions, cut fuel shipments entirely, and stepped up its military campaign. Increased air strikes and use of internationally proscribed tank shell ammunition has led to a drastic increase in civilian deaths and injuries in hopes of eroding support for Hamas in Gaza. Combined with dangerous shortages of fuel, food, water, and basic supplies, the coastal region has fallen into catastrophe.

World Bank Responsible for Theft of Congo Forests

Sources:
The Guardian, April 11, 2007
Title: "Vast Forests With Trees Each Worth £4,000 Sold for a Few Bags of Sugar"
Author: John Vidal

The Guardian, October 4, 2007
Title: "World Bank Accused of Razing Congo Forests"
Author: John Vidal

The World Bank financed and encouraged foreign companies to destructively log the world's second largest forest, destroying the home of up to 600,000 Congolese Pygmies, according to an independent inspection panel report on an internal investigation by senior bank staff and outside experts. The report accuses the bank of drastically misleading the Congo government about the value of its forests, of deceptive and unethical business practice, and of breaking its own rules regarding protection of environments and alleviation of poverty. The report on the bank's activities in the Democratic Republic of Congo since 2002 follows complaints made by an alliance of twelve Pygmy groups. The groups claim that the legally questionable World Bank system of awarding vast logging concessions to companies to exploit the forests causes "irreversible harm" to rainforests that nearly 40 million people depend on for medicines, shelter, timber, and food.

Languages Facing Extinction

Source:
International Herald Tribune, September 19, 2007
Title: "Linguists identify endangered-language hot spots"
Author: John Noble Wilford

Of the estimated 7,000 languages spoken in the world today, nearly half are in danger of extinction and are likely to disappear within this century. They are, in fact, now falling out of use at a rate of about one every two weeks, as indigenous tongues are overwhelmed by the dominant languages at school, in the marketplace, and on television. Research supported by the Living Tongues Institute for Endangered Languages and the National Geographic Society identified five regions where languages are disappearing most rapidly and are concentrating on recording and preserving these. More than half of these languages have no written form. When they disappear, they leave behind no dictionary, no text, no record of the accumulated knowledge and history of a vanished culture. Thousands of languages now face extinction at a rate that exceeds that of birds, mammals, fish, or plants.

Chevron is Burmese Regime Lifeline

Source:
King Features Syndicate, truthdig.com, October 2, 2007
Title: "Chevron's Pipeline Is the Burmese Regime's Lifeline"
Author: Amy Goodman

While George Bush and Condoleezza Rice make headlines calling for sanctions against the brutal Burmese regime, Chevron plays a vital role as its lifeline. The Burmese regime, in partnership with the US multinational oil giant, Chevron, delivers extracted gas to Thailand through Burma's Yadana pipeline. It is Yadana and related gas projects that have kept the military regime afloat to buy arms and ammunition and to pay its soldiers. The pipeline was built by people forced into servitude by the Burmese military. The original pipeline partner, Unocal, was sued for use of slave labor. As soon as the suit was settled out of court, Chevron bought Unocal. The US government has had sanctions in place against Burma since 1997. A loophole exists, though, for companies grandfathered in. Unocal's exemption from the Burma sanctions has been passed on to its new owner, Chevron. Despite the recent brutal crackdown, Chevron maintains it has no intention to cut ties.

Africa Says No

Source:
Le Monde Diplomatique, January 2008
Title: "Africa Says No"
Author: Ignacio Ramonet

Africa refused to sign trade agreements with the European Union during the second European Union–Africa summit in Lisbon, in December 2007. The EU pressured African countries to agree to the Economic Partnership Agreements, which would allow European Union goods and services exports to enter African markets without any customs duty. Several African governments, starting with those represented by the presidents of Senegal, South Africa, and Namibia, made it clear that they refuse to sign such an agreement. They have also gained the support of France's president, Nicolas Sarkozy. This rebellion against the Economic Partnership Agreement won the field as the summit adjourned on a note of failure for the EU. European Commission President José Manuel Barroso was forced to back down and agree to the African countries' demand to continue the discussion at a later date.

New Bomb Blasts

Source:
Citizen's Watch, August 2007
Title: "Stopping New Radioactive Bomb Blasts"
Author: Loulena Miles

Lawrence Livermore Lab, run by the University of California–Berkeley, proposes conducting bigger, open-air bomb blasts at the lab's Site 300, a high-explosives testing range near Tracy, California. Livermore Lab is proposing to raise the annual limit for high explosives detonated at Site 300 by 800 percent, from 1,000 to 8,000 pounds. And the daily limit will rise by 350 percent, from 100 to 350 pounds. According to the Lab, these blasts will be so powerful they will blow the walls and roof out of Site 300's Contained Firing Facility—hence the plan to detonate them in the open. What makes these bomb tests so terribly dangerous are the toxic and radioactive materials they contain. According to the permit application, the test explosions will contain up to 5,000 pounds of deadly depleted uranium (uranium-238). This nuclear test expansion greatly increases the risk of danger to Northern California residents, as tests will be conducted without safeguards to contain the radioactive material.

Electricity Triples in Cost After Deregulation

Source:
Power in the Public Interest, November 2007
Title: "Gap in Electricity Prices For Industrial Customers Between Deregulated and Regulated States Has Tripled Since 1999"
Author: Marilyn Showalter

According to a Power in the Public Interest (PPI) study, the cost of electricity for deregulated industrial customers has tripled since 1999—an increase of $55 billion by the end of 2007. Industrial customers in the eleven deregulated states (California, Connecticut, Delaware, Maine, Maryland, Massachusetts, Michigan, New Hampshire, New Jersey, Rhode Island, and Texas) pay roughly $7.2 billion more annually for their power than their counterparts in regulated states pay for the same amount of energy. The PPI executive director states, "This gap in purchasing power explains why industrial customers are hurting as they try to compete with their counterparts in regulated states."

Possibility for Profound Change in Nepal

Sources:
Revolution Newspaper, May 1, 2008
Title: "Nepal: Expectations For Profound Change Soar To The Sky"

Revolution Newspaper, February 24, 2008
Title: "The 12th Anniversary of the People's War in Nepal and Its Unsettled Outcome"

On April 10, 2008, elections were held in Nepal for the first time in nine years. But these were not ordinary elections. For ten years, beginning in 1996, the Communist Party of Nepal waged a people's war. The goal of the war was to free Nepal from imperialism, feudalism, and capitalism. The war was based in the countryside but there was also a massive leftist political movement that swept the urban areas. The revolution has brought about dramatic positive changes. Women joined the ranks, becoming political leaders and learning to write. The caste system based on the Hindu religion was challenged. New forms of power grew. A people's court, formed by villagers, was established to settle disputes. Alcoholism, which had been a big problem, has been reduced. And, although it still continues in some areas, child marriage has been made illegal and people may choose partners without reference to caste.

CHAPTER 2

Censored Déjà vu
What Happened to Previous *Censored* Stories

by Peter Phillips and Project Censored

INTRODUCTION TO GUEST ARTICLE

Project Censored has covered election fraud on several occasions over the past four years. *Censored 2005*, #6, reported on the close ties between the electronic voting machine companies and key players in the Republican Party. *Censored 2006*, #3, covered the 8 million vote discrepancy between the exit polls and the results of the 2004 presidential election. Additionally, we covered the voter purges in Florida in 2000. Updates on election fraud were completed in the 2007 yearbook. As Larry Beinhart describes below, the corporate media is still deliberately covering up election fraud in the US.

New York Times Perpetuates the Myth that George Bush Won the 2000 Election

by Larry Beinhart

They buried the truth about the 2000 election, and they're still burying it today.

"In 2001, painstaking postmortems of the Florida count, one by the *New York Times* and another by a consortium of newspapers, concluded that Mr. Bush would have come out slightly ahead, even if all the votes counted throughout the state had been retallied" (Alessandra Stanley, *New York Times*, May 23, 2008, in a review of the HBO television movie *Recount*).

That's not true.

The *New York Times* did not do its own recount. It did participate in a consortium. Here's what the consortium actually said: "If all the ballots had been reviewed under any of seven single standards, and combined with the results of an examination of overvotes, Mr. Gore would have won, by a very narrow margin" (Ford Fessenden and John M. Broder, *New York Times*, November 12, 2001).

Why did Ms. Stanley make such an important and fundamental error?

It is a common piece of misinformation. Many, many people believe it. Now a few more do, as a result of Ms. Stanley's review. It is not a trivial matter. Because that misinformation was created by one of the most bizarre, and still completely unexplained, journalistic events in modern times.

Here's what happened.

George Bush appeared to have won Florida, and therefore the presidency.

The law in Florida was actually quite simple and direct:

> $f(4)$ If the returns for any office reflect that a candidate was defeated or eliminated by one-half of a percent or less of the votes cast for such office . . . the board responsible for certifying the results of the vote on such race or measure shall order a recount of the votes cast with respect to such office or measure.

That is one of the simplest and most clearly written bits of legislation I've ever seen anywhere. The Florida court thought so too, and ordered a recount. Then the United States Supreme Court stepped in and shut the recounts down. Bush was left as the victor and became the president. But, presumably, the whole world wanted to know who actually did get the most votes. It would make a great and important story. But getting the truth was too time-consuming and expensive for any single news organization, so a consortium was formed. It consisted of the *New York Times*, the *Wall Street Journal*, the Tribune Company, the *Washington Post*, the Associated Press, the *St. Petersburg Times*, the *Palm Beach Post*, and CNN. It took almost a year and cost more than a million dollars. All the news organizations had the same information: Al Gore got more legal, countable votes than George Bush. Here are the headlines:

New York Times: STUDY OF DISPUTED FLORIDA BALLOTS
FINDS JUSTICES DID NOT CAST THE DECIDING VOTE

Wall Street Journal: IN ELECTION REVIEW, BUSH WINS
WITHOUT SUPREME COURT HELP

Los Angeles Times: BUSH STILL HAD VOTES TO WIN IN A
RECOUNT, STUDY FINDS

Washington Post: FLORIDA RECOUNTS WOULD HAVE
FAVORED BUSH

CNN.com: FLORIDA RECOUNT STUDY: BUSH STILL WINS

St. Petersburg Times: RECOUNT: BUSH

If you were still interested after the headlines and bothered to read
the stories, it didn't get much better. I read the *New York Times* article.
I missed the key paragraph, until I saw it pointed out in an article by
Gore Vidal. The *Times* spent the first three paragraphs supporting the
headline, and they explicitly stated that Bush would have won even with
a statewide recount. Finally, in the fourth paragraph—if you got that
far—was the statement quoted above:

> If all the ballots had been reviewed under any of seven single
> standards, and combined with the results of an examination of
> overvotes, Mr. Gore would have won, by a very narrow margin.

There it was. A very simple statement. Al Gore got more votes in
Florida than George Bush. It is also very well buried. After reading
the statement, I went back and read all the coverage of the study. The
Times was the worst in terms of active misdirection. It had arcana
about chads on both sides of it. Even so, as if in a panic to make sure
that nobody might think that it mattered that Al Gore got more votes
than George Bush, the *Times* dismissed what the consortium had
spent a million dollars to find out: "While these are fascinating findings, they do not represent a real-world situation. There was no set
of circumstances in the fevered days after the election that would have

produced a hand recount of all 175,000 overvotes and undervotes." That would seem to be a fairly obvious interpretation of the law, and it is what was found when someone actually did sit down and count the votes.

The rest of the story detailed a variety of other possible recounts, all partial recounts—these counties, but not those counties—that the Gore lawyers or the Bush lawyers asked for at various times. Bush would have won all of those variations; he just didn't get the most votes in Florida. Not that the variations mattered much. The Florida court had ordered a statewide hand recount.

The news story spinners hung their hat on a technicality.

Florida law, as affirmed by the courts, says a vote must be counted if there is "a clear indication of the intent of the voter." When the questions and lawsuits started, they were about undervotes. An undervote is when a voter has tried to vote but for some reason the counting machines fail to accept it. In Florida, the most common cause was the punching system's failure to consistently make clear holes in the voting cards. This resulted in hanging, broken, and dented chads. While the machines couldn't discern the "intent of the voter," the human eye often could. If only the undervotes were counted, by some standards of judging them, then Bush would have won.

But the consortium recount came across something else: overvotes. An overvote is when someone punches in the name of the candidate, and then, just to make sure, writes the candidate's name on the ballot. The machines could only read that the ballots had been marked in two places, and so threw them out.

But a human being could see that the place to vote for Gore had been punched and that Gore's name had been written in, and could easily determine the intent of the voter. The reporters for the consortium kept track of overvotes, too, and found out that Gore actually won.

Did the people inspecting the votes in the actual recount also notice overvotes? Did they also ignore them? The answer appears to be yes.

Newsweek has uncovered hastily scribbled faxed notes written by Terry Lewis, the plain-speaking, mystery-novel-writing state judge in charge of the Florida recount just hours before the US Supreme Court issued its order, showing that Lewis was actively considering directing the counties to count the so-called "overvotes":

Judge, if you would, segregate 'overvotes' as you describe and indicate in your final report how many where you determined the clear intent of the voter," Lewis wrote in a note to Judge W. Wayne Woodard, chairman of the Charlotte County Canvassing Board on the afternoon of December 9, 2000. "I will rule on the issue for all counties, Thanks, Terry Lewis" (*Newsweek*, "The Final Word?" by Michael Isikoff, November 19, 2001).

That leaves us with a big question.

The largest, most prestigious news organizations in the United States—pretty much in the world—discovered a great and exciting story: The wrong guy was president of the United States. Also, that the Supreme Court of the United States had interfered in an election to frustrate the actual will of the voters. (Justice Antonin Scalia wants us to get over it.) Why did they so distort the story—by using misleading headlines, burying the lead, fostering fog and confusion around the subject that almost everybody who read or heard the story walked away with the false impression instead of the truth?

There is no hard, on-the-record answer to that. None of the editors or publishers have come forward and said, "This is why we spun the story the way we did, even if it meant pissing away the million dollars we spent to get it." Nobody has, and nobody can, sue them for gratuitous misinformation and malfeasance and put them in the witness box under oath to get to the bottom of it. There is only speculation. The story is dated November 12, 2001, just two months after September 11, 2001. We can imagine that they universally felt it was not the time to announce a pretender was on the throne and that the system was rotten, right to the top. But I sure would love to know how they all got on the same page about it. That would make a terrific story. Not as great as the one they threw away, but good enough.

I wrote to the *Times* and suggested a correction. As of the time that I submitted this update, none has appeared. However, the Gray Lady did correct an article that appeared the same day about the number of television seasons of *Sex and the City*. You have to know when accuracy is important.

Republished with permission from AlterNet. Posted May 29, 2008.

LARRY BEINHART is the author of *Wag the Dog*, *The Librarian* and *Fog Facts: Searching for Truth in the Land of Spin*, all available at nationbooks.org. His new novel, *Salvation Boulevard*, will be published in September by Nation Books. Responses can be sent to beinhart@earthlink.net.

Censored #1 2008

No Habeas Corpus for "Any Person"

In *Censored 2008*, Project Censored reported on the Military Commissions Act (MCA), signed by George W. Bush on October 17, 2006. Ushering in military commission law for US citizens and non-citizens alike, the MCA effectively does away with habeas corpus rights for "any person" arbitrarily deemed to be an "enemy of the state." The judgment on who is deemed an "enemy" is solely at the discretion of the president. Robert Parry writes: "Under the cloak of setting up military tribunals to try al-Qaeda suspects and other so-called unlawful enemy combatants, Bush and the Republican-controlled Congress effectively created a parallel legal system for 'any person'—American citizen or otherwise—who crosses some ill-defined line." In one of the most chilling public statements ever made by a US attorney general, Alberto Gonzales opined at a Senate Judiciary Committee hearing on January 18, 2007, "The Constitution doesn't say every individual in the United States or citizen is hereby granted or assured the right of habeas corpus. It doesn't say that. It simply says the right shall not be suspended." (See Chapter 5 for an analysis of habeas corpus in the news.)

Original Sources: Robert Parry, "Who Is 'Any Person' in Tribunal Law?" Consortium, October 19, 2006; Robert Parry, "Still No Habeas Rights for You," Consortium, February 3, 2007; Thom Hartmann, "Repeal the Military Commissions Act and Restore the Most American Human Right," Common Dreams, February 2, 2007.

Update by Sarah Maddox:
Senator Arlen Spector of Pennsylvania introduced the Habeas Corpus Restoration Act of 2007 (S. 185) in January of 2007. The proposed legislation would have repealed provisions of the Military Commissions Act of 2006 that stripped US civilian courts from jurisdiction to hear or

consider applications for a writ of habeas corpus filed by aliens detained as enemy combatants. In September of 2007, the bill was defeated with a vote of 56–43, enough to block a cloture motion. Of the forty-three votes against the bill, forty-two were Republican and the remaining vote was cast by an Independent, Senator Joe Lieberman of Connecticut. Additional bills were introduced into the House of Representatives in 2007 by Representative Jerrold Nadler of New York, including the Restoring the Constitution Act (H.R. 1415) in March, and the Habeas Corpus Restoration Act (H.R. 1416) introduced in June. Both of these bills have been referred to subcommittees. On June 12, 2008, The Supreme Court ruled that foreign terrorism suspects held at Guantanamo Bay have rights under the Constitution to challenge their detention in US civilian courts. In its third rebuke of the Bush administration's treatment of prisoners, the court ruled 5–4 that the government is violating the rights of prisoners being held indefinitely and without charges at the US naval base in Cuba. The court's liberal justices were in the majority.

Justice Anthony Kennedy, writing for the court, said, "The laws and Constitution are designed to survive, and remain in force, in extraordinary times."

Sources

John Nichols, "Habeas Corpus and a Senate Race in Maine," *The Nation*, September 20, 2007, http://www.commondreams.org/archive/2007/09/20/3983/; Brian Beutler, "Congress Pushes Ahead on Detainee Rights," The Media Consortium, June 27, 2007, http://www.motherjones.com/news/update/2007/06/detainee_rights_beutler.html; William Fisher, "Battle Over Habeas Corpus Returns," truthout.org, April 2, 2007, http://www.truthout.org/ docs_2006/040207J.shtml; Mark Sherman, "High Court sides with Guantanamo detainees again," Associated Press, June 12, 2008.

Censored #2 2008

Bush Moves Closer to Martial Law

On October 17, 2006, President Bush signed the John Warner Defense Authorization Act of 2007. One of its goals was the revision of the Posse Comitatus Act of 1878, which constructed strict regulations for the use of military troops as domestic law enforcement. The new Defense Authorization Act gave the president the ability to order military troops to any place in the country, without the permission of any state governor or local authorities, in order to "suppress public disorder." The following are listed as justifiable events for the invocation of martial law: natural disasters, epidemics and/or serious public health issues, terrorist attacks, or any time domestic violence occurs to the extent that the state or local authorities can no longer control the situation. Senator Leahy was one of the few to speak out against this legislation, stating, "There is good reason for the constructive friction in existing law when it comes to martial law declarations. Using the military for law enforcement goes against one of the founding tenets of our democracy. We fail our Constitution, neglecting the rights of the States, when we make it easier for the President to declare martial law and trample on local and state sovereignty."

Original Source: Frank Morales, "Bush Moves Towards Martial Law," *Uruknet*, October 26, 2006.

Update by Sarah Maddox:
There were two significant updates to this story in 2007–2008. The good news is that in January 2008, President Bush signed into law the annual defense authorization bill that included the Leahy-Bond National Guard Empowerment reforms introduced into the Senate in 2007. In addition to the reforms being passed, Leahy also achieved repeal of the so-called "Insurrection Act Rider," attached to the 2006 defense policy bill, which had made it easier for presidents to take control of the National Guard from governors and to use the US military for domestic law enforcement. In 2007, in a Senate Judiciary Committee hearing organized by Leahy, key national military and law enforcement officials testified against the 2006 policy change. The nation's governors also unanimously supported the Leahy-Bond bill to repeal the Insurrection Act changes.

There was bad news as well, though, in the form of a new document entitled "National and Homeland Security Presidential Directive" (NSPD-51/HSPD-20), which was released on May 9, 2007. In the National Security Presidential Directive, Bush laid out his plan for dealing with a "catastrophic emergency." It defines a "catastrophic emergency" as "any incident, regardless of location, that results in extraordinary levels of mass casualties, damage, or disruption severely affecting the US population, infrastructure, environment, economy, or government function." The document emphasizes the need to ensure "the continued function of our form of government under the Constitution, including the functioning of the three separate branches of government." It continues: "The President shall lead the activities of the Federal Government for ensuring constitutional government." The document is vague about the need to work closely with the other two branches, saying there will be "a cooperative effort among the executive, legislative, and judicial branches of the Federal Government." However, this effort would be "coordinated by the President, as a matter of comity with respect to the legislative and judicial branches and with proper respect for the constitutional separation of powers."

Sources

"Bush Signs Bill Enacting Leahy-Bond National Guard Empowerment Reforms, and Their Repealer of the 'Insurrection Act Rider,'" PR Newswire, January 30, 2008, http://www.foxbusiness.com/article/bush-signs-enacting-leahybond-national-guard-empowerment-reforms-repealer_457791_1.html; Matthew Rothschild, "Bush Anoints Himself as the Insurer of the Constitutional Government in Emergency," The *Progressive*, May 18, 2007, http://www.progressive.org/mag_wx051807.html; Larry Chin, "National Security and Homeland Security Presidential Directive Establishes National Continuity Policy," Global Research, May 21, 2007, http://www.globalresearch.ca/index.php?context=viewarticle&code =CHI20070521&articleId=5720.

Censored #3 2008

AFRICOM: US Military Control of Africa's Resources

In February 2007, the White House announced the formation of the US African Command (AFRICOM), a new unified Pentagon command center in Africa, to be established by September 2008. This military penetration of Africa is being presented as a humanitarian guard in the Global War on Terror. However, critics charge that the real objective is the procurement and control of Africa's oil and its global delivery systems.

The most significant and growing challenge to US dominance in Africa is China. An increase in Chinese trade and investment in Africa threatens to substantially reduce US political and economic leverage in that resource-rich continent. The political implication of an economically emerging Africa in close alliance with China is resulting in a new cold war in which AFRICOM will be tasked with achieving full-spectrum military dominance over Africa.

From the *Censored 2008* update by Bryan Hunt:
By spring 2007, US Department of Energy data showed that the United States now imports more oil from the continent of Africa than from the country of Saudi Arabia.

The Department of Defense states that a primary component of AFRICOM's mission will be to professionalize indigenous militaries to ensure stability, security, and accountable governance throughout Africa's various states and regions. Stability refers to establishing and maintaining order, and accountability, of course, refers to US interests. This year alone, 1,400 African military officers are anticipated to complete International Military Education and Training programs at US military schools.

Original Source: Bryan Hunt, "Understanding AFRICOM," MoonofAlabama.org, February 21, 2007.

Update by Carmela Rocha:
After the White House announced the formation of the US Africa Command (AFRICOM) in February 2007, the National Conference of Black Lawyers (NCBL) decided to take a closer look at its mission and goals. After a year of inspection, NCBL has concluded that AFRICOM violates the sovereignty of African nations by interrupting international law standards that protect rights to self-determination and that prohibit unprovoked military aggression. It suggests that the current administration is more likely interested in working through AFRICOM to push forward three primary goals. First, it wants to open Africa as another front in the administration's "war on terrorism." Second, it intends to protect and expand US access to African oil, mineral wealth, and other raw materials. Third, it wants to put the US in a better military position in order to compete with China for domination of Africa's resources.

According to Gerald LeMelle, executive director of Africa Action, an organization in Washington, DC, that supports peace and development in Africa, "neither African governments nor the UN were consulted on the announcement of AFRICOM." One of the purposes of AFRICOM is to identify and develop African governments that will function as US surrogates. So far the concept of AFRICOM has been received with skepticism and hostility by most African governments. The only country that has expressed a clear willingness to provide a location for AFRICOM headquarters is Liberia. This is said to be the result of a quid pro quo in which the US is willing to cover Liberia's financial debts.

Currently, the amount of oil imported by the US from the Persian Gulf is about 16 percent of its total imports. By the year 2015, it is projected that 25 percent of US oil imports will be from West Africa. The two largest oil producers on the continent, Nigeria and Angola in West Africa, receive the most US aid.

Sources
"NCBL Statement: AFRICOM Threatens the Sovereignty, Independence and Stability of the African Continent," Pan-African News Wire, January 17, 2008; Haider Rizvi, "US Military Plan for Africa Panned," OneWorld.net, February 25, 2008.

Censored #4 2008

Frenzy of Increasingly Destructive Trade Agreements

The Oxfam report, "Signing Away the Future," revealed that the US and European Union (EU) are vigorously pursuing increasingly destructive regional and bilateral agreements, outside the auspices of the World Trade Organization (WTO). These agreements are requiring enormous irreversible concessions from developing countries, while offering almost nothing in return. During 2006, more than one hundred developing countries were involved in Free Trade Agreement (FTA) or Bilateral Investment Treaty (BIT) negotiations. "An average of two treaties are signed every week," the report says. "Virtually no country, however poor, has been left out."

Double standards in the intellectual-property rights chapters of most trade agreements are glaring. As new agreements limit developing countries' access to patented technology and medicines—while failing to protect traditional knowledge—the public-health consequences are staggering. The US-Colombia FTA is expected to reduce access to medicines by 40 percent and the US-Peru FTA is expected to leave 700,000 to 900,000 Peruvians without access to affordable medicines. New rules also pose a threat to essential services as FTAs allow foreign investors to take ownership of healthcare, education, water, and public utilities.

From the *Censored 2008* update by Laura Rusu of Oxfam International:

In the United States, the new Democratic leadership in Congress recently negotiated changes in the areas of labor, environment, and intellectual property in regard to access to medicines that are to be incorporated into the completed FTAs awaiting Congressional ratification. The US administration hopes to bring FTAs with Peru, Panama, Colombia, and Korea to a vote this year, although it remains doubtful whether there would be sufficient congressional support to move the latter two.

Original Sources: "Signing Away The Future," Oxfam International, March 2007; Sanjay Suri, "Free Trade Enslaving Poor Countries," Inter Press Service coverage of Oxfam Report, March 20, 2007.

Update by Kat Pat Crespán:

The trade agreement with Peru passed in November 2007 in Congress with a vote of 285–132. It is likely that this ratification will ease the passage of other FTAs in Latin America. The ultimate goal is to have a US-dominated Free Trade Area of the Americas while blocking the development of any alternative agreements in Latin American countries. According to Amazon Watch, passage of this agreement permits oil companies to drill in the Peruvian Amazon, which may cause massive deforestation and road construction, failing to protect endangered species. US corporations that stand to benefit include Hunt Oil, ConocoPhillips, Occidental Petroleum and Newmont Mining.

As for the Colombian FTA, Oxfam America has called upon members of the US Congress to reject the deal since it will "undermine development in Colombia and national security interests here at home." Though the bill was supposed to help the local communities, it has only further subjugated them. Poor farmers who cannot compete with US exports to sell their food crops, such as corn and rice, will have few other options to survive. Calling on the US Congress to reject the Colombia Free Trade Agreement, Oxfam said the deal would stall development and fail to reduce poverty, affecting women, indigenous, and Afro-Colombian communities. Instead, it says, the US needs a new trade policy that will expand economic opportunity for the poor and be inclusive of the most economically disadvantaged nations.

In Costa Rica, the United States campaigned to pass the Central American Free Trade Agreement (CAFTA). A delegation from the US-based Alliance for Responsible Trade and the Stop CAFTA Coalition said the passage is an example of dirty campaigning aimed at undermining publicly-run utility, phone, and healthcare systems. "We are not accepting the results of the referendum because of the way in which the Costa Rican and US governments behaved during the final three days of the referendum," said Jorge Arguedas Mora, president of the ANTTEC union of electrical and telephone workers and coordinator of the No CAFTA campaign. "Both violated laws regulating the referendum, the constitution, and even existing international agreements. The media colluded in the government manipulation and unfortunately the Supreme Electoral Tribunal looked the other way."

Throughout Africa, regions have continued to say no to agreements such as the Economic Partnership Agreements (EPAs) proposed by western countries. While the World Trade Organization argued that the trade agreements are necessary at the EU-Africa summit in late 2007, the president of Senegal, Abdoulaye Wade, refused to sign and stormed out of the meeting. South Africa's Thabo Mbeki supported his stand, as did the country of Namibia. This was a bold move, considering that an increase in EU customs duties would make it impossible for Namibia to export or continue to produce beef. The African countries' refusals were met with support from French president Nicolas Sarkozy, saying he was in favor of globalization but not the despoilment of countries that have nothing left. Ultimately, the summit ended in failure when social movement and trade union organizations joined in the mutiny against the proposed EU agreements.

As of June 2008, the South Korea FTA is still in the negotiations process and waiting for approval before the end of 2008. Former president Roh Moo-hyun was hoping for ratification on February 26, 2008, when the nation's National Assembly took place, but that did not happen. As of April 22, 2008, President Lee Myung-bak was confident the US Congress would ratify the free trade agreement with South Korea later in 2008. He was convinced after hearing that "several opponents in the US Senate and House are expected to change their position toward the FTA on account of the envisioned benefits for the United States." While the deal has not yet been ratified by either country, Lee's administration hopes to have it ratified before the end of Bush's term in January 2009.

Sources

Kim Yon-se, "Leaders Reiterate early FTA Ratification," *Korea Times*, February 18, 2008; Kim Ji-hyun, "Lee confident of FTA with US," *Korea Times*, April 22, 2008; Laura Rusu, "US-Colombia Free Trade Agreement Bad Deal for Development and National Security," Oxfam America, April 2008; Jennifer Gunderman and April Howard, "US Congress Passes Free Trade Deal with Peru," *Upside Down World*, November 14, 2007; David T. Rowlands, "Peru: Free Trade Deal an Andean Tragedy," *Upside Down World*, February 6, 2008; Ignacio Ramonet, "Africa Says No," *Le Monde Diplomatique*, January 2008.

Censored #5 2008

Human Traffic Builds US Embassy in Iraq

The US embassy in Iraq will be the most expensive and heavily fortified embassy in the world—and it is being built by a Kuwait contractor repeatedly accused of using forced labor trafficked from South Asia under US contracts. By using bait-and-switch recruiting practices, thousands of citizens from countries that have banned travel or work in Iraq are being tricked and smuggled into brutal and inhumane labor camps, and subjected to months of forced servitude—all in the middle of the US-controlled Green Zone.

On April 4, 2006, the Pentagon issued a contracting directive following an investigation that officially confirmed that contractors in Iraq, many working as subcontractors to Halliburton or KBR, were illegally confiscating worker passports, using deceptive, bait-and-switch hiring practices, and charging recruiting fees that indebted low-paid migrant workers for many months or even years to their employers. However, the Pentagon has yet to announce any penalty for those found to be in violation of US labor trafficking laws or contract requirements.

The problem of labor abuse has been found to be "widespread" among contractors in the theater of war in Iraq. Unfortunately, not one contractor has been penalized; in fact, many are being rewarded with new US-funded contracts.

Original Source: David Phinney, "A US Fortress Rises in Baghdad: Asian Workers Trafficked to Build World's Largest Embassy," *CorpWatch*, October 17, 2007.

Update by Melissa Willenborg:

Nicknamed "George W.'s Palace," the US Embassy in Iraq is likely to become an enduring symbol of the worst excesses of the Bush administration. Initially scheduled to launch in January 2007, opening of the

embassy was delayed until June, then September, and now vaguely sometime late in 2008. Yet there has been no public explanation for these continued postponements.

The embassy will occupy 104 acres. It will be six times larger than the UN complex in New York. It is ten times the size of the new US Embassy being built in Beijing, which, at ten acres, is America's second-largest embassy.

In December 2007, a senior State Department official certified that embassy construction was "substantially complete," but department inspectors found "major deficiencies" at the unoccupied embassy, according to their inspection report. "It appears that the State Department is concealing from Congress basic information about the status of the embassy project and the activities of officials and contractors involved. This continued intransigence is inappropriate," wrote Rep. Henry Waxman, who threatened to call the State Department official before his panel.

The White House originally requested $1.3 billion to build the compound, but Congress allotted $592 million for the project in 2005. Now, according to documentation provided to Congress by the State Department, an additional $144 million is needed for completion and the embassy may cost as much as $1 billion each year to operate.

In addition, construction has been complicated by a dispute between Ambassador to Iraq Ryan Crocker and James L. Golden—the top Washington-based official charged with the project's oversight. Golden has been barred from Iraq by Crocker for allegedly destroying evidence in the case of an embassy worker's death.

After the death of the embassy worker, and the possible violations of other workers' rights, attorneys Andrew Kline and Michael J. Frank in the Justice Department's civil rights division were charged with investigating allegations of labor trafficking. On September 18, 2007, Rep. Henry Waxman, chairman of the Oversight and Government Reform Committee, wrote a fourteen-page letter to Howard Krongard, inspector general at the State Department, requesting Krongard's cooperation with an investigation into allegations regarding his conduct. Howard Krongard was subsequently removed from the State Department at the end of January, 2008.

The embassy in Baghdad represents a sea change in US diplomacy. While it is larger in scope than other US embassies opening around the world, it is hardly unique. Since al-Qaeda bombed the American embassies in Kenya and Tanzania in 1998, the State Department has been aggressively replacing obsolete or vulnerable facilities with ones designed under a program it calls Standard Embassy Design. The United States opened fourteen newly built embassies in 2007 alone, and long-range plans call for seventy-six more, including twelve to be completed in 2008–09. The result will be a radical redesign of the diplomatic landscape—not only in Baghdad, but in Bamako, Belmopan, Cape Town, Dushanbe, Kabul, Lomé, and elsewhere.

If architecture reflects the society that creates it, the new US embassy in Baghdad makes a devastating comment about America's global outlook.

Sources

Allen McDuffee, "Empire's Architecture," *In These Times,* January 2008; Warren P Strobel, "Even Kitchens are Fire Hazard at New US Embassy in Iraq," Tribune News Service, February 29, 2008; Dow Jones & Company, Inc., "The Waxman Method," Wall Street Journal, February 9, 2008; Jane C Loeffler, "Fortress America," *Foreign Policy,* September/October, 2007.

Censored #6 2008

Operation FALCON Raids

Under the codename Operation FALCON (Federal and Local Cops Organized Nationally), three federally coordinated mass arrests occurred between April 2005 and October 2006. In an unprecedented move, more than 30,000 fugitives were arrested in the largest dragnets in the nation's history. The operations directly involved over 960 agencies (state, local and federal) and were the brainchild of Attorney General Alberto Gonzales and US Marshals Director Ben Reyna.

Operation FALCON II, carried out the week of April 17 to 23, 2006, arrested another 9,037 individuals from twenty-seven states, mostly west of the Mississippi River. Operation FALCON III, conducted during the week of October 22 to 28, 2006, netted another 10,733 fugitives in twenty-four states east of the Mississippi River.

From the Censored 2008 update by Mike Whitney:

Operation FALCON presents the first time in US history that all of the domestic police agencies have been put under the direct control of the federal government. The operation serves little purpose but to centralize power and establish the basic contours of an American police state. It is not an effective way of apprehending criminals.

Original Sources: Artificial Intelligence, "Operation Falcon," *Source-Watch*, November 18, 2006; Mike Whitney, "Operation Falcon and the Looming Police State," *Ukernet*, February 26, 2007.

Update by Darcy Newton:

According to the US Marshals' official website, "The emphasis centered on gang related crimes, homicides, crimes involving use of a weapon, crimes against children and the elderly, crimes involving sexual assaults, organized crime and drug related fugitives, and other crimes of violence." As of June 2008, Operation Falcon has largely consisted of arresting 36,516 minor criminals and continues on a regional basis. According to the Operation Falcon website, "FALCON 2007 continued to promote these important efforts, but took on a more focused, long-term approach by targeting twenty-seven cities and regions experiencing elevated levels of criminal activity. Working in conjunction with the Department of Justice, the National Center for Missing & Exploited Children, and other agencies, the US Marshals' Service identified and targeted the communities most in need of assistance. The Marshals then reached out to their many partners in federal, state, and local law enforcement to coordinate a sustainable push designed to safely apprehend the maximum number of violent predators."

FUGITIVES ARRESTED

FALCON I* (April 4–10, 2005): 10,340
FALCON II (April 13–17, 2006): 9,030
FALCON III (October 22–28, 2006): 10,733
FALCON 07: 6,406

TOTAL ARRESTED: 36,516

BREAKDOWN OF FUGITIVES ARRESTED BY AGENCY

	F-I	F-II	F-III	07
FALCON Team Members	3,100	2,126	3,100	NA
Federal Agencies	25	25	30	22
State Agencies	206	120	103	70
Local Agencies	366	312	482	242
County Agencies	362	330	430	206

* Operation covered entire United States

Source
See http://www.usmarshals.gov/falcon/index.html.

In a May 2, 2008, press release, Senator Hillary Rodham Clinton joined a coalition of her colleagues in calling on the Senate Appropriations Committee to provide funding for the Adam Walsh Act to strengthen the United States Marshals Service (USMS) and aid their programs to apprehend child predators and other dangerous felons. Clinton's release stated, "Operation Falcon is a successful national fugitive apprehension initiative, which has resulted in the collective capture of more than 36,500 dangerous fugitive felons." (States News Service, May 2, 2008)

The AP reported on November 26, 2007, that Washington state's Governor Chris Gregoire and law enforcement in five counties were launching Operation Crackdown to catch dozens of sex offenders who are back on the streets, but haven't registered with authorities. The state program was patterned after the US Marshals' Operation FALCON. The cost, including overtime, could reach $100,000.

Source
"Marshals' operation nets 6,400 fugitives since June," *Washington Times*, November 3, 2007.

Censored #7 2008

Behind Blackwater Inc.

As was well-covered in the latter part of 2007, Blackwater Inc. is the largest of the three US private military companies. The company is headed by Erik Prince, a neo-conservative ex–Navy Seal. Created in 1996 as a private military training facility, last year it boasted approximately 20,000 soldiers, a fleet of twenty military aircraft, and is considered to be the most powerful mercenary group in the world.

Private contractors currently constitute the second-largest "force" in Iraq. At last count, there were about 100,000 contractors in Iraq, of which 48,000 work as private soldiers, according to a Government Accountability Office report. These private contractors, including Blackwater, have operated largely without any oversight as it is unclear if they should fall under civilian or military law. This means that Blackwater soldiers can do as they please without fear of legal retribution.

As of 2007, the privatization of the US military was well underway. The Center for Public Integrity reported that since 1994 the US Defense Department has entered into contracts worth $300 billion with twelve private military contractors. These contractors do everything from peeling potatoes to fighting on the front lines.

Original Source: Jeremy Scahill, "Our Mercenaries in Iraq: Blackwater Inc. and Bush's Undeclared Surge," *Democracy Now!*, January 26, 2007.

Update by Luke Plasse:
Blackwater has had a busy year. Reports filed by the company exposed 195 "escalating force" incidents in which Blackwater admitted to firing shots in Iraq. In 80 percent of these incidents, Blackwater said that they fired the first shot despite their contract saying that they can only use defensive force. In many such cases, Blackwater contractors fired from moving vehicles and did not take the time to assist the wounded or check for civilian casualties.

In one case, a drunken Blackwater contractor shot and killed the guard of Iraqi Vice President Adil Abd-al-Mahdi. Within thirty-six hours of the shooting, Blackwater was allowed to transport the contractor out of Iraq in order to avoid any consequences. It was recommended that Blackwater make a payment to the man's next-ofkin in an attempt to quiet the situation. Charge d'Affaires recommended that $250,000 be given to the grieving family but the Department's Diplomatic Security Service thought that this was too much. They warned that such an amount could result in Iraqis trying to get themselves killed. In the end, $15,000 was given to the family.

On September 16, 2007, Blackwater personnel reported killing a number of armed Iraqi civilians including a mother and son. Blackwater claims to have acted in self-defense, only returning fire after being fired upon by armed Iraqi civilians. An investigation was launched after discrepancies were found in Blackwater's report. The investigation uncovered another version of the September 16 events that directly opposes Blackwater's account of what happened that day. According to reports, Blackwater personnel were attempting to clear a path for their convoy when a Kia sedan began slowly driving towards them on the wrong side of the road. The car did not heed yells or warning shots fired by the Blackwater mercenaries. The men then opened fire on the car, killing the occupants, including a mother and her son. Following this, Blackwater began using non-lethal stun grenades to clear the area. Mistaking the stun grenades for real grenades, nearby Iraqi Army Soldiers began to fire on the Blackwater men. Reports differ, but approximately seventeen Iraqi civilians were killed in the resulting gunfight.

Crimes committed by US contractors operating in a war zone still fall into a gray area. Any soldier who is part of the US armed forces is subject to a code of laws that is separate from civilian law. These laws

are appropriately called military law and they govern such things as what a soldier can and cannot do when acting in a war zone. The problem arises when deciding which set of laws to apply to Blackwater, who are not part of the armed forces, but are not quite civilians either.

Costs to the Taxpayer

The cost of a Blackwater mercenary is significantly higher than that of an analogous army officer. According to contract documents, Blackwater bills the United States government $1,222 a day for one individual security specialist. That works out to around $439,920 annually. The jobs these individuals do would usually be done by army sergeants whose pay ranges between $140 and $190 per day. On an annual basis, the salary, housing, and subsistence pay of an army sergeant ranges from $51,100 to $69,350 per year.

Despite the significantly increased cost of hiring Blackwater over the use of the US Army, Blackwater's contracts continue to grow larger and larger. In 2001, the US paid $736,906 in Blackwater contracts. In 2006, the US paid $593.6 million in Blackwater contracts, an 800-fold increase. In total, Blackwater has received over a billion dollars from the federal government during the years 2001 to 2006. Of this total, 51 percent of the money was rewarded in the form of no-bid contracts, discouraging even cursory competition between Blackwater and its rivals.

Questions are being raised about whether there is a benefit to using Blackwater contractors that justifies the extra expense. Some people in Congress see it as a misappropriation of taxpayer money and maintain that this reason alone is enough to put a stop to the use of Blackwater contractors.

Censored #8 2008

KIA: The US Neoliberal Invasion of India

Farmers' cooperatives in India are defending the nation's food security and the future of Indian farmers against the corporate invasion of genetically modified (GM) seeds. When India's Prime Minister Singh met with President Bush in March 2006 to finalize nuclear agreements, they also signed the Indo-US Knowledge Initiative on Agriculture (KIA), backed by Monsanto, Archer Daniels Midland (ADM), and Wal-Mart. The KIA allows for the acquisition of India's seed sector by Monsanto, of its trade sector by giant agribusiness ADM and Cargill, and its retail sector by Wal-Mart.

Over the past decade, with the involvement of Monsanto, ADM, and Cargil in India's agriculture sector, as many as 28,000 Indian farmers have committed suicide as a result of debt incurred from failed GM crops and competition with subsidized US crops.

Through the KIA, Monsanto and the US have asked for unhindered access to India's gene banks, along with a change in India's intellectual property laws to allow patents on seeds and genes, and to dilute provisions that protect farmers' rights. The KIA has also paved the way for Wal-Mart's plans to open 500 stores in India, starting in August 2007, which will compound the outsourcing of India's food supply and threaten the livelihoods of 14 million small family venders.

Original Sources: Vandana Shiva with Amy Goodman, "Vandana Shiva on Farmer Suicides, the US-India Nuclear Deal, Wal-Mart in India," *Democracy Now!*, December 13, 2006; Arun Shrivastava, "Genetically Modified Seeds: Women in India take on Monsanto," October 9, 2006; Suman Sahai, "Sowing Trouble: India's "Second Green Revolution," SciDev.Net, May 9, 2006.

From the *Censored 2008* update by Vandana Shiva:

The Indo-US Knowledge Initiative on Agriculture impacts 650 million farmers of India and 40 million small retailers and it is redefining the relationships between people in the two biggest democracies in the world.

A new movement on retail democracy has begun in India that is bringing together small shopkeepers, street hawkers, trade unions, and farmers' unions. On August 9, 2007, which is Quit India Day, the movement organized actions across the country, telling Wal-Mart to Quit India.

For more information, visit our website at www.navdanya.org.

Update by Michele Salvail:

Anuradha Mittal writes in *Earth Island Journal*, spring 2008, "After years of speculation, the figure is now official: Between 1997 and 2005, nearly 150,000 farmers in India committed suicide, according to data from the National Crime Records Bureau. Many farmers' organizations believe the number of suicides to be even greater. The number of farmers whose livelihoods have been devastated by debts, crop failures, government indifference, and skewed global trade policies is possibly much higher. Every five hours, one farmer commits suicide somewhere in the country," Devinder Sharma, a food and trade policy analyst based in New Delhi, writes in an e-mail. "Farmers are failing because of the anti-farming policies that are being propagated. The tragedy is that the hand that feeds the nation is being deliberately chopped off."

Mittal goes on to say, "the free trade system continues to expose Indian farmers to lopsided global trade rules under which poorer countries are forced to open their markets while richer countries are able to maintain lavish export subsidies. At the same time, the WTO and World Bank agreements have allowed multinational corporations, such as Monsanto, to penetrate the Indian seed market; the sophisticated marketing of genetically modified seeds and other expensive inputs has dramatically raised Indian farmers' costs even as they try to survive amid harsh new competition."

Censored #9 2008

Privatization of America's Infrastructure

Over twenty states have enacted legislation allowing public-private partnerships to build and run highways. Investment firms including Goldman Sachs, Morgan Stanley, and the Carlyle Group are lobbying states to sell off public highway and transportation infrastructure. Investors, most often foreign companies, are charging tolls and insisting on "noncompete" clauses that limit governments from expanding or improving nearby roads.

On June 29, 2006, Indiana's governor Mitch Daniels announced that Indiana had received $3.8 billion from a foreign consortium made up of the Spanish construction firm Cintra and the Macquarie Infrastructure Group (MIG) of Australia. In exchange the state handed over operation of a 157-mile Indiana toll road for the next seventy-five years. With the consortium collecting the tolls, which will eventually rise far higher, the privatized road should generate $11 billion for MIG-Cintra over the course of the contract.

Across the nation, there is now talk of privatizing the New York Thruway to the Ohio, Pennsylvania, and New Jersey turnpikes, as well as of inviting the private sector to build and operate highways and bridges from Alabama to Alaska.

The Bush administration and private contractors plan to build a huge ten-lane NAFTA Super Highway through the heart of the US along Interstate 35, from the Mexican border at Laredo, Texas, to the Canadian border north of Duluth, Minnesota, financed largely through public-private partnerships. The Texas Department of Transportation will oversee the Trans-Texas Corridor as the first leg of the NAFTA Super Highway, which will be leased to the Cintra consortium as a privately operated toll road.

Original Sources: Daniel Schulman and James Ridgeway, "The Highwaymen," *Mother Jones*, February 2007; Jerome R. Corsi, "Bush Administration Quietly Plans NAFTA Super Highway," *Human Events*, June 12, 2006.

Update by Peter Phillips:
The continuing effort by private corporations to acquire public infrastructure was in the news in 2007–2008:

The *Boston Herald* reported on September 11, 2007, that Governor Deval Patrick was launching a detailed examination of options for leasing the state's cash-starved bridges and roads to private companies.

On June 27, 2007, the *Dallas Morning News* detailed efforts by the Texas Transportation Commission to overrule a local commission regarding the privatization of State Highway 121 in a deal with the Spanish company Cintra. On August 23, 2007, the Texas Transportation Commission rescinded and terminated the comprehensive development agreement with Cintra to develop SH 121 (see www.txdot.gov/services/texas_turnpike_authority/sh121_prop _files.ht).

After the August 1, 2007, collapse of the Interstate 35W Bridge in Minneapolis there were some efforts to privatize the bridge after reconstruction (*Star Tribune*, August 15, 2007).

Democracy Now! covered the issue on August 3, interviewing Daniel Schulman and James Ridgeway on the privatization issues after the Minneapolis bridge collapse. Ridgeway and Schulman claimed that efforts to prevent increasing taxes are a deliberate attempt to force the selling off or our public infrastructures.

Bloomberg.com reported on May 19, "Pennsylvania officials said a $12.8 billion bid from Citigroup Inc. and Abertis Infraestructuras SA won an auction to lease the state's only toll road (the Pennsylvania Turnpike) in what would be the biggest agreement of its kind in the US. New York-based Citigroup, the biggest US bank by assets, and Barcelona-based Abertis, which operates toll roads in Europe and Latin America, topped two other offers. The next-highest bid was $12.1 billion by New York's Goldman Sachs Group Inc. and Transurban Group, Australia's second-largest toll-road operator"

(see www.bloomberg.com/apps/news?pid=20601103&sid=aa7KegrkckgE
&refer=us).

The claim by author Jerome Corsi that the Bush administration supports a NAFTA Super Highway, while true from a private interests perspective, has been somewhat discredited by an article in the *Nation* by Christopher Hayes on August 9, 2007. According to Hayes, the NAFTA Super Highway story became a hyper-conservative conspiracy theory of mythic proportion. However, as with many theories, there were some elements of truth. The North America's Super Corridor Organization (NASCO) does exist and proudly claims that they "assisted in the lobbying effort to bring hundreds of millions of dollars to the NASCO Corridor since 1994. The group's efforts resulted in High Priority Corridor designated status for all 1,500 miles of I-35 from Laredo, Texas to Duluth, MN in 1995, and inclusion of same within the National Highway System under the Intermodal Surface Transportation Efficiency Act (ISTEA)." NASCO has in fact received some money from the US Government (see www.nascocorridor .com/commondetail.asp?id=2168).

However, the US government denies supporting the NAFTA Super Highway. In a State Department press release from April 22, 2008, Walter Bastian, deputy assistant secretary for the western hemisphere, US Department of Commerce; Alfonso Martinez-Fonts, is quoted as saying,

> Are we as a federal government planning a NAFTA super highway? No. . . . Have we been transparent in the process? I think the answer is absolutely yes, even though we've been accused of holding meetings with our Canadian and Mexican counterparts behind closed doors, private meetings. [Inaudible] from the private sector. . . . Let me add to that, however, that there are a number of communities, community leaders, governors and mayors out there that see business development and job creation as a good thing. Surprising, huh? They are very happy, recognizing the benefits of trade, trade to their communities, jobs, doing everything they can, one to attract foreign investment in there; two, to attract foreign business in there.

Censored #10 2008

Vulture Funds Threaten Poor Nations' Debt Relief

Vulture funds, under the guise of "distressed-debt investors," have been taking aid money from poor countries through a loophole in the law. Vulture funds are western companies that buy debts from investors at a fraction of the cost, and then sue the debtors for the original amount owed. This business practice, which typically liquidates assets of defaulted companies, has recently been extended to reap the money developing nations reclaim through debt cancellation initiatives. In February 2007, Donegal International (owned by American Michael Sheehan and based in the US Virgin Islands) sued Zambia for $40 million, a debt it bought for $4 million, and was awarded $15 million by the English High Court.

Original Source: Greg Palast with Meirion Jones, "Vulture Fund Threat to Third World," *BBC Newsnight*, February 14, 2007.

Update by April Pearce:
Following the English High Court's ruling, and Greg Palast's reporting, members of the British Parliament and the US Congress voiced opposition to vulture fund investing in developing countries. Recognizing that Donegal International exploited British law, eighty-five members of the British Parliament demanded Prime Minister Gordon Brown prohibit vulture fund activities in poor nations. Across the Atlantic, US Congress members John Conyers and Donald Payne, angered by the misappropriation of African development funds, confronted George Bush. They took him to task on the issue including his relationship with the largest vulture fund owner: Paul Singer, his largest financial donor. Legislators from both countries urged their leaders "to close the legal loopholes that allow 'Vulture Funds' to flourish," at the G-8 Summit later in the year. No direct action was taken at the summit to halt vulture fund activities.

In May 2007, a British Court ruled that Zambian President Chaluba must pay back $46 million that he stole from Zambia's Treasury. At this time the US Government started to look into whether Michael Sheehan violated the Foreign Corrupt Practices Act because he admitted money he donated to President Chaluba's charity (upon Chaluba's acceptance of Zambia's debt to Donegal) might have been used in a corrupt manner.

The Jubilee Act for Responsible Lending and Expanded Debt Cancel-lation, H.R. 2634/ S. 2166, was introduced to Congress in June and to the Senate in October of 2007. The Jubilee Act increases the number of countries eligible for debt cancellation and stipulates accountability and transparency from creditors and debtors. The House of Representatives passed the Act, by 285–132, on April 16, 2008. The Senate Committee on Foreign Relations held hearings on the Jubilee Act on April 24, 2008, and as of June 2008, it is in committee. Under current debt relief poli-cies, established at the G-8 Summit of 2005, eighteen of the forty countries eligible for relief do not receive it due to their unwillingness to implement harsh economic conditions, including privatizing basic ser-vices, to qualify for debt cancellation. The Jubilee Act extends debt cancellation to all of the sixty-seven countries that need it to reach the Millennium Development Goals, without imposing such conditions.

Sources
Greg Palast, "Conyers Hunts Bush's Vultures," *BBC Newsnight*, June 11, 2007; "Jubilee Act Summary," Jubilee USA Network.

Censored #12 2008

Another Massacre in Haiti by UN Troops

On December 22, 2006, eyewitness testimony confirmed indiscrimi-nate killings by UN forces in Haiti's Cité Soleil community. Reports on the ground indicated that this was a collective punishment against the community for a massive demonstration of Lavalas supporters in which about 10,000 people rallied for the return of President Aristide in clear condemnation of the foreign military occupation of their country. According to residents, UN forces attacked their neighborhood in the early morning, killing more than thirty people, including women and children. Footage taken by Haiti Information Project (HIP) videogra-phers shows unarmed civilians dying as they tell of extensive gunfire from UN peacekeeping forces (MINUSTAH). Frantz Michel Guerrier, spokesman for the Committee of Notables for the Development of Cité Soleil based in the Bois Neuf zone, said "It is very difficult for me to explain to you what the people of Bois Neuf went through on Decem-ber 22, 2006—almost unexplainable. It was a true massacre. We counted more than sixty wounded and more than twenty-five dead, among [them] infants, children, and young people."

"We saw helicopters shoot at us, our houses broken by the tanks," Guerrier told Inter Press Service (IPS). "We heard detonations of the heavy weapons. Many of the dead and wounded were found inside their houses. I must tell you that nobody had been saved, not even the babies. The Red Cross was not allowed to help people. The soldiers had refused to let the Red Cross in categorically, in violation of the Geneva Convention." Several residents told IPS that MINUSTAH, after conducting its operations, evacuated without checking for wounded.

Original Sources: Haiti Information Project, "UN in Haiti: Accused of Second Massacre," HaitiAction.net, January 21, 2007; Wadner Pierre and Jeb Sprague, "Haiti: Poor Residents of Capital Describe a State of Siege," Inter Press Service, March 2, 2007.

Update by Sarah Maddox:

The situation in Haiti has become increasingly oppressive as political tensions multiply. Riots erupted in April 2008 over high food and fuel prices, which left at least six people dead and augmented the continuing plea to have Aristide returned to the Haitian people. The *Miami Herald* reported in February 2008 that 5,000 supporters of Aristide marched through Port-au-Prince to demand the return of their president. Chanting Aristide's name and waving signs, marchers took their protest to the gates of the US Embassy in Port-au-Prince and Haiti's National Palace to remind President René Préval—a one-time supporter of the former priest now living in South Africa—that Aristide's Fanmi Lavalas party helped elect him two years ago. "I believe he heard us," said thirty-two-year-old marcher Jean-Michel Porfil. "The people . . . are hungry. They don't have work, but they protested because their president isn't here. We are asking for him to be returned."

In April 2008, an article in the *Guardian* of London reported that the United Nations peacekeepers fired rubber bullets and used tear gas to control mobs rioting over rising food prices in Haiti. Food prices have risen 40 percent on average since the middle of 2007, causing unrest around the world, with riots seen in countries such as Burkina Faso, Cameroon, and Egypt. For months, Haitians have compared their hunger pains to "eating Clorox [bleach]" because of the burning feeling in their stomachs. The World Food Programme (WFP) made an emergency appeal for donations for Haiti. "Riots in Haiti underline the additional need for lifesaving food assistance," said WFP executive director Josette Sheeran. "At this critical time, we need to stand with the people of Haiti and other countries hardest hit by rising food prices."

The situation in Haiti was thrown into further confusion on April 12, when the Haitian parliament passed a vote of no confidence against then–Prime Minister Jacques-Edouard Alexis, led by rightists in Haiti's parliament. President Préval, following controversial UN-sponsored elections in 2006, had appointed Alexis as prime minister. Alexis served for an administration touted as a coalition government, backed by the United States and the international community, that included members of the so-called opposition that forced former president Jean-Bertrand Aristide into exile in 2004. Alexis's administration gave the final appearance of a legal veneer to the ouster of Aristide and his political movement known as Lavalas by co-opting former grassroots leaders into his government.

But observers fear that the proposed alternative may be worse. On May 25, after some political shuffling, Préval nominated his long-time friend and close advisor Robert "Bob" Manuel to be Haiti's next prime minister. Manuel's political arc has brought him from the left to the right, and perhaps now the extreme right. Sources who have worked closely with Manuel over the years report that he is now deeply distrustful and dismissive of popular demands and fiercely opposed to the return of former President Aristide from exile in South Africa. "One thing is for sure," said one well-placed former Haitian government security source, "If Manuel becomes Prime Minister, Aristide will not be returning to Haiti while Préval is president."

Sources

"Haiti's PM Nominee #2: A Contradictory History: Preval's Friend & Aristide's Foe Bob Manuel," Haiti Action, Kim Ives, May 31, 2008, http://www.haitiaction.net/News/KI/5_31_8/5_31_8.html; "Haiti: Aristide and the removal of Alexis," The Haiti Information Project, April 13, 2008, http://www.haitiaction.net/News/HIP/4_13_8/4_13_8.html;Orla Ryan, "Food Riots Grip Haiti," The Guardian, April 9, 2008, http://www.guardian.co.uk/world/2008/apr/09/11; "Haiti MPs Reject New PM Candidate," BBC News, May 13, 2008, http://news.bbc.co.uk/2/hi/americas/7397541.stm; Jacqueline Charles, "Aristide Supporters Demand His Return To Haiti," Miami Herald, February 29, 2008.

Censored #13 2008

Immigrant Roundups to Gain Cheap Labor for US Corporate Giants

The National Campesino Front estimates that between 1994 and 2005, two million farmers were displaced by the North American Free

Trade Agreement (NAFTA), in many cases related to the increase in US imports. Between 2000 and 2005, Mexico lost 900,000 rural jobs and 700,000 industrial jobs, resulting in deep unemployment throughout the country. Desperate poverty forced millions of Mexican workers north in order to feed their families.

This combination of unemployment in Mexico, the huge gap between salaries in the United States and Mexico, and US demand for cheap labor to compete on global markets has created a demand for undocumented labor in the US economy which is structurally unlikely to be temporary. It is not just a few companies seeking to cut corners. These are not just jobs that "US workers won't take." Migrants work in nearly all low-paying occupations and have become essential to the US economy in the age of global competition.

In the wake of 9/11, Immigration and Customs Enforcement (ICE) has repeatedly conducted workplace and home invasions across the country in an attempt to round up "illegal" immigrants. ICE justifies these raids under the rubric of keeping the homeland safe and preventing terrorism. Critics charge that the real goal of these actions is to disrupt the immigrant work force in the US and replace it with a tightly regulated non-union guest worker program. Immigrant rights organizations have noted that the crackdown has led to serious human rights violations. Families are separated. Hearings are slow, and often families do not know for long periods of time where their loved ones are being held.

From the *Censored 2008* update by David Bacon:

US immigration law is being transformed into a mechanism for supplying labor to some of the country's largest corporations. Immigration law is creating a two-tier society, in which millions of people are denied fundamental rights and social benefits, because they are recruited to come to the US by those corporations on visas that condemn them to a second-class status. Those guest workers face increased poverty and exploitation, and their status is being used to put pressure on wages, benefits, and workplace rights for all workers.

Original sources: David Bacon, "Which Side Are You On?" Truthout.org, January 27, 2007; David Bacon, "Workers, Not Guests," *The Nation*, February 6, 2007; Laura Carlsen, "Migrants: Globalization's Junk Mail?" Foreign Policy in Focus, February 26, 2007.

Update by April Pearce:

While the workplace and ICE home raids continue, rights advocates are working to protect the children, citizens, and lawful permanent residents who have suffered from such raids. The National Commission on ICE Misconduct and Violations of 4th Amendment Rights, a privately convened commission of labor and immigration advocates, began a series of nationwide hearings on February 25, 2008, to publicize allegations that US immigration officials routinely violate constitutional protections against unreasonable search and seizure during workplace raids. During large-scale raids, ICE often detains all employees, some of whom are citizens or lawful permanent residents, to seek out those without documentation. The commission will publish a report when the scheduled hearings have been completed.

On April 25, 2008, 114 US citizens and lawful permanent residents filed claims for damages with the Department of Homeland Security and ICE alleging that they were illegally detained and harassed during a large-scale raid at Micro Solutions Enterprise in Los Angeles on February 7, 2008. Armed ICE agents sealed off the company and issued orders directing everyone where to go and did not allow those detained to use their phone or computer. Of more than 700 employees at Micro Solutions, 130 were detained in this raid.

The Committee on House Education and the Labor Subcommittee on Workforce Protections heard testimony on May 20, 2008, on the impact of immigration enforcement on children. Included in the testimony was a report that the National Council of La Raza commissioned the Urban Institute to conduct, based on a study of the three communities where large-scale work site raids occurred in 2007. The report, released in October 2007, confirmed the inevitability of hardship to children resulting from an immigration raid. There are approximately 5 million children in the US with an undocumented parent; the vast majority are US citizens under ten years old. The report found that for every two immigrants detained as a result of work site raids, approximately one child is left without a parent. The Urban Institute also found that our nation's social institutions—such as school and child welfare agencies—that are tasked with protecting and nurturing children, are playing the role of first responders in the aftermath of a raid.

There is also growing alarm about ICE's engagement in intimidation and enforcement tactics near public schools and Head Start programs. ICE agents have been seen parked near schools and Head Start centers during drop-off and pick-up times. Schools have reported extremely high absence rates following ICE sightings.

Censored #20 2008

Terror Act Against Animal Activists

The Animal Enterprise Terrorism Act (AETA), signed into law on November 27, 2006, broadens punishment present under the Animal Enterprises Protection Act (AEPA) of 1992. One hundred and sixty groups, including the National Lawyers' Guild, the Natural Resources Defense Council, the League of Humane Voters, the Physicians' Committee for Responsible Medicine, and the New York City Bar Association, oppose this act on grounds that its terminology is dangerously vague and poses a major conflict to the US Constitution. The broad definition of an "animal enterprise," for example, may encompass most US businesses: "any enterprise that uses or sells animals or animal products." The phrase "loss of any real or personal property," is elastic enough to include loss of projected profit. Concerns deepen as protections against "interference" extend to any "person or entity having a connection to, relationship with, or transactions with an animal enterprise."

Hoch and Wilkens explain that in spite of the fact that 160 groups opposed its passage, the House Judiciary Committee placed AETA on the suspension calendar, under which process, bills that are non-controversial can be passed by voice vote. The vote on the bill was then held hours earlier than scheduled, with what appears to have been only six (out of 435) congresspersons present. Five voted for the bill, and Dennis Kucinich, who said that "[t]his bill will have a real and chilling effect on people's constitutionally protected rights," voted against it. Kucinich went on to say, "My concern about this bill is that it does nothing to address the real issue of animal protection but, instead targets those advocating animal rights."

Original Sources: Will Potter, "US House Passes Animal Enterprise Terrorism Act With Little Discussion or Dissent," Green is the New Red, November 14, 2006; David Hoch and Odette Wilkens, "The AETA is Invidiously Detrimental to the Animal Rights Movement (and Unconstitutional as Well)," *Vermont Journal of Environmental Law*, March 9, 2007; Budgerigar, "22 Years for Free-Speech Advocates," *Earth First! Journal*, November 2006.

Update by Sarah Maddox:

When five mansions caught fire in March of 2008, the FBI and the mainstream media immediately said this was more than a simple case of arson: it was terrorism. To be exact, it was eco-terrorism by the infamous Earth Liberation Front (ELF). Three houses were gutted and two were damaged, creating a total cost of $7 million in damage. These $2 million, 4,500–square foot homes were promoted as being "green" homes. Left at the scene was a large spray-painted bedsheet reading: "Built green? Nope black. McMansions in RCDs r not green." It was signed "Elf"—the Earth Liberation Front.

The Seattle Joint Terrorism Task Force, working with the FBI and the US Bureau of Alcohol, Tobacco, and Firearms, said in April that they were indeed working on the theory that it was "eco-terrorism," carried out by a cell of environmentalists using the catch-all title of the Earth Liberation Front. According to the FBI, "eco-terrorism," or "ecotage," is now the number one domestic terrorism threat in the US, greater than that of right-wing extremists, anti-abortion groups and animal rights organizations, and on a par with al-Qaeda. The US building industry, right-wing political groups, and the mainstream media all leapt to condemn the ELF after the arson.

But the jury on the McMansions arson is very much out. Although right-wing commentators and libertarian bloggers have used the attack as ammunition in their ideological war against environmentalists and the Left, few others think it is so simple. The more anyone looks into the arson, the more they suspect that it has probably got more to do with fraud or political smearing and dirty tricks than with terrorism.

The case for the McMansion fires being ecotage is weak, because this form of radical protest has all but died out. While animal rights extremism has continued, in the past seven years, the FBI admits, there have been only a handful of attacks on property that could have been committed by environmentalists. The silence is said to be partly as a result of ELF groups voluntarily giving up arson as a tactic following an undefined "mistake." But activists say 9/11 had the most chilling effect of all.

The attack on the twin towers led directly to the draconian USA

PATRIOT Act, which created a new category of domestic terrorism and allowed the FBI to expand its domestic and international powers. Many actions previously considered vandalism (with sentences of two to four years) can now be classed as major acts of terror, and life sentences can be given. The new terror laws have also allowed the FBI and the federal government to target people it had given up on years before and to use new surveillance methods.

Civil liberty groups expect the green scare to worsen. The Animal Enterprise Terrorism Act now raises any attacks against the profits of any animal-based industry to the level of terrorism, and a little-known bill making its way through US Congress with virtually no debate is expected to lead to a new crackdown on any dissident activity, under the guise of fighting terrorism.

The Orwellian-sounding Violent Radicalization and Homegrown Terrorist Prevention Act, passed by an overwhelming 400–6 vote in March 2008, will soon be considered by the Senate. Rather than seeking to criminalize "extremist" acts, it targets beliefs, or what many people are calling "thought crimes." "It proposes initiatives to intercede before radicalized individuals turn violent. It could herald far more intrusive surveillance techniques, without warrants, and has the potential to criminalize ideas and not actions. It could mean penalties for a stance rather than a criminal act," the American Civil Liberties Union and the Centre for Constitutional Rights have jointly said.

Sources

John Vidal, "The Green Scare," *The Guardian*, April 3, 2008, http://www.guardian.co .uk/environment/2008/apr/03/greenbuilding.ethicalliving.

Censored #23 2008

Feinstein's Conflict of Interest in Iraq

Dianne Feinstein—the ninth wealthiest member of Congress—has been beset by monumental ethical conflicts of interest. As a member of the Military Construction Appropriations subcommittee (MILCON) from 2001 to the end of 2005, Senator Feinstein voted for appropriations worth billions of dollars to her husband's firms.

From 1997 through the end of 2005, Feinstein's husband Richard C. Blum was a majority shareholder in both URS Corp. and Perini Corp. She lobbied Pentagon officials in public hearings to support defense projects that she favored, some of which already were or subsequently became URS or Perini contracts. From 2001 to 2005, URS earned $792 million from military construction and environmental cleanup projects approved by MILCON; Perini earned $759 million from such projects.

In 2000, Perini earned a mere $7 million from federal contracts. After 9/11, Perini was transformed into a major defense contractor. In 2004, the company earned $444 million for military construction work in Iraq and Afghanistan, as well as for improving airfields for the US Air Force in Europe and building base infrastructures for the US Navy around the globe. In a remarkable financial recovery, Perini shot from near penury in 1997 to logging gross revenues of $1.7 billion in 2005.

From the *Censored 2008* update by Peter Byrne:
In March 2007, right wing bloggers by the thousands started linking to and commenting upon these stories, agitating for a congressional investigation of Feinstein. In just two days, the stories got 50,000 online hits. Michael Savage and Rush Limbaugh did radio segments on my findings. I declined to appear on their shows, because I do not associate with racist, misogynist, or homophobic demagogues. Fox News's Bill O'Reilly invited me to be on his national TV show, but quickly dis-invited me after I promised that the first sentence out of my mouth would frame Feinstein as a neoconservative war-monger just like O'Reilly.

As the storm of conservative outrage intensified, Joe Conason from the Nation Institute, which had commissioned the Feinstein investigation, asked to have the tag thanking the Nation Institute for funding removed from my stories because, he said, Katrina vanden Heuvel, the *Nation's* editor and publisher, did not want the magazine or its non-profit institute to be positively associated with Limbaugh. I told Conason that not only was I *required* to credit the Nation Institute under the terms of our contract, but that the *Nation's* editors should be proud of the investigation and gratified by the public reaction.

The back story to that encounter is that, in October, vanden Heuvel had abruptly killed the Feinstein story, which had been scheduled to run as a cover feature before the November 2006 election in which Feinstein was up for reelection.

Original Source: Peter Byrne, "Senator Feinstein's Iraq Conflict," *North Bay Bohemian*, January 24, 2007.

Update by Darcy Newton:

Peter Byrne's controversial exposé, "Feinstein's Conflict of Interest in Iraq," confirmed that while US Senator Diane Feinstein served as the chairperson of the Military Construction Appropriations (MILCO) subcommittee, her husband, Richard Blum, received multimillion dollar defense contracts. Although Byrne's report established that Feinstein and Blum had been profiting from the war on Iraq, the article has been largely dismissed by the corporate media and has unleashed a flurry of bipartisan media criticism. Byrne stated that after his article came out, right- and left-wing bloggers and talk show hosts attacked the Feinstein story, and Feinstein's office sent Byrne a twelve-page letter refuting his claims. While Feinstein has resigned from the MILCO subcommittee, she continues to deny any unethical behavior.

However, the implications of Byrnes's article are far reaching and are being revived in the media. Marcus Stern reported on Feinstein's denial of any wrongdoing in the *San Diego Tribune* in July 2007, and the *San Francisco Bay Guardian* made the story visible again in "Project Censored: The Byrne ultimatum" in September 2007. And in December 2007, Judicial Watch ranked Senator Feinstein as one of Washington's "Ten Most Wanted" Corrupt Politicians for 2007 based on Byrnes's solid investigative work.

In 2007, Investigative Reporters and Editors (IRE), a nonprofit organization committed to excellence in journalism, recognized Peter Byrne for his outstanding investigative work on the Feinstein story. Byrne says that it was gratifying to get the IRE award because it is a validation of good reporting and confirmation that his assertion that Feinstein had a conflict of interest in Iraq was correct.

Sources

"The Diane Feinstein War Profiteering Scandal," Rush Limbaugh, Transcript, March 29, 2007, http://www.projectcensored.org/top-stories/articles/23-feinsteins-conflict-of-interest-in-iraq/; Marcus Stern, "Feinstein denies helping husband's firms," *San Diego Union Tribune*, July 1, 2007, http://www.signonsandiego.com/uniontrib/20070701/news_1n1difi.html; Amanda Witherell "The Byrne ultimatum," Project Censored, September 5, 2007, http://www.sfbg.com/entry.php?entry_id=4454; "Judicial Watch Announces List of Washington's 'Ten Most Wanted Corrupt Politicians' for 2007," December 19, 2007, http://www.judicialwatch.org/judicial-watch-announces-list-washington-s-ten-most-wanted-corrupt-politicians-2007; see http://www.ire.org/contest/07winners.html for information on the 2007 IRE Awards.

CHAPTER 3

Junk Food News and News Abuse

by Kate Sims, Luke Plasse, April Pearce, Melissa Willenborg, and
Margo Tyack

One of the complaints news reporters and editors have had about the
Censored List over the years is that, they claim, it unfairly criticizes
news professionals for the hard choices they have to make on a regular
basis. It is not that stories are "censored" they assert, it is just that there
is not enough time or space to cover all of the important stories that
come up in a day.

In 1985, Carl Jensen rethought this aspect of the project's analysis.
Maybe news producers, scrambling hard to cover the most salient, pro-
foundly impactful information, simply cannot capture it all. Some of
the journalistic gems are bound to slip through their fingers, and perhaps it is simply a matter of priority and a difference of opinion. So the
project undertook to examine the stories that were deemed important
by mainstream-corporate media.

Over the twenty-some years since Project Censored started taking a
look at the news that was covered *instead* of the twenty-five selected by
the organization, it has become painfully apparent that the selection of
news stories within the mainstream media has little to do with a difference of opinion about what is important. Simply put, the priorities
of the corporate news networks are skewed.

It is not opinion that local communities are losing their access to
fresh water because it is being bought and exported by a small handful of multinational companies. It is not opinion that the number of
media company owners has dwindled from about fifty in the early
1980s to no more than five in 2007. It is not opinion that the wealth
gap in the US has risen ten-fold in the last twenty years, or that this gap
correlates directly to one's life expectancy. There are dozens of stories
like these that made it into the ranks of the Top 25 but got barely a mention in the mainstream-corporate press.

What does make it into the corporate press is "horse race" election coverage, partisan political squabbles, the latest tragedy or catastrophe, and pundits dressed up as experts on any given subject. Trumping all of this, of course, is everything celebrity. Once relegated to *Tiger Beat*–style magazines and a handful of television programs dedicated to "entertainment news," the minutiae of celebrity lives are now respectable material for all news programming—including "serious" cable and network coverage.

Just as fast food has slowly replaced the balanced diets of previous Americans, junk news is replacing the good, wholesome news stories that keep the arteries of democracy unclogged and flowing free. Such malnourishment is making the American brain obese and flabby.

Here are the Junk Food news stories of the 2007–2008 cycle as selected by Project Censored's online community:

1. The Britney Spears saga (eternally)
2. The pregnancy of Jamie Lynn Spears
3. Paris Hilton goes to jail
4. Lindsay Lohan goes to rehab
5. Anna Nicole Smith's baby and inheritance
6. Brad Pitt and Angelina Jolie get pregnant
7. Jessica Simpson distracts her football star boyfriend
8. The redemption of Nicole Richie
9. Alec Baldwin insults his daughter
10. David Hasselhoff falls off the wagon

1) Topping the Junk Food list for the second year in a row is media spectacle Britney Spears. Despite multiple traffic violations, stints in rehab, and her father becoming co-conservator of herself and her estate following two hospitalizations, most of the attention has been focused on Britney's custody troubles. During the first week of October 2007 more mainstream-corporate media coverage was given to the court ruling that gave Spears's ex-husband Kevin Federline custody of the children than to Bush's veto of a bipartisan children's health insurance bill. The bill would have expanded the number of children eligible for the State Children's Health Insurance Program from 6.6 million to over 10 million.

Receiving even less coverage, *Democracy Now!* reported on the connection between Chevron and the turmoil in Burma. The Burmese

CENSORED 2009 | 163

regime, in partnership with the US multinational oil giant Chevron, delivers extracted natural gas to Thailand through Burma's Yadana pipeline. It is Yadana and related gas projects that have kept the military regime afloat to buy arms and ammunition and pay its soldiers.

Here are some of the other headlines from around the country the first week of October 2007 that television news programs could not find time for:

➤ Venezuela Defends Iran, Blasts 'Hypocritical' US Policy On Terror
➤ Abu Ghraib Prisoners Accuse US Companies of Torture
➤ Ex-White House Lawyer Speaks of 'Legal Mess' of Illegal Spying
➤ New Details In The Blackwater Shootings Don't Mesh With Firm's Version
➤ Citigroup, Bank of America Raked Over Coal
➤ Ecuadoran President Celebrates Victory After Reform Vote

Sources:
"Britney in the News," www.cnn.com/2008/SHOWBIZ/Music/02/02/spears.father.ap/index.html#cnnSTCOther1; David Scott, "Bush Vetoes Children's Health Bill," *New York Times*, October 3, 2007, http://www.nytimes.com/2007/10/03/washington/03cnd-veto.html?hp; Amy Goodman, "Chevron's Pipeline Is the Burmese Regime's Lifeline" King Features Syndicate, truthdig.com, October 2, 2007, http://www.truthdig.com/report/item/20071002_chevrons_pipeline_is_the_burmese_regimes_lifeline/.

2) In one of the most shocking displays of "not learning from an older sibling," Jamie Lynn Spears announced on December 18, 2007, that she was twelve weeks pregnant. The Father, eighteen-year-old Casey Aldridge, met Spears while they were both attending church. "I can't say it was something I was planning to do right now," the sixteen-year-old confessed to *OK!* magazine. "But now that it's in my lap and that it's something I have to deal with, I'm looking forward to being the best mom I can be." Shortly after the announcement, Lynne Spears, Britney and Jaime Lynns' mother, declared that her book on parenting had been delayed indefinitely.

Meanwhile, hidden in all the Spears hysteria, was a report by veteran CIA officer Ray McGovern that stated that evidence for the impeachment of President Bush is overwhelming. McGovern said that he witnessed a "prostitution of his profession" as the Bush administration lied about what information the CIA's intelligence reports contained concerning weapons of mass destruction. "Don't let anyone tell you the President was deceived by false intelligence . . . they knew," McGovern said.

Here are some of the other headlines from around the country on December 18, 2007 that television news programs could not find time for:

➤ FCC Votes for Monopoly, Congress Must Vote for Democracy
➤ World Food Stocks Dwindling Rapidly, UN Warns
➤ Iraq: "Bad" Women Raped and Killed
➤ US Corn Boom Threatens Sea Life: Pesticide Runoff Continues To Pollute Gulf
➤ Iraq, Afghanistan War Costs Top Vietnam

Sources

"World Exclusive: Jamie Lynn Spears—"I'm Pregnant" *OK!*, December 18, 2007, www.okmagazine.com/news/view/3425/World-Exclusive:-Jamie-Lynn-Spears-%E2%80%94-; Monica Hesse, "The Other Spears Does the Bump," *Washington Post*, December 20, 2007; Brian Stelter, "Cash Counts in Battle for Celebrity Shockers," *International Herald Tribune*, January 3, 2008; "Lynne Spears' Book about Parenting Delayed Indefinitely," *USA Today*, December 19, 2007, www.usatoday.com/life/people/2007-12-19-spears-book_N.htm; Gretyl Macalaster, "Former CIA Analyst Says Evidence Abounds for Impeachment," *Foster's Daily Democrat* (New Hampshire), December 21, 2007, www.commondreams.org/archive/2007/12/21/5940/.

3) On June 3, 2007, heiress and socialite Paris Hilton quietly turned herself in to the Men's Central Jail in downtown Los Angeles to begin serving a sentence for driving under the influence. The next day media sources everywhere exploded into a titanic tizzy arguing over what this meant for Paris and who, if anyone, was responsible for this.

A less provocative report released that week told a much more frightening story. A consensus of studies revealed that global warming is progressing at a rate three times faster than earlier predicted. Carbon emissions are three times what they were in the 1990s, the Arctic ice caps are melting three times as fast and ocean waters are rising twice as fast. Measurements show that carbon dioxide emissions increased by about 1.1 percent each year during the 1990s. Now carbon dioxide is increasing by about 3 percent. This exceeds the worst case scenario outlined in the 2007 reports by the Intergovernmental Panel on Climate Change (IPCC). It means that shortages of food and water supplies and loss of species are likely to be worse than predicted.

Here are some of the other headlines from around the country on June 3–4, 2007 that television news programs could not find time for:

➤ Top Retired General Says US Can Forget About Winning in Iraq
➤ Melting Ice, Snow to Hit Livelihoods Worldwide: UN
➤ Global Wildlife Trade Talks Focus on Species Survival, Human Livelihood
➤ Gorbachev Criticizes US "Empire"
➤ Thousand Hurt in Anti-G8 Protest, Police Arrest 128 People

Sources
"Paris Begins Jail Sentence After MTV Awards" *US Magazine*, June 4, 2007, http://www.usmagazine.com/paris_begins_her_sentence_after_mtv_awards; Steve Gorman, "Paris Hilton Fashionably Early for Jail," *The Toronto Star*, June 5, 2007; Chris Ayres, "The Perfect Fate for Paris Hilton," *Times* (London), May 8, 2007; Geoffrey Lean, "Global Warming 'Is Three Times Faster Than Worst Predictions,'" *The Independent*, June 3, 2007, www.independent.co.uk/environment/climate-change/global-warming-is-three-times-faster-than-worst-predictions-451529.html.

4) On May 26, 2007, actress Lindsay Lohan crashed her Mercedes-Benz SL65 on a curb on Sunset Boulevard in Beverly Hills, CA. The police found her in possession of cocaine and suspected her of driving under the influence. ABC News, Fox News, and MSNBC published pictures and headlined articles regarding Lindsay's status. In the months that followed, network and cable news programs provided detailed updates on her rehab, relapses, and second and third attempts at rehab. On-air discussions with psychological "experts" discussed the phenomenon of celebrity substance abuse and debated the potential causes for this national tragedy.

Here are some of the headlines from around the country on May 26, 2007 that television news programs could not find time for:

➤ GOP Presidential Candidates Repeat Unproven Iraq-9/11 Tie
➤ Abortion Decision Could Pave Way for More Restrictions
➤ Intel Agencies Warned of Post-War Risks
➤ Greenpeace Posts Leaked US Objection to G8 Climate Statement
➤ Protesters Barred From Cheney's West Point Speech

Sources
Associated Press, "Lindsay Lohan Cited on Suspicion of DUI," May 26, 2007.

5) As many well remember, the saga of Anna Nicole Smith and the search for her baby's father was a favorite preoccupation of news shows throughout 2006. On March 5, 2007, a Los Angeles judge ruled that the child, Dannielynn, was to be the sole heir to the estate of Anna Nicole, a multimillion-dollar fortune. Two days later, on March 7, Fox news covered a story that speculated on potential fathers to Dannielynn. These potential fathers included O.J. Simpson, Nicole's former attorney Howard K. Stern, documentary filmmaker Norm Pardo, and (the eventual winner of the paternity prize) ex-boyfriend Larry Birkhead.

On March 7, the same day as the Fox News report, an English newspaper published a story about the new US National Intelligence Estimate on Iraq. Apparently, since an official report on conditions in Iraq could include public access to the government documents, US officials had decided not to release the information.

Here are some of the other headlines from around the country that did not appear on US television news programs from May 5–7, 2007:

➤ Palestinians 'Routinely Tortured' in Israeli Jails
➤ Whistle-Blower on Student Aid Is Vindicated
➤ American Dream Sours as Housing Market Collapses (long before it was reported on corporate television)
➤ Survey Shows Iraq War Strain Leads Troops to Abuse Civilians
➤ Rove Prepped Justice Dept. Official for Testimony

Sources

Associated Press, "Report: O.J. Simpson Says Anna Nicole Smith's Baby Might Be His," March 7, 2007; "US Officials Lean Toward Keeping Iraq Report Quiet," *Washington Post*, March 7, 2007.

6) 2007 was a busy year for Brad Pitt and Angelina Jolie. Few other people received as much press as they did. From their borderline bizarre baby adoptions to marriage rumors and relationship gossip, nary a week went by without another story on what the media have named "Brangelina." Stories about the pair reached a pinnacle in September of 2007 when reporters seem to be able to write just about anything concerning these two people or their children and it would fly off the newsstands.

Here are some of the headlines from around the country the first week of September, 2007 that television news programs could not find time for:

> ➤ Climate Activists Target Asia-Pacific Summit in Australia
> ➤ Iraqi Children Starved of Childhoods
> ➤ More "Megafires" To Come, Say Scientists
> ➤ US Poverty Data Raise New Questions About Cost of War
> ➤ Government Secrecy Up Despite Exposure of Issue

Sources
Tashi Singh, "Angelina Jolie Honor Tattoos: Angelina Has Tat For Lover Brad Pitt" *The Post Chronicle*, June 4, 2007; Wendy Cook, "Angelina Jolie Still Taking More Shots at 'Blob' Shiloh, An Outcast?" *The National Ledger*, December 11, 2007; Brenda Jones, "Angelina Jolie & Brad Fed Up: Pitt Attacks SUV, Frightens Housewife," *The National Ledger*, August 8, 2007.

7) On December 16, 2007 at an NFL Cowboy's game against the Philadelphia Eagles, Jessica Simpson showed off her Tony Romo replica jersey to the eager media. Within moments, boyfriend and NFL star athlete Tony Romo injured his thumb and played what analysts deemed as one of his worst games of the season. According to sports psychologists, the "Simpson jinx" is more than just a typical superstition. A detailed account of the story was covered by Fox news, ABC news, CBS, and MSNBC.

In Paris, meanwhile, major world leaders and key donors met for a conference to raise billions of dollars to help the emergence of a viable Palestinian state. The goal was to promote the newly re-launched peace process with Israel. The US has offered to pay 500 million dollars toward the stabilization of the Palestinian economy and to urge Israel to gradually lift restrictions on movement between Palestinian towns and villages. This potentially Middle East–changing event received barely a whisper in US media.

Here are some of the other headlines from around the country on December 16, 2007 that television news programs could not find time for:

> ➤ Tasers Don't Reduce Shootings, Despite Police and Politicians' Claims
> ➤ Officials Seek to Protect Firms Aiding NSA Spying
> ➤ Army Knew of Cheating on Tests for Eight Years
> ➤ Oceans' Growing Acidity Alarms Scientists

Sources

Agence France Presse, "World Powers Gather in Paris to Bankroll Palestinian State," December 16, 2007; Associated Press, "Jessica Simpson Attends Dallas Cowboys Game to Cheer on Tony Romo," December 17, 2007.

8) On January 11, 2008, corporate media preoccupied itself with the birth of Harlow Winter Kate Madden, the first child of celebrity debutante, former bad girl, and recovering heroine addict Nicole Richie. Reporting on her pregnancy and birth focused on how the baby had changed Nicole's rampant ways (in July 2007 she had pled guilty to her second DUI after driving the wrong way on a Los Angeles freeway). On February 29, 2008, news anchors informed the public about the latest edition of *People* magazine that had exclusive photos of Harlow (for which *People* reportedly paid $1 million).

That same day, Nobel Prize-winning economist, Joseph Stiglitz, and Professor at Harvard's Kennedy School of Government, Linda Blimes, debuted their new book, *The Three Trillion Dollar War*, which places the conservative cost of the Iraq and Afghanistan Wars at $3 trillion. They claim the Bush administration has repeatedly low-balled the cost of the wars by mentioning only the operational costs and hiding others. Hidden costs include: interest the US has to pay other countries for money borrowed, long-term healthcare and disability services for veterans, in addition to, the cost of salaries and insurance for the estimated 100,000 no-bid contractors operating in the countries.

Here are some of the other headlines from around the country on January 11, 2008 that television news programs could not find time for:

➤ In Voiding Suit, Appellate Court Says Torture is to be Expected
➤ Iraqi Civilian Deaths Massive by Any Measure
➤ Pakistan Warns US Not to Enter Northwest
➤ UN Remains Impotent as Captive of US
➤ Abu Ghraib Officer: Probe Was Incomplete

Sources

"Madden, Pregnancy Made Richie Change Her Ways," *Good Morning America*, ABC News, August 2, 2007, http://abcnews.go.com/GMA/story?id=3433390; "Nicole Richie Introduces Baby Harlow, Says She's Not a Wild Child Anymore," Fox News, February 28, 2008, www.foxnews.com/story/0,2933,333469,00.html; Kevin G. Hall, "Nobel Laureate Estimates Wars' Cost at More than $3 Trillion," *McClatchy Newspapers*, February 27, 2008, http://www.mcclatchydc.com/staff/kevin_hall/story/28891.html.

9) On April 20, 2007, actor Alec Baldwin is caught on a phone message audiotape leaving a blistering and insulting message for his twelve-year-old daughter Ireland within which he called her a "thoughtless little pig." Within a day, Baldwin's outburst at his only child caused a family court judge in Los Angeles to suspend his visitation rights temporarily. Baldwin and ex-wife Kim Basinger had been locked in a vicious custody and visitation battle over Ireland since the couple divorced in 2002. Baldwin has regularly accused Basinger of playing games with scheduling, and this was the subject of the tirade.

During the week that surrounded the Baldwin brouhaha, the US released Posada Carriles from jail. He is the former CIA operative connected with the bombing of a Cuban airliner that killed seventy-three people. Both Cuba and Venezuela had victims from the crash and wanted him extradited in order to stand responsible for his actions.

Here are some of the other headlines from around the country on April 20, 2007 that television news programs could not find time for:

- ➤ Vermont Senate Calls for Bush, Cheney Impeachment
- ➤ Audit Finds Many Faults in Cleveland's '06 Voting
- ➤ Rights Group Sues Yahoo Over Arrests in China
- ➤ World Bank May Target Family Planning
- ➤ Iraq Refugees: The Hidden Face of the War
- ➤ World Opposed to US as Global Cop

Sources
Roger Friedman, "411: Caught on Tape: Alec Baldwin Calls Daughter a 'Rude, Thoughtless Pig'" Fox news, April 20, 2007; Amy Goodman, "Cuban Militant Posada Carriles Released," *Democracy Now!*, April 23, 2007.

10) On May 4, 2007, the country was alerted to information about a high priority drama—the one taking place in actor David Hasselhoff's bedroom. Apparently, Mr. Hasselhoff's daughters had finally reached the end of their tolerance regarding his alcoholism and had decided to videotape him in the throes of a drunken junk food binge. CNN, MSNBC and Fox News looped the low-grade web video ad nauseum. Days later, network and cable news outlets followed up with a "debate between experts" about the pressures of Hollywood and the plague of celebrity substance abuse.

Here are some of the other headlines from around the country on May 4, 2007 that television news programs could not find time for:

➤ Chavez Threatens to Nationalize Banks
➤ Murder of Mexican Union Organizer Alarms Workers, Activists
➤ Crucial Climate Change Agreement Reached After Fierce Debate
➤ US Oil Company Accused of Dumping Waste in Amazon
➤ Karl Rove Prepped Justice Department Official for Testimony

Sources
Associated Press, "David Hasselhoff Says Tape of Him Drunk Made Him Think," May 3, 2007; Tucker Carlson, Willie Geist, "Tucker For May 4, 2007," MSNBC, May 4, 2007; A. J. Hammer; Brooke Anderson, Richelle Carey, "David Hasselhoff Needs Help for his Drinking Problem," CNN, May 4, 2007; Michelle Malkin, "Hasselhoff's Battle Filmed," Fox News Network, May 4, 2007; CBS News Transcripts, "Mark Steines of *Entertainment Tonight* Discusses Home Video Showing a Drunk David Hasselhoff," May 4, 2007.

NEWS ABUSE

In 2001, addressing concerns that some of the stories overplayed in the media could not appropriately be called Junk Food, Project Censored writers added a list of stories that became labeled News Abuse. These are potentially valid news stories that eventually consumed more space and air time than their importance would seem to warrant.

The News Abuse for 2008:

1. Elliot Spitzer
2. Michael Vick dog fights
3. Heath Ledger death
4. Kanye West mother's death
5. Dog the Bounty Hunter racist tirade

1) New York Governor Eliot Spitzer resigned March 12, 2008 after his involvement in a high-class prostitution ring became public. Spitzer was caught on a federal wiretap arranging to meet with Emperor's Club VIP prostitute, Ashley Alexandra Dupre, at the Mayflower Hotel in Washington DC on February 13, 2008. The media frenzy surrounding the Spitzer scandal involved his performance as governor, his wife's reaction, and the identity of the prostitute. While mainstream-corporate

media discussed minuscule details such as how many hits were on Dupre's MySpace page, they failed to mention that Spitzer had cancelled a major address he was supposed to give at the annual meeting of Family Planning Advocates of New York State. He was going to speak to one thousand citizens who had gathered to lobby their legislators preceding the New York State Assembly vote on the Healthy Teens Act, which would "provide comprehensive, age-appropriate, medically accurate and 100 percent truthful information about sex to teens." Overwhelmed with news of the scandal, the Assembly did not pass the act as scheduled.

Hiding in the shadows of the Spitzer scandal was the release of a report by the UN Committee on the Elimination of Racial Discrimination (CERD) that stated the United States is failing to meet international standards on racial equality. The CERD is responsible for monitoring global compliance with the 1969 Convention on the Elimination of Discrimination, an international treaty that has been ratified by the US. Criticisms include racial discrimination against indigenous communities, environmental racism and degradation of indigenous areas of cultural and spiritual significance, sentencing minors to life without parole, and indefinitely detaining non-citizens at Guantanamo. The panel said the US needs to implement training programs for law enforcement officials, teachers, and social workers to raise awareness about the treaty and obligations the US is required to uphold. The CERD also recommended the establishment of an independent human rights body that could help eliminate racial disparities.

Sources

Danny Hakim and William Rashbaum, "Spitzer is linked to Prostitution Ring," *New York Times*, March 10, 2008, http://www.nytimes.com/2008/03/10/nyregion/10cnd-spitzer.html; Michael M. Grynbaum, "Spitzer Resigns, Citing Personal Failings," *New York Times*, March 12, 2008, http://www.nytimes.com/2008/03/12/nyregion/12cnd-resign.html?hp; Amy Goodman, "A Cause Bigger Than Any Scandal," *Democracy Now!*, March 12, 2008, http://www.democracynow.org/blog/2008/3/12/a_cause_bigger_than_any_scandal; Haider Rizvi, "Rights-US: UN Panel Finds Two Tier Society," IPS, March 11, 2008, http://ipsnews.net/news.asp?idnews=41556.

2) On August 24, 2007, NFL football player Michael Vick pled guilty to charges of dog fighting. During the investigation it was revealed that Vick had established an enterprise called Bad Newz Kennels with the intention of buying and training pit bulls to fight and kill in the ring. For those dogs that did not measure up, Vick oversaw the destruction of the animals by hanging or drowning.

Michael Vick was a star quarterback on the Atlanta Falcons. Said to be in the prime of his football career, Vick's future had been bright. After Vick signed a guilty plea agreement, NFL commissioner Roger Goodell was swift to act, banning Vick from the NFL indefinitely. "Your admitted conduct was not only illegal, but also cruel and reprehensible. Your team, the NFL, and NFL fans have all been hurt by your actions," Goodell said.

At the same time that US news programs obsessed over this very sad case of animal cruelty, CARE, one of the world's largest food aid distributers, shocked the rest of the world when it turned down 46 million dollars in food subsidies from the US government. The US allocates 2 billion dollars to buy food from US growers for distribution to poverty-stricken areas of the world but the crops must be grown in the US only and 75 percent must be shipped using US shipping lines. CARE claimed that such protectionist US food distribution methods meant that food aid often failed to reach its intended destination, and the subsidies undercut local farmers who could have raised and sold the food themselves, strengthening their local economy.

Other headlines from across the country on August 24, 2007, for which mainstream corporate television could find no room, include:

➤ Role of Telecom Firms in Wiretaps Is Confirmed
➤ How Iraq War Backers Morphed Into "Critics"
➤ World Faces Threat From New Deadly Diseases As Scientists Struggle To Keep Up
➤ Democratic Presidential Contenders Trash NAFTA
➤ More Iraqis Said to Flee Since Troop Increase

Sources

Gary Mihoces, "NFL Bans Vick Indefinitely after Plea Agreement," *USA Today*, August 25, 2007 http://www.usatoday.com/sports/football/nfl/falcons/2007-08-24-vick-friday_N.htm; The United States District Court for the Eastern District of Virginia "Summary of the Facts," August 24, 2007, http://www.usatoday.com/sports/football/nfl/vick-summary-of-facts-070824.pdf; Ellen Massey, "Mutiny Shakes US Food Aid Industry," Inter Press Service, August 24, 2007, http://www.commondreams.org/archive/2007/08/21/3395/.

3) On January 22, 2008, twenty-eight-year-old actor Heath Ledger was found dead by his housekeeper in a Lower Manhattan apartment. An autopsy later determined that he had died of a probably-accidental overdose of prescription medication. There was no note and no signs of

foul play. Ledger's family called his death "very tragic, untimely and accidental." They asked to be left alone, but to no avail. Over the following months, network and cable news programs poured through every detail of the actor's life and death.

Here are some of the headlines from across the country the week of January 22, 2008 for which mainstream corporate television could find no room:

➤ Gaza: No Rights, Little Mercy
➤ Contractor Abuses Rarely Punished, Groups Say
➤ Pre-Emptive Nuclear Strike a Key Option, NATO Told
➤ Globally, Topsoil is Disappearing
➤ US Censors Arctic Scientists' Findings as it Prepares for Oil and Gas Auction

Sources

Nancy Grace, Richard Roth, Mike Brooks, "Actor Heath Ledger Found Dead In Apartment," CNN, January 22, 2008; Heather Nauert, John Gibson, Jill Dobson, Greta Van Susteren, Mark Fuhrman, Bill McCuddy, Rick Leventhal, Jeanine Pirro, Andrew Napolitano, "Heath Ledger Dies," Fox News Network, January 22, 2008.

4) On November 9, 2007, Donda West, the mother of well-known Hip-Hop artist Kanye West, died after undergoing surgery. Over the following week, the story of how she may have died from surgical complications was covered by CNN, Fox News, CBS and MSNBC. Coverage expanded to include stories of her planned autopsy and the many songs by Kanye that she had inspired. This was a terrible family tragedy that became overhyped and abused by corporate news organizations.

Here are some of the headlines from across the country the week of November 9, 2007 that did not make it onto mainstream corporate television:

➤ The death of author and political critic Norman Mailer
➤ 2007 Deadliest for US in Afghanistan
➤ FCC's Copps & Adelstein Rip Into Chairman Martin at Media-Ownership Hearing
➤ Burma: Keeping the Revolution Flame Alive Over Radio, Internet
➤ Cheney Tried to Stifle Dissent in Iran NIE
➤ Violence Erupts After Bhutto's Arrest

Sources
Associated Press, "Kanye West's Mother May Have Died of Surgery Complications," November 10, 2007; CNN.com, "Autopsy Planned for Kanye West's Mom," November 11, 2007.

5) On November 1, 2007 A&E halted production of its popular reality series *Dog the Bounty Hunter*. According to Duane "Dog" Chapman's lawyer, the bounty hunter's son had taped a private phone conversation in which the reality star used the "N-word." Chapman, fifty-four, repeatedly used the racial slur during a March phone call to his son, Tucker, urging him to break up with a black girlfriend. The son then sold the tape in November to a tabloid for "a lot of money." Every detail of the conversation—Chapman's apology, the response by black leaders, and the debate over the shows cancellation—became fodder for debate by mainstream pundits.

Here are some of the headlines from across the country on November 1–2, 2007 that did not make it onto mainstream corporate television:

➤ Retired General Says Guantanamo Mission Came Straight From Bush, Rumsfeld
➤ USAF Struck Syrian Nuclear Site
➤ Poll Shows Majority OK with Birth Control for Schools
➤ Did Blackwater Sneak Silencers Into Iraq?
➤ In Nicaragua At-Risk Pregnancy Means Death or Prison
➤ Nordic Nations Sound Alarm Over Melting Arctic

Sources
"Duane 'Dog' Chapman Apologizes for Using Racial Slur in Taped Conversation With Son," The Insider Online, CBS studios, November 1, 2007, http://www.theinsideronline.com/news/2007/11/13796/index.html; "Lawyer: Son of TV bounty hunter Sold 'N-word' tape," AP Newswire, November 2, 2007, http://www.cnn.com/2007/SHOWBIZ/TV/11/01/dog.chapman.ap/index.html; "Chapman Apologizes for Using Racial Slur," ABC News, November 8, 2007, http://abcnews.go.com/Entertainment/wireStory?id=3836394

To learn more about each of the headlines listed within the stories above, please visit the CommonDreams web site. Click on "archives" and "headlines" for the date listed.

CHAPTER 4

The News is Good!
Stories of Hope and Change from 2007 and 2008

edited by Kate Sims and the people of *Yes! Magazine*

There are widespread indications that the world may be fast approaching the tipping point of understanding so many of us have been waiting for. You wouldn't know it from reading the daily news, but around the world, people have quit waiting for political and financial elites to solve the problems we face and are instead assuming the mantle of leadership at the grassroots level. They are developing renewable energy alternatives, promoting real health care solutions, and bringing the struggle for equity together with the work of saving the environment.

Perhaps the world owes a debt of gratitude to the Bush administration and its neoconservative associates. Their exploits have made the folly of the "pro-empire" agenda so painfully clear that it may have finally forced the global population into a different, post-empire mode of thinking; one that could give birth to a whole new way of life for humankind. And while change of this magnitude will be difficult, there are strong indications that people are now ready to face this challenge.

This global shift in perception is revealing the emergence of a new, people-centered sociopolitical agenda. While pro-empire foreign policy means perpetual wars of aggression for resources and global power, the new agenda is calling for the US to rejoin the community of nations. While pro-empire proponents press for trade agreements that favor large corporations, the new agenda favors strong local economies that put families and the environment first.

The mainstream media, as usual, avert their eyes from anything painful, complex, or "controversial," and this growing movement is no exception. But in the end, it may not matter. Change is happening on a global scale despite attempts to contain it. And it is in the independent media that one can see the new stories unfolding.

People are now beginning to come out of the fear-induced trance they have been in since 2001, and they appear to be ready for a dose of reality.

Poll after poll reveals that people want to change directions. In 2008, *Yes! Magazine* reported on a study that shows that, on a series of key domestic issues, Americans are far more progressive than one might think, given the range of political debate in mainstream media. The polling results, compiled by the Campaign for America's Future and Media Matters, show Americans hold deeply progressive values on issues including national defense, energy, the environment, health care, and criminal justice.

As author and progressive theorist David Korten often mentions to his audiences, "We are not the representatives of an alternative 'fringe' minority. We are the cutting edge of a national super-majority—and it is appropriate for us to begin acting accordingly."

Here are this year's top stories about people who are stepping up to the task of building a world that works for all.

1. COMMUNITIES TAKE ON CORPORATE POWER

➤ Small town citizens are claiming the right to govern themselves by adopting laws that protect their voting rights and their natural resources while challenging the laws stacked in favor of corporations. The courts have not yet ruled on some of these measures. If they are challenged, no one knows what the outcome will be. But these new activists point to the abolitionist and women's suffrage movements, which also were viewed as radical challenges to well-settled law. In the best tradition of the patriots of the thirteen colonies, these communities are asserting their right to govern themselves and to make sure their votes count. (Doug Pibel, "Communities Take Power," *Yes! Magazine* #43, fall 2007)

➤ Farmers and small-town residents in rural Pennsylvania resisted the encroachment of corporate feedlots and the dumping of sewage sludge from other states. With the help of the Community Environmental Legal Defense Fund, they drafted model ordinances asserting community rights to self-governance and banning corporations from damaging operations in townships. Since that time, more than one hundred Pennsylvania townships have adopted similar ordinances. And in New Hampshire, citizens are using local laws to keep corporate giants from bottling up their water. Such actions ban unwanted corporate operations, not based on regulation, but on a declaration that human beings have the right to control their local resources, and that corporations are not people and not entitled to rights the Constitution grants to humans. (Kaitlin Sopoci-Belknap, "Democracy Unlimited," *Yes! Magazine* #43, fall 2007, www.YesMagazine.org/43corporateban)

➤ In 2006, Humboldt County, California, became the largest jurisdiction to abolish the legal doctrine known as "corporate personhood" with the passage of local Measure T. Now human beings and local businesses, but not out-of-district corporations, may determine the outcome of elections in Humboldt County. (www.YesMagazine.org/43Humboldt)

2. THE ENVIRONMENTAL MOVEMENT: NOW THERE'S A PLACE FOR EVERYONE

Since the blockbuster success of the 2007 documentary *An Inconvenient Truth*, the attitude toward global climate change has turned a corner. It seems like everyone is suddenly, and ostentatiously, "going green." Mainstream media programs are promoting "environmental alternatives," and even Fortune 500 CEOs are talking about their efforts to reduce their companies' "carbon footprint." What isn't making it into the national conversation is a core cause for the global crisis: the inequality of wealth, power, and consumption. Yet millions of environmental activists know that the climate crisis can't be solved without also taking on the poverty crisis. These hard-working groups from all parts of the world aren't waiting for the mainstream to catch up. They're putting these issues on the agenda now.

➤ Climate negotiators representing the nations of the world met in Bali, Indonesia, and hammered out a fragile climate agreement that takes on global poverty and aims to build just climate solutions. This is a case where the world will either swim or sink together. (Tom Athanasiou, "Global Fairness," *Yes! Magazine* #45, spring 2008, www.YesMagazine.org/45Bali)

➤ People left out of the fossil fuel economy are taking their place in the green economy—this time, jobs are to go to the poor and to people of color. The environmental movement meets the social justice movement, and the marriage is changing everything. (Ian Kim, "Green Jobs for All," *Yes! Magazine* #45, spring 2008, www.YesMagazine.org/45GreenJobs)

➤ The community organizers of the Industrial Areas Foundation are gathering their grassroots clout to insist that the nation retools for green jobs that serve the poor and working people. (Doug Pibel, "Unions, Churches, and Schools," *Yes! Magazine* #45, spring 2008, www.YesMagazine.org/45unions)

➤ Young people are literally fighting for their lives and their futures when they organize to protect the climate. The author is one of those youth, and she tells of the growing power of young people with a passion for climate protection. (Shadia Fayne Wood, "Youth Feel the Power," *Yes! Magazine* #45, spring 2008, www.YesMagazine.org/45youth)

➤ As climate change and worldwide shortages loom, will people fight over water or join together to protect it? A global water justice movement is demanding a change in international law to ensure the universal right to clean water for all. (Maude Barlow, "Life, Liberty, Water," *Yes! Magazine* #46, summer 2008, www.YesMagazine.org/46water)

3. FOOD: CONSUMERS SAY YES TO LOCAL AGRICULTURE, NO TO GMOS

A consensus is building around the world about the dangers facing our global food chain. The small farmers at the front lines of this historic struggle are beginning to make important headway—for which we may all owe them a debt of gratitude.

➤ On May 3, 2007, Monsanto took a blow to its monopolistic practices. The European Patents Office's appeals tribunal finally revoked Monsanto's monopoly on genetically modified soy, a huge victory in the worldwide struggle for food sovereignty. (Hope Shand, "Challenging Monsanto's Monopoly," *Z Magazine*, July/Aug. 2007, http://zmagsite.zmag.org/JulAug2007/shand.html)

➤ Percy Schmeiser has a check for $660 and a Right Livelihood Award to prove that sometimes the little guy wins. In a modern version of the David vs. Goliath story, the Saskatchewan farmer and his wife are now considered folk heroes, following settlement of their legal battle with agribusiness giant Monsanto Canada Inc. (Barbara L. Minton, "Small Farmer Wins Moral Victory Over Monsanto," NaturalNews.com, April 01, 2008, http://www.naturalnews.com/022918.html)

➤ Forty-one of the world's largest rice exporters, processors, and retailers promised in February not to purchase genetically engineered (GE) rice. Also, farmers in Mali, located in Sub-Saharan Africa, recently voted against allowing GE crops. (Rik Langendoen, "No to Genetically Engineered Rice," Yes! Magazine #42, summer 2007, www.YesMagazine.org/42Rice)

➤ The state government of the Spanish islands of Mallorca, Menorca, and Ibiza declared the islands a GMO-free zone. They are the latest participants in a campaign, supported by Friends of the Earth and Greenpeace, that now includes 236 regions, over 4,200 municipalities, and tens of thousands of farmers and food producers in Europe who have declared themselves "GMO-free," banning the use of genetically modified organisms in agriculture and food in their territories. ("Spanish Islands Go GMO-Free," Yes! Magazine #44, Winter 2008, www.YesMagazine.org/44GMO-free)

For more information, see www.gefoodalert.org and www.gmo-free-europe.org.

4. INDIGENOUS PEOPLES: THE FIGHT FOR RECOGNITION BEARS FRUIT

The global movement to recognize and respect the rights of indigenous peoples took a dramatic step forward in 2007 with the adoption of the UN Declaration on Indigenous Rights. Many corporations and governments continue to exploit and appropriate the lands of native people—which include some of the world's most biodiverse and environmentally productive regions. But the recognition of the rights of first peoples is growing, and the indigenous peoples of the world are joining forces.

➤ After two and a half decades of work by indigenous peoples and UN member states, the United Nations General Assembly passed the

Indigenous Rights Declaration on September 13, 2007. Only four countries (Australia, Canada, New Zealand, and the United States) voted
against it. (Poka Laenui, "UN Declaration on Indigenous Rights," *Yes! Magazine* #44,
Winter 2008, www.YesMagazine.org/44UN; see also *Censored 2009*, Chapter 1, #17)

▶ Bolivians voted on a new constitution that fully recognizes the indigenous sovereignty of the thirty-six nations within Bolivia. The innovative
document also requires basic services to be delivered on a not-for-profit
basis and bans GMOs, giving priority to small organic farmers and protecting natural resources. (Juliette Beck, "Bolivia Adopts New Constitution," *Yes!*
Magazine #45, Spring 2008, www.YesMagazine.org/45Bolivia)

▶ The indigenous nations of "Abya Yala" (the Americas) meeting in La
Paz, Bolivia, call on the people of the world to adopt a Culture of Life—
while there is still time. (Jallalla Indigenous Pueblos and Nations of Abya Yala,
"Declaration of La Paz," *Yes! Magazine* #42, summer 2007, www.YesMagazine.org/42LaPaz)

5. ENERGY ALTERNATIVES TAKE HOLD

While the "pain at the pump" is allowing the debate about energy to
broaden once again in the mainstream media, think tanks like the
American Enterprise Institute are working hard to position nuclear and
coal as the only "alternatives." Commuters, school districts, home owners, and others who are paying the financial, security, and
environmental costs of oil dependence are "getting it" though. Real
alternatives and opportunities are taking hold around the world, and
even here in the US.

▶ The solar industry is poised for rapid growth and price reductions
that will make it cost-competitive in the next few years, according to
a new assessment by the Worldwatch Institute in Washington, DC,
and the Prometheus Institute in Cambridge, Massachusetts. (Alisa
Gravitz, "Solar Power Surge," *Yes! Magazine* #43, fall 2007, www.YesMagazine.org/
43solar, www.coopamerica.org)

▶ There is enough wind, solar, deep geothermal, and tidal power available to power the US many times over. Recent innovations include
photovoltaic "paint," underground wind-energy storage, and concentrated

solar plants. The biggest barrier is the sunk investment in dirty, fossil-fuel burning energy, not the technology. (Guy Dauncey, "Electricity: an Astonishing Abundance," *Yes! Magazine* #45, spring 2008, www.YesMagazine.org/ 45electricity)

➤ Kansas Secretary of Health and Environment Roderick Bremby has blocked the building of two coal-fired power plants, a $3.6 billion project. Concerns about carbon emissions and the public's health spurred Bremby's controversial decision, the latest in a trend of resistance against Big Coal. (Margit Christenson, "Blocking Big Coal," *Yes! Magazine* #44, Winter 2008, www.yesmagazine.org/article.asp?ID=2115, www.YesMagazine.org/44coal)

➤ Plug-in hybrids can run on wind or solar power, and in their off hours, they can feed power back to the grid. An innovation that can get us places without carbon while providing distributed battery power for the renewables electrical grid. (Sherry Boschert, "The Secret Life of Plug-in Hybrids," *Yes! Magazine* #45, spring 2008, www.YesMagazine.org/45hybrids)

➤ Buildings are responsible for 30-40 percent of the climate change problem—but around the world, builders, residents, and communities are deploying energy-saving innovations that are reducing their carbon footprint by as much as 93 percent. The US Conference of Mayors has endorsed Architecture 2030's campaign to have all US buildings 100 percent carbon neutral by 2030. (Guy Dauncey, "Smart, Green Buildings," *Yes! Magazine* #45, Spring 2008, www.YesMagazine.org/45buildings)

6. ALTERING THE MEDIA LANDSCAPE

As the corporate media increasingly acts as stenographers and spinmeisters for the status quo; people are looking elsewhere for reliable sources of information. Independent media outlets are becoming the news source of choice for many. Meanwhile, people power and citizen pressure are beginning to chip away at the monolithic structure of big media multinationals (see chapter 11 for more on how this movement is building).

➤ In June, Maine's legislature became the first in the nation to express strong support for preserving net neutrality. Network neutrality means no discrimination on the Internet. Internet providers are prevented from speeding up or slowing down Web content based on its source, ownership, or destination. The big telecom firms want to eliminate net neutrality so they can charge content providers additional fees for preferred access. (Jon Bartholomew, "Maine Leads on Net Neutrality," *Yes! Magazine* #43, fall 2007, www.YesMagazine.org/43Net)

➤ Comcast Corporation has been airing pre-packaged video news releases (VNRs), and the Federal Communications Commission (FCC) is cracking down with a small but unprecedented $4,000 fine. In 2007, non-profit organizations Free Press and the Center for Media and Democracy documented nearly 140 undisclosed VNRs. The $4,000 fine is the first-ever penalty imposed by the FCC for airing fake news. (Margit Christenson, "FCC Fines Comcast for Fake News," *Yes! Magazine* #44, winter 2008 www.YesMagazine.org/44FCC)

➤ Hundreds of citizens from across the political spectrum turned out in Seattle to tell the FCC they want no more media consolidation. The raucous hearing lasted from mid-afternoon until late into the night. ("The People Speak Out at FCC Hearing in Seattle," *Yes! Magazine*, www.YesMagazine.org/FCC)

7. REAL HEALTHCARE SOLUTIONS ARE ON THE TABLE

The debate about healthcare is receiving more diverse coverage in the media than it has in many decades. It cannot be denied that the much-maligned Michael Moore documentary *Sicko* created an opportunity to change the conversation. Programs like the PBS series *Unnatural Causes: Is Inequality Making Us Sick?* and Frontline's *Sick Around the World* are digging deep into the reality of the situation. Healthcare activists are building on this national movement.

➤ Michael Moore's film *Sicko* opened the door to organizing in hundreds of communities, including unexpected cities like Gainesville, Boca Raton, and Louisville, along with ones we might expect like Chicago, Indianapolis, Atlanta, Pittsburgh, New York, Sacramento, and Boston. People are realizing that single-payer health care is not just a dream but a real possibility. (*"Sicko* Paves the Way," *Yes! Magazine* #43, fall 2007, www.YesMagazine.org/article.asp?id=1848. See www.healthcare-now.org and, for six ways you can get involved: www.yesmagazine.org/43sicko)

➤ San Francisco is the first city in the nation to offer health care to all of its uninsured residents. The funding comes from redirecting money previously spent on emergency hospital visits by the uninsured into a more complete medical safety net. (Brooke Jarvis, "San Francisco's Health Care for All," *Yes! Magazine* #45, winter 2008, www.YesMagazine.org/45health)

➤ Cuba is exporting its healthcare system to poor communities in Latin America, the Caribbean, Africa, and even the United States. Tens of thousands of students from poor communities in more than thirty countries are studying medicine in Cuba, and teams of Cuban doctors are responding to natural disasters and to ongoing needs for medical care. In the summer of 2007, about one hundred US students were in Havana studying to be doctors, with the promise that they would return to serve underserved communities at home. (Sarah van Gelder, "Health Care for All; Love, Cuba," *Yes! Magazine* #42, Summer 2007, www.YesMagazine.org/42Cuba)

8. DEVELOPING COUNTRIES TAKE CHARGE OF THEIR ECONOMIES

For years, "developing nations" in Africa and South America have been challenging the neocolonial economic policies that have hindered their growth and autonomy. In 2007 and 2008, many countries pulled away from the old models with a speed that left transnational corporations, multi-lateral agencies (and the US media) speechless.

➤ The International Monetary Fund (IMF) once called the shots in Latin America. Governments, fearful of being cut off from international finance, bowed to IMF mandates that starved education and health care, and turned agriculture and natural resources over to corporate interests. No more. The IMF's loan portfolio worldwide has shrunk by more than two thirds. The global justice movement's opposition to the agency has won out, but that victory is going almost completely unreported. (Sarah Anderson, "IMF: Paid in Full," *Yes! Magazine* #42, summer 2007, www.YesMagazine.org/ 42IMF)

➤ NAFTA has devastated the rural economy of Mexico. On the fourteenth anniversary of the trade agreement, as the final provisions took effect, there were mass protests in Mexico's capital. But in the countryside, farmers and small businesses are working to rebuild the rural economy, with cooperatives and fair trade as the foundation. (Wendy Call, "New Light in the Sky," *Yes! Magazine* #46, summer 2008, www.YesMagazine.org/ 46NAFTA)

➤ In Lisbon in December 2007, during the second European Union-Africa summit, twenty-seven industrialized nations were demanding from the African (and Caribbean and Pacific) countries that they allow European Union goods and services exports to enter their markets without any customs duty. The poor countries said no. (Ignacio Ramonet, "Africa Says No," *Le Monde Diplomatique*, January 2008; "Promises and Poverty," Tom Knudson, *Sacramento Bee*, 9/23/2007; www.truthout.org/docs_2006/122807G.shtml; www.sacbee .com/101/story/393917.html)

➤ Ethiopia recently shook up the industry with a new tactic: trademarking its specialty coffees, overcoming resistance to the idea from distributors—notably Starbucks. In May 2007 Ethiopia won a battle with Starbucks over trademark entitlement, which could help the country's coffee growers to earn some $88 million more per year. (Matthew Clark, "In Trademarking its Coffee, Ethiopia Seeks Fair Trade," *Christian Science Monitor*, November 9, 2007, http://www.csmonitor.com/2007/1109/p01s06-woaf.html)

9. MOVING BEYOND WAR

While the Iraq conflict sparked large protests throughout the world, the larger "war on terror" has had a quieter, more profound impact that has grown largely unnoticed in recent years. Now, even the hawks of yesterday are recognizing the worth of the anti-war movement and its call for a move beyond war.

➤ Former Secretary of State George Shultz, along with Sam Nunn, Henry Kissinger, and others are calling for the abolition of nuclear weapons, which Shultz says are making us dangerously less secure. ("George Shultz Calls for the Abolition of Nuclear Weapons," an interview with Sarah van Gelder, *Yes! Magazine* #46, summer 2008, www.YesMagazine.org/46Shultz)

➤ The congressional class of 2006 was elected with a mandate to end the war. Now a team of candidates for the 2008 election have made a commitment to a plan that goes further than the current congressional leadership in assuring that no "enduring" military presence would remain in Iraq. (Erik Leaver, "Candidates for Congress Show the Way Out," *Yes! Magazine* #46, summer 2008, www.YesMagazine.org/46Iraq)

➤ Americans who think the federal government has made a travesty of foreign relations are taking matters into their own communities, passing resolutions for peace and voting to bring their National Guard home. (Ben Manski and Karen Dolan, "Cities Declare Peace," *Yes! Magazine* #46, summer 2008, www.YesMagazine.org/46Cities)

➤ There are billions of dollars that could be saved if we cut waste and abuse out of the military budget and converted our spending to real defense. (Miriam Pemberton, "Raiding the War Chest," *Yes! Magazine* #46, summer 2008, www.YesMagazine.org/46WarChest)

10. SEATTLE: THE BEGINNING OF A NEW CULTURE OF ACTIVISM

The "Battle in Seattle" against the WTO was but a single event in an ongoing struggle to take back power from global corporations and finance agencies. Nonetheless, the 1999 mass protest, direct action, and popular education events marked a turning point in activism. People around the world are taking notice.

➤ According to author Paul Hawken, there are currently a million (or more) grassroots green and social organizations throughout the world that act as an immune system, working to stop injustice and pollution. The author says it is the biggest movement in the history of humankind and has come just in time. (Paul Hawken, "Remembering the Battle of Seattle," *Ode Magazine*, June 2007, www.odemagazine.com/doc/44/remembering_the_battle _of_seattle)

➤ Tens of thousands of people from grassroots movements throughout the United States gathered in Atlanta under the banner: "Another World is Possible—Another US is Necessary!" The US Social Forum took place in June 2007, and with it the United States joined the world as full participants in the World Social Forum process. The Forum was led and shaped by Americans who have been historically left out or left behind, providing a space for all who wanted to collaborate in sharing their work and their visions for a better US and a better world. (Sarah van Gelder, "We Saw Another World in Atlanta," *Yes! Magazine* #43 Fall 2007, www.YesMagazine.org/43USSF)

➤ A group of activists who have worked for years to save rainforests, to abolish toxic chemicals, to defend labor rights, and to block destructive global trade agreements came to a stark realization. Unless they took on the underlying cause—excess corporate power—they would not succeed. They have joined forces to do something about it. (Michael Marx and Marjorie Kelly, "Who Will Rule," *Yes! Magazine* #43, fall 2007, www.YesMagazine.org/43CorporateRule)

CHAPTER 5

Oiling the Dangerous Engine of Arbitrary Government
Newspaper Coverage of the Military Commissions Act

by Andrew Roth, with Sarah Maddox and Kaitlyn Pinson

The suspension of habeas corpus for "any person" by the 2006 Military Commissions Act (MCA), as reported by Robert Parry and Thom Hartman, was Project Censored's top-ranked story of 2006–2007.[1] Habeas corpus protects individuals against unlawful exercises of state power. It is so fundamental to the United States that the framers wrote it into the Constitution, establishing that it could only be suspended "in cases of rebellion or invasion."[2] Identifying habeas corpus as the greatest security to "liberty and republicanism" contained in the Constitution, Alexander Hamilton drew insight from the eighteenth-century British legal scholar Blackstone, who championed habeas as a protection against the "dangerous engine of arbitrary government."

Civil rights activists, constitutional law experts, and the public have been outspoken in their criticisms of the MCA. For example, in analyzing how it "purports to confer rights that, upon close inspection, prove illusory," one legal scholar concludes that the Act is "an exercise in misdirection. It is, in a word, 'Orwellian.'"[3] Deceptive though its language may be, the Act's political significance is straightforward, as Michael Dorf concludes: "It is difficult to imagine a greater denial of individual liberty than the prospect of indefinite executive detention without recourse to the judiciary."[4]

To what extent have corporate media done an adequate job of informing the public about the MCA? William Parry and Thom Hartman's stories earned the #1 spot in Project Censored's 2006–2007 rankings precisely because corporate media were not adequately covering the MCA and, in particular, its suspension of habeas corpus.

Parry and Hartman's reportage reveals both (a) how little the corporate media did to inform the public about the Act's sweeping implications, and that (b) good reporting can convey the necessary understanding to a lay public, despite the Act's Orwellian logic. Furthermore, in reporting on the Act's suspension of habeas corpus, Parry noted that "the public's lack of a clear understanding of the law's scope has undercut efforts to build a popular movement for repeal or revision of the law" (*Censored 2008*, p. 39).

Inspired by Parry and Hartman's work, and committed to the belief that habeas corpus for all persons is a cornerstone of democratic government, we examined subsequent newspaper coverage of the MCA to determine how adequately corporate news media fulfills its interconnected functions as (1) a watchdog against abuse by those in positions of power, (2) a source of substantial information for citizens about social and political issues, and, (3) a forum in which diverse opinions are communicated to others.[5] In this chapter, we examine three fundamental causes for the public's lack of understanding and consequent inaction:

(1) a continued deficit in coverage of the MCA by corporate news media, compounded by
(2) reliance on a narrow range of sources in stories that do report on the MCA, resulting in
(3) the framing of public discourse about the Act as legitimate controversy, rather than the unconstitutional, counter-democratic law that it is.

MEDIA STANDING AND SPHERES OF CONSENSUS, CONTROVERSY, AND DEVIANCE[6]

Media scholars pay attention to the role that news sources play in the construction—and slant—of news stories. Following the research of sociologist William Gamson, we use the term "media standing" to refer to those who gain status as a regular media source, especially those whose claims and views journalists quote directly. According to Gamson, media standing is "a measure of achieved cultural power." Journalists grant media standing to individuals and organizations because these sources are understood to "speak as, or for, serious players in any given policy domain. In other words, individuals or groups who have enough political power to make a potential difference in what happens."7

Typically journalists bestow the cultural power of media standing on sources whose official, bureaucratic statuses already establish them as "serious players" due to their political power. Thus, sociologists who study news production typically conclude that elites are both "the sources and subjects of most political stories"8 because, for journalists, "'news' is about what those in power say and do."9

By treating news as primarily, if not exclusively, a matter of what the powerful elite say and do, corporate news media provide the public with distorting perspectives on crucial issues in at least two ways. First, and most obviously, by affording media standing to a partial range of sources, news media can convey a false sense of consensus. Second, and perhaps less obviously, by presenting a narrow range of competing perspectives, news media can convey a sensation of robust debate even as such coverage functions to define narrowly the limits of acceptable political debate.10

In his influential study of US media during the Vietnam War, Daniel Hallin conceptualized three spheres of news coverage: (1) the sphere of legitimate controversy, in which journalists seek conscientiously for balance and objectivity, (2) the sphere of consensus, in which journalists take for granted shared values and assumptions, and (3) the sphere of deviance, in which journalists understand themselves as authorized to treat marginal figures or positions without regard for professional commitments to balance and objectivity.11

Where journalists adhere most closely to professional norms of balance and objectivity, they contribute to the definition of the story, or the issues the story addresses, as a matter of legitimate controversy. One way journalists accomplish this is by quoting multiple, often competing sources to represent "both sides" of an issue, a standard practice for achieving "balance."12 In doing so, journalists contribute to the framing of the issue as one outside of shared consensus, but worthy of serious news coverage.

Though this might seem to exemplify how a free press ought to function in a democratic society, this scenario is not always ideal. Most relevant for the purposes of this study, if individuals or groups come to (re)frame the protections afforded by habeas corpus as subject to political debate, then the suspension of habeas corpus is repositioned as a (potentially) legitimate legal and political act.

Informed by Gamson's and Hallin's research, we examined news-paper coverage of the Military Commission Act in order to determine the breadth of perspectives concerning the Act. We reviewed the *Los Angeles Times, New York Times,* and *Washington Post,* and analyzed whether these papers treated the Act as a matter of consensus, legitimate controversy, or deviance.

DATA AND METHODS

Our data consist of news stories in the *Los Angeles Times, New York Times,* and *Washington Post* between September 17, 2006, and November 17, 2007. We selected these three newspapers as exemplars of corporate news media. The date range was chosen to span the time between the month before the MCA became law (on October 17, 2006) and one month after the first anniversary of its passage.

Using Lexis/Nexis Academic and Proquest Newstand, we searched for all print news references to the MCA in the three newspapers during that period. Our search generated 189 records, comprised of seventy-six items from the *New York Times,* sixty-two from the *Washington Post,* and fifty-one from the *Los Angeles Times.* We excluded a number of these items from analysis because they were not news stories (such as editorials, opinion pieces, and letters to the editor) or they were news stories that made only passing reference to the MCA. This left us with a data collection of seventy-five relevant news stories (thirty-six from the *Los Angeles Times,* twenty-one from the *Post,* and eighteen from the *New York Times*).

Following prior work on "media standing," we were most interested in how each article identified its news sources and whom journalists quoted directly. Thus our unit of analysis is the individual quotation. The seventy-five stories in our data collection include 237 direct quotations. We coded each quotation for its source identification using the following categories: *legal* (with subcategories for lawyers, judges, constitutional rights advocacy organizations, and professors), *congress, executive, military, other government officials, human rights advocacy groups,* and *other source types,* a residual category.

We also coded each quotation for its position toward the Act (pro, con, or neutral) and whether it made explicit reference to habeas corpus or not. In determining each quote's position toward the Act, which involves some subjective judgment on the coder's part, we sought to minimize ambiguity by restricting use of the "pro" and "con" categories to quotations that clearly took one position or the other. All other quotations were treated as "neutral." We only coded quotations as making reference to habeas corpus if the source referred to it by name, synonym (e.g., "the great writ" or "the writ"), or pronoun.

Finally, we coded for the location within the newspaper of the story in which each quotation appeared. This last coding category gives an imprecise but useful measure of the quotation's prominence. The measure is 'imprecise' because we cannot determine the exact location of specific quotations based on electronic reproductions of the original newsprint stories. The measure is useful, nonetheless, because front-page stories are more likely to attract the reader's attention.

Working as a team to code the data, we sought to develop coding categories that required a minimum of subjective interpretation. We met regularly to compare coding decisions and to refine our shared sense of how to code ambiguous, "borderline" cases. When tested, this effort paid off with a high degree (93.5 percent) of inter-coder reliability. Even our most difficult, subjective category—position toward the MCA—yielded a solid 82.2 percent inter-coder reliability score. Thus, we report the findings that follow with strong confidence in their reliability.

WHO'S QUOTED?

The range of sources quoted in stories concerning the MCA is typical of conventional news coverage: it reflects the strong journalistic bias for sources with official, bureaucratic statuses. Table 1 summarizes our findings regarding whom the three newspapers treated as newsworthy sources of quotations. The legal category accounts for nearly a majority (49 percent) of the 237 quotations in our data collection. Government officials (including representatives of the executive and congressional branches) constituted the next largest (28 percent) source category. Within this category, Congress accounted for 14 percent, the executive branch accounted for 5 percent, and other government officials (e.g., State Department officials) accounted for 9 percent of the total quotations in our data. Spokespersons for human rights advocacy groups—such as Human Rights Watch, Amnesty International,

Human Rights First, and the International Council of the Red Cross—
contributed 9 percent of the quotations.

TABLE 1. Distribution of Quotations by Source Type

Source Type	Quotes	Total (%)
Legal	115	49
Government*	67	28
Military	23	10
Human Rights	22	9
Other	10	4
TOTAL	237	100

*Government category excludes military sources

Notably, in the *Other* category, we found just a single instance of a
direct quotation attributed to a detainee: describing Salim Hamdan as
an "ambassador of sorts for frustrated detainees," the *New York Times*
quoted him as saying, "There is no such thing as justice here," during
a war crimes court hearing.

The preponderance of quotations by legal sources warrants a closer
look at this category, as provided in Table 2.

TABLE 2. Distribution of Quotations by Legal Sources

Source Type	Quotes	Total (%)
Detainee Lawyer	28	24
Judge (non-military)	26	23
Professor	23	20
ACLU/CCR*	12	10
Military Lawyer	10	9
Other Lawyer	6	5
Attorney General	5	4
Military Judge	3	3
Other	2	2
TOTAL	115	100

*CCR refers to the Center for Constitutional Rights

Detainees' legal counsel were the most frequently quoted subcategory of legal sources (24 percent), followed closely by non-military judges (23 percent) and law professors (20 percent). Spokespersons for the CCR and the American Civil Liberties Union accounted for 10 percent of the legal category.

Though detainees almost never achieved media standing in our data, journalists frequently quoted their lawyers. Notably, a majority of the quotations attributed to judges, and many of the quotations attributed to lawyers, was derived from transcripts of legal proceedings.

The preceding distributions give a clear picture of who achieved media standing. Overwhelmingly, the three newspapers we examined treated legal experts and political officials as the most frequently quoted source types. Next we turn to examine the positions of these quoted sources toward the MCA itself.

WHAT POSITIONS DO SOURCES TAKE ON THE MCA?

We were initially surprised to find that most of the quoted sources (43 percent) in our data collection expressed opposition to the MCA in one way or another; and just 22 percent of the quoted sources expressed support for the Act, as summarized in Table 3:

TABLE 3. Distribution of Quotations by Position on MCA

Position	Quotes	Total (%)
Opposes MCA	102	43
Neutral	82	35
Supports MCA	53	22
TOTAL	237	100

We had expected that quoted sources would split evenly between support for and opposition to the Act, reflecting journalists' commitment to the objectivity norm of "balance." Instead, by nearly a 2–1 ratio, quoted sources spoke in opposition to the Act, which might be interpreted as evidence of the newspapers fulfilling their "watchdog" role. This interpretation is complicated by a more in-depth study of the variation in the degree of criticism expressed in the oppositional quotations. To exemplify this point, consider the similarities and differences between the following two quotations:

"Navy Lt. Cmdr. Charles Swift, Hamdan's defense attorney, said the Military Commissions Act 'demonstrates once again that if you put a statute together in three weeks and rush it through . . . you end up with a process that doesn't work'" (*Los Angeles Times*, June 5, 2007, ellipses in the original).

"'Habeas corpus was recklessly undermined in last year's legislation,' said Sen. Patrick J. Leahy (D-VT), the [Judiciary] committee's chairman, referring to the Military Commissions Act. 'I hope the new Senate will reconsider this historic error and set the matter right'" (*Los Angeles Times*, June 8, 2007).

Both quotations identify the sources in terms of their official statuses, quote those sources directly, and the quotations themselves express criticisms of the Act. By contrast, however, the first quotation expresses what might be understood as a *limited* criticism: The "process doesn't work" because it was put together hastily. Though this comment registers a criticism of the Act, it is one with a relatively ready remedy, namely slower, more careful revision of the statute. By contrast, the second quotation assesses "last year's legislation" (i.e., the MCA) as having "recklessly undermined" habeas corpus. Furthermore, Leahy's call for the Senate to "set the matter right" can only be understood, in context, as a call to fundamentally revise the Act by restoring habeas corpus. The second quote is, in sum, a more *fundamental* criticism of the Act.

Qualitative analysis of the quotations that referenced habeas, such as the previous quotation from Senator Leahy, led us to employ references to habeas corpus as indicators of more fundamental critiques of the MCA. We sought to determine how often quoted sources invoked habeas corpus. Table 4 summarizes our findings on the frequency with which quoted sources invoked habeas corpus.

TABLE 4. Distribution of Quotations by Invocation of Habeas Corpus

Invocation	Quotes	Total (%)
No Mention of Habeas	193	81
Mentions Habeas	44	19
TOTAL	237	100

Overwhelmingly the sources quoted in our data do not mention habeas corpus (81 percent): Just 19 percent of the quotations refer to it, by name, synonym, or pronoun.

Does the position of the quoted source toward the MCA bear any significant relationship to the source's likelihood of mentioning habeas corpus explicitly? Based on qualitative analysis, we expected that the MCA's opponents would be more likely than supporters to mention habeas. The data (summarized in Table 5) confirm our expectation of a strong correlation between position on the MCA and reference to habeas corpus.

TABLE 5. Position on Military Commissions Act and Invocation of Habeas Corpus

Position on MCA	Mention Habeas	No Mention	Total
Support MCA	6 (11%)	47 (89%)	53 (100%)
Oppose MCA	26 (25%)	76 (75%)	102 (100%)

x^2 (1, N=155) = 3.45, $p < 0.031$

We found a 14 percent difference between mentions of habeas corpus by position on the MCA; a difference of considerate importance. (A chi-square test yields a p-value of 0.031, well within the conventional standard [0.05] of statistical significance.)

Quoted sources' invocations of habeas corpus typically represented the strongest critiques of the MCA. (Recall, for example, Leahy's characterization of it as "reckless.") These quotations raised fundamental questions about the counter-democratic consequences of the Act and its questionable constitutionality.

By contrast, supporters of the MCA seldom referenced habeas corpus. The following two instances may be treated as exemplary. The first comes from a news story that recalled an exchange in January 2007, between President Bush's nominee for attorney general, Alberto Gonzales and Senator Arlen Specter, during Gonzales's confirmation hearing:

"Gonzales responded by suggesting the Constitution does not protect habeas corpus at all. 'The fact that the Constitution—again, there is no express grant of habeas in the Constitution. There is a prohibition against taking it away'" (*Los Angeles Times*, January 30, 2007).

The article went on to report Specter's challenging response (e.g., "'Now wait a minute,' Specter interrupted, 'The Constitution says you can't take it away except in case of rebellion or invasion. Doesn't that mean you have the right of habeas corpus?'") and to report other legal scholars' positions on Gonzales's assertion (e.g., "'He is completely wrong on the history,' said Eric Freedman, a Hofstra law professor and expert on habeas corpus").

A second case: In December 2007, Solicitor General Paul Clement urged the Supreme Court to uphold the federal appeals court's February 2007 decision that detainees had no constitutional rights in the first place. Clement argued that the MCA provided detainees more access to judicial review than afforded by habeas corpus:

"'This is the remarkable liberalization of the writ, not some retrenchment or suspension of the writ,' Mr. Clement declared" (*New York Times*, December 6, 2007).

To describe the tribunals established by the MCA as a "liberalization" of habeas corpus echoes the Orwellian "doublespeak" of the Act itself.

In sum, we proceeded by treating invocations of habeas corpus as indicators of the strongest critiques of the MCA. Their relative scarcity in our data, despite the preponderance of quotations expressing opposition to the MCA, suggest that the newspapers we studied were not providing their readers with as full a range of the critical perspectives on the Act as existed. Subsequent analyses build on this finding.

HOW PROMINENTLY PLACED ARE CRITIQUES OF THE MCA?

We hypothesized that quotations expressing support for the MCA would be more likely to appear in prominently located stories (front-page stories) while quotations expressing opposition to the Act would be more likely to appear in less prominently located stories. However, our data does not support this hypothesis. Of forty-nine quotations from stories originating on a newspaper's front page, 53 percent expressed opposition to the MCA, and 27 percent voiced support for it. (The remaining 20 percent were neutral.) Of 188 quotations from stories not originating on the front page, 41 percent expressed opposition to and 21 percent voiced support for the Act (with 38 percent neutral).

Three aspects of these findings are important. First, stories originating on the front page are more likely to feature quotations that take a definite position, accounting for 80 percent of the "front-page" quotes. In contrast, just 62 percent of the quotes in stories not originating on the front page took a definite position. This correlation makes sense in the context of news values, where the clash of competing views on a contentious social issue probably contributes to an editor's sense of the story's appeal to readers and, hence, its deserving more prominent placement. Second, as previously noted, quotations expressing opposition to the Act appear more frequently in stories that originate on the front page, than on other pages by a difference of 12 percent (i.e., the percentage difference of 53 percent and 41 percent).

Third, and finally, before concluding that the prevalence of oppositional quotes in prominently positioned stories constitutes evidence of the newspapers' oppositional stance, note that (a) quotations supporting the MCA are also more likely to appear in stories originating on the front page, by a difference of 6 percent, and (b) we found little difference between front-page and other stories in the frequency with which quotations invoked habeas corpus. Of quotations from front-page stories (N=49), we found 16 percent that mentioned habeas, compared with 19 percent of the quotations from stories not originating on the front page (N=188). The slight difference (3 percent) in mentions of habeas corpus by story location is most likely a product of random variation. What is significant, though, is that the greater proportion of oppositional quotes in prominently placed stories did not yield an increase in the frequency with which quoted sources invoked habeas corpus. Since we understand references to habeas as indicative of more fundamental criticisms of the MCA, this finding suggests that, although the newspapers in our data gave prominent placement to quotations critiquing the MCA, those critiques were not the most fundamental ones. This dynamic contributes to the overall frame established by the papers in covering the Act: namely, the appearance of healthy debate, including frequent—albeit relatively superficial—criticism of the Act and its consequences.

THE 2006 ELECTION AS REFERENDUM

Many pundits, and perhaps also the American public, oriented to the

November 2006 midterm elections as a referendum on the Bush administration's policies in general and its "Global War on Terror" in particular. Thus, we sought to determine whether corporate media were more likely to afford media standing to critical perspectives on the MCA after the Democrat Party's convincing November victories. We found this to be true, as Table 6 documents:

TABLE 6. Position on MCA Before and After 2006 Election

Time Period	Support MCA	Oppose MCA	Total
Before Election	16 (46%)	19 (54%)	35 (100%)
After Election	37 (31%)	83 (69%)	120 (100%)

x^2 (1, N=155) = 2.67, $p < .051$

When compared with the period before the election, quotations expressing opposition to the Act increased by 15 percent in the period after the election. Before the election, the newspapers in our data presented an almost evenly divided spectrum of expert opinion on the merits of the MCA, with a slight tilt toward critique (54 percent opposed versus 46 percent supportive). After the election, the 15 percent increase in sources critical of the Act shifted the balance strongly toward opposition (69 percent opposed versus 31 percent supportive).[13] Consistent with our prior findings, this post-election increase in the percentage of quotations opposing the MCA might be interpreted as evidence that the newspapers, spurred by public opinion, roused to fulfill their role as "watchdogs" against governmental abuses of authority. Unfortunately, a secondary analysis cautions against any hasty embracing of this conclusion. As before, we use explicit references to habeas corpus as our indicator of more serious critiques of the MCA. Comparing mentions of habeas, before and after the election, reveals no significant change, as evident in Table 7:

TABLE 7. Mentions of Habeas Corpus Before and After 2006 Election

Time Period	Mention Habeas	No Mention	Total
Before Election	10 (20%)	41 (80%)	51 (100%)
After Election	34 (18%)	152 (82%)	186 (100%)

In fact, there was a very small (2 percent) decrease in the frequency of quotations that referenced habeas corpus after the 2006 election. This difference is much too small to rule out the possibility of random variation as the best explanation.

Combining the findings summarized in Tables 6 and 7, we conclude that although the newspapers in our data did increase the number of quotations opposing the MCA after the 2006 elections, this did not result in an equivalent increase in fundamental critiques of the Act. Consistent with our prior findings, the coverage gives the appearance of healthy, legitimate political debate, with the balance shifting toward an oppositional perspective after the elections—but with no more room for critiques that frame the Act, with its unconstitutional suspensions of habeas corpus, as beyond the pale of legitimate political debate.

CONCLUSIONS

The patterns of corporate newspaper coverage identified in this study provide an important contribution to understanding why the US public continues to lack a strong grasp of the MCA's significance. Our examination of 237 direct quotations regarding the Act, drawn from three major newspapers over a fifteen-month period, leads us to conclude that, although the papers present critical perspectives on the Act,

(1) these oppositional quotations only infrequently invoke the most fundamental criticisms against it, including especially its suspension of habeas corpus for "any person," and,

2) ironically, in this context, the relative balance of supportive and critical quotations contributes to the framing of public discourse about the MCA as a matter of *legitimate* controversy.

Should the suspension of habeas corpus, historically a pillar of western democratic government, be subject to the type of political debate—not to mention journalistic coverage—usually reserved for mundane partisan politics? Does presenting it that way fulfill the functions of a free press in a democratic society, including the media's responsibility as watchdog, information source, and forum of diverse public opinion?

Blackstone warned against secret, indefinite government detention without recourse to judicial review as "a dangerous engine of
arbitrary government." Extending his metaphor, we understand news
coverage of the type analyzed in this chapter as oiling the dangerous
engine. Incomplete coverage of the (full range of critical) perspectives on the MCA, framed in a context of legitimate controversy,
keeps the public inadequately informed and thus aids the powerful
elite in their efforts to extend governmental authority at the expense
of individual liberties.

If the American public is to mount an effective, popular movement for repeal of the MCA, it must first understand the Act. As this
chapter shows, two crucial steps in that direction are, first, to expand
the scope of sources whom journalists treat as worthy of media standing, to include more frequently those who will voice fundamental
critiques of the Act; and, second, drawing on Hallin's theoretical
model, to reposition public discourse about the Act's suspension of
habeas from the sphere of legitimate controversy to the sphere of
deviance, because habeas corpus is a cornerstone of American law.
Its affirmation as such is all the more important in the context of the
current administration's unconventional, unlimited "Global War on
Terror."

Notes

1. See Chapter Two, "Censored Déjà Vu," in this volume for an update on "No Habeas Corpus for 'Any Person.'"
2. See, for example, Jonathan Hafetz, "Ten Things You Should Know about Habeas Corpus," Bren-nan Center for Justice, New York University School of Law, White Paper, 2007, http://www.nimj.org/documents/HabeasPaperFinal.pdf.
3. Michael C. Dorf, "The Orwellian Military Commissions Act of 2006," *Journal of International Criminal Justice*, 5 (2007): 10–18.
4. Ibid., 18.
5. For a critical discussion of the functions of the free press, see David Croteau and William Hoynes, *By Invitation Only: How the Media Limit Political Debate* (Monroe, ME: Common Courage, 1994), 10–22.
6. This section extends prior work by Andrew Roth and Emilie Vander Haar, "Media Standing of Urban Parkland Movements," *City & Community*, vol. 5, no. 2 (June 2006):129–151.
7. William Gamson, "Media and Social Movements," in N.J. Smelser and P.B. Baltes. *International Encyclopedia of the Social Sciences*, (Amsterdam: Elsevier Science, 2001), 9468–9472.
8. Robert Entman and David Paletz, "Media and the Conservative Myth," *Journal of Communica-tion*, vol. 30, no. 4 (1980):154–165.
9. Croteau and Hoynes, *By Invitation Only*, 177.
10. Ibid.

11. Daniel Hallin, *"The Uncensored War": The Media and Vietnam* (New York: Oxford University Press, 1986); see also Stuart Hall, "A World at One with Itself," in S. Cohen & J. Young, *The Manufacture of News* (Beverly Hills, CA: Sage, 1973), 85–94.

12. See, e.g., Robert Entman, "Objectivity, Bias, and Slant in the News," in Entman, *Democracy without Citizens* (New York: Oxford University Press, 1989), 30–38.

13. A chi-square test of this distribution yields a p-value of .051, a hair's breadth short of the conventional standard (.050) of statistical significance. Put another way, it is extremely unlikely that the observed distribution is the product of random variation in the data.

CHAPTER 6

Universal Healthcare, Media, and the 2008 Presidential Campaign

by Peter Phillips, Kat Pat Crespán, Carmela Rocha, Corey Sharp
Sabatino, and Bridget Thornton

> I once tried to explain to a Norwegian woman why it was so hard
> for me to find health insurance. I'd had breast cancer, I told her,
> and she looked at me blankly. "But then you really need insur-
> ance, right?" Of course, and that's why I couldn't have it.

—Barbara Ehrenreich, journalist and author

INTRODUCTION

This study examines the corporate media coverage of the 2008
presidential candidates' positions on universal healthcare vis-à-vis
single-payer healthcare. We look at the organizational structures of
private, for-profit versus "nonprofit" insurance companies that
dominate the healthcare industry and the strategies these firms use to
maintain their $401 billion annual revenue. Finally, we explore the role
of US corporate media in maintaining this private, for-profit system.

Health and disability insurance is an extremely large and profitable
businesses. Increasingly, the health and disability insurance industry
has come under scrutiny for mismanagement and blatant abuse of its
policyholders. Michael Moore's top-grossing movie *Sicko* is only one
example of the growing concern surrounding healthcare in the US.

In 2002, the World Health Organization (WHO) put the cost of
healthcare at 15.2 percent of the US gross domestic product (GDP)
(WHO 2006). WHO reports, "The health-care industry, including
biopharmaceutical and medical device companies, now represents the
third-largest sector among the 1,000 largest US firms, behind only
energy and retailing" (See Appendix A).

In order to understand how insurance companies strategize to maximize profits and limit payouts for benefits, we examined the evolution of the industry and the socioeconomic power base of the top health insurance companies in the US.

A BRIEF HISTORY OF HEALTH INSURANCE IN THE US

The United States has been slow to implement national social welfare programs compared to European countries. The creation of social welfare and rudimentary public health services with the Social Security Act of 1935 set the US on a path similar to what European countries had had in place for several decades. With the Social Security Act, the US government instituted the Public Health Service to conduct "investigation of disease and problems of sanitation," yet national healthcare for all people has remained an elusive goal (Social Security Act, Section 603-1935). Findings by the Public Health Service in 1938 reported widespread incidences of sickness and disability among the American people and closely linked these to poverty conditions (Hirsh, 1939).

In 1965, President Johnson signed legislation for senior and low-income healthcare, Medicare and Medicaid, respectively. While the wealthy and upper middle classes have generally been able to afford necessary healthcare in the US, the bottom one-third of American society (100 million people) faces limited access to necessary healthcare. This bottom 100 million people, 47 million of whom have no health insurance whatsoever, are disproportionately people of color and single women with children. These inequalities of race and gender have led some researchers to conclude that racism and sexism have historically played a major role in US healthcare policy (Quadagno, 1994).

Throughout the twentieth century, there has been discussion around building a national healthcare system in the US. The National Conference on Charities and Corrections in 1911 called for the establishment of social insurance programs in the US including provisions against sickness and disability (Hirsh, 1939).

During the first half of the twentieth century, the American Manufacturing Association and the US Chamber of Commerce intensely opposed attempts at national- and state-level healthcare legislation. (Trattner, 1989) Additionally, many physicians opposed national health insurance for financial and professional reasons, though this did not include all doctors. The American College of Surgeons supported prepaid health insurance for hospitalization in 1934, but leaders in the American Medical Association generally opposed national healthcare efforts (Thomasson, 2002).

The beginning of employer-sponsored health insurance plans started in the 1920s. At Baylor University Hospital in Dallas, local teachers paid six dollars per year for the guarantee of twenty-one days of hospitalization. In 1929, Blue Cross was the first organization to offer prepaid health insurance. Before World War II, only twenty private insurance companies offered health insurance plans in the US. This changed rapidly after the war, as private insurance companies began to compete with Blue Cross and Blue Shield groups plans by offering health insurance at lower rates to pre-screened healthy individuals. By 1958, prepaid health insurance plans covered 75 percent of Americans (Thomasson 2002).

The insurance industry in the US remains severely underregulated at the federal level. Instead, each state adopts laws and regulations that govern insurance companies in their states. A national insurance company may adopt a business practice that one state deems legal while that same practice may be illegal in another state.

While countries around the world offer citizens necessary healthcare as a basic right, the US has not adopted the same philosophy. According to the Universal Declaration of Human Rights, healthcare is a vital right for every human being:

> Everyone has the right to a standard of living adequate for the health and well-being of himself and of his family, including food, clothing, housing, and medical care and necessary social services, and the right to security in the event of unemployment, sickness, disability, widowhood, old age or other lack of livelihood in circumstances beyond his control (Article 25, adopted by the United Nations on December 10, 1948).

What is the best way to insure that all people in society have equal access to necessary healthcare regardless of income? The Institute of Medicine estimates that as many as 18,000 Americans die prematurely each year because they do not have health insurance. (Institute of Medicine, 2004) The number of Americans without health insurance is increasing—47 million at last count, or some 16 percent of the population. The cost of health insurance is rising two to three times faster than inflation, and unpaid medical bills are the number one cause of personal bankruptcy in the country (Walter 2007).

PRIVATIZATION VERSUS SINGLE-PAYER

In the US, private insurance companies sell health insurance to individuals and employers. Insurance companies do not provide any healthcare goods or services. They are the broker between the consumers and the providers of healthcare. Most people obtain health and disability insurance through employment-related group plans. However, if one is not a member of a group plan, one must purchase an individual policy. Often, one cannot afford to purchase health or disability insurance. A person must be very low-income or elderly to qualify for state-subsidized care.

The issue of public single-payer healthcare versus private insurance company involvement is gaining momentum. The private insurance companies and health maintenance organizations (HMOs) have a desire to remain in the system and continue to make huge profits. In Massachusetts, private insurance companies pushed forward mandatory universal healthcare by requiring that everyone purchase health insurance. Other states are considering following suit.

In 2002, President Bush, with the support of Congress, reformed Medicare, which increasingly privatized the system and boosted the profits of insurance companies. Bush also promised to veto a bill that expanded healthcare coverage to low-income children. In both cases, the president insisted that the private sector is better at managing healthcare than the government. According to Bush, "Expansion of government in lieu of making the necessary changes to encourage a consumer-based system is not acceptable" (Lee 2007).

Private insurance companies are motivated to make as much money as possible and do so by systematically delaying, diminishing, and denying payment for promised services, and by blaming individuals for their misfortunes. The state officiates this process by maintaining healthcare for the poorest and protecting profits of the major providers with limited enforcement of regulation (Phillips and Thornton, 2007).

However, most of the industrialized countries in the world manage to provide all their citizens (and in some countries, immigrants) with relatively efficient, state-of-the-art healthcare that is paid for with taxes. While many proponents of private insurance argue that the citizens in these countries pay higher taxes, the individual cost to taxpayers is actually substantially less than the amount individuals and employers pay in health and disability care premiums and related expenses in the US. The total per capita healthcare costs in the US exceed healthcare costs of all other industrial countries, yet we leave huge gaps in service and systematically deny benefits to many of those in need (WHO, 2006).

Countries with common-pool or single-payer healthcare systems provide similar levels of service to every person. In the US, insurance companies are not required to sell policies to people with preexisting conditions, leaving many without care unless they qualify for Medicare, Medicaid, or other public programs. Private insurance companies are in fact motivated to delay, diminish, and deny care whenever they can. States assist them in this process by supporting limitations on access to the courts and adequate redress, and by engaging in minimum or illusory regulatory enforcement.

Countries with common-pool or single-payer systems do not tie health insurance to employment. In such countries, it is the responsibility of society as a whole to provide healthcare for each individual. In these societies it is understood that a person without access to proper healthcare is likely to become less productive and a bigger financial burden on the society in the future.

One single-payer advocacy group, Physicians for a National Health Program, reports that private insurance corporations spend an enormous amount of money on business-oriented expenses rather than health-related investments. Competition among private companies creates waste and duplication. According to a physician advocacy group, "When, for example, hospitals compete they often duplicate expensive equipment in order to corner more of the market. This drives up overall medical costs to pay for the equipment. They also waste money on advertising and marketing. The preferred scenario has hospitals coordinating services and cooperating to meet the needs of the public" (Physicians for a National Health Program, 2007).

A 2003 study in the *New England Journal of Medicine* estimates that spending for the administrative costs associated with healthcare amounts to over $320 billion per year, or about 31 percent of overall healthcare costs in the US. This figure includes hospital administrative costs and time spent by doctors, nursing homes, and other home health providers on administering insurance claims. The study also takes into account the amount of money private insurers spend on costs not found in single-payer systems: "Underwriting and marketing account for about two-thirds of private insurers overhead." The administrative costs in the Canadian national healthcare system amount to 16.7 percent, or about half, of the administrative overhead of insurance costs in the US (Woolhandler 2003).

The figure above does not consider the time and out-of-pocket expenses incurred by individuals and families related to personal administration of the policies and claims. A January 2007 article by Bloomberg News reported, "A new study says that $2.3 billion worth of time is spent in waiting rooms, doctors' offices, hospitals and transportation in the first year after cancer is diagnosed. The study did not look at the value of time spent by members of a patient's family" (Bloomberg, January 3, 2007).

Inflated healthcare costs and limits on care in the US have very negative consequences for many families. A 2001 study conducted by professors from Harvard and Ohio Universities revealed that medical bills lead to one-half of the bankruptcies filed in the US:

> In 2001 1.458 million American families filed for bankruptcy. . . . About half cited medical causes, which indicates that 1.9–2.2 million Americans (filers plus dependents) experienced medical bankruptcy annually. Among those whose illnesses led to bankruptcy, out-of-pocket costs averaged $11,854 since the start of illness; 75.7 percent had insurance at the onset of illness. Medical debtors were 42 percent more likely than other debtors to experience lapses in coverage. Even middle-class insured families often fall prey to financial catastrophe when sick (Himmelstein, 2005).

State legislators, such as Shiela Kuehl of California, have introduced legislation for a single-payer system for their states.* Of the 2008 presidential candidates, only Dennis Kucinich advocated for a single-payer system.

---

* Shiela Kuehl's single-payer legislation (S.B. 840) can be found at her website, which includes studies, reports, fact sheets, and further reading. http://dist23.casen.govoffice.com/.

HEALTHCARE POSITIONS OF 2008
PRESIDENTIAL CANDIDATES

We examined the media coverage of the three final presidential candidate (Obama, Clinton, and McCain) plans on healthcare reform in the context of the single-payer healthcare proposed by Dennis Kucinich. Both Clinton and Obama promoted their plans for "universal healthcare" as a right that all American citizens should have, insisting that everyone should have the option to purchase healthcare insurance, regardless of age or preexisting conditions. They both propose that healthcare should be affordable, and their approaches involve rolling back tax cuts in the high income brackets. Clinton wants to implement mandates for all who do not purchase health insurance, and Obama wants healthcare for all children and would make it available to those who would like to purchase it without mandates. Obama feels that mandates will only increase financial pressure and struggle for the majority of uninsured Americans.

John McCain would essentially like to keep the system as is, believing that maintaining a free market system without mandates will increase the competition among insurance companies so that eventually the competition between businesses will make the prices more affordable.

Support for single-payer healthcare was not in any of the main candidate's plans. Dennis Kucinich was the primary supporter of a single-payer system until he stepped down from the presidential race at the beginning of 2008.

2008 PRESIDENTIAL CANDIDATES'
MAIN STANCES ON HEALTHCARE

McCain
➤ Pay only for quality
➤ Care intended to improve health
➤ Variety of insurance choices
➤ Companies responsive to needs
➤ Lower costs
➤ Emphasis on preventive care

Kucinich
➤ Universal, single-payer, not-for-profit healthcare system

➤ $10, $20, $30 for prescription, no matter what the drug's actual cost
➤ Social service

Clinton
➤ Choice to preserve existing coverage
➤ Offer choice of public plan option similar to Medicare
➤ Improve quality and lower costs
➤ Ensures that job loss or family illness will never lead to a loss of coverage or exorbitant costs
➤ No American will be denied coverage, refused renewal, unfairly priced out of the market, or forced to pay excessive insurance company premiums
➤ End discrimination based on preexisting conditions or expectations of illness and ensure high value for every premium dollar
➤ Drug companies offer fair prices and give accurate information
➤ Providers work collaboratively with patients
➤ Government ensures affordable healthcare that never burdens families and provides improvement of quality and lower cost
➤ Businesses to deliver high-quality, affordable care
➤ Employers will help finance the system
➤ Large employers provide insurance or contribute to coverage costs
➤ Small business receive tax credit or begin to offer coverage

Obama
➤ Rely on investor-owned companies
➤ Accessible regardless of illness or preexisting conditions
➤ Affordable premiums, co-pays and deductibles
➤ Requirement of all children to have coverage
➤ Young adults covered under their parents' coverage until age twenty-five
➤ Reimburse employer health plans for a portion of the costs they incur if they guarantee savings that are used to reduce the cost of workers' premiums
➤ Hospitals and providers required to collect data on preventable medical errors, nurse staffing ratios, hospital-acquired infections, and disparities in care
➤ Hospitals and providers to publicly report measures of healthcare costs and quality
➤ Providers required to report preventable medical errors and support

hospital and physician practice improvement to prevent future occurrences
➤ Lower prices
➤ Increased competitiveness
➤ Ability to purchase medications from other developed countries if the drugs are safe and prices are lower
➤ Promotion of generic drugs

POWER OF THE HEALTH INSURANCE COMPANIES

In order to understand the money and power connections of the health insurance industry, we reviewed the political campaign donations of the boards of directors of nine of the largest insurance companies. In our earlier research (Phillips and Thornton, 2007), we found 113 board members in the top nine health and disability insurance companies. These directors in turn held, or currently hold, 150 positions with major financial or investment institutions, including such major firms such as J. P. Morgan, Citigroup, Lord Abbett, Bank of America, and Merrill-Lynch (Department of Commerce, 2006).

Additionally, these board members had or have connections to some of the largest corporations in the world, including General Motors, IBM, Ford, Microsoft, and Coca-Cola. We found direct corporate affiliations among the 113 health insurance directors to thirty-four corporations on the Fortune 500 list for 2007.

The board members also held or hold eighty-two government or government-related positions. These positions range from members of the US House and Senate to cabinet positions, ambassadors, governors, state insurance commissioners, and posts in the Democrat and Republican Parties showing a deeply embedded interconnectedness between the government and the health insurance industry. Additionally, many board members were or are affiliated with influential policy organizations such as the Trilateral Commission, the Brookings Institute, the US–China Business Council, the US Chamber of Commerce, and the Business Roundtable. The board members of the major health and disability insurance firms in the US are a core element of the socioeconomic-political elite in the US and are uniquely positioned to dominate healthcare policy-making decisions for the American people.

Adding to their direct power in the government, major financial institutions, and across many industries in the US, the health insurance company directors also maintain some thirty direct connections to media organizations in the US ranging from local newspapers, radio, and TV stations to major corporations such as ABC, the *Washington Post*, Cox Communications, and AOL Time Warner. Thus, they are in a strong position to influence national media editorial policy and news reporting perspectives on key health and disability issues of the day.

Many of the board members have cross-affiliations with the nine companies we researched, whereby board members of one company serve on boards of other companies such as Wellpoint, Unum, Blue Cross–Blue Shield, and Kaiser Permanente, along with maintaining many connections to the pharmaceutical industry, health policy organizations, and hospitals.

These board members tend to hold industry-wide perspectives on protecting health insurance company profits, maintaining a healthy business environment for long-term economic growth, and ensuring that any movement for expanded healthcare in the US will maintain their companies as the primary officiators.

Health and disability insurance companies maintain an ongoing lobbying effort in state capitals and provide continuing campaign support to both parties. According to the Center for Responsive Politics, the insurance lobby industry spends $130,588,217 per year to influence state and federal politicians (CRC Lobby Database, 2006). Additionally, directors of health insurance companies are very active in the 2008 presidential campaign.

INSURANCE COMPANY BOARD MEMBERS CAMPAIGN CONTRIBUTIONS 2007–08

Period: January 2007 to May 2008

Director	Amount	Candidate
Aetna		
Frank Clark	$2,300	Obama
Earl Graves	$4,600	Obama
Ellen Hancock	$2,300	Romney

AIG

Martin Feldstein	$2,000	McCain
Richard C. Holbrooke	$4,600	Clinton
Fred H. Langhammer	$2,100	McCain
George Miles Jr.	$1,000	Obama

Berkshire Hathaway

David Sokol	$4,600	Obama
Ronald Olson	$2,300	Obama
	$2,300	Clinton
Donald Keough	$2,300	McCain
	$1,000	Romney
William Gates III	$2,300	Clinton
	$2,300	Obama
Susan Decker	$1,000	Clinton

Cigna

Roman Martinez IV	$2,000	McCain
	$1,000	Romney

Humana

Michael McCallister	$2,300	Romney

Prudential

Gilbert Casellas	$2,300	Clinton
William Gray III	$2,600	Clinton

Unum Groupv

Gloria C. Larson	$2,300	Obama

Wellpoint

Julie Hill	$2,300	Obama
Sheila Burke	$2,300	McCain
John Zuccotti	$4,600	McCain

Source: www.opensecrets.org/indivs

Warren Buffett (Berkshire Hathaway) is the only director/company to appear on a lobbyist bundler list. His name and company appear on Clinton's list for $100,000.

Additionally, several health insurance companies were listed as donors in lobbyist bundling of money for the campaign.

Blue Cross–Blue Shield	McCain	Amount not listed
AMN Healthcare (Healthcare staffing)	McCain	Amount not listed
Amerisure (Workers' comp)	McCain	Amount not listed
Federation of American Hospitals (National reps for investor-owned hospitals)	McCain	Amount not listed
Direct Meds Inc. (Mega online pharmacy)	McCain	Amount not listed
TriWest Healthcare Alliance (Military)	McCain	Amount not listed
Pfizer (Pharma)	McCain	Amount not listed
FHC Health Systems (Behavioral health)	Clinton	$100,000+
Biogen Idec (R&D therapy/products)	Clinton	$100,000+
United Health Group (Health industry)	Obama	$50,000+
Sandy River Health Sytems (Health industry)	Obama	$100,000+

It is safe to say that health insurance companies and their directors have taken a keen interest in supporting 2008 presidential election candidates who favor maintaining the current $400+ billion revenue for private insurance companies in the US.

The fact that so much special interest profit protection is involved in 2008 presidential election is simply not being covered by the corporate media in the US. Instead, the corporate media dismisses single-payer healthcare and tends to reinforce the negative myths of a single-payer system in coverage of universal healthcare issues.

We examined all the newspaper coverage of universal and single-payer healthcare during the election period of this study, 2007 to May 2008, in the *New York Times*, the *Washington Post*, and the *Los Angeles Times*. We found a continual denial of the efficacy of a single-payer system and the continuing inclusion of negative stereotypical clichés.

NEGATIVE MYTHS OF SINGLE-PAYER HEALTHCARE

Washington Post (April 13, 2007): Some say such plans violate the idea that people should be able to choose whether they want insurance, and that costs hurt businesses.

Washington Post (July 10, 2007): Republicans are wary of large plans that call for tax increases and have depicted the Democrats' proposals as "socialized medicine."

Washington Post (July 1, 2007): Inequities occur through emergency room visits. People worry that they won't get what they need, and that the government will ration Healthcare, like now, but with more stress and anxiety.

Washington Post (November 13, 2007): There are long waits for treatment under a single-payer system. Republicans call single-payer "socialized medicine," and claim it would inevitably deliver inferior care

Washington Post (September 13, 2007): Single-payer systems are cold, impersonal, and uncaring. Eighty percent of Americans have a regular doctor whom they usually see. Long waits for treatment occur under single-payer healthcare.

Washington Post (November 2, 2007): Giuliani speaks of his personal experience with prostate cancer and cites an ear-grabbing statistic. "My chances of surviving prostate cancer—and thank God I was cured of it—in the US: 82%. My chances of surviving prostate cancer in England: only 44% under socialized medicine."

Washington Post (July 25, 2007): Academic medical journals routinely publish studies that supposedly document the cupidity and ignorance of practicing physicians while lauding the virtues of single-payer healthcare systems, such as those in Canada or Britain, where physicians are paid only by the government.

New York Times (January 25, 2007): Republicans and policy strategists have raised the specter of "socialized medicine," and depicted the Democratic plans as a back-door route to a so-called single-payer system. A Medicare-style plan would compete ferociously with private plans on price.

New York Times (December 13, 2007): Federation of American Hospitals opposed proposals to place healthcare under an umbrella of Medicare-style "single-payer" financing. Government safety nets should not be allowed to "crowd out private insurance care."

New York Times (September 23, 2007): The Democrats' goal is to head off opposition from those who fear that their own coverage might suffer in the course of covering some 47 million uninsured people.

New York Times (September 7, 2007): Some liberals, believing that government should step in as employers withdraw, support a European-style, single-payer, which would be fine if we were Europeans. But Americans, who are more individualistic and pluralistic, will not likely embrace a system that forces them to defer to the central government when it comes to making fundamental healthcare choices.

Los Angeles Times (June 28, 2007): Bush said that Democrats want government-run healthcare for every American, but it's the wrong path for our nation. He said it would eliminate choice and competition in healthcare, and cause huge increases in government spending that could lead to higher taxes, "resulting in rationing, inefficiency and long waiting lines."

Los Angeles Times (April 5, 2007): Some suggest that when people without health insurance receive treatment, the cost of their care is passed along to the rest of us.

Los Angeles Times (July 1, 2007): A single-payer system discourages innovation and causes long waits for treatment through shortages and bureaucratic delay. The idea of the federal government completely replacing the private health insurance industry is so far outside the American experience that even the vast majority of health reform advocates consider it politically dead on arrival for the foreseeable future.

Los Angeles Times (September 18, 2007): Republicans say it's a "European-style socialized medicine plan—that's where it leads—and that's the wrong direction for America."

Without the corporate media accurately or objectively informing the American people of the facts of single-payer vis-à-vis universal healthcare, the profits of the health insurance elites are protected and the presidential debate remains filled with one-sided platitudes promoting healthcare for all.

CONCLUSION

People in the US have a choice. But we are often unaware of the full range of choices and of what would be in our own best interests. We can continue with the profit-driven private insurance healthcare system leaving many millions to languish without care, and many millions more to face the frustrations of systematic delays, diminishment, and denials of promised benefits. Alternatively, we can build a common-pool healthcare system that provides necessary healthcare to everyone—for less than we are paying now.

Health and disability insurance companies are for-profit entities, despite some organizations operating under tax-exempt status. Customer care and quality of service falls to second place under this profit-driven model of healthcare. These practices are part of a growing structural arrangement between private business, media, and government that is unlikely to be undone without extensive public outcry.

The 2008 presidential campaign is a perfect example of how the power of media and the healthcare industry are combined. The candidates know which side of the bread the butter is on and act accordingly in the campaign.

At the beginning of this study, Barbara Ehrenreich, former State University of New York professor, journalist, and author of several books, states that she was unable to procure insurance because she had breast cancer. She goes on to state,

> This is not because health insurance executives are meaner than other people, although I do not rule that out. It's just that they're running a business, the purpose of which is not to make people healthy, but to make money, and they do very well at that. Once, many years ago, I complained to the left-wing economist Paul Sweezy that America had no real health system. 'We have a system all right,' he responded, 'it's just a system for doing something else.' A system, as he might have put it today, for extracting money from the vulnerable and putting it into the pockets of the rich. (Ehrenreich, 2007)

Private insurance has a structural motivation to delay, diminish, and deny payment for promised benefits, in order to maintain profit margins. They use these profits to propagandize the American public and to influence voters through scare tactics of "socialized medicine" and long delays of service that supposedly occur in single-payer systems. Using corporate media and massive political donations to both parties, private health insurance companies have increased profits and maintained their influence in the system.

In times of crisis, the people in the US have joined social movements to demand justice and government action. The progressive movement in the early twentieth century gained stronger regulations on medicines, medical education, and healthcare delivery systems. During the Depression, the labor movement won the Social Security Act and the expansion of disability and healthcare benefits for employees. The civil rights movement and the "war on poverty" led to Medicare and Medicaid.

Adequate healthcare for everyone is a human right, acknowledged by the world in the 1948 United Nations' 1948 Declaration of Human Rights. Most Americans pay higher combined taxes, health and disability insurance premiums, co-payments, and various health-related expenses than citizens in common-pool, single-payer systems, yet those countries allow all their citizens equal access to services. When the American people collectively decide that healthcare and basic social security is a right that belongs to everyone, the health and disability system can be changed to provide necessary benefits for all.

References

Barnes, Jared. "Insurance Companies Register Record Profits 10 Years After Tort Reform." *World Internet News Cooperative*, October 12, 2006. Retrieved July 2, 2007 (http://soc.hfac.uh.edu/artman/publish/article_403.shtml).

Bloomberg News. "Cancer Patients' Wait Times Cost Billions." January 3, 2007. Retrieved October 9, 2007. (http://www.nytimes.com/2007/01/03/science/03brfs-cancer.html).

Ehrenreich, Barbara. "Healthcare vs. the Profit Principle." *Huffington Post*, July 12, 2007. Retrieved July 15, 2007 (http://www.huffingtonpost.com/barbara-ehrenreich/health-care-vs-the-profi_b_55941.html).

Ericson, Richard V., Aaron Doyle, and Dean Barry. *Insurance As Governance*. Toronto: University of Toronto Press, 2003.

Heller, Douglas. "Insurance Profits Reveal Gouging, Need for Reforms." *The Foundation for Taxpayer and Consumer Rights*, April 25, 2005. Retrieved June 22, 2007 http://www.saynotocaps.org/newsarticles/insurance_profits_reveal_gouging.htm.

Himmelstein, David, et al. "Illness And Injury As Contributors To Bankruptcy." *Health Tracking Market Watch*. February 2, 2005. http://content.healthaffairs.org/cgi/content/full/hlthaff.w5.63/DC1

Hirsh, Joseph. 1939. "The Compulsory Health Insurance Movement in the United States." *Social Forces* 18: 102–114.

Institute of Medicine, Fact Sheet 5. Uninsurance Facts and Figures. http://www.iom.edu/CMS/ 17645.aspx

Phillips, Peter and Bridget Thornton. *Practices in Health and Disability Insurance: Deny, Delay, Diminish and Blame.* 2007. http://www.projectcensored.org/articles/story/practices-in-health-care/

Physicians for a National Health Program, 2007. http://www.pnhp.org/

Quadagno Jill. *The Color of Welfare.* London: Oxford University Press, 1994.

Social Security Administration. "Legislative History Social Security Act of 1935." 1935. Retrieved July 14, 2007. (http://www.ssa.gov/history/35actvi.html)

Thomasson, Melissa. 2002. "From Sickness to Health: The Twentieth-century Development of US Health Insurance." *Explorations in Economic History* 39: 233–253.

Trattner, Walter. *From Poor Law to Welfare State.* New York: Free Press, 1989.

United Nations, "Universal Declaration of Human Rights." Retrieved July 16, 2007, http://www.un.org/Overview/rights.html.

Walter, Kevin. "Insurance Breakdown." *The Buffalo News,* June 24, 2007. Retrieved June 26, 2007 (http://buffalonews.typepad.com/opinion/viewpoints/index.html).

Woolhandler, Steffie, MD, MPH, Terry Campbell, MHA, and David U. Himmelstein, MD. 2003. "Costs of Health Care Administration in the United States and Canada." *New England Journal of Medicine.* 349: 768–775.

World Health Organization. Annex Table 2 Selected indicators of health expenditure ratios, 1999–2003. *World Health Report 2006.* Retrieved July 6, 2007: http://www.who.int/whr/2006/annex/06_annex2 _en.pdf

APPENDIX A

2006 Income and Profits of Major Health and Disability Insurance Providers

(Source: 2007 Fortune 500 Companies) **$ in millions**

	Profits	Revenue
AIG	14,048.0	113,194.0
Berkshire Hathaway	11,015.0	98,539.0
Prudential	3,428.0	32,488.0
Hartford	2,745.0	26,500.0
Cigna	1,155.0	16,547.0
Wellpoint	3,094.9	56,953.0
Aetna	1,701.7	25,568.6
Humana	487.4	21,416.5
Unum Group	411.0	10,718.8
TOTAL	$38,086.0	$401,924.9

CHAPTER 7

US Media Bias, Human Rights, and the Hamas Government in Gaza

by Janeen Rashmawi, Nelson Calderon, Sarah Maddox, Christina Long, Andrew Hobbs, and Peter Phillips

> The world is witnessing a terrible human rights crime in Gaza, where a million and a half human beings are being imprisoned with almost no access to the outside world. An entire population is being brutally punished.
>
> —Jimmy Carter, 2008

In June of 2007, Israel imposed full sanctions on the Gaza Strip, creating a virtual prison camp of 1.5 million people. Food, fuel, medical supplies, and basic essentials are all in short supply. Intermittent electricity makes daily work mostly impossible, resulting in an almost total collapse of the economic infrastructure, massive human suffering, and daily deaths. This study reviews the history of the Gaza Strip over the past two and half years and the US television news coverage of this human rights tragedy in the Middle East.

Nora Barrows-Friedman reports from the Jebaliya Refugee Camp, Gaza on June 11, 2008: "In the brightly painted new intensive care unit wing of al-Awda, northern Gaza's only emergency medical facility in the massive Jebaliya refugee camp, doctors, nurses, aides, and administrators are ready to provide emergency surgery services for the area's 300,000 people.

"But the metal bed frames remain empty of patients—and of mattresses, and IV bags, and heart monitors, and other basic supplies needed at a basic medical facility. The equipment has been purchased, but remains in the occupied West Bank city Ramallah, prevented by Israel from being taken into Gaza. 'In the last year, the service burden on al-Awda was tripled. We had difficulty, especially after the Fatah-

222 | CENSORED 2009

Hamas fighting, and through the closures beginning last year,' says Nehal Mehanna, program officer at al-Awda tells IPS as she walks around the empty rooms. 'Israel is not letting certain medication and supplies into Gaza, through any checkpoint. For example, we have been waiting for seven months to have the operation tables to be shipped and enter Gaza through the Erez checkpoint—the equipment is only one hour away by car, but we've been waiting for seven months. Sometimes we can get supplies through the Red Cross, but they're helping many organizations at the same time. They have limited supplies. It's a long, complicated procedure, and it all has to be approved by the Israeli authorities.'

"According to doctors in Gaza, over 180 patients have died as a result of lack of essential supplies since the Israeli-led blockade began in June 2007. Palestinians seeking medical treatment for cancer, heart disease, and kidney failure, among other illnesses, cannot access the services they need—as Israel has prevented chemotherapy, heart, and dialysis medications from entering Gaza. They have to look for treatment abroad, either in Egypt or in Israel. But since the blockade, even with written permission and international coordination, Israel has shut the borders to Palestinian patients coming from Gaza, resulting in many preventable deaths.

"'We try to provide the best services we can,' Mehanna tells IPS. 'We have a colleague here, a nurse at the hospital, who has kidney failure. She has received written permission four times to leave and get treatment in Egypt, but the Israelis have prevented her from leaving. We hope she can get out and get treatment. She's our friend. It's a difficult situation.'

"Al-Awda hospital staff says they are quickly running out of anesthesia. The hospital's pharmacist, Dr. Akram Naffar, shows IPS his small cache of anesthetic medications, small boxes stacked on a spare white shelf at the back of the storage room. 'We only have enough left for two, maybe three weeks,' Naffar says. 'I don't know what will happen at the end of the month. We can only live day by day.'

"Naffar tells IPS that if another massive Israeli attack comes soon, people may not get even present levels of treatment.

"'When other hospitals around Gaza have medicine we need for an operation, or for emergency services, we trade with them,' Naffar tells IPS. He says this is both a dangerous and a demoralizing system, but there is no alternative until the Israeli blockade is lifted.

"Mehanna tells IPS that the medical staff at al-Awda is under extreme stress. 'We try to provide as much care as we can,' she says. 'We have a procedure for receiving medicines and supplies. We make a list every six months and update it, but lately we've needed more and more emergency medications. We have an obstetrics department, and we need labor and delivery medication. Also for emergency needs—we anticipate more Israeli incursions and attacks, so we need to be ready.'

"Riyad al-Adassi, of the Union of Health Work Committees in Gaza City, expects the situation to get much worse. 'A hundred and eighty patients died in twelve months, and this number is expected to increase day by day. In the past, 300 to 400 patients a day used to travel abroad to get treatment. Now, we can hardly get thirty people to travel out of Gaza. They're prevented from leaving. There are many waiting lists to get special permission from the Israeli side.'

"IPS asked al-Adassi to define the effects of Israel's policies towards Gaza from the health workers' perspective. 'Palestinians are dehumanized. In the past, we used to have a concept of freedom, having a state, fighting for our rights. Now, it's shifted to providing for our families and surviving. We live in a jungle—and the concept of living in a jungle is to try and adapt to survive. All of us are frustrated and suppressed. This is not healthy at all, even for Israel itself. At a certain point, it will explode. And who will take responsibility? Those with the keys to the occupation.'"

Circumstances in Gaza are significantly under-covered by the US media. Other than NPR's *All Things Considered* airing on May 16, 2006, and a *Washington Times* article on January 22, 2000, no mention of the healthcare crisis in Gaza has occurred in US corporate media over the past two and half years, since Hamas democratically won the Palestinian general election in January 2006. Americans know very little about this de facto prison camp of 1.5 million people in the Gaza Strip.

The following is a short historical timeline of the Gaza situation since January 2006:

2006

January 25: Hamas wins Palestinian general elections gaining seventy-six of 132 seats.

January 29: Western governments threaten to halt financial aid to Palestinians.

January 30: The UN, EU, US, and Russia announce "all members of a future Palestinian government must be committed to non-violence, recognition of Israel, and acceptance of previous agreements and obligations."

March 18: Hamas submits its cabinet to President Mahmoud Abbas (twenty-four ministers including eight members of parliament). In response, the US, the EU, and Israel boycott the new government and say they will suspend aid to the government.

April 16: Iran announces an offer of $50 million in aid to the Palestinian Authority.

May 8: Three Palestinians are killed and ten wounded in clashes in southern Gaza, near Khan Yunis, between rival Hamas and Fatah supporters.

May 17: Hamas deploys a new 3,000-strong force on the streets of Gaza.

May 11: Prominent Palestinian prisoners in Israeli jails release a document calling for a national unity government between Hamas and Fatah.

June 3: A new security force loyal to Abbas is deployed in the West Bank.

June 16: The EU endorses a new policy to channel aid directly to the Palestinians, bypassing the Hamas government.

June 25: Palestinian fighters launch an attack in Israel that results in the deaths of two Israeli soldiers and the capture of another, Corporal Gilad Shalit.

June 27: Hamas and Fatah reach an agreement based on the May 11 prisoners' document, which includes the forming of a national unity government.

June 28: Israel launches Operation Summer Rains, in what it claims is an attempt to recover the captured Corporal Shalit. The ongoing operation initially consists of heavy bombardment of bridges, roads, and the only power station in Gaza. Hundreds of Palestinians are killed during aerial and ground attacks over the following months.

June 29: Israel detains sixty-four Hamas officials, including eight Palestinian Authority cabinet ministers and up to twenty members of the Palestinian Legislative Council.

September 1: Abbas says Hamas and Fatah have agreed on the principles of a power-sharing government and may soon form a new cabinet to lead the Palestinian Authority. Under the plan, Abbas is to dissolve the current Hamas-led cabinet within forty-eight hours.

September 8: UN officials say Gaza is at a "breaking point" after months of economic sanctions and Israeli attacks.

September 23: The agreement breaks down. It is reported to be Hamas's refusal to recognize Israel at the heart of the continued disagreements.

October: A number of mediation attempts take place. Egypt and Qatar send their foreign ministers to meet both sides. Other Palestinian groups such as Islamic Jihad and the Popular Front for the Liberation of Palestine mediate between the two sides to stop the clashes.

October 1: Eight people are killed in Gaza in factional fighting between Hamas and Fatah as a new wave of violence erupts.

November 13: Following talks between Hamas and Fatah, both sides agree to form a government of technocrats unaligned with either party. Muhammad Shbeir, a Gaza academic who is close to Hamas but not a party member, accepts the offer to head the government.

November 14: Hamas again asserts that it will not recognize Israel and the agreement stalls.

December 15: Hamas accuses Fatah of involvement in a gun attack on Ismail Haniyah, Palestinian prime minister, as he crosses the border from Egypt into Gaza.

December 16: Abbas calls for new elections as a solution to the ongoing crisis.

2007

January 21: Abbas meets Khaled Meshaal of Hamas in Damascus in response to an invitation by Bashar al-Assad, the Syrian president.

January 30: Fatah and Hamas reach a ceasefire agreement mediated by Egypt after a series of clashes lead to the death of thirty-two Palestinians. Both sides welcome a Saudi initiative to meet in Mecca.

February 8: Hamas and Fatah agree to a deal in Mecca to end factional warfare that has killed scores of Palestinians and to form a coalition, hoping this would lead Western powers to lift crippling sanctions imposed on the Hamas-led government.

February 9: The Quartet welcomes the role of the Kingdom of Saudi Arabia in reaching the agreement to form a Palestinian National Unity government. It later reaffirms that it must obey international demands to recognize Israel, renounce violence, and abide by previous peace agreements.

February 15: Haniyah and his cabinet resign. Haniyah is reappointed by Abbas and begins the process of forming a new Palestinian unity government.

March 15: Palestinians reach agreement on the formation of the government.

March 20: Jacob Walles, the US consul general to Jerusalem, meets Salam Fayad, the Palestinian finance minister, marking the first contact between the US and the recently formed Palestinian Unity government.

March 21: The EU and UN hold talks with non-Hamas cabinet ministers.

March 22: Fighting erupts again between Hamas and Fatah fighters, with one Fatah fighter killed and seven people injured.

April 10: US announces it is to give Abbas $60 million to boost his presidential guard and for other security expenses.

April 23: Interior Minister Hani al-Qawasmi resigns, citing resistance to his planned reforms for the security services.

April 24: The Izz al-Din al-Qassam Brigades, the military wing of Hamas, fires scores of rockets into Israel, saying a truce "no longer exists." At the same time, the Hamas-led Palestinian government calls for the truce to be restored.

April 30: Palestinian teachers hold a one-day strike over unpaid wages. This prompts Azzam al-Ahmad, the deputy prime minister and a member of Fatah, to suggest that the unity government be disbanded if the Western embargo is not lifted.

May 10: The unity government deploys a joint Hamas-Fatah police force to deal with growing lawlessness in Gaza.

May 11: Clashes erupt between Fatah and Hamas factions.

May 13: Factions agree to a truce, brokered by Egypt, but skirmishes continue to be reported and the ceasefire quickly disintegrates. Over the next few days, ceasefires are continually agreed to but broken hours later. Meanwhile Israel continues to bomb Gaza in response to rockets fired by Hamas fighters.

May 24: Abbas calls for Hamas rockets to be stopped, but is rebuffed as factional fighting continues.

May 30: The UN Security Council calls for an "immediate end" to the faction fighting in Gaza.

June 7: A Fatah fighter is killed, the first person killed in internal fighting in more than two weeks.

June 10: Further clashes between the rival factions leave more dead and scores injured.

June 12: Fatah declares it is withdrawing from the unity government until there is an end to recurring street battles.

June 13: Hamas's Izz al-Din al-Qassam Brigade, which has gained ground across much of Gaza, orders Fatah security forces to surrender their weapons. The group launches attacks on a number of Fatah bases.

June 14: Abbas sacks the Hamas-led unity government and declares a state of emergency. Haniya defies Abbas and promises the government will continue to function.

June 15: Hamas seizes several senior officials and appears effectively in control of Gaza. The group declares an amnesty for Fatah fighters.

June 16: Abbas, in the West Bank, signs a decree allowing a Palestinian emergency government to take office without parliamentary approval. Fayad, an independent parliamentarian, is made prime minister. The Palestinian territories have become split between the West Bank, controlled by Fatah; and Gaza, run by Hamas.

2008

January: Israel announces that it will close all border crossings into Gaza, intensifying a six-month blockade imposed on the territory.

It says this is in response to continued rocket fire from the territory. Severe fuel and food shortages are reported in Gaza.

Managers at Gaza's only power plant, which supplies a third of the territory's electrical supplies, shut down its generators saying there is a lack of fuel. UN officials in Gaza say the measure amounts to collective punishment of the territory's population of 1.5 million people.

At night, much of Gaza City is plunged into darkness because of electrical shortages.

Palestinians hold candlelight vigils in the city protesting the embargo.

Israeli officials insist there is enough fuel to keep the power plant running and blame Hamas, Gaza's de facto rulers, of staging the crisis.

Palestinian Leader Mahmoud Abbas wins international support for a proposal to take responsibility for the Palestinian side of all Gaza's crossings. However Hamas says that past arrangements imposing a blockade on Gaza were "history" and it must have a role in future border control.

Hamas fighters cooperate with Egyptian forces to patch up parts of the frontier barrier. People continue to pass into Egypt through Rafah, though in greatly reduced numbers.

Shops in eastern Sinai start running low on supplies, prompting complaints from local people about the situation.

Egyptian roadblocks in the Sinai Peninsula prevent thousands of Palestinians from traveling to mainland Egypt.

Rival Palestinian delegations head for Cairo, where Palestinian leader Mahmoud Abbas says talks with Hamas are out of the question unless it ends its "coup d'état" in Gaza.

February: Egyptian forces use barbed wire and metal barricades to seal the last remaining gap on the Egyptian side of the frontier at Rafah, ending twelve days of freedom of movement for Palestinians.

The Egyptian authorities say that their nationals visiting Gaza, and Gazans who traveled to Egypt, would be allowed to return home.

Senior Hamas leader Mahmoud Zahhar says Hamas has reached an understanding with Egypt to control the breached border between

Egypt and Gaza. This is denied by Palestinian Authority President Mahmoud Abbas, who lost control of Gaza in June and refuses to negotiate with the de facto rulers, Hamas.

March 2008: Israeli occupational forces kill over 120 Palestinians in one week, twenty-seven of which are children.

Sources
BBC, Al Jazeera, and Reuters.

US MEDIA COVERAGE OF HAMAS

The *New York Times* ran a front page story on June 15, 2008, entitled, "A Year Reshapes Hamas and Gaza," by Ethan Bronner. The article focuses on how the Hamas government is enforcing strict laws, such as those prohibiting kissing in public and improper behavior in the streets. Essentially the article criticizes the Hamas government as fundamentally extremist, but acknowledges that it is more solidly in place than ever. Bonner writes, "Whereas Hamas says it will never recognize Israel, its leaders say that if Israel returned to the 1967 borders, granted a Palestinian state in Gaza, the West Bank and East Jerusalem, and dealt with the rights of refugees, Hamas would declare a long-term truce. This is not much different from what the rest of the Arab world says or the Fatah positions in peace talks with Israel."

Given that the *New York Times* acknowledges that Hamas is willing to accept the existence of the state of Israel and that Hamas's position really isn't any more radical than many other Arab states, why do so many Americans see Hamas as a terrorist organization dedicated to Israel's total destruction?

The words "Palestinians" or "Hamas" are translated into "terrorists" and "violence" in the minds of many people in the United States. This translation did not simply appear on its own. US television news media continuously reinforce a mindset in the American people that dehumanizes Palestinians. This dehumanization allows for a democratically elected government, such as Hamas, to be labeled endlessly as a terrorist organization. Palestine is seen as a breeding ground for violence and terror. American mass media portrays an image of Palestinians as victimizers rather then victims of an oppressive military occupation. Even when it is clear that Palestinians are the victims of the Israeli military,

American television has a way of twisting the story and blaming Palestinians for the violence.

On June 27, 2006, the *Jim Lehrer News Hour* reported that 3,000 Israeli troops had just entered Gaza. The program reported that Israeli warplanes, flying over Gaza, had completely sealed off all the borders. Yet, after Lehrer described Israel's actions, he justified it as a form of collective punishment by reporting on the two Israeli soldiers captured prior to the invasion. Framed in this way, Israel's cruel treatment of Palestinians, specifically in Gaza, then becomes acceptable.

On March 3, 2008, when ABC reported on the deaths of over one hundred Palestinians in the Gaza Strip, these deaths were justified as a retaliation to Hamas rockets that had been previously fired into Israel. In almost all of the news reports regarding Hamas, the media has referred to Hamas using negative language. The same terms are used repeatedly: violent, extremist, and terrorist.

Political commentator and MIT professor Noam Chomsky writes in "Elite Policy and the 'Axis of Evil'" (*Z Magazine,* February 5, 2008), "in a remarkable act, tens of thousands of the tortured people of Gaza broke out of the prison to which they had been confined by the US-Israel alliance as a punishment for the crime of voting the wrong way in a free election in January, 2006." It goes unrecognized that Palestinians have the right to elect their own representative government. Instead, Palestinians are punished for electing a government that supports them and their right for autonomy, "failing to recognize the people of the Middle East are too backward to appreciate democracy— another principal that traces back to 'Wilsonian Idealism,'" scathes Chomsky.

Hamas, in most US television news programs, is not even presented as a democratically elected government. On June 15, 2007, CBS news reported on the chaos in Gaza. In this report the elected Hamas government was referred to as a forced government: "Masked Hamas gunmen have taken over Gaza Strip." Not only was there no acknowledgment that Palestinians elected the Hamas government, the adjectives used to describe Hamas created a violent image justifying its vilification. In the same CBS news report, the reporter Charles Osgood interviewed Mr. Michael Oren, a Middle East analyst, in which he stated that the violence and deaths in Gaza are to be blamed on Hamas: "Hamas has to stop terrorizing the Palestinian people."

The following are descriptive terms and editorial comments regarding Hamas used by US television news stations over the past two-and-a-half years. Stories also link Hamas to other Middle Eastern "terrorist" organizations and countries. Negative terms are italicized.

ABC News Now, World View

May 9, 2006
"Hamas Versus Fatah; Factions Fight For Control"
Anchor: Mike Lee; Reporter: Simon McGregor Wood (Gaza, Jerusalem)

MIKE LEE: The situation has deteriorated significantly. As you say, since the Hamas organization won the Palestinian elections, what we've had is almost daily clashes between armed gunmen from the Fatah organization, which lost power in the elections, *and gunmen from Hamas.* And, in the last two days, yesterday, three people were killed. And this morning's incident produced nine injuries and we read from the sources that we have in Gaza that up to five or six of those were school children.

VOICEOVER: *Of course, the danger is that the Palestinians will become ungovernable and that could lead to further chaos.*

MIKE LEE: And, in many cases, we've seen, particularly recently in Gaza, they're refusing to play *Hamas's game.* And there is this enormous tension on the streets almost every day now because the guys with the guns are not necessarily obeying the orders of the new government.

(Off-camera) And, because *Hamas is in control, refuses to amend its charter, saying that Israel should be abolished.* The West is still withholding hundreds of millions of dollars in funds that should be going to the Palestinian people. Now, there is a medical crisis there, as you've reported before. President Bush says he's going to send some emergency medical aid but is that going to be enough?

The News Hour with Jim Lehrer

June 27, 2006
"Hamas and Fatah Struggle for Power within Palestinian Government"
Jim Lehrer, Jonathan Miller, Margaret Warner, Kwame Holman, Alexis Bloom, Jeffrey Brown

JIM LEHRER: A major Israeli military strike into Gaza appeared imminent late today. Warplanes attacked a bridge in central Gaza, and tanks began moving nearby.

Meanwhile, there were conflicting reports about Hamas accepting a plan that implicitly recognizes Israel. The *militant group* now runs the Palestinian Authority.

CNN, *The Situation Room*
June 29, 2006
"Supreme Court Rules on Military Tribunals for Terror Suspects"
Wolf Blitzer, John Vause, Brian Todd, Ed Henry, Jack Cafferty, John Roberts, Susan Roesgen, Zain Verjee, Andrea Koppel, Bill Schneider, Mary Snow, Paula Zahn, Chris Lawrence

JACK CAFFERTY: And this just coming in, the Israeli Defense Forces telling CNN that a third and fourth Israeli air strike have been launched. One target, according to the Israelis, one target including a Hamas training site in Gaza. Another target, Hamas offices in Gaza City.

JOHN VAUSE: In the short time since then, there's been a total of five air strikes tonight in and around Gaza. Apparently a Hamas training camp in the north has also been targeted; an Hamas office; and, also, possibly, a *storage house used by Hamas militants for explosives and other weapons*—Wolf.

WOLF BLITZER: The Israelis say, John, they're doing this to try to get their one kidnapped Israeli soldier released. . . . We have been told by the IDF that they've targeted a Hamas training ground. They've also targeted a Hamas office, as well as what could have been a storage place for *Hamas ammunitions, and bomb-making facilities* as well, that kind of thing . . .

JOHN VAUSE: Well, really in many ways Palestinians are split about what to do with Gilad Shalit, the nineteen-year-old soldier, who's currently being held by the *militant wing of Hamas*. Some say if it avoids bloodshed, hand him back, enough is enough.

ABC News Now, World View
July 28, 2006
"Crisis in The Middle East; Al Qaeda Announces Holy War Against Israel"
Anchor: Nick Watt, Reporters: Jeremy Bowen (Gaza Strip)

. . . Hezbollah's Hassan Nasrallah is not his leader because he's fighting Israel to help the Palestinians. Secular Palestinian nationalists in this camp are turning to *resistance movements inspired by Islam, their own homegrown Hamas, and Lebanon's Hezbollah.* The al-Qaeda broadcast suggests it's trying to get on the bandwagon.

CNN, *Anderson Cooper 360°*
July 14, 2006
"Hezbollah Drone Packed with Explosives Hits Israeli Gunship; Hezbollah Fires Rockets at Israeli Towns; Hezbollah Leader Declares Open War on Israel; Two Wildfires Consume Over 60,000 Acres in California"
Anderson Cooper, Nic Robertson, Paula Hancocks, Suzanne Malveaux, Candy Crowley, John Roberts, Joe Johns, John Vause, John King, Chris Lawrence
Guests: Martin Indyk, Edward Djerejian, Robert Baer, Clayton Swisher

ANDERSON COOPER: *A video from Gaza where Hamas had a demonstration calling for people to take to the streets, to support Hezbollah and praise them for what they have done with the kidnapping of Israeli soldiers.*

It may represent a growing *linkage between Hamas and Hezbollah,* a linkage which worries many not only here in Israel but also in the US government and in this region.

JOHN KING: Now this additional common ground. Both Hezbollah and Hamas are holding kidnapped Israeli soldiers, looking to exchange them for prisoners held by Israel and looking to draw attention to their shared political agenda.

CLAYTON SWISHER, MIDDLE EAST INSTITUTE: *Hamas is blamed for more than 350 attacks in the past dozen years, killing more than 500.*

JOHN KING: Iran has offered Hamas more support since its dramatic gains in January's Palestinian elections, saying it would make up for any aid the West cuts off because of *Hamas ties to terrorism.*

The News Hour with Jim Lehrer
June 13, 2007
"Fighting Between Palestinian Factions Rages Out of Control"
Jim Lehrer, Kwame Holman, Margaret Warner, Tom Bearden, Jeffrey Brown
Guests: Ghaith al-Omari, Mark Perry, Damien Cave, Barbara Goff

JIM LEHRER: Battles spread across Gaza today, as fighting between Palestinian factions raged out of control. The *Islamic militant group Hamas* gained ground everywhere against its rival, Fatah. Hamas forces attacked three security bases in Gaza City and took control of a number of key positions. They also captured a main north-south road to block Fatah from moving reinforcements . . . The conflict between Fatah and Hamas has paralyzed the already-fragile Palestinian National Unity government. Fatah, the nationalist, largely secular party, led by President Mahmoud Abbas, appeared to be losing significant ground in northern Gaza to the *Islamist movement Hamas*, which won control of the Palestinian Legislative Council in elections in January 2006.

Fox News Network, *Fox Special Report with Brit Hume*

June 15, 2007 Friday
"Panel Discussion on Latest Palestinian Crisis"
Brett Baier
Guests: Fred Barnes, Charles Krauthammer, Mort Kondracke

BRETT BAIER: This gun battle is finished. Those were Hamas leaders holding a very unique news conference in the Gaza Strip today, fully masked, as you say there. Hamas now in control there, Fatah in the West Bank, what now?

CHARLES KRAUTHAMMER: That clip is an extreme example of "we're the government, and we're here to help you." *Imagine a government run by masked terrorists. It's* ominous because you have men like that who are terrorists, run by a *terrorist party, who are in control of Gaza*, and even worse, this is an *Iranian client*, so Iran now has essentially a frontier with Israel in the south, and Egypt as well. . . . You now have *Gaza, which is all Hamas, all rejectionist, all terrorists*, and you've got the West Bank, run but Fatah, which is a lot stronger than the West Bank, run by Abbas.

MORT KONDRACKE: Well, what I'm afraid of is that it's (peace) not going to last for very long, that Hamas is on the ascendancy. In Gaza they're going to get *aid from the Iranians*—it will be smuggled in, but they'll get aid. Military aid as well as, probably, economic aid.

KRAUTHAMMER: Well, no. Look, I think Fred is right. People have always assumed what the *Palestinians wanted was a state. What they actually had wanted was the destruction of the Israel.*

CBS News, *The Osgood File*

June 15, 2007
"Chaos in the Gaza Strip as Hamas Takes Control"
Charles Osgood

CHARLES OSGOOD: *Masked Hamas gunmen have taken over the Gaza Strip, raiding and looting Fatah strongholds, dragging men into the street and shooting them. Hamas calling this liberation, the arrival of Islamic rule in Gaza.*

CNN, *Late Edition With Wolf Blitzer*

June 17, 2007
"Interview With Fatah, Hamas Spokesmen; Interview With Hoshyar Zebari"
Wolf Blitzer, Ben Wedeman, Ed Henry, Donna Brazile, Terry Jeffrey, Atika Shubert
Guests: Ahmed Yousef, Saeb Erekat, Seymour Hersh, Hoshyar Zebari, Jack Reed, Duncan Hunter, John Cornyn

WOLF BLITZER: But it comes at a time of extreme tension throughout the region. A new Palestinian government was sworn in today, a government, though, without Hamas. While the *radical Islamic Palestinian faction remains firmly in control of Gaza* right now, its rival group, Fatah, is intent on maintaining control on the West Bank.

What is happening in Gaza now is a state of emergency. It is a situation out of our hands. You have seen who are sitting in Abu Mazen's office—President Abbas's office yesterday, *gangsters* and so on.

These descriptions of Hamas as a radical militant group, bent on the destruction of the state of Israel and supported by Iran and Hezbollah, are typical of the ongoing coverage of Middle East issues on US television news. Increasing the blame of Hamas eases the responsibility of Israel for the dire humanitarian situation currently existing in Gaza. The fact that Israel's continuing attacks and economic boycott, which has strangled the Gaza Strip and created an unlivable situation for Palestinians, is accepted by most in the US as fully justified.

For the most part, Americans do not recognize the bias inherent in everyday reporting regarding the situation in Israel and Palestine. Therefore when former US President Jimmy Carter visited with Hamas leaders in April 2008, the result was puzzlement and disgust in corporate media.

On April 13, 2008, Jimmy Carter landed in Israel at the start of a nine-day tour of the Middle East. The former president's itinerary took him to Palestine, Egypt, Syria, Saudi Arabia, and Jordan, where he met a number of political leaders from each of the countries, including Egyptian President Hosni Mubarak, Jordan's King Abduallah II, and Syria's President, Bashar al-Assad.

However, Carter's meeting with top leaders of Hamas took center stage as the defining event of his trip. Carter stated that he believes that Hamas can no longer be shut out of talks, if peace is to be established between Israel and Palestine. The former president tried to be clear that he was not going as a negotiator, but hoped that his visit would result in Syria and Hamas being included in talks that cannot succeed without them. On April 17 and 18, former President Carter met with Mahmoud Al-Zahar, Siad Siam, and Ahmed Yousef in Egypt, and Mashaal and other Hamas leaders in Syria. American mass media has focused almost exclusively on these meetings, just one part of his voluntary assistance, and the coverage has been almost entirely negative.

Fox News Network, *Fox Hannity & Co.*
January 15, 2007
"Is Jimmy Carter Anti-Semitic?"
Sean Hannity, Alan Colmes
Guests: Steve Berman

SEAN HANNITY: Steve, I want to specifically go—explain in detail why you think he (Carter) supports terrorism.

STEVE BERMAN: I wouldn't say that Jimmy Carter supports terrorism. What Jimmy Carter does is he supports the underdog in this conflict. But what he fails to recognize, that the underdog in this particular conflict has choices and has made choices. . . .

SEAN HANNITY: When Israel withdrew from the Gaza Strip, unilaterally, how was that greeted? It was greeted with the election of Hamas, and it was greeted with the Kassam missiles falling on Sderot, the Israeli town . . .

STEVE BERMAN: Well, Israel is the victim of terror. But you know what? This is a—this is a complicated story, Sean, with dual narratives at work here, dual claims to—legitimate claims to the land. And to unwind this all to get to an essential truth where we can find, perhaps, a peaceful way of dealing with this situation, both sides have to be held accountable . . .

ALAN COLMES: Steve, did Jimmy Carter deserve the Nobel Peace Prize?

STEVE BERMAN: At the time—at the time I was very proud of him. Three years ago I traveled to Geneva to witness the—witness and support the signing of the Geneva Peace Accord that was authored by very brave Israelis and Palestinians. The president was the keynote speaker. *I think in that interim he's lost his way.*

The corporate media, during the week of President Carter's trip, focused heavily on his meeting with Hamas leaders. Most of the network news stressed that President Carter is a private citizen and was acting in direct defiance of America's foreign policy with regards to Hamas.[1] Many of the news stories featured US politicians who called for action against the President for meeting with Hamas while neglecting to present an opposing view on his trip.

A search of Lexis/Nexis found that no major news sources had a guest speaker who supported the president's meeting with Hamas. Many news stories did not even touch on the reasons stated by President Carter for his meeting with Hamas.

Fox News had Representative Sue Myrick of North Carolina calling for his (Carter's) passport and stating, "He is just deliberately undermining [US] policy. And it's wrong."[2] Guest speakers like Sue Myrick and the accompanying negative attention were common on all the major news networks. Most of the networks reported that President Carter was told by the State Department prior to his trip that he shouldn't meet with Hamas.[3] However, this was not the case: President Carter had contacted the State Department before leaving and informed them of his intended meetings with Hamas and he was never contacted back. While this information was made available and reported on, the major news channels did not correct this story and continued to report that President Carter was acting in direct defiance of the US State Department, after being told not to talk to Hamas.[4]

The tone of most of the stories that covered President Carter's trip was negative and hostile to the former president. President Carter was accused of "engage[ing] with terrorists,"[5] and "radical diplomacy."[6] He was blasted as a "horrible President" who "is a stooge"[7] as a result of his meetings with Hamas leaders. This kind of language was common on news shows, presenting the issue as ridiculous rather than treating it as a serious news story. President Carter's trip to the Middle East was reduced, in America's mass media, to a couple meetings with Hamas that received little fair or serious coverage.

Current US corporate media coverage is as much a bias in favor of Israel as it is negative towards the democratically elected Hamas government in Gaza. Both sides reflect a US policy of continuing $3 billion in annual military support to Israel, making it the fourth most powerful military in the world. The negation of Hamas becomes itself a justification for the continued funneling of US tax dollars to Israel, most of which come back to the US military-industrial complex in the form of weapons purchases.

Without truthful, unbiased disclosures of the Israel-Palestine conflicts in the US media, massive human rights abuse in Gaza will likely continue unabated.

Notes

1. CNN, *American Morning*, April 22, 2008, 7:00 AM EST.
2. Fox News Channel, "America's Pulse" Interview with Representative Sue Myrick (R-NC),April 17, 2008.
3. *Good Morning America*, April 19, 2008, 8:31 AM EST.
4. *Fox Special Report with Brit Hume*, April 24, 2008, 6:00 PM EST.
5. Fox News Channel, "Your World" Interview with Representative Eric Cantor (R-VA), April 17, 2008.
6. Fox News Channel, "America's Pulse" Interview with Representative Sue Myrick (R-NC), April 17, 2008.
7. Glenn Beck, "Carter Doing More Harm than Good in Middle East," April 21, 2008.

CHAPTER 8

The Gardasil Sell Job

by Judith Siers-Poisson, associate director, Center for Media and
Democracy & PR Watch

Chances are that if you watch any amount of television, skim through
popular magazines, or glance at banner ads on websites, you have seen
ads for Gardasil. Often erroneously called a "vaccine against cancer,"
Gardasil has been marketed by its maker, Merck, through an impecca-
bly designed and executed PR campaign that culminated in the "I
Chose" ads. But there is much more behind the upbeat ads that show
girls and young women drumming, shooting hoops, hip hop dancing,
and, of course, asking for Gardasil by name.

    Gardasil is a vaccine against human papillomavirus, or HPV, a virus
spread primarily through sexual contact. More than one hundred
strains of HPV exist, and as many as 50 percent of sexually active men
and women become infected with HPV at some point in their lives.
According to the Center for Disease Control and Prevention, by age
fifty, at least 80 percent of women will have acquired a genital HPV
infection.

    Most people know very little about HPV, and Merck has been eager
to fill the knowledge vacuum to its own advantage. A 2005 survey by
the National Cancer Institute found that only 38.3 percent of US
women had heard of HPV and less than 50 percent thought it caused
cervical cancer. The survey also found that nearly 80 percent of women
mistakenly thought that medical treatment was needed to resolve an
infection. In fact, the body's own immune system usually eliminates
HPV infections without treatment. In more than 90 percent of cases,
infected individuals never even notice that they have had HPV.

    Moreover, HPV does not lead directly to cervical cancer. It causes
cell abnormalities (called dysplasia), which can become cancerous if
left undetected and untreated. However, dysplasia can be detected by a
simple Pap smear and is 100 percent treatable. Cervical cancer was
once one of the most common causes of death for US women, but
thanks mostly to the Pap test, its death rate declined by 74 percent
between 1955 and 1992, and it continues to decline at a rate of about 4

percent a year. Even today, however, more than 11,000 women are diagnosed each year in the US with cervical cancer, and nearly 4,000 die. In developing countries, it is still often the deadliest cancer for women, mainly due to inadequate basic screening.

Unfortunately, Merck's PR and advertising blitz around Gardasil has created confusion between HPV infection and cervical cancer, with many people thinking of them as one and the same. The resulting panic is not particularly good for women's health, but it serves Merck's interests well. Healthcare resources are finite, and the best way to use them to save lives is to ensure that all women receive consistent and reliable access to Pap tests. However, Pap tests have been around for decades, and although they are safe and effective, there is little profit in them for drug companies. So Merck is pushing its new vaccine instead.

WHAT IS GARDASIL?

Gardasil, Merck's wonder drug, is a vaccine given in a series of three injections. It protects against four of the more than thirty strains of genital HPV—types 6, 11, 16, and 18. According to the US Food and Drug Administration (FDA), "HPV Types 16 and 18 cause 70 percent of cervical cancer cases, and HPV Types 6 and 11 cause 90 percent of genital warts cases." Currently it is the only vaccine approved by the FDA against HPV.

For Merck, Gardasil provides both a public image and financial response to the company's ongoing Vioxx debacle. Vioxx, its anti-inflammatory drug, was pulled from the market in 2004 after the FDA belatedly discovered that it raised the risk of heart attack in people who took it. Worse still, the company has been accused of concealing that risk while executing an aggressive direct-to-consumer advertising campaign to increase demand for the drug. The recall alone cost Merck an estimated $2.5 billion in annual revenue. In 2007, the company admitted that it "has been named as a defendant in approximately 27,250 lawsuits, which include approximately 45,700 plaintiff groups alleging personal injuries resulting from the use of Vioxx, and in approximately 266 putative class actions alleging personal injuries and/or economic loss." Additional lawsuits involving billions of dollars more are likely. In May 2008, the *Canadian Press* reported that Saskatchewan's Chief Justice is allowing a class action suit to proceed that would include users in every Canadian province except Quebec (where a lawsuit is already pending).

For Merck, therefore, Gardasil promises to fix both its financial and its image problems. In the court of public opinion, it is anxious to be seen as the first drug company to sell a vaccine against cancer. Financially, Gardasil is also a potentially huge cash cow—especially if Merck succeeds in getting states to make the vaccine mandatory. Glaxo-SmithKline has developed a competing vaccine, Cervarix, but it continues to face delays in FDA approval. In the meantime, Gardasil remains the only HPV vaccine on the market, giving Merck an effective monopoly on a product with an estimated market value of $2 billion to $4 billion. The company expects 2008 sales of Gardasil to reach $1.9 billion to $2.1 billion, and is currently asking the FDA to approve the vaccine for women ages 26 to 45, which would double the market.

MERCK'S PR JUGGERNAUT

Dr. Diane Harper, a professor at the Dartmouth Medical School, has been studying HPV for almost twenty years. She was involved in drug trial design with both Merck and GlaxoSmithKline and was a principal investigator at the clinic site for the phase II and III trials for both Gardasil and Cervarix. In a June 2007 interview, she told me emphatically, "The vaccines are good and will indeed prevent cervical cancer." However, she expressed serious concerns about Merck's marketing tactics:

> I'll give Merck credit—there is absolutely nothing factually incorrect in Merck's advertisements. But the interpretation of the rock stars, and the media, and of everyone else is that this vaccine will completely eliminate cervical cancer. I've worked with ABC, with NBC, and even on their nightly news, their headline is "HPV vaccine prevents cervical cancer." It's true, that is a true headline, but it is not accurate.

This popular misconception is no accident. Even before the FDA approved Gardasil, Merck began using its deep pockets to sow concern—one might even say fear—about HPV among US women and girls.

FROM CONNECTION TO COMMITMENT

The marketing juggernaut was multifaceted and meticulously planned. In 2005—a full year before the FDA approved Gardasil—Merck financed a national campaign in the US called "Make the Connection," which was run by the Cancer Research and Prevention Foundation (CRPF) and the Step Up Women's Network (SUWN), a celebrity charity. The campaign used the standard formula of a celebrity spokesperson and a medical professional. By using nonprofits, doctors, and a celebrity, Merck reached audiences that could have rightly been suspicious of the message if it had come directly from a pharmaceutical company. (In the PR trade, this strategy of using proxies to deliver a client's message is known as the "third-party technique.")

For the nonprofits that participated in this campaign, the financial benefits are obvious. CRPF's 2006 annual report lists several pharmaceutical companies as funders, including Merck, GlaxoSmithKline, Pfizer, Roche, Eli Lilly, and Sanofi-Aventis. Each gave in excess of $100,000 in 2006. CRPF also received more than $100,000 from the drug industry's main lobbying group, the Pharmaceutical Research and Manufacturers of America (PhRMA).

Merck's other campaign partner, the Step Up Women's Network, describes itself as a "nonprofit, membership organization dedicated to strengthening community resources for women and girls." Its founder, Kaye Popofsky Kramer, is a former talent agent (and associate producer of the 2001 film *Kissing Jessica Stein*). SUWN boasts a stable of celebrity supporters including Jessica Alba, Courteney Cox-Arquette, Geena Davis, Anjelica Huston, Brooke Shields, and Aisha Tyler. This celebrity roster served Merck well. The SUWN website features a video montage of celebrities hitting the news and talk show circuits. Their participation took SUWN's message to 563 million people who saw the TV spots or read the print coverage in popular women's magazines.

"Make the Connection" eventually morphed into "Make the Commitment," which urged women to take a pledge to "talk with my healthcare professional in January about ways that I can prevent cervical cancer, including getting regular cervical cancer screenings." January is designated as Cervical Health Awareness Month in the US. The pledge for women to talk with their doctors ensured that medical practitioners would be approached from all sides—from Merck's drug reps, from patients, and (as a result of additional lobbying at the political level) by state legislators.

NEXT PHASE: TELL SOMEONE

The "Make the Connection/Commitment" campaigns were low-key efforts compared to the most significant preapproval effort—Merck's "Tell Someone" commercials. The "Tell Someone" spots did not mention Gardasil (since it was not yet FDA approved), but they did include Merck's name and logo. The ads featured actors portraying everyday women saying they were shocked that HPV is so prevalent and that there is a link to cervical cancer. "I was stunned at how many people have HPV. I was stunned. Millions? That's insane," said one woman. With a sense of urgency, the women in the ads pledge to tell someone they love.

Not everyone was taken in. Gary Ruskin, executive director of Commercial Alert, criticized the campaign in comments to Bloomberg News reporters Angela Zimm and Justin Blum in May 2006. Ruskin said Merck's promotional website was "deceptive and dishonest. Merck doesn't tell you why the site exists, which is to sell Gardasil."

The Bloomberg article also quoted Merck's Richard Haupt, who said that the company had "invested in public affairs and consumer education more than we've done *for any vaccine* in the past" (emphasis added). The Bloomberg reporters calculated that Merck spent $841,000 in the first quarter of 2006 alone for Internet ads on HPV's link to cervical cancer. In April 2006, Merck bought 295 TV advertising spots for the HPV campaign, followed by 788 spots in May. The following month, the FDA approved Gardasil.

ONE LESS

Once it was legal to sell Gardasil, Merck could finally make its message overt. On November 13, 2006, Merck launched a direct-to-consumer mixture of television, print, and online advertising called "One Less." The upbeat ads feature young women and girls engaged in a variety of activities—playing soccer, shooting baskets, skateboarding, drumming, and dancing, while declaring that they want to be "one less statistic," "one less woman who will battle cervical cancer." Young women are shown writing "one less" on a gym shoe, and appliquéing "one less" on the front of a hoodie. Young African American girls jumping rope at the end chant "I want to be one less, one less! O-N-E-L-E-S-S!" While some of the girls are pictured with parents or other adults, the ads are clearly meant to convey a sense of girls talking to other girls.

The Gardasil commercials have clearly had an impact. Writing for the *Daily Record* in Morristown, New Jersey in May 2007, Tien-Shun Lee told of a fourteen-year-old girl who talked to her mom and her friends about HPV after she "first heard about the human papillomavirus, or HPV, vaccine from a television commercial that features a woman saying 'I just found out that cervical cancer is caused by certain types of a common virus.'" Lee also spoke to an eighth-grade health teacher who said HPV "came up in discussion because of the commercials."

PAY NO ATTENTION TO THE FLACKS
BEHIND THE CURTAIN

Who created this culture of fear and panic on Merck's behalf? The genius behind all stages of Merck's campaign is the PR giant Edelman, the world's largest independent PR firm. Edelman reported $299 million in revenues for its 2006 fiscal year, boasting of its expertise at building "health relationships with healthcare companies, advocacy organizations, foundations, NGOs and academic institutions."

Edelman positions itself as a PR firm that can create partnerships between businesses and nonprofits. It spelled out its strategy bluntly in a December 2000 press release: "You've got an environmental disaster on your hands. Have you consulted with Greenpeace in developing your crisis response plan? Co-opting your would-be attackers may seem counter-intuitive, but it makes sense when you consider that NGOs (nongovernmental organizations) are trusted by the public nearly two-to-one to 'do what's right' compared with government bodies, media organizations and corporations."

A September 2002 article titled "Forging Alliances" in *Pharmaceutical Executive Magazine* quotes Nancy Turett, Edelman's Global President for Health. "So what does PR stand for?" Turett says. "It stands for powerful relationships. The heart of PR is third-party credibility." She continued, "Third-party messages are an essential means of communication for validating scientific credibility, for legitimizing products, for building brand and disease awareness, and for building defenses against crises. As advocates develop louder voices, pharma companies must forge alliances and win allies."

Edelman's work for Gardasil has gained attention and adulation for itself and for Merck. *Pharmaceutical Executive Magazine* gave Gardasil its first annual Brand of the Year award in February 2007. In a lengthy article by Beth Herskovits, the magazine noted, "The disease aware-ness effort did more than just play on cancer fears, but drew on themes of safeguarding your children (for moms) and empowerment (for girls)." Herskovits went on to quote Bev Lybrand, Merck's vice presi-dent and general manager for Gardasil. "Of course everyone understands cancer and is scared of cancer," Lybrand said, "but we learned early on that moms really wanted to protect their daughters— that protective insight is important. For young women, they want to empower themselves to take control of their own destiny."

On May 3, 2007, Merck and Edelman also received several Pharma-ceutical Advertising and Marketing Excellence (PhAME) Awards. PhAME gave the "Tell Someone" campaign awards for Public Health, Best Integrated Campaign, Best Multicultural Campaign, and Best Unbranded Ad. Merck also took home best Marketer of the Year. Edel-man's Nancy Turett was inducted into the "Hall of PhAME."

SECOND FRONT: LOBBYING AT THE STATE LEVEL

In addition to targeting individual consumers, Merck has also pursued an even more lucrative goal. It wants states to require that girls get vaccinated for HPV as a prerequisite for attending school. Mandatory vaccination for more than half of the population is the financial equivalent of the Holy Grail for a pharmaceutical company. (The price tag for a three-shot regi-men of Gardasil is at least $400 per person, not including doctor and other appointment costs.) The *Washington Times* reported in February 2007 that Gardasil is the most expensive vaccine on the market. Dr. Harper told me that GlaxoSmithKline's competing vaccine, Cervarix, is showing longer efficacy than Gardasil in the trials. Since Cervarix is not yet FDA approved, however, a mandate "would mean that all the vaccine would be purchased from Merck because they are currently the sole provider."

For its state-level lobbying, Merck once again turned to the third-party technique, this time using a different nonprofit partner called Women in Government (WIG). According to WIG's website, it is "a national 501(c)(3), non-profit, bi-partisan organization of women state legislators providing leadership opportunities, networking, expert forums, and educational resources to address and resolve complex public policy issues." WIG launched its "Challenge to Eliminate Cervical Cancer" in 2004. The WIG website features a legislative policy toolkit with sample legislation, and maps showing states with cervical cancer related bills pending or laws enacted. WIG's efforts do not focus exclusively on passing HPV vaccine mandates, but mandates are one of the campaign's main components.

In March 2007, I interviewed WIG President Susan Crosby. She told me that WIG lets legislators "call in and get totally unbiased information . . . to be able to make decisions that are the best for their state." She continued, "That's one thing that we at Women in Government have always tried to do, is try to give them the full picture, the balanced picture—the good, the bad, and the ugly. Because nothing's worse than to give a legislator, a woman legislator in particular, part of the story, and have her go back to her state, standing up at the mike, proposing something, and all of a sudden this question comes flying out of left field and she has no idea what it was."

But does WIG really provide that service, or do its corporate contributors help set its agenda? WIG's business council over the past four years has included Amylin Pharmaceuticals, Cinergy Corporation, Digene Corporation (maker of the HPV test), ExxonMobil, GlaxoSmithKline, Merck Vaccine Division, Verizon Communications and Wellpoint, Inc. Other corporate donors include agribusiness, energy companies, alcohol manufacturers, telecom, and big box retailers, but there is little doubt that the pharmaceutical industry is its bread and butter. The list of current WIG sponsors for 2008 includes at least thirty pharmaceutical companies, their foundations, and lobbying associations such as PhRMA.

WIG's funders also get direct access to individual state legislators through the organization's Legislative Business Roundtable. The roundtable, Crosby told me, is "people that come together to help the women legislators identify what the cutting edge issues are. For instance, we might have someone from Verizon saying, 'OK, we're looking at telephone deregulation—this may be an issue you want to get more information on to help educate your legislators.' . . . So they float those topics out there and we say, 'Oh, that's something we definitely need more information on.'"

Some of the close ties between Merck and WIG came to light in Texas, where Governor Rick Perry signed an executive order on February 2, 2007, mandating HPV vaccination for girls entering seventh grade. His move angered his conservative base, which opposes mandatory vaccination of girls against HPV on the grounds that protection from a sexually transmitted virus might encourage promiscuity. Details of Perry's connections to Merck and WIG soon became public. "It turned out that Perry's former chief of staff is now a lobbyist for Merck," wrote Ellen Goodman in the *Boston Globe*. "Did that look bad? Whoa, Nellie. Did it look bad that Merck had funded an organization of women legislators backing similar bills? Whoa, Merck." *USA Today* reported that the mother-in-law of Perry's chief of staff was a state director for WIG, and that Perry's wife addressed a WIG summit on cervical cancer. Perry also received $6,000 from Merck's political action committee during his reelection campaign.

The flap over Perry prompted Merck to backpedal, announcing on February 20 that it would no longer lobby directly for vaccine mandates at the state level. "Our goal is to prevent cervical cancer. Our goal is to reach as many females as possible. Right now, school requirements and Merck's involvement in that are being viewed as a distraction to that goal," said Richard Haupt, Merck's Executive Director for Medical Affairs. In March 2007, the nonprofit Center for Medical Consumers assessed Merck's lobbying tactics as having "moved from the usual pharmaceutical industry hucksterism (hype the disease, hype the new drug) to blatantly purchasing a public policy that is clearly a windfall for the one and only company that sells a cervical cancer vaccine."

WHAT'S THE HARM?

The main danger posed by the marketing hype around Gardasil is that it creates confusion about what actually causes cervical cancer. Some 30 percent of cervical cancer cases occur in women who have *not* been infected with the strains of HPV that Gardasil prevents. Additionally, girls and women can already be infected with a strain of HPV without knowing it. Since the vaccine is only effective before exposure and does not help eliminate the infection if it is already present, they may have a false sense of security after getting the shots. Gardasil offers imperfect protection, and all women will need to continue receiving regular Pap screens if they want to avoid the disease. The false notion that Gardasil is a "vaccine against cancer" could breed complacency that prevents women from getting regular screens.

Dr. Harper, the Dartmouth professor who has worked on clinical trials for Gardasil and Cervarix, said she took those concerns to Merck, but they fell on deaf ears. "I think those are very valid concerns. I've heard it myself. You go through the grocery store aisles, to the beauty shop, to the local concert and if anyone's talking about the vaccine, what you hear is, 'I think I'm going to get that vaccine because I won't have to get my Paps anymore.' I think the risk of that is really very high."

The Spring 2007 issue of *Ms. Magazine* contained an article written by Cindy Wright that shows how Gardasil's potential has been over-simplified and misinterpreted. Wright discussed the controversy in Texas over Perry's executive order mandating vaccination, but she blames the "firestorm" on social conservatives—not to the controversial ties linking Perry to Merck and its allies. In response to Gardasil's daunting price tag, Wright opined, "Even if I had to pay full price, how could I say no to the first-ever cancer vaccine? How could anyone? Who would consider not giving our daughters the best chance of avoiding a deadly disease?" The implication, of course, is that parents are negligent if they fail to get their daughters vaccinated. Wright concludes her article by saying, "Meanwhile, my daughter has gotten her second booster. That's one less life-threatening illness to worry about." Her use of the phrase "one less" shows how thoroughly Merck's marketing slogan has penetrated, and how easily it translates into complacency. We can only hope that Wright's daughter, even with the vaccine, continues to "worry about" cervical cancer enough to keep getting Pap smears.

Legislators pushing for HPV vaccine mandates aren't necessarily any better informed. In 2007, Minnesota legislators were considering a mandate, but public concern forced the bill off the table when details of the cozy relationship between Governor Perry and Merck came out. The bill's sponsor, State Senator Yvonne Prettner Solon, was surprised when there was not overwhelming support for a mandate. But her understanding of the vaccine seems dangerously limited. She told the *Minneapolis Star-Tribune* in February 2007 that "this is the first time that we're able to actually eradicate or eliminate a cancer in known history. So I got very excited about that."

Gardasil may well be a worthwhile vaccine, as Harper believes. It may save lives. Nevertheless, there are serious issues about the push to vaccinate girls at the age of eleven or twelve. "This is a vaccine that will prevent disease in women of all ages," Harper explains. "So the target, and the extreme emphasis on twelve-year olds, is misleading to the public in making them feel that this is a vaccine that you have to get before anyone . . . has touched your genitals." She added, "We also have some evidence now that Gardasil is losing efficacy after five years. So if you need a booster shot later, are we really providing the best protection by vaccinating at an early age?" If the vaccine is given too early, its efficacy could decline before a girl even becomes sexually active.

IT'S NOT THE SEX

In America's polarized political and religious climate, the debate over Gardasil has taken the form of absurd posturing over "promiscuity" from conservative groups, provoking in turn an equally ridiculous knee-jerk defense of Gardasil from some on the Left. Rather than carefully examining the issue, some people endorse the vaccine simply because the Right is against it.

Nevertheless, reputable and important voices oppose mandating the vaccine. An editorial in the May 2, 2007, edition of the *Journal of the American Medical Association* speaks positively about the vaccine's potential, but adds that "the rush to make HPV vaccination mandatory in school-aged girls presents ethical concerns and is likely to be counterproductive." It also notes that the drug has not been extensively tested on girls between the ages of nine to fifteen—the target population for which it is now being recommended. If Gardasil were mandated nationwide, the editorial points out, "it would be administered to some 2 million girls and young women, most of them between eleven and twelve years old and some as young as nine years old. The longer-term effectiveness and safety of the vaccine still need to be evaluated among a large population, and particularly among younger girls."

The *JAMA* editorial also asserts that the push for mandates is a direct result of Merck's efforts, and is not in the best interest of the population it claims to serve.

Public health authorities, pediatricians, and infectious disease specialists, rather than political bodies, should drive mandatory vaccination decisions and policies. The Centers for Disease Control and Prevention recommend routine use of HPV vaccinations, but that is not equivalent to mandatory use. Merck, the manufacturer of the HPV quadrivalent vaccine, lobbied legislatures to make the vaccine mandatory before withdrawing its campaign when it became controversial. Since the manufacturer stands to profit from widespread vaccine administration, it is inappropriate for the company to finance efforts to persuade states and public officials to make HPV vaccinations mandatory, particularly so soon after the product was licensed. Private wealth should never trump public health.

JAMA is not alone. In February 2007, the American Academy of Family Physicians released the "AAFP Policy Statement Regarding Consideration of the Mandated Use of HPV for School Attendance." They stated, "The AAFP feels it is premature to consider school entry mandates for human papillomavirus vaccine (HPV)."

In March 2007, the American Medical Association released a statement that while generally very favorable toward the vaccine's potential, does not specifically call for mandates. In a personal communication to me on June 5, 2008, Mollie Turner, Public Information Officer for the AMA, confirmed that they do not support mandated vaccination.

In 2007, the Minnesota legislature directed the state's commissioner of health to study whether the HPV vaccine should be mandated for middle school–aged girls. Its conclusion, announced publicly on February 1, 2008, was that "adding HPV to the school immunization schedule should not be mandated at this time for several main reasons. . . . More time is needed for the public to become aware of the vaccine, accept it and understand its limitations."

THE DRUMBEAT GOES ON

The push for mandatory vaccination continues, and many of its supporters are people who have received money from Merck. Following a legislative debate over the issue in Indiana, the *Indianapolis Star* reported that "support for a mandatory HPV vaccine . . . came from doctors, the state health commissioner, professors, and other health officials—some of them with ties to Merck."

There has been a palpable turning of the tide against mandates, but Women In Government still swims against the current. In a 2008 report titled "State of Cervical Cancer Prevention in America," WIG continued to push for mandates and gave higher scores to states that have introduced or passed legislation for this purpose.

WIG reports that twenty-seven states, plus the District of Columbia, saw legislation introduced in 2007 that would have mandated HPV vaccination. To date, Virginia and the District of Columbia are the only places where the mandate has passed. In Virginia, it is already the law. In DC, it needs Congressional approval to take effect. In the other states, legislation died in committee, was referred on to the next legislation session, was withdrawn, or was modified to focus on education and availability of funds instead of the mandate.

Merck is also continuing and expanding its ad and PR juggernaut. Building on the "One Less" ad campaign, Gardasil is now being pushed in the "I Chose" commercials. There are two versions of the spots. One is aimed primarily at mothers and includes adult women saying "I chose to get my daughter vaccinated because I want her to be one less woman affected by cervical cancer." A second version has no adults to be seen—all the people featured are young women, including one who says that she chose to be vaccinated because her "dreams don't include cervical cancer." Again Merck is counting on parents' desires to protect their children and girls' need to feel independent and empowered. The first ad ends with a montage of women and girls saying "O-n-e-l-e-s-s. One less. Gardasil." In the end, women are told, "You have the power to choose. Ask your daughter's doctor about Gardasil." The fact that there are no adults in the second ad plays directly on girls' desire to feel independent and that they can make important decisions for themselves.

The New Jersey *Star Ledger* reported on June 5, 2008, that Merck has bought a sixty-second ad slot to be screened before the blockbuster film *Sex and the City*. The trailer is based on the "I Chose" TV ads. A long awaited "chick flick," *Sex and the City* allows Merck to reach the perfect demographic for the vaccine, and through a very effective medium. The company says that its "research showed 76 percent of young women between the ages of nineteen and twenty-six described advertising they saw before a movie as entertaining. But here's the clincher: The same young women said they pay more attention to ads on a movie screen than on television."

Merck and its supporters would have you believe that time is of the essence and that we should move more quickly to ensure that every young girl gets vaccinated. However, its own overly aggressive PR campaign, its deceit in pushing for mandates through a non-profit front, and its willingness to overhype its product are reasons enough to avoid embracing the so-called "vaccine against cancer."

No one, myself included, seriously doubts that the development of a vaccine against even some of the high-risk strains of human papillomavirus holds great potential for women's health. As both the mother of a teenaged girl and someone who has personally needed treatment to address a pre-cancerous cervical condition, I welcome this development on one level. Medical advances that truly benefit women in the area of reproductive health are rare enough that they ought to be cause for celebration when they do occur. In this case, however, the drug itself is not the problem. Merck's marketing and PR, by hyping and oversimplifying Gardasil's role in addressing the risk of cancer, threatens to undermine its potential health benefits and even introduce new risks.

JUDITH SIERS-POISSON is the associate director of the Center for Media and Democracy, a nonprofit public interest organization that watchdogs the PR industry and its role in corporate spin and government propaganda. She wrote a four article series called "The Politics and PR of Cervical Cancer" in 2007, which is available at www.PRWatch.org.

Sources

American Academy of Family Physicians policy statement regarding consideration of the mandated use of HPV for school attendance, February 7, 2007, http://www.aafp.org/online/en/home/ clinical/immunizationres/mandatedhpv.html; S. Begley "Antidepressants: Beware the file-drawer effect," *Newsweek*, January 17, 2008.

"Cervical cancer," Medline Plus, a Service of the US National Library of Medicine and the National Institutes of Health,June 9, 2006, http://www.nlm.nih.gov/ medlineplus/ency/article/000893.htm#Causes, percent2oincidence, percent2oand percent2orisk percent2ofactors.

J. Coste, B. Cochand-Priollet, P. de Cremoux, C. Le Galès, I. Cartier, and V. Molinié, et al, "Cross sectional study of conventional cervical smear, monolayer cytology, and human papillomavirus DNA testing for cervical cancer screening," *British Medical Journal*, 2003, 326, 733.

T. Cox, "Forging alliances," *Pharmaceutical Executive*, September 1, 2002, http://pharmexec.findpharma .com/pharmexec/article/articleDetail.jsp?id=29974&pageID=1&sk=&date=&searchString=Forging percent2oAlliances.

"Genital HPV infection - CDC fact sheet," Centers for Disease Control and Prevention, April 10, 2008, http://www.cdc.gov/std/HPV/STDFact-HPV.htm#common.

E. Goodman, "A dose of reality on HPV vaccine," *Boston Globe*, March 2, 2007.

L. Gostin and C.D. DeAngelis, "Mandatory HPV Vaccination: Public Health vs Private Wealth," *Journal of the American Medical Association*, 2007, 297, 1921–1923.

"Health information national trends survey," National Cancer Institute, US National Institutes of Health, 2005, http://hints.cancer.gov/questions/cks-cv.jsp.

B. Herskovits, "Brand of the year," *Pharmaceutical Executive*, February 1, 2007, http://pharmexec.findpharma.com/pharmexec/article/articleDetail.jsp?id=401664.

S. Hupp, "Committee OKs weaker vaccine bill: Parents of girls would be able to opt out of HPV vaccinations," *Indianapolis Star*, February 1, 2007.

T. Lee, "Morris women join HPV debate," *Daily Record*, March 21, 2007.

M. Lerner, "States have 2nd thoughts about requiring cancer shots," *Minneapolis Star-Tribune*, February 27, 2007.

G. Lopes, "CDC doctor opposes law for vaccine," *Washington Times*, February 27, 2007.

"Merck Frosst to seek review of Sask court ruling to expand Vioxx lawsuit," *The Canadian Press*, May 30, 2008.

"Merck reports strong financial results for first-quarter 2007," Merck News, April 19, 2007, http://www.merck.com/newsroom/press_releases/financial/2007_0419.html.

"Health department report recommends not mandating HPV vaccine as part of school immunization requirements at this time," Minnesota Department of Public Health, February 1, 2008.

M. Napoli, "How vaccine policy is made: The story of Merck and Gardasil, the HPV vaccine," Center for Medical Consumers, March 2007, http://www.medicalconsumers.org/pages/howvaccinepolicyismade.htm.

"New data presented on GARDASIL®, Merck's cervical cancer vaccine, in women through Age 45," Merck News, November 5, 2007, http://www.merck.com/newsroom/press_releases/product/2007_1105.html.

S. Pettypiece, "Merck profit jumps 94 percent on AstraZeneca payment," Bloomberg News, April 21, 2008, http://www.bloomberg.com/apps/news?pid=20601103&sid=aErm1_TQK4M0&refer=us.

"Prescription drugs and mass media advertising 2000: A research report by the National Institute for Health Care Management," National Institute for Health Care Management Foundation, November 2001, http://www.nihcm.org/publications/prescription_drugs.

Product approval information, Center for Biologics Evaluation and Research, US Food and Drug Administration, June 8, 2006, http://www.fda.gov/CBER/products/hpvmer060806qa.htm.

B. Steinberg and S. Vranica, "Not such a 'beautiful morning'," *Wall Street Journal*, October 1, 2004.

"Texas governor orders anti-cancer vaccine for schoolgirls," *USA Today*, February 2, 2007

R. Thomaselli, "Merck, Schering wage PR battle after Vytorin backlash: Newspaper ads look to comfort consumers worried about drug," *Advertising Age*, January 22, 2008.

J. Todd, "Industry insider: Gardasil's girl talk hits big screen," *Newark Star-Ledger*, June 5, 2008.

"What are the key statistics about cervical cancer?" American Cancer Society, March 26, 2008, http://www.cancer.org/docroot/CRI/content/CRI_2_4_1X_What_are_the_key_statistics_for_cervical_cancer_8.asp?sitearea=.

R. Winslow and A. Johnson, "Merck's publishing ethics are questioned by studies," *Wall Street Journal*, April 16, 2008.

"The "state" of cervical cancer prevention in America," Women In Government, 2008.

C. Wright, "Lifesaving politics," *Ms. Magazine*, April 24, 2007, 12-13.

A. Zimm and J. Blum, "Merck promotes cervical cancer shot by publicizing viral cause," Bloomberg News, May 26, 2006, http://www.bloomberg.com/apps/news?pid=10000103&sid=amVj .y3Eynz8&refer=us.

CHAPTER 9

Fear & Favor 2007
How Power Still Shapes the News

by Janine Jackson and Peter Hart

US journalists seeking to fulfill the profession's traditional goal of telling the truth and "letting the chips fall where they may" have powerful forces to contend with, starting with their corporate employers and the corporate advertisers who fuel the enterprise, both of whom have an investment in maintaining a political climate favorable to their profitability. There are also legislators who maintain the pro-corporate policy that media owners rely on to thrive, local political players with axes to grind, and well-funded public relations (PR) campaigns from all corners. Each year these entities renew and refine their efforts to shape news media coverage—and public opinion—to suit their interests. Each year some journalists fight back, and some don't.

Fear & Favor is by no means a comprehensive compilation of violations of journalistic ethics; indeed, often when people in the news business compromise their integrity, word never leaves the news room. But this sampling of what got out should encourage news audiences to maintain a critical attitude as we read and watch the news, not only about what might be left out of the story, but about what's in it—and why.

IN ADVERTISERS WE TRUST

It's been a while since commercial sponsors were happy with a thirty-second spot; now it's all about subtler forms of encroachment into programming, the more unavoidable, the better: product placement, "video news releases" (VNRs), tie-ins.

Sometimes these compromises seem simply inane: It's hard to know what the *Register-Guard* of Eugene, Oregon, was thinking when they ran an ad for the Sacred Heart Medical Center (October 29, 2007) featuring a graphic of a bandaged index finger that "poked up" several inches beyond the ad's margin into the news columns above. Other incidents seem less silly and more troubling.

➤ "It doesn't blur the line. It obliterates it," stated *Washington Post* ombud Deborah Howell (*Washington Post*, September 24, 2007). "It" was a six-page General Motors (GM) advertising supplement (September 20, 2007) in the paper that touted the automaker's environmental credentials. Howell's and many newsroom staffers' problem: the section was filled with articles bearing bylines of *Post* writers, giving the appearance of a partnership between the paper and a company it covers. Executive editor Leonard Downie Jr.'s official justification was unsatisfying: because the stories had been previously published, he told the *Post*'s Howard Kurtz (September 24, 2007), "We were not doing journalism specifically for this section." But his response on the ethics of such editorial/advertising hybrids was priceless: "I'm not sure where the line is on that, and that's why I agreed to go this far."

➤ GM's successful charm offensive didn't stop with the *Washington Post*. A cover story by Mary Connelly in the trade paper *Automotive News* (August 6, 2007) described how the automobile company gave radio talk show hosts free use of new cars and trucks in addition to buying ads during their shows. There's no reason not to draw a straight line from that to, for example, Rush Limbaugh's effusion to listeners: "Believe in General Motors, folks. They're a classic American company doing it all." As consumer advocate and longtime GM nemesis Ralph Nader pointed out (*CounterSpin*, August 24, 2007), it "would be clearly illegal for disc jockeys to take freebies in order to promote certain songs. . . . I don't see anything different when it comes to a product, like a GM car."

Sam Mancuso, GM's director of brand marketing alliances and operations, told *Automotive News* the company wooed hosts (of various ideological stripes, including liberals Ed Schultz and Whoopi Goldberg, as well as Limbaugh, Bill O'Reilly, and Sean Hannity) because "radio personalities have unique relationships with their listeners. They make a real emotional connection. The audience knows they are being genuine."

➤ Glenn Beck hasn't done much for CNN *Headline News*' ratings, but he did snag the cable channel one first in 2007: in June and July, Beck delivered the channel's first ever on-air plugs for a sponsor, Select Comfort mattresses. A CNN spokesperson told *Hollywood Reporter* (July 20, 2007), "Select Comfort is Glenn Beck's/*Headline News*' first and only advertiser to have an on-air entitlement, and it's specifically targeted for his show." But the PR flak went on to suggest that they hoped to fix that, saying that *Headline News* will "evaluate advertiser interest" in similar deals for Beck's show, as well as for others, including Nancy Grace and *Showbiz Tonight*.

▶ Somehow, ever since Providence Health Systems began sponsoring a weekly medical report during newscasts on KOIN-TV in Portland, Oregon, Providence spokespeople seem to keep showing up in those reports. In one segment, according to *OPB News* (June 25, 2007), an informational phone number given out at the end of a story on inner ear disorders turned out to be for Providence. Likewise, a segment on Montessori schools featured one operated by Providence. At the time of *OPB News'* story, each of the station's previous fourteen health reports had featured at least one Providence source.

KOIN news director Jeff Alan declared, "These are not advertisements whatsoever. These are reports." He admitted that the sponsor's experts were likely to be featured, because "they're looking to be available," but he claimed that "if other hospitals and other people were more available to us, yeah, they would be in the reports." However, according to *OPB News'* investigation, the station "does not appear to have trouble finding non-Providence medical experts for health reports that air at times when Providence is not a sponsor."

▶ News director Greg Caputo of WGN-Channel 9 in Chicago didn't see what the fuss was about. "We're not going to be promoting the Bureau of Tourism, for God's sake," Caputo exclaimed (*Chicago Sun-Times*, March 23, 2007). Caputo was responding to concerns about two-minute segments the station planned to air April through July, sponsored by the state tourism bureau. WGN would retain "total editorial control" over the segments about travel in and around the state, he argued, though the sponsoring agency wouldn't be shut out: "We may ask them for some of their ideas." No word on whether that's the relationship the news department usually maintains with advertisers.

▶ Amanda Congdon may have had a modern job title—she was a "videoblogger" for *ABC News*—but she has an old-fashioned conflict of interest. According to *Ad Age* (March 19, 2007), she had a sideline hosting a series of what she called "infotainmercials" for the website of the chemical company DuPont. As *Radar* magazine put it (RadarOnline.com, March 20, 2007), the deal "naturally raises questions about how aggressively the network covers DuPont's role in, say, building up Iraq's nuclear program or its part in giving thousands of people cancer."

But it wasn't a problem for *ABC News*; network spokesperson Jeffrey Schneider told *Radar* that Congdon was "a unique contributor who had deals prior to working for ABC, and continues to do so"—though Congdon's videoblog segments were also featured on ABC's twenty-four-hour digital news channel, *ABC News Now*, and her segments were co-produced, at least according to her, by an *ABC News* senior producer.

➤ When the *Philadelphia Inquirer* was sold in 2006, some readers may have hoped the paper would bring in some new voices. They probably didn't imagine that one of those new "voices" would be a bank. In what their own staff writer called an "unusual arrangement" (April 14, 2007), the *Inquirer* began running a column paid for by Citizens Bank in 2007. The column, which focuses on news about local businesses, carries a Citizens Bank label and is boxed in green—that's "Citizens Bank's color," the paper informed readers (in a story whose main subject was the paper's decision to start running ads on page one, "once considered the sacred province of news").

➤ CNBC anchor Maria Bartiromo seemed to be a walking conflict of interest in 2007. In January, details of her close relationship with top Citigroup officer Todd Thomson were revealed (*Wall Street Journal*, January 24, 2007). Citigroup is a major CNBC advertiser, as well as the subject of reporting on any financial news network. Thomson often brought Bartiromo to company functions and meetings with clients, in one case flying her to private Citigroup luncheons in Hong Kong and Shanghai.

The conflict seems obvious, but CNBC defended their star anchor, even chalking the engagements up to "source development" (*Wall Street Journal*, January 26, 2007). One anonymous CNBC source told the *Washington Post* (January 26, 2007): "I don't think there's even the appearance of a conflict of interest. . . . We paid our way. This is what we cover. This is what we do."

New York Times columnist David Carr had a different take (January 29, 2007), pointing to "an implicit contract at play here. By making huge advertising buys on CNBC, Citigroup obtained access to its biggest star. Clearly, an exchange of brands was under way." Added

Carr: "CNBC has positioned itself as an adjunct to business, the glowing friend in the corner with the sound off and a ticker at the bottom. . . . It is companion media rather than the source of oversight or rigorous coverage."

THE BOSS'S BUSINESS(ES)

For some, the *Wall Street Journal*'s failure to break the story of its own parent company's imminent purchase by Rupert Murdoch (CNBC was first with the story of Murdoch's ultimately successful bid for Dow Jones on May 1, 2007) was the perfect example of corporate media outlets' inability to report on themselves. *Slate*'s Michelle Tsai (July 10, 2007) cited self-censorship on matters of their boss's business as an all-too-common media reality. "Thirty-five percent of respondents [to a journalists' survey] said journalists they knew often or sometimes avoided stories that would hurt the financial interests of their employers." The flip side, of course, is all those stories they actually report on that serve those financial interests, which become more various all the time.

➤ It seems the biggest sacred cow of the press really is the press itself, even if the press is just a giveaway subway tabloid like *Metro*. *New York Magazine* reported (August 13, 2007) that *Metro* humor columnist (and *Daily Show* producer) Elliott Kalan had been summarily dropped from the paper after a column in which he declared: "Nobody reads newspapers anymore. As this very copy of *Metro* shows, the only way to get people to read a newspaper is to literally force it into their hands."

A *Metro* staffer told *New York* that Kalan's column was seen by the interim CEO of the Stockholm-based Metro International, in New York on business, who told the paper's New York publisher to fire the columnist immediately; Kalan was told the next week his column was finished. Says Kalan, "My assumption is the wrong person saw it and didn't get the joke."

And they know funny, those *Metro* execs. The global newspaper chain is notorious for in-house "humor," like that of leading North American executive Steve Nylundh, who opened a 2003 speech to a group of top representatives: "There were two niggers standing by a pool, and they took their dicks out" (AlterNet, January 10, 2005).

➤ The worst examples of a conflict of interest are when the public has no way of knowing of a behind-the-scenes link between the content of a news story and some other entity. But sometimes disclosure just doesn't seem like enough. When NBC's *Today Show* launched its "Where in the World is Matt Lauer?" feature by having Lauer "earn his wings" at the Boeing factory in Everett, Washington (April 30, 2007), the show's acknowledgement of their corporate closeness to the matter consisted of Lauer, after telling viewers he was "standing right now inside one of the engines of a 777," continuing: "Full disclosure, it's actually made by our parent company, General Electric. One hundred fifteen thousand pounds of thrust."

But that disclosure seemed more like a plug when it was followed by Lauer's assurances that "these planes will make flying more comfortable" and that "you don't have to be nervous on a plane like this, because they have put these things through rigorous and extensive testing." Another correspondent declared that new Boeing planes "will actually not only deliver passengers a better ride, but also cost savings for airlines," while a third reporter described Boeing as "a single company contributing an awful lot to the U.S. bottom line." By the time Lauer thanked Boeing employees "who love what they do and make a great product," and signed off with "a saying around here . . . 'If it ain't Boeing, we ain't going,'" viewers may have felt that no amount of disclosure could have been sufficient.

➤ Timing is everything. Had ABC's news division decided to devote five hours in the heart of primetime to NASCAR in 2006, that might've been one thing. But the fact that the network launched the five-part documentary series *NASCAR in Primetime* in August 2007, just weeks after ABC corporate cousins ABC Sports and ESPN began a $560 million–a-year contract to carry the sport, made it seem like another thing altogether. A *New York Times* reviewer (August 15, 2007) found the series offered "nothing new about NASCAR"—though it seemed newsworthy enough to *Good Morning America* (also in ABC's news division), which aired a segment the day of the first installment (August 15, 2007) that concluded with reporter Chris Cuomo telling viewers to "make sure to watch it."

➤ The Catholic Church shouldn't be in the business of fibbing, but that's what some suspected when the Brownsville, Texas, PBS affiliate KMBH, owned by the Roman Catholic Diocese of Brownsville, claimed that they didn't air the *Frontline* documentary *Hand of God* because PBS failed to provide the video feed in time (*Valley Morning Star*, January 18, 2007). Critics suspected the station's actual reason had to do with the documentary's subject matter: Catholic priest molestation scandals. The station re-aired a program about the Taliban instead.

➤ It's by now an open joke that the Super Bowl will have urgent "news value" to the news division of whatever network is sponsoring it that year. Too bad the joke's on the public, who are poorly served by such open acceptance of non-journalistic priorities. In 2007, CBS's supposedly austere Sunday political talk show *Face the Nation* signed on as just another part of what one paper rightly termed "today's NFL infomercial" (*Newport News, Virginia Daily Press*, February 4, 2007). Host Bob Schieffer, broadcasting from the Indianapolis Colts cheerleader dressing room, hardly made a pretense of journalistic justification:

> We usually concentrate on the news we believe you need to know. The Super Bowl, on the other hand, is big news that millions upon millions of Americans want to know. Since someone had to do it, we volunteered to help tell the story. Now, how is that for a high-minded excuse for being here?

Not great.

➤ The network tie-in is no longer limited to "light" morning show segments. Call it rooting for the home team, but one has to ask what stories are being squeezed out as chunks of the newscast are devoted to in-house cheerleading. Several writers on ABC's *Good Morning America*, responding anonymously to a 2007 Writers Guild of America–East (WGA–E) survey (July 2007), reported that "any domestic story without a crime component is expected to find a way to use a clip from the popular ABC television series *Desperate Housewives.*" Journalists at WABC-TV in New York noted the station had "reported" on magician David Blaine's Manhattan underwater-living stunt each of the eight nights leading up to an ABC primetime special in which he re-surfaced. ABC Network Radio staffers were "instructed to write about" betting on the National Spelling Bee, coincidentally airing on ABC that week.

➤ The WGA–E survey also found accounts of parent company tie-ins at CBS, where respondents "took particular exception to the requirement that they regularly write interviews with the previous night's *Survivor* or *Amazing Race* loser, stories about the 'real-life missing person' featured on that Sunday's episode of *Without a Trace*, and numerous feature stories incorporating syndicated daytime talk show host Dr. Phil."

➤ *Buried in the Bitter Waters: The Hidden History of Racial Cleansing in America*, a 2007 book by Cox Newspapers reporter Elliot Jaspin, expanded on "Leave or Die," Jaspin's remarkable 2006 series on racial cleansing in fourteen American counties in Texas, Missouri, Indiana, and Georgia. In the book, Jaspin describes how "Leave or Die," which ran in Cox and non-Cox papers, came to be spiked in the chain's largest daily, the *Atlanta Journal-Constitution (AJC)*. The decision was especially noteworthy since Forsyth County, featured in the series, is part of the paper's distribution area.

The problem, according to Jaspin (*Creative Loafing*, March 7, 2007): In reporting the terrible history of racial violence against blacks in the early twentieth century, during which many were driven from their homes, the series also noted the Journal-Constitution's record of ignoring and whitewashing that history.

Beyond killing the series locally, recounts Jaspin, *AJC* editors inveighed upon Cox to tone down criticisms of the paper in Cox's reporting, in order to "obscure the Atlanta newspaper's lackadaisical coverage." Behind the scenes, executives went so far as to plan an "anti-marketing" strategy to keep Atlanta readers from even finding out about the series, and Jaspin was forbidden to "proactively mention" the *Journal-Constitution*'s reporting in public discussion.

AJC managing editor Hank Klibanoff doesn't deny Jaspin's charges, but dismisses the reporter as overzealous and "cranky" (*Creative Loafing*, March 7, 2007). As for whether the paper was unfairly portrayed, however, Jaspin's book quotes David Pasztor, who edited "Leave or Die" for Cox's *Austin American-Statesman*:

> Why are [we] pounding on the *Atlanta Journal-Constitution* for being apologists who look at race relations in Forsyth County through rose-colored glasses? The reason we are doing that is because the *Atlanta Journal-Constitution* have been apologists

who look at race relations in Forsyth County through rose-colored glasses. It's just true.

The paper's actions around the series tend to corroborate that.

GOVERNMENT PRESSURE

In March 2007, a Missouri circuit judge ordered two media outlets (the *Kansas City Star* and alternative weekly the *Pitch*) to refrain from publishing print stories about the Board of Public Utilities that were based on a confidential document. The papers were going to report that the power company may have been operating several plants in violation of federal environmental laws. The stories had already been published on each paper's website, so the judge ordered those removed as well, citing the need to protect the utility company from being "irreparably harmed." The decision was later reversed (*Editor & Publisher*, March 6, 2007).

Cases of such direct, specific intervention may be rare, but only because the influence official power exerts on news media is so general and pervasive. Reporters rely on government officials for much of what is considered news, and maintaining friendly relationships with these sources is considered an essential part of the job. Obvious "favors" extended to politicians include the infamous "beat sweeteners"—soft stories full of glowing testimonials from (often unnamed) aides and supporters. But what is it if not a favor when journalists routinely take their cues from official pronouncements—for example, reporting the Bush White House's assertions about Iran's nuclear ambitions with nary a dissenting voice (*FAIR Action Alert*, February 16, 2007)?

Fear of losing access is often cited as the driving force behind such timidity, and there's something to that. Reporters at the Knight Ridder chain stood apart from their mainstream media colleagues for their skeptical analysis of the weapons of mass destruction (WMD) rationale for the Iraq War. The chain was swallowed up by McClatchy Newspapers, but Pentagon officials apparently aren't ready to make up. *Editor & Publisher* reported last year (May 23, 2007) that the bureau's reporters have been barred from the defense secretary's plane for "at least three years" due to their critical coverage of the Pentagon.

➤ The *Lowell Sun* had a novel approach to celebrating the birthday of hometown Rep. Marty Meehan (D-MA): a special section dedicated to the life and good works of Marty Meehan. The section was described by the *Columbia Journalism Review* (March–April 2007) as "56 besotted pages of gushing articles" that also included special advertisements from local businesses and politicians paying tribute to Meehan. Finally, a portion of the ad revenue went to the Marty Meehan Educational Foundation.

➤ The Canadian Broadcast Corporation (CBC) pulled a documentary about the Chinese Falun Gong spiritual movement hours before it was scheduled to air (*New York Times*, November 9, 2007). The CBC didn't exactly say what was objectionable about the report, though they did say that Chinese diplomats in Canada had lobbied them to cancel the airing of *Beyond the Red Wall: The Persecution of Falun Gong*. The *New York Times* quoted some observers who wondered if the CBC's upcoming broadcasts of the Beijing Olympic games could have played a role. One CBC official's comment was: "I'm happy we didn't air it. I'm happy we stepped into the process. In the end, we got the journalism right."

➤ When New York City mayor Michael Bloomberg wanted to garner press attention for his annual State of the City speech, his office decided there was one sure way to get the kind of coverage they'd like: float advance copies of his speech to reporters a day early, on the condition that they not interview potential critics about his proposals.

Reporter Liz Cox Barrett of the *CJR Daily* website (January 18, 2007) found just one local—the *New York Sun* (January 17, 2007)—that filled readers in on the deal, even as they played along. The *Sun* included no analysis or comment from outsiders in their story, but did state that Bloomberg's remarks were "released to reporters on the condition that nobody would be called to comment on them until today."

As for other papers (all January 17, 2007), the *New York Times* indicated only that they were briefed "on the condition of anonymity"; the *New York Post* had it they were "briefed . . . on a background basis" by "an unnamed mayoral aide," while *Newsday* and the *Daily News* simply quoted these unnamed Bloomberg officials.

As Cox Barrett put it: "You can't beat a day's worth of stories in the press highlighting the crowd-pleasing parts of a speech, free of outside analysis or criticism. (Wait, aren't those called press releases?)"

JANINE JACKSON is the program director at Fairness & Accuracy in Raeporting (FAIR) and a frequent contributor to FAIR's magazine, *Extra!* She co-edited *The FAIR Reader: An Extra! Review of Press and Politics in the '90s* (Westview Press), and she co-hosts and produces FAIR's syndicated radio show, *CounterSpin*—a weekly program of media criticism airing on more than 150 stations around the country. Jackson has testified to the Senate Communications Subcommittee on budget reauthorization for the Corporation for Public Broadcasting. She has appeared on ABC's *Nightline*, CNBC's *Inside Business*, and CNN's *Headline News*, among other outlets.

PETER HART is the activism director at FAIR. He writes for FAIR's magazine, *Extra!*, and is also a co-host and producer of FAIR's syndicated radio show, *CounterSpin*. He is the author of *The Oh Really? Factor: Unspinning FOX News Channel's Bill O'Reilly* (Seven Stories Press, 2003). Hart has been interviewed by a number of media outlets, including NBC's *Nightly News*, FOX News Channel's *O'Reilly Factor*, the *Los Angeles Times*, *Newsday*, and the Associated Press. He has also appeared on Showtime and in the movie *Outfoxed*.

Reprinted from *Extra!* March/April 2008, Fairness & Accuracy In Reporting (FAIR), http://www.fair.org.

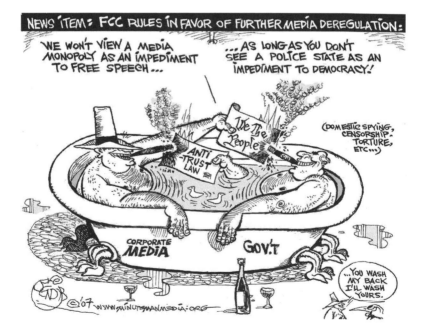

CHAPTER 10

Index on Censorship 2007–08

by Padraig Reidy

One can build up a dispassionate picture of the big issues in freedom of expression by citing the most frequently tagged categories on the Index on Censorship website (www.indexoncensorship.org). Top? "Media" and "journalist," which make sense, as the mission of Index on Censorship is to campaign for the rights of journalists and free media. After that? "Terrorism."

Here in the United Kingdom, where Index on Censorship is based, prevention of terrorism, and the somewhat vague concept "extremism" have been cited as the motivating factors in a string of dubious convictions and attempted convictions. Unfortunately, the fragmented, nebulous nature of the perceived threat to national security has led to the introduction of new measures that are, at best, panicked, and at worst, mendacious.

In December 2007, Index reported on the case of Samina Malik, a young Muslim woman who worked at Heathrow Airport. Malik, portrayed in the newspapers as the "lyrical terrorist"—her own nom de plume in Internet chat rooms—was convicted of having materials "likely to be of use to a terrorist." The materials in question were all widely available on the Internet, and none were illegal—in fact, some were downloaded from US government websites. Interestingly, the judge in Malik's case, in handing down the verdict, acknowledged that "The Terrorism Act and the restriction it imposes on personal freedom exists to protect this country. . . . Its protections embrace us all . . . its restrictions apply to us all, regardless of political or religious conviction."

Malik received a suspended sentence and is awaiting the results of an appeal at the time of this writing. But the broader media response was notable: rather than view Malik as a dangerous jihadist, most saw this woman of twenty-three, who looked even younger, as a misguided young girl.

In February 2008, five students convicted of holding materials for terrorist purposes had their convictions quashed. Like Malik, the young men had downloaded various materials from the Internet and had expressed admiration for jihadis in chat rooms and forums. Also like Malik, this was as far as they had gone: there was no definite plan, merely a shared, admittedly sinister, interest. The youngest of the group had written a letter to his parents expressing his wish to become a holy warrior before setting out from London to Bradford, in the north of England, to meet his Internet associates. But there was no plan after that.

As Index editor Jo Glanville noted at the time: "[The] judgment breaks the link (which until now has gone virtually unquestioned) between extremism and terrorism. The Internet is seen as the hub of extremist activity—an underworld of activity that must be controlled. Jihadi material is viewed as such a toxic force that viewing it—'possessing' it—has become a criminal act. The Court of Appeal has poured cold water on these assumptions and demanded a much more rigorous, restricted interpretation of the law. The public response to the Samina Malik case last year marked the first shift in attitude towards extremist literature and any connection with terrorism. The Court of Appeal has now fundamentally called into question the application of the law."

The law in question is the 2000 Terrorism Act, specifically Sections 57 and 58, which concern possession and dissemination of materials "likely to be of use to a terrorist"—materials never defined beyond that. Considering the vast amount of materials available on the Internet for the mildly curious mind, it's not difficult to see how one could find one's self in trouble.

It is not just those suspected of extremism who have found themselves the subject of police attention. Spring 2008 saw the Greater Manchester police pursue a broad range of media, searching for journalistic materials related to self-confessed ex-Islamic extremist Hassan Butt. Police investigated the BBC's flagship current affairs program, *Newsnight*, along with the *Sunday Times* and the intellectual monthly magazine *Prospect*. But the police's main target was freelance journalist Shiv Malik. Malik, who had been writing a book with Butt, bravely stood by his commitment to protect sources and was backed in his efforts by Index on Censorship, English PEN, and, most importantly, the National Union of Journalists, which provided a fighting fund for the young reporter.

In September 2007, Index reported a story that appeared to go unnoticed in the UK. Esteemed academic publishers Cambridge University

Press had pulped all copies of a book, *Alms for Jihad*, after threats of libel from Saudi billionaire Khalid bin Mahfouz. Bin Mahfouz claimed that the book linked him to funding for jihadism. Cambridge University Press (CUP), mindful of Britain's unsympathetic libel laws, immediately backed down, without even attempting to defend the book or its authors, Americans Robert O. Collins and J. Millard Burr. In fact, CUP's intellectual property director went so far in his apology as to describe the claims in the book as "entirely and manifestly false." Collins was, understandably, upset about this, telling Index that CUP's lawyers had "spent a month in 2005 vetting the book."

Publishers were not the only ones afraid to discuss the issue. Apart from political magazine *Private Eye*, and the trade publication *Bookseller*, which reproduced Index's article on its website, not a single national publication even mentioned the story of Khalid bin Mahfouz. Indeed, one national newspaper journalist told Index that he twice attempted to write about the case in his weekly column, and twice the "offending" paragraphs were removed from his copy by fearful editors acting on the advice of their lawyers.

Good research and reporting are vital in the age we live in, and restrictive laws on what we can read or write will only serve to leave us dangerously ignorant of the myriad facets of the War on Terror.

GLOBAL UPDATES ON CENSORSHIP AND FREEDOM OF MEDIA

Afghanistan

On January 23, Sayed Parvez Kambakhsh of *Jahan-e Naw* was sentenced to death for distributing blasphemous material. He had been arrested the previous October for downloading an article that addressed the role of women in Islamic societies. It is widely believed that the charges against Kambaksh were an attempt to stop his brother Yuqub Ebrahimi from reporting for his employer, the Institute of War and Peace. (BBC, CPJ)

Armenia

Protests following the disputed presidential election were subject to a virtual blackout by state-run media. Protests began peacefully on February 20, but on March 1, police dispersed the crowds, firing shots into the air and using tear gas. At least eight people were killed and dozens injured. The government established a state of emergency, blocking central streets with tanks, and imposing severe restrictions on the media, ordering that only state-provided information be used in reports. Restrictions on freedom of movement and assembly were also implemented (*International Herald Tribune*).

Azerbaijan

Ilgar Nasibov, a journalist for Radio Free Europe/Radio Liberty, was released from prison on December 10, four days after he was sentenced to ninety days' imprisonment for defamation of the Nakhchivan city police chief in an e-mail to President Ilham Aliyev. The e-mail appealed to the president to address the harassment of journalists by the city's police. Nasibov was also handed down a one-year suspended sentence in response to separate charges of defaming a university official and university employees in a newspaper article he claims he did not write. Nasibov was the tenth journalist imprisoned in the country in 2007 (CPJ, RFE/RL).

Belarus

On August 22, police interrupted a performance of *Eleven Vests* by Edward Bond. Armed officers raided the Free Theatre, located in the Minsk suburbs, and arrested fifty people, including the performers and audience. They were released three hours later (*Guardian*).

Burma

Japanese news photographer Kenji Nagai was killed on September 27, after security forces opened fire on protesters in the center of Rangoon. Nagai worked for the Japanese photo and video agency APF and had been in the country for two days. On September 30, Japan's deputy foreign minister arrived in Burma to investigate the death, resulting in speculation over the future of Japan's role as a major donor to the country (BBC, RSF).

Chad

In October, authorities declared a state of emergency in three regions in the north and east of the country following clashes between rival ethnic groups. The state of emergency was ordered for twelve days after a special cabinet meeting, and included a blanket suppression of media across the country (AllAfrica.com).

China

On April 3, human rights activist Hu Jia was sentenced to three and a half years' imprisonment. The previous December 27, the day of Hu's arrest, police raided his house and disconnected his phone and Internet. He was accused of "subverting state authority," partly because of his participation in European parliamentary discussions on the country's human rights situation (RSF).

Colombia

Throughout August, there were numerous reports of threats made against television and radio broadcasters. During the first week, a faction of the guerrilla group FARC told media outlets in Arauca that if they didn't agree to broadcast the contents of a pamphlet, they would become a target for violence. Two radio stations broadcast the propaganda, stating that they had been pressured into doing so, but Álvaro Pérez García, director of Meridiano 70 radio station, refused (IPYS).

Cuba

Six journalists were among approximately thirty people detained on September 27 at the Justice Ministry in Havana following a protest in support of political prisoners. The six journalists—freelancer Idania Yanes Contreras; Roberto de Jesús Guerra Pérez, correspondent for the websites Payolibre and Nueva Prensa Cubana, and Radio Martí; Alvaro Yero Felipe and Belinda Salas Tapanes, of Agencia Libre Asociada (ALAS); and Yoel Espinosa Medrano and Felix Reyes Gutierrez, of the independent news agency Cubanacán Press—were released the next day. People who joined the demonstrations in front of the ministry and in front of Cubanacán's offices in Havana were also detained (RSF).

Denmark

On February 12, police arrested three people suspected of planning an attack on cartoonist Kurt Westergaard. Westergaard's caricatures of the

Prophet Mohammed, published in September 2005, sparked world-wide protests. He and his wife were under police protection for three months prior to the arrests (BBC, *New York Times*).

Egypt

The editors of fifteen opposition and privately owned newspapers agreed not to publish on October 7 in order to protest government harassment of the press. The decision came in the run-up to the trial of Ibrahim Issa, editor of *al Dustour*, who prosecutors claim undermined national security by printing stories alleging the president was in poor health. Issa's trial, which was due to take place on December 5, was postponed (BBC).

France

Investigative journalist Guillaume Dasquié, the founder and editor of the news website geopolitique.com, was under investigation for compromising state secrets and faced five years' imprisonment and a 75,000-euro fine if convicted. The Directorate for Territorial Surveillance (DST) carried out a five-hour search of Dasquié's Paris home on December 5, before taking the journalist into custody for forty-eight hours. On December 6, the investigating magistrate filed preliminary charges. Although the confidentiality of sources is protected under Article 109 of the penal code, Dasquié was pressured to reveal his sources and was investigated for divulging classified information from the General Directorate for External Security (DGSE) in an article in *Le Monde* the previous April 17. According to the article, French intelligence services had alerted their US counterparts as early as January 2001 to a hijacking plan by al-Qaeda. An unnamed DGSE agent was also questioned under caution (CPJ, *Le Monde*, *Le Nouvel Observateur*, RSF).

India

Protests in Calcutta followed the publication of an open letter that discussed the case of Taslima Nasreen and allegedly insulted Islam. The *Bengali Patho-Sanket* magazine initially published the article, but protests were staged only after the story reached a wider audience in an Urdu daily on November 7. On November 9, the state government ordered the seizure and ban on distribution of all copies of the original article (*Asian Age*).

Indonesia

On November 16, Australian coroner Dorelle Pinch issued a report detailing the findings of an inquest that found the Indonesian army responsible for the 1975 killings of five British, Australian, and New Zealander journalists in East Timor. The report determined that the journalists were not incidental casualties of war, but were deliberately captured and executed to prevent information from being released about the army's conduct in East Timor. The Indonesian government has dismissed the findings (RSF).

Iran

American academics Haleh Esfandiari and Kian Tajbakhsh were released on bail on August 21 and September 20, respectively. Interviews with the Iranian-American academics were broadcast on July 18 as part of a documentary that argued they were involved in a US plot to overthrow the government. Both were detained for spying and endangering national security (AP, BBC, Index [March 2007]).

Iraq

On February 27, Shihab Al Tamimi, the president of the Iraqi Journalists Union, died from wounds sustained in a gun attack. He was shot on February 23 as he left a meeting in a cultural center near the Turkish embassy in the north Baghdad district of al Waziria (RSF).

Ireland

Eleven journalists were arrested in Donegal on March 16, as part of an investigation into paramilitary activity. Among them were BBC journalists, who were working on a current affairs report on Northern Ireland. All were arrested under the Offences Against the State Act (Reuters).

Israel

Following air strikes in Syria on September 6, the military censor ordered a media blackout on the incident, instructing press to forward all relevant articles to its offices. Media workers risked charges and imprisonment if they violated the ruling, and foreign news organizations were permitted to operate within the country only under the agreement that they abide by the emergency rules. The ban was lifted on October 2 (*Guardian, New York Times, Telegraph*).

Italy

The Pope cancelled a planned speech inaugurating the new academic year at La Sapienza University in Rome on January 17, following protests from students and academics over controversial remarks he had made in 1990 when he was then Cardinal Ratzinger.. In charge of Catholic doctrine, Ratzinger had condoned Galileo's 1633 conviction for heresy, describing the verdict as "rational and just" (BBC).

Kenya

It was reported on January 22 that during the run-up to the December 27 elections, vernacular radio stations broadcast hate speech. Broadcasts referred to communities as "baboons," "weeds," or "animals of the West" and were said to be a contributing factor to the ethnic cleansing that occurred in late December and early January. On January 14, the government ordered an investigation into the claims (AllAfrica.com, BBC).

Kosovo

Vesna Bojicis, correspondent for the Serbian-language service of Voice of America (VOA) radio, was attacked by an unidentified assailant on October 16. The masked attacker forced his way into her apartment in the village of Caglavica, and beat and threatened to kill her because of her reporting. He reportedly accused Bojicis of a "bias in favour of Albanians" and threatened to abduct her child if she did not stop her work for VOA. Bojicis has worked for VOA for seven years and says she will continue (CPJ).

Kyrgyzstan

Alisher Saipov, an ethnic Uzbek journalist, a reporter for Voice of America radio, and an editor of Uzbek-language newspaper *Siyosat*, was shot dead on October 24. The twenty-six-year-old wrote about torture in Uzbek prisons and the plight of Uzbek refugees living in Kyrgyzstan. He was also openly critical of the Kyrgyz authorities. Two days before he was killed, Saipov told friends he thought he was being followed by Uzbek security services (BBC).

Malaysia

On November 13, the Internal Security Ministry banned seven books, including *The Muslim Jesus*, saying they could potentially cause offense and anxiety amongst the country's large Muslim population (*Star*).

Mexico

As reported on November 29, the Supreme Court ruled that Lydia Cacho had suffered "no serious violation of her individual rights" following her arrest and detention in 2005 on the orders of the Puebla state governor. Cacho received threats following the publication of a book linking prominent citizens, including businessman Kemal Necif, to a pedophile ring. The case commanded widespread public interest after tapes were leaked to the media featuring Governor Mario Marin and Necif laughing about Cacho's detention and joking about paying someone to rape her while in prison (RSF, *Washington Post*).

Morocco

Fouad Mourtada was jailed on February 5 for creating a fake Facebook profile of the king's brother. Upon his arrest, Mourtada was sentenced to three years' imprisonment for insulting the royal family. He was released on March 19, after receiving a royal pardon prior to a holiday marking the birth of the Prophet Mohammed, a traditional date for pardons (BBC, Global Voices, RSF).

Nepal

During late September and early October, the Kantipur press group, publisher of the *Kantipur* and *Kathmandu Post* daily newspapers, was the subject of violent attacks. On September 30, members of the Maoist-affiliated All Nepal Communication, Printing and Publications Workers' Union (ANCPPWU) sabotaged electrical installations at the press group's printing press and vandalized the car of the group's managing director. On October 1, Shalik Ram Jamkatel, a Maoist member of the interim parliament, gave a speech in which he threatened to kidnap a Kantipur executive and to attack the group's TV station, Kantipur

Television. That same day, Maoist activists burned hundreds of copies of regional editions of the dailies in Bharatpur and Biratnagar. Over 2,000 copies were torched in Pokhara (RSF).

Pakistan

Over 180 journalists in Karachi were jailed on November 20 for protesting against the state of emergency and crackdown on the media (CPJ).

Palestine

Alan Johnston was released to Hamas officials on July 4, after 114 days in captivity. Johnston was captured on March 12 by the Army of Islam (BBC, Index 3/2007).

Paraguay

Radio reporter Tito Alberto Palma was shot to death on August 22 in Mayor Otano. Palma was a reporter for the local radio station and a correspondent for the Asuncion-based Radio Chaco Boreal (CPJ).

Philippines

Up to fifty media workers were arrested and detained after a failed coup attempt in Manila on November 29. Journalists were covering the standoff at the Peninsula Manila Hotel, between government forces and a group led by Senator Antonio Trillanes IV and Brigadier General Danilo Lim. The standoff took place after a walkout from Trillanes's trial for his role in the failed 2003 rebellion. After the rebels surrendered, government troops confiscated video footage of the siege and are said to have harassed reporters and their news crews. Those arrested on November 29 included eleven people from ABS-CBN News. One official explanation for the arrests was that it prevented the escape of soldiers involved in the coup attempt, who were believed to be disguising themselves as journalists, but journalist associations condemned the statement. The Philippine National Police issued an apology to media representatives and crews, but maintains that their actions were necessary (Seapa).

Russia

It was reported on January 10 that the Vladimir regional prosecutor's office opened a criminal case against local television station TV-6 Vladimir. The lawsuit was filed following accusations that news reporter Sergei Golovinov insulted President Putin during his coverage of a rally on November 30. The station's staff were not charged, but if convicted under Article 319, which relates to insults to public officials, they could face up to one year of "corrective labour" (CPJ).

Somalia

The head of the Shabelle press group, Bashir Nur Gedi, was shot dead by unknown attackers on October 19. News editor Isse Abdullahi Mohammed, station manager Abdi Farah Jama Mire, and producer Mohammad Dahir Yusuf, all of Radio Garowe, were arrested on October 19. Mire and Yusef were later released; Mohammed was released the next day. Radio Garowe was shut down for twenty-four hours (AllAfrica.com).

South Africa

On July 23, a gang of three people shot Abel Matsakani in Johannesburg. Matsakani is editor of ZimOnline, an independent online news agency operating from the city, and former managing editor of the *Daily News*, banned in Zimbabwe in 2003 (AllAfrica.com, *Guardian*).

Sri Lanka

On the night of January 29, two armed people entered the house of Duleep Dushantha, a media worker at the state-owned Sri Lanka Rupavahini Corporation (SLRC). Dushantha had been highly critical of the government minister who assaulted the news director at the SLRC offices the month before, on December 27. He was not home at the time but the intruders threatened his mother with death if she reported the incident to the police. On the night of January 25, Hemantha Mawalage, a news producer who condemned the minister's actions on behalf of the SLRC staff, was stabbed and required extensive medical treatment (FMM).

Tunisia

Sihem Bensedrine and her husband Omar Mestiri were seized by customs officials upon their arrival at la Goulette port on March 3. Bensedrine is president of the Working Group on Press Freedom in North Africa and Mestiri is managing editor of the newspaper *Kalima*. The two were detained for six hours and assaulted by police. Authorities also seized and copied the hard disks of their laptops without providing a docket for the confiscated property as the law requires (RSF).

Turkey

In June 2007, employees of the newspaper *AGOS*, including Arat Dink, the son of the paper's former editor, Hrant Dink, were in court for "insulting Turkish identity." The prosecution followed the reprint in *AGOS* of an interview in which Dink referred to the 1915 Armenian genocide (RSF).

United Kingdom

On July 26, four men were jailed for their involvement in the protests outside the Danish embassy in London in February 2006. They were protesting against Danish cartoons depicting the Prophet Mohammed. Mizanur Rahman, Umran Javed, and Abdul Mahid were jailed for six years for soliciting murder. Abdul Saleem was jailed for four years for stirring up racial hatred (BBC).

United States

Chauncey Bailey, editor of the weekly newspaper the *Oakland Post*, was shot and killed on August 2 in the city's downtown area. His murder was connected to his reports on gang violence and corruption (CPJ, *San Francisco Chronicle*).

Uzbekistan

Russian-language religious news website portal-credu.ru was blocked in March 2007, joining the list of websites blocked by authorities. Internet companies blame the state-run Uznet, through which all Internet service providers have to connect to the Internet, but Uznet claims the National Security Service is responsible (Forum 18).

Venezuela

On May 28, President Hugo Chávez stopped the broadcast of Radio Caracas TV after it was refused a license. It was replaced by a state-run station on the same day. Chávez also accused Globovision television of calling for his murder and filed a lawsuit against CNN for allegedly linking him to al-Qaeda (BBC, RSF).

Zimbabwe

President Robert Mugabe signed into law the Interception of Communications Act on August 3. The law entitles government authorities to intercept all phone calls, e-mails, and faxes on grounds of protecting national security (RSF).

PADRAIG REIDY is the news editor for the Index on Censorship, London, England.

CHAPTER II

Truth Emergency Meets Media Reform

by Peter Phillips, Mickey S. Huff, Carmela Rocha, Andrew Hobbs,
April Pearce, Kat Pat Crespán, Nelson Calderon, and David Kubiak

> Reformers who are always compromising, have not yet grasped
> the idea that truth is the only safe ground to stand upon.

—Elizabeth Cady Stanton

In the United States today, the rift between reality and reporting has
reached its end. There is no longer a mere credibility gap, but rather a
literal truth emergency. Americans cannot access the truth about the
issues that most impact their lives by relying on the mainstream corporate media. This truth emergency is a culmination of the failures of
the fourth estate to act as a truly free press. Our truth emergency exists
not only as a result of phony elections, illegal preemptive wars, torture
camps, and doctored intelligence, but also around issues that intimately
impact our lives at home, from healthcare to education. Further, most
Americans have been faced with a thirty-five-year decline in real wages,
while the top 10 percent now enjoy unparalleled wealth with strikingly
low tax burdens, and some 50 million Americans lack healthcare resulting in the deaths of 18,000 people a year. These truths are a wake up
call to all citizens.

Many economists now doubt that government measures can prevent a major recession given the continuing slump in the housing
market, the subprime mortgage crisis, and the greater humanitarian
costs of growing unemployment, declining consumer spending, and
record-high oil prices. Even harder times for working people are
undoubtedly at hand, yet mainstream corporate media continues to lavish more attention on the Super Bowl and celebrity misadventures than
measures to protect Americans from grave personal economic harm.
We are spun, mislead, propagandized, and amused to death by our
media conglomerates. As a result the US has become the best enter-
tained and least informed society in the world (Postman, 1985).

Now, however, a growing number of activists are finally saying "enough!" and joining forces to address this truth emergency by developing new journalistic systems and practices of their own. They are working to reveal the common corporate denominators behind the diverse crises we face and to develop networks of trustworthy news sources that tell the people what's really going on. These activists know we need journalism that moves beyond forensic inquiries into particular crimes and atrocities to expose wider patterns of corruption, propaganda, and illicit political control.

Truth exposed can arouse a nation to reject a malignant corporate status quo. American investigative journalist George Seldes once said, "Journalism's job is not impartial 'balanced' reporting. Journalism's job is to tell the people what is really going on."

Millions of Americans engaged in various social justice issues constantly witness how corporate media marginalize, denigrate, or simply ignores their concerns. Activist groups working on issues like 9/11 truth, election fraud, impeachment, war propaganda, civil liberties, and torture, and many corporate-caused environmental crises have been systematically excluded from mainstream news outlets and the national conversation in the country as a whole.

The Truth Emergency Movement held its first national strategy summit in Santa Cruz, California from January 25 to 27, 2008 (see the website at http://truthemergency.us). Further representation was present at the National Conference for Media Reform in Minneapolis, Minnesota, in early June 2008.

At the Santa Cruz Summit, organizers gathered key media constituencies to devise coherent decentralized models for distribution of suppressed news, synergistic truth-telling, and collaborative strategies to disclose, legitimize, and popularize deeper historical narratives on power and inequality in the US.

During the Minneapolis conference, a sociological survey was conducted to better assess media democracy activists' understandings and expectations of truth seeking in the US.

The truth movement is seeking to discover, in this moment of Constitutional crisis, ecological peril, and widening war, ways in which top investigative journalists, whistle-blowers, and independent media activists can transform how Americans perceive and defend their world.

META-NARRATIVES/UNDERSTANDINGS FROM THE
SANTA CRUZ TRUTH EMERGENCY CONFERENCE

At the Santa Cruz conference, a process was employed to bring the opinions, goals, and needs of all the 300-plus individual attendees together for purposes of comparison.

Individuals were asked to summarize their feelings and thoughts, discuss them with fellow panelists, and submit them to a central area for organization. Participants quickly discovered tremendous synergies in their desires, as shape and form began to emerge out of the once scattered statements. These meta-narratives (defined by the social science dictionary as a story, narrative or theory which claims to be above the ordinary or local accounts of social life) are outlined below. The narratives include some of the key quotes that helped to form them. These statements are collective understandings from over 300 activists framed into core areas. They do not represent a permanent manifesto, but rather a working document from the voices of the people.

Vox Populi: The Voice of the People

Undemocratic media is a form of mind control for the powerful. The greater the distance between the media and the people it supposedly serves, the weaker the democracy. We extolled the virtue of cooperation in media—"unity to get out the truth." "We need to rethink the institutions which control our lives," pushing society past the entertainment, material-centered existence which modern commercial media has sold us. We must "provide an immune response to the virus/cancer of corporate control" and reform the media so that it has its own safeguards, from the inside, against the decline of truth.

Mindfulness: Personal and Community

Mindfulness is the interdependence, interconnectedness, of the issues and the people. We honor the power of dialogue, listening, and collaborative active work. We must find and get to know others. A powerful force exists within each of us: an ability to choose and consider at each point in our lives the greater impact of our decisions. Mindfulness has been promoted in almost every culture in the world, and the truth movement seems to be no exception.

Democratic Renaissance

The system, including the FCC, media, elections, and the economy, must work for the people. Responsibility for change lies with the electorate. The US, as a democracy, should always act and fight for the common good.

The people must continually act instead of waiting for others to do so, or for politicians to solve our problems. Threats to liberty are constantly unfolding, so the activist culture must always be leading the fight. We must "put truth back on the table," as truth is the foundation on which progress and mindfulness will be built. "Now is the opportunity through shared public grassroots efforts to create/articulate, public/shared, social/personal, positive change through humor and mutual respect."

New Media Solutions: From the Ground Up

There would be no truth emergency had the media, ostensibly set up to profit from public awareness, not become that which it used to deplore: a mouthpiece for corporate and political interests. New ways to address this deficiency are being explored by independent news outlets all over the world, from pamphlet publishers handing out leaflets to individuals building new news sources.

The Internet has been a strong tool for this expansion, but still does not reach a broad enough audience to be a complete solution.

Foremost, we call for the "visibility of independent media, reporting reality, truth, [and] factual issues." We need the media to be a gadfly and to give positive credit where it is due, so that it will encourage people to do the right thing, not just to avoid disgrace.

We hope for "standards and training for truthful journalism," a journalism dependent on the benefits of collaboration. We require the "FCC to serve the public better" rather than serving the goals of the highest bidder in its bandwidth auctions. The FCC's secret preservation of competitive advantage is antithetical to the needs of the people. The people should not have to be at the right place at the right time to receive accurate news from competing sources.

We cry for "progressive collaboration—tell [the] truth to all citizens," as there is but "one planet, one people, one future." Indeed, global awareness to the greater effects of our actions and choices may be a powerful catalyst for worldwide progress.

We challenge the global elite "built on domination, greed and alienation by long standing groups who maintain secrecy, control and the preponderance of wealth."

We must reframe existing narratives and myths and tell the truth from the bottom up by engaging our collective voice.

Environmental Interests: Not Any One of Ours

The ecological reality of the planet essentially frames the future: we have one Earth, and it is apparently undergoing serious changes due to our ignorance and hubris. Whereas the long-term effects of our environmental wastefulness may never be known, most individuals seem to know precisely where to point the finger: unregulated capitalism (profit motive) is killing the earth and all life. The "life vs. profit" struggle calls for regulations to prevent massive abridgments in responsibility as to make money a life or death decision. We recognize an undeniable truth, that "we are reaching ecological limits." "We are all one human family," and our species' success rises and falls on the backs of each other. Americans must see that our position of luxury is in fact a burden to others in less advantaged situations.

Economic Evolution: Quality not Quantity

The consolidation of media and business has not escaped the watchful eyes of the Truth Movement. Visualizing the idea that profit-seeking institutions will generally have similar interests goes a long way to understanding the insidious nature of media consolidation. "Consolidation of wealth and power (including media) keeps the general public from knowing and accessing the truth."

We must "eliminate corporate dominance," especially that one particularly vicious relationship between lawmakers and profiteers. Referencing the founding fathers' concerns about religion, we ask for the "separation of corporations and government."

Imperialism is unacceptable coming from America. "The empire is in us; we have to get it out."

By continuing to participate in the great resource and money grab—by not actively refusing the coercive forces of corporate society, by continuing to buy filthy goods and crooked services, and by filling our cars with gas and bellies with corn and beef, we live the empire. Only by refusing to participate in the grab will the empire fail, and be replaced by democratic liberty and opportunity. "Empire [is] not geography, [but] a process internalized!"

Change: Ours for the Taking

"If the New World Order is so great, why don't they share the plan?" "The world is a dangerous place: we can feel it." "We need to counter the corporate political party's meta-narrative, that what is good for corporations is good for America—trust us!"

"We must reach and motivate folks to talk about the need to decide how we spend our national money."

Consider Radical Ideas: For Radical Times

"The US is too large and diverse to have such an overpowering federal government."

We must "march away from Washington." We must build and expand the perspective that what we are facing is the elite engaging in class warfare from the top down. We must take over media power to tell the truth. The oligarch will not relax his tenuous grip voluntarily.

ACTION STEPS

On the final day of the Truth Emergency Conference in January 2008, participants entered into action teams to formulate specific ideas for truth actions needed in the US.

Key Action Steps included:

➤ Take back the media.
➤ Reform our national media policy.
➤ Build a spiritual component into the Truth Movement.
➤ Reduce consumerism by knowing the four Rs—Reduce, Reuse, Recycle, and Rot.
➤ Support a consciousness around the terms we use for the Truth Movement.

We will also build a truth emergency website that publishes news feeds from trustworthy, dependable noncorporate sources, providing the kind daily news that is adequate for anyone in a democratic society. Plenty of truth sites already exist on the Internet, and we need to figure out which of those sites are consistently the most trustworthy/truthful sites. From there, we will formulate an Internet-based news service that pulls the best of the truth sites into one comprehensive service for daily news. The goal is to move from the corporate top-down daily news sources going to most people, to on-site, grassroots-supported, and self-generated bottom up news sources. We'll publish that which encourages our spirituality, non-consumerist behaviors, democratic knowledge, mindfulness, self-actualization, diversity, and social justice and equality.

SUMMARY FROM SANTA CRUZ

It is amazing what more than 300 truth emergency activists can do in three days. We were able to study numerous political perspectives, serious truth issues, and varying levels of spiritual and activist sentimentalities, ultimately reaching an understanding of the importance of a Truth Emergency movement. The statements include philosophical, spiritual, and practical levels of understanding that were generated from a broad selection of people from all over the US and several countries.

TRUTH EMERGENCY POLLS THE
MEDIA REFORM CONFERENCE

During the 2008 National Conference for Media Reform (NCMR) in Minneapolis, Project Censored interns conducted a sociological survey designed to gauge conference participants' thoughts on the status quo of the news media as well as the truthfulness of corporate media news. The survey also sought to determine the level of belief and support in a truth emergency in the US and the varying degrees of support for key truth issues.

Project Censored researchers looked to NCMR 2008 as an opportunity to explore media democracy activists' feelings concerning the corporate media's systematic failure to support full disclosure on important key issues in society.

This survey was completed by 376 randomly selected NCMR attendees out of the 3,500 people registered for the conference. The survey has a statistical accuracy of plus or minus 5 percent at a 95 percent confidence interval. The survey instrument used is included below.

For discussion purposes, questions are grouped by their intention and reviewed in the context of other similar questions. They are numbered as they were on the survey form on the table of results below.

Strong support was shown for the premise of a truth emergency in the US. We asked: Has corporate media failed to keep the American people informed on important issues facing the nation? Does a truth emergency exist in the US?

The response was staggering. Ninety-nine percent strongly agreed, or agreed with the first question, and only 7 percent of responders disagreed with the characterization of current events as a truth emergency. This indicates to us that the attendees at the NCMR strongly believe in the failure of corporate media and support the idea that a truth emergency exists in the US, and that every possible avenue should be investigated to bring access to truth and fair reporting.

Truth emergency addresses a number of issues that most directly threaten democracy. Further surveys conducted within the truth emergency context may focus on other subjects such as undocumented workers, health insurance profiteering, mortgage officer impropriety, judicial and executive malfeasance, energy policy corruption, and other hot-button topics.

Questions 7–12 in the initial survey addressed several truth emergency topics. Participants were asked to state whether they strongly agreed, agreed, felt neutral, disagreed, or strongly disagreed with the following statements:

7. Unanswered questions regarding 9/11 are an important truth emergency issue in the US.

8. Discovering the truth about the reasons the Bush administration decided to invade Iraq is an important truth emergency issue in the US.

9. Investigating allegations of election fraud in the 2000 and 2004 presidential elections is an important truth emergency issue in the US.

10. Addressing torture by US officials as a violation of basic human rights is an important truth emergency issue in the US.

11. Full healthcare for all residences of the US is a vital truth emergency issue.

12. Who profits from the increasing cost of gasoline is a vital truth emergency issue in the US.

Response varied a little more on this panel of issues. Torture (question 10) received the most widespread condemnation, with 98 percent of respondents agreeing that its use constitutes a truth emergency. Ninety percent of the NCMR participants agreed with the statements on healthcare concern, election fraud, gas pricing, and Iraq lies. The 9/11 question was the most polarizing, drawing the lowest overall agreement and the most negative responses. However, over 79 percent of the responders strongly agree or agreed that unanswered questions on 9/11 constitute part of a truth emergency in the US.

Movement strategy questions showed strong understanding and support from the media democracy crowd as well. They included:

3. A media democracy movement is occurring in the US that specifically supports the expansion and development of independent media from the bottom up. (Ninety-one percent of the participants chose Strongly Agree or Agree.)

4. Reform of the FCC and changing of laws to break up concentrated corporate media in the US is an important strategy for the media democracy movement. (Ninety-five percent of the participants chose Strongly Agree or Agree.)

5. The media democracy movement can have both a reform segment and an activist independent media segment. (Eighty-nine percent of the participants chose Strongly Agree or Agree.)

6. The media democracy movement should focus on using the Internet to build independent news sources. (Eighty-three percent of the participants choose Strongly Agree or Agree.)

14. A truth emergency exists in the US and can best be addressed by deep investigative research done by independent media. (Ninety-three percent of the participants chose Strongly Agree or Agree.)

Discovering the most effective ways to chisel at the bulwark of corrupt corporate media will require continued thought and effort. It is clear from our survey that media democracy activists strongly support the continuing development of independent media combined with aggressive reform efforts as part of an overall media democracy movement. Activists also believe that both reform and grassroots independent media efforts will take on the truth emergency theme and work together to conduct investigative research into critical social justice issues. One activist said, "We cannot be afraid; democracy is in the balance."

While we recognize that this survey was done at an independent media activist "reform" conference, where a high level of agreement on the questions was expected, we were amazed at the total agreement for grassroots media efforts in addition to reform work.

The overall positive response to our own Project Censored yearbook was heartening and further validates the importance of our annual effort.

Question 15, which asked whether a military-industrial-media complex exists in the US for the promotion of the US military domination of the world, received a 87 percent agreement rating. This result shows that research done by Project Censored (*Censored 2006*) about the US government, the US media, and the national policy structure is widely accepted by participants at the NCMR.

SURVEY RESULTS: TRUSTED NEWS SOURCES

A valuable resource generated by the NCMR 2008 survey was a list of participants' most trusted new sources. Survey takers were asked to list their five most trustworthy/truthful news sources. These sources were tabulated for frequency.

Number of participants=376

Democracy Now!	119
The Nation	44
BBC	43
NPR	43
Common Dreams	34
Bill Moyers	26

PBS	22
Truthout.org	22
The New York Times	20
Alternet	15
Huffington Post	15
The Daily Show	15
Mother Jones	13
FAIR	12
Freepress.net	12
The Guardian (UK)	12
The Progressive	12
Air America	11
Daily Kos	10
The Colbert Report	9
FSTV	8
In These Times	7
Keith Olbermann	7
Al Jazeera	6
CNN	6
Indymedia.org	6
Truthdig.com	6
Z Magazine	6

The continuing agenda for the Truth Emergency Movement will be to expand our findings on trustworthy/truthful news sites from Minneapolis (June 2008) and from our listings in Santa Cruz (January 2008) into a full source list, which will ultimately lead to a comprehensive web-based source of noncorporate daily news that can be used by Internet readers and downloaded by independent newspapers, radio stations, and activist organizations for secondary distribution worldwide. Much work is needed before trustworthy, truthful news will be fully accessible. However, the agenda is clearly set for further action.

The media conferences organized by Free Press have been an outstanding effort to push media reform lobbying efforts in the US. Undoubtedly these efforts on Internet neutrality, media consolidation, and FCC rule-making have had some significant successes. Our survey shows that the 3,500 participants at the NCMR in Minneapolis in June 2008 strongly support these efforts.

However, efforts by the Santa Cruz Truth Emergency Conference organizers to hold an informational panel in Minneapolis were denied by Free Press. While this may well have been due to an overwhelming number of proposals for panels at the June conference, it may also have been due to a hesitation to cover some of the truth issues represented among the Santa Cruz Truth Emergency organizers.

Our survey shows that the media reform activists in Minneapolis, in addition to supporting continued development of grassroots media, also strongly support the building of a national Truth Emergency Movement and are not shy at all about finding the truth on key issues that the corporate media is failing to cover. We think that independent media development and the Truth Emergency Movement should be more widely addressed at future media democracy conferences.

Bibliography

Neil Postman, *Amusing Ourselves to Death*, (London: Methuen Publishing Ltd, 1985), 224.

Peter Phillips, Bridget Thornton, and Lew Brown, "The Global Dominance Group and US Corporate Media," in *Censored 2007*, (New York: Seven Stories Press, 2006), 432.

MEDIA REFORM CONFERENCE SURVEY DATA

Number of participants=376

	Strongly Agree	Agree	Neutral	Disagree	Strongly Disagree
1.	328	44	3	1	0
2.	270	72	15	13	6
3.	160	179	29	3	5
4.	289	70	12	4	1
5.	250	87	39	0	0
6.	175	138	54	8	1
7.	194	106	49	23	4
8.	265	81	21	8	1
9.	272	80	21	2	1
10.	314	53	7	2	0
11.	284	69	21	2	0
12.	221	121	27	6	1
13.	211	117	45	3	0
14.	230	121	20	5	0
15.	251	78	38	7	2

SURVEY DATA BY PERCENTAGE

	Strongly Agree	Agree	Neutral	Disagree	Strongly Disagree
1.	87.23%	11.70%	.80%	0.27%	0.00%
2.	71.81%	19.15%	3.99%	3.46%	1.60%
3.	42.55%	47.61%	7.71%	0.80%	1.33%
4.	76.86%	18.62%	3.19%	1.06%	0.27%
5.	66.49%	23.14%	10.37%	0.00%	0.00%
6.	46.54%	36.70%	14.36%	2.13%	0.27%
7.	51.60%	28.19%	13.03%	6.12%	1.06%
8.	70.48%	21.54%	5.59%	2.13%	0.27%
9.	72.34%	21.28%	5.59%	0.53%	0.27%
10.	83.51%	14.10%	1.86%	0.53%	0.00%
11.	75.53%	18.35%	5.59%	0.53%	0.00%
12.	58.78%	32.18%	7.18%	1.60%	0.27%
13.	56.12%	31.12%	11.97%	0.80%	0.00%
14.	61.17%	32.18%	5.32%	1.33%	0.00%
15.	66.76%	20.74%	10.11%	1.86%	0.53%

TRUTH EMERGENCY SURVEY FOR THE MEDIA REFORM CONFERENCE, JUNE 6-8, MINNEAPOLIS

Background: Over 300 media democracy activists met in Santa Cruz California in January 2008 to hold a Truth Emergency Summit. The purpose of the summit was to address unresolved issues in US society, including torture, election fraud, the Iraq war, and 9/11. The following questions were designed to measure the support for truth emergency efforts by media democracy activists attending the NCMR.

1. The corporate media has failed to keep the American people informed on important issues facing the nation.

○ Strongly Agree   ○ Agree   ○ Neutral   ○ Disagree   ○ Strongly Disagree

2. A national truth emergency on important unresolved issues exists in the US today.

○ Strongly Agree   ○ Agree   ○ Neutral   ○ Disagree   ○ Strongly Disagree

3. An activist media democracy movement is occurring in the US that specifically supports the expansion and development of independent media from the bottom up.

○ Strongly Agree   ○ Agree   ○ Neutral   ○ Disagree   ○ Strongly Disagree

4. Reform of the FCC and changing of laws to break up concentrated corporate media in the US is an important strategy for the media democracy movement.

○ Strongly Agree   ○ Agree   ○ Neutral   ○ Disagree   ○ Strongly Disagree

5. The media democracy movement should have both a reform segment and an activist independent media segment.

○ Strongly Agree   ○ Agree   ○ Neutral   ○ Disagree   ○ Strongly Disagree

6. The media democracy movement should focus on using the Internet to build independent news sources.

○ Strongly Agree   ○ Agree   ○ Neutral   ○ Disagree   ○ Strongly Disagree

7. Unanswered questions regarding 9/11 are an important truth emergency issue in the US.

○ Strongly Agree   ○ Agree   ○ Neutral   ○ Disagree   ○ Strongly Disagree

8. Discovering the truth about the reasons the Bush administration decided to invade Iraq is an important truth emergency issue in the US.

○ Strongly Agree   ○ Agree   ○ Neutral   ○ Disagree   ○ Strongly Disagree

9. Investigating allegations of election fraud in the 2000 and 2004 presidential elections is an important truth emergency issue in the US.

○ Strongly Agree   ○ Agree   ○ Neutral   ○ Disagree   ○ Strongly Disagree

10. Addressing torture by US officials as a violation of basic human rights is an important truth emergency issue in the US.

○ Strongly Agree   ○ Agree   ○ Neutral   ○ Disagree   ○ Strongly Disagree

11. The absence of action to address the truth emergency crisis in the US threatens democracy.

○ Strongly Agree ○ Agree ○ Neutral ○ Disagree ○ Strongly Disagree

12. Who profits from the increasing cost of gasoline is a vital truth emergency issue in the US.

○ Strongly Agree ○ Agree ○ Neutral ○ Disagree ○ Strongly Disagree

13. Project Censored's annual release of the most important under-covered news stories is an important media democracy event.

○ Strongly Agree ○ Agree ○ Neutral ○ Disagree ○ Strongly Disagree

14. A truth emergency crisis can best be addressed by deep investigative research done by independent media.

○ Strongly Agree ○ Agree ○ Neutral ○ Disagree ○ Strongly Disagree

15. A military-industrial-media complex exists in the US for the promotion of the US military domination of the world.

○ Strongly Agree ○ Agree ○ Neutral ○ Disagree ○ Strongly Disagree

CHAPTER 12

Winter Soldier
Iraq & Afghanistan—Eyewitness Accounts of the Occupations

by Elizabeth Stinson

This chapter includes the testimony and statements of Iraq Veterans Against the War (IVAW) members, speaking at the National Labor College in Silver Spring, MD, in March of 2008. Those giving testimony included Kelly Dougherty, Adam Kokesh, Joe Wheeler, Adrianne Kinne, Vincent Emanuele, Steve Mortillo, Vincent Manelli, Jason Washburn, Jesse Hamilton, Jose Vasquez, Michael Leduc, Mark Wilkerson, Clifton Hicks, Steven Casey, Geoff Millard, Zollie Goodman, Jason Hurd, Camilo Mejia, and Sergio Corrigan. Dahr Jamail and Dahlia Wahdi, not members of IVAW, also provided expert testimony.

None of the statements, observations or responses would exist without the dedicated intentions and ongoing efforts of IVAW and its members. If I were asked to give a profile of the IVAW members I met who testified at Winter Soldier, I would say that each was sensitive, intellectual, idealistic, honest and in need of support. I hope that all who read their testimonies are able to take a piece of what they have given us and work to help their collective voices become an agent of change.

What should have been the most media-covered and thought-provoking accounts, those of returning Iraq War Veterans, instead resulted in a corporate media blackout in which the testimonies of Iraq Veterans Against the War were virtually ignored by major US media.

The event has been named Winter Soldier to honor a similar gathering thirty years ago of veterans of the Vietnam War. Winter soldiers, according to founding father Thomas Paine, are the people who stand up for the soul of their country, even in its darkest hours (IVAW press release, March 2008).

The hearings were held at the labor hall in Silver Springs, MD a mere ten miles from downtown Washington, DC, and the White House. All congresspersons and major and minor media were invited, according to IVAW testifier and media team member, Joe Wheeler. Although the hearings were attended and covered by alternative, international as well as many military outlets, there was a nearly complete blackout by the mainstream corporate media.

This writer observed testifiers in disbelief as they were asked to be interviewed by media from the UK, France, Australia, El Salvador and many Asian and Mideastern outlets as well as "Big Noise Films," while no major US media were present at all.

IVAW hearing attendees had timed their gathering to coincide with the fifth anniversary of the invasion of Iraq. Yet the personal testimony of hundreds of Iraq and Afghanistan war veterans garnered scant mainstream media coverage. A few notable exceptions included *Time*, National Public Radio's *All Things Considered*, the *Boston Globe*, and the *Washington Post*, which buried an article on Winter Soldier in their Metro section.

Meanwhile, the *New York Times*, ABC, CNN, NBC, and CBS ignored the hearings completely. At some point it is important to ask ourselves: What was the role and intention of the media in perpetuating this deception of the American people?

Testimonies were vetted in advance by Iraq Veterans Against the War. Ongoing legal support was provided to testifiers by attorneys from the Military Law Task Force of the National Lawyers Guild along with attorney J. E. McNeill from the Center on Conscience & War in Washington, DC. While in Silver Spring, I met privately with many who came to testify who had not yet received their final DD214 (military discharge) and many who were advised to not yet make public statements.

Psychiatric and emotional support was provided by therapists, counselors, and by many of us who maintained a table outside the hearing rooms to provide counseling for those who attended the hearings and had not yet gained their discharges. Support for the IVAW members was a "Who's Who" of the national antiwar movement. Although we have all communicated on the internet and by phone, many of us had not seen each other since Crawford, Texas, when the last series of events took place around Cindy Sheehan.

This should have been a long overdue "tipping point" in the minds of the American people, but it was kept hidden from them by an irresponsible corporate-owned media, believed by many to be responsible, along with the Bush administration, for the blind charge to occupy Iraq. If people want the truth, they can find it on the IVAW website at www.ivaw.org. We cannot underestimate the power of corporate-owned media to misshape and mislead public opinion.

Iraq Veterans Against the War was founded in 2004 to give those who have served in the military since September 11, 2001, a way to come together and speak out against an unjust, illegal and unwinnable war. Today, IVAW has over 700 members in forty-nine states, Washington, DC, Canada, and on military bases overseas. Iraq Veterans Against the War call for three things:

1. The immediate withdrawal of all occupying forces from Iraq
2. Full benefits for returning veterans
3. Reparations for the Iraqi people.

As more and more IVAW members join in resistance to their military mission, the need to tell and hear the truth becomes even more compelling. Security for IVAW members who came to Silver Spring to testify was provided by red-shirted members of Veterans for Peace and Gulf War I Veterans, both inside and outside the hearing rooms. One security person was Gulf War I resister Jeff Patterson from Courage to Resist. Jeff is well-known for having sat down, rather than board a plane for Iraq, with fellow Marines in Gulf War I.

Lori Hurlebaus, of Courage to Resist, went from being the stage manager at Winter Soldier, shuffling and protecting struggling IVAW members before and after they testified, to a position with IVAW staff in Pennsylvania—even more determined to facilitate their growing voice of resistance. Retired Colonel Ann Wright was present, as was Suzanne Swift to give support to women testifying about sexual harassment and abuse by and within the military.

How do the IVAW members feel and why were they compelled to testify?

Vincent Emanuele, a former Marine who testified at the Iraq/Afghanistan Winter Soldier hearings states: "This is not about being unpatriotic. I think this is about being as patriotic as you can possibly be. Being honest and saying, 'Hey, listen, our government has been doing some bad things in a Middle Eastern country,' and that's ok to admit that. Because if we don't admit that, and don't learn from that, we're going to continue down this very same path."

While in England in January of '08, this writer was contacted by three young men who had gone AWOL from a hospital in Italy after they had been told that they would be redeployed to Iraq, rather than sent home for medical leave. They were searching for an IVAW branch and have no intention of returning to this country. We will miss those who consciences have driven them from our culture. I have thought often of the many human losses from this misled occupation and I am all the more grateful to IVAW and its members who continue to push for the truth to be heard and to make a difference.

IVAW has members on active duty, in the Reserves, in the Guard, and in every branch of service. They are the only organization of veterans of the Global War on Terror that requires proof of service for membership.

According to Adam Kokesh, current board member of IVAW, members consider it their duty to speak out, to cut through the lies, spin, and propaganda that are being used to manipulate society into supporting a war that is not in our best interest as a nation. They firmly believe that if America could see what the "boots on the ground" really thought of this occupation, it would not continue for another day.

"We've heard from the politicians, from the generals, from the media—now it's our turn," said Kelly Dougherty, executive director of IVAW. Dougherty, who served in Iraq in 2003 as a military police officer, said, "It's not going to be easy to hear what we have to say. It's not going to be easy for us to tell it. But we believe that the only way this war is going to end is if the American people truly understand what we have done in their name."

The Winter Soldier Hearings panels, each consisting of five to seven persons giving testimony, covered: Rules of Engagement: Parts One and Two, the Crisis in Veterans' Healthcare, Corporate Pillaging and Military Contractors, Divide To Conquer: Gender and Sexuality in the Military, Racism and War: the Dehumanization of the Enemy: Parts One & Two, the Breakdown of the Military, and the Future of GI Resistance.

The first hearing on Thursday, March 13 was on the Rules of Engagement: Part One

This panel covered the killing and injuring of innocent civilians and unarmed combatants, as well as the destruction of the property, infrastructure, and natural resources of Iraq and Afghanistan. The speakers were Adam Kokesh, James Morriss, Jason Lemieux, Jason Hurd, Clifton Hicks, Steve Mortillo, Jose Vasquez, Michael Leduc, and Jesse Hamilton.

Adam Kokesh was a Marine reservist attending Claremont McKenna

College in January 2004 when he volunteered to transfer from November Battery 5/14 (artillery), which was not deploying, to the 3rd Civil Affairs Group which was leaving in less than a month. He served in the Fallujah area from February to September, 2004, and received the Combat Action Ribbon and Navy Commendation medal for his service. He says, "While as soldiers who have taken an oath we all have a responsibility to support the system that ensures us the quality of life that we enjoy in America, we also have a responsibility as citizens to ensure that the system is held accountable to the American people and to the highest moral standard."

Adam originally signed up in 1999. He states, "The only people that knew Iraq was in my future were the NeoCons." Adam believes that a lot of the folks that have joined since he did have been lied to by recruiters. (Adam can be reached at adam@ivaw.org. See also kokesh.blogspot.com.)

Clifton Hicks was a tank driver, a humvee .50cal gunner, and an amateur infantryman in southern Baghdad in 2003 and 2004. He lives in Gainsville, Florida. Clifton's profile page for IVAW reads—"The whole damned thing was a tremendous waste of time, energy, and human life. Too many of my friends and acquaintances have been slain for naught and too many spineless, neck-tied curs have profited from their blood." In Clifton Hicks IVAW profile, he states: "Too many of my friends have been slain for naught and too many worthless cowards have grown fat on their blood."

RULES OF ENGAGEMENT PART 2

Logan Melatori, from Camden, Missouri, was an E-3 in Afghanistan. He had applied for Conscientious Objector status while in Tikrit. He had also requested noncombatant assignment. For this he was diagnosed with a "maladjustment disorder." Logan had very strong feelings about his will to provide alternatives to violence in the military. He was acutely aware of the capacity to abuse rank. Logan felt that he was suffering injury to his physical and spiritual health by being part of an institution that was profiting from war.

THE BREAKDOWN OF THE MILITARY

Steve Mortillo thinks the world of the leaders of his platoon in Iraq. "They're some of the most honorable people I think I'll meet in my life," he says. "I'll never forget the camaraderie and the tough times we went through together." So it hit him hard when he returned from R & R (rest and recuperation) in the United States and was told that while he was gone, his platoon leader was critically wounded by an IED. "The first thing I said, the first thing everyone says, is, 'Stop lying to me! I don't want to hear that.' There's this feeling of guilt: while you're living it up back in the States, one of your comrades got hit." A few weeks later, he was awakened in the middle of the night to be told another comrade had been fatally wounded.

Mortillo says the military's willingness to stage house raids based on flimsy intelligence contributed to the growing American casualties. "I hope the American people can understand the impact that this occupation is having on the military," he said. "It's tearing us apart."

Daniel Fanning served in Iraq with a Wisconsin National Guard transportation unit. When he got there, the trucks had no armor. Only after a soldier embarrassed Donald Rumsfeld in front of the media did the Pentagon send armor. Fanning was trained in bayonet fighting, which no one has done for decades. He learned how to kick down walls and destroy rooms, but "never one second of culture or language training. We had no idea how to respect (Iraqis)."

The soldiers saw third world contractors exploited while American contractors made three or four times the pay of a GI. All of this damaged morale. "I enlisted [after 9/11] to be part of the solution, not part of the problem," Fanning says, but I feel like I did just the opposite, and many of the people in my unit feel the same way.

Kristofer Goldsmith saw the World Trade Center towers collapse on September 11, 2001. He enlisted in the Army and went to Iraq in 2005. In Sadr City, he witnessed abuse of Iraqi civilians. On one occasion, he was assigned to take pictures of Iraqis who had been found in a shallow grave, ostensibly for intelligence purposes, but they were only used as trophies by those who received them. After repeated commendations, he was expecting to return to civilian life and college when President Bush announced the "surge," and the military adopted its stop-loss policy, essentially making Goldsmith a prisoner of war. Goldsmith attempted to kill himself rather than return to Iraq, but survived. He was diagnosed with depression, anxiety, and post traumatic stree disorder (PTSD), but then was discharged for misconduct as a malingerer. He now delivers pizzas and struggles to overcome his persisting symptoms with treatment through the Veterans Administration (VA).

Lars Ekstrom was a strong supporter of the Iraq War. He reported to boot camp in November 2003, six months after graduating high school. However, Ekstrom's faith in the military and the US mission steadily eroded during his training and subsequent deployment to Iraq. The young corporal became troubled by a lack of accountability on the part of a culture he says is too "indoctrinated" to reform itself. Training was inadequate, equipment and supplies were substandard, and, most damaging, Ekstrom was on the receiving end of a hazing campaign by other servicemen. Disillusioned and depressed, Ekstrom made repeated requests for assistance but was brushed off. Soon, he began to wonder if this and other forms of negligence were a greater risk to his personal safety than the enemy he had been trained to fight. After his discharge, Ekstrom waited six months for VA benefits and continues to overcome bureaucratic obstacles as he seeks treatment for his depression.

Former Marine, Matt Howard says the Marine Corps "bases itself on dehumanization and subjugation and abuse of its lower enlisted in order for it to function." He had been severely beaten in a hazing incident.

Howard took part in the invasion of Iraq. He says the very first tank was destroyed mistakenly by a Marine helicopter. Fortunately, no one died that time. Shortly thereafter, however, the first casualty of the war was a soldier who stepped on a cluster bomblet dropped by Americans. Howard says American ammunition and armor both contained depleted uranium (DU), which is radioactive. He believes depleted uranium is "the agent orange of this occupation," and that the military is poisoning its soldiers, the people of Iraq, and the whole world with depleted uranium. On impact, tiny particles of DU go up into the atmosphere and eventually spread over the entire planet.

Captain Luis Carlos Montalvan notes that IVAW critics have challenged the speakers to testify under oath, subject to the penalties of perjury. He says he would love to do that. (He and other IVAW member were given a brief chance to testify before the House Out of Iraq Caucus on May 15, following the pressure exerted on members of the caucus by the Winter Soldier hearings). He discusses several military reports and his own experiences that show the shortcomings of the military. Because young people don't want to join, he says the military accepts many who don't meet its qualifications. American soldiers in Iraq show a wider range of competency than any of the other contributing countries. There is a severe shortage of mid-level officers, many of whom are leaving the service. Montalvan also says the military knows that it needs to protect the civilian population and win friends, but when Americans are killed, it often resorts to ferocious attacks that kill civilians and create enemies.

Geoff Millard served with the New York Army National Guard for nine years including a year in Tikrit. After coming home from Iraq and attending an anti-war event, he was made to fear for his life from his fellow soldiers. Mark Wilkerson served in Tikrit and Samarra with the 401st Military Police Company. When he came home, he decided to apply for Conscientious Objector status, but was threatened and harassed in such a way that he had no choice but to go AWOL when his application was denied. Thomas J. Buonomo graduated from the US Air Force Academy with a degree in Political Science and Middle East Studies and a minor in Arabic. After graduation, he volunteered to cross-commission into the Army in order to support our ground forces. Shortly after qualifying as a Military Intelligence Officer, his security clearance was suspended, and he was involuntarily discharged for expressing views contrary to the administration.

Bearded and calm, Jason Hurd came to the hearings to testify and support fellow IVAW members in their quest. Jason was born in Kingsport, TN where he lived his entire life until enlisting in the US Army in 1997 at the age of seventeen. In November 2004 he deployed to central Baghdad with Bristol, Tennessee's Troop F 2/278th Regimental Combat Team after a five-month long train-up. He served as a medic in Baghdad. Jason testified about the practice of shooting civilians from convoys, as well as the abduction of young male Iraqis. His father, a former veteran, opposed his activation to Iraq. Jason is the president of IVAW's chapter in Asheville, North Carolina. Jason has been actively opposing recruiter fraud in his community in Tennessee since his return from Iraq.

THE CRISIS IN VETERANS' HEALTHCARE

This panel looked at neglect and abuse of veterans and service members with regards to their mental and physical health. Testimonies included accounts about the impact of an under-funded Veterans Administration, injured soldiers being forced back into combat without fully recovering from their wounds, cases of the military's denial of mental healthcare for those suffering from PTSD, and exposure of service members to depleted uranium munitions and other hazardous materials. Speakers included: Martin Smith; Adrienne Kinne, IVAW member and a Veterans Administration employee; Eugene Martin, national organizer with American Federation of Government Employees, AFL-CIO; Joyce and Kevin Lucey, parents of a son who committed suicide after being denied treatment for PTSD; Zollie Goodman; and Tod Ensign.

Speaking about the crisis in mental health and healthcare in the military, Naval Officer Zollie Goodman maintained that he had been promised his family would have medical coverage when he joined the Navy. Yet when his pregnant wife started bleeding and thought she was miscarrying, the base hospital refused to send an ambulance, then refused to treat her when she arrived in a friend's car, because it was almost closing time. She lost the baby.

After Goodman was discharged, when he asked for treatment for PTSD, he was offered an appointment in three months. When he found out that the law guarantees no more than a thirty-day wait, he was given one thirty days later, at which a doctor prescribed three drugs and said there was no way to tell which might work. His personal research revealed that all three are associated with suicidal thoughts. Now, Goodman has a fifteen-minute therapy appointment every thirty days. When he arrives, he finds fifteen Vietnam Vets waiting with him, all with the same 8:00 a.m. appointment.

Also addressing the Crisis in Healthcare was Eric Estenzo. During his tour of duty in Iraq in 2003, Marine Corps reservist Eric Estenzo suffered a non-combat-related back injury. The thorough and prompt treatment Estenzo received at Camp Pendleton in California lived up to his trust in the VA health care system. After his honorable discharge in 2005, Estenzo had no reason to believe that the system wouldn't continue to take care of him. As his injury lingered, however, Estenzo faced repeated brush-offs, bureaucratic hurdles, and redundant paperwork.

The adjustment to civilian life was also proving to be unexpectedly challenging. Estenzo's savings dried up as meaningful employment eluded him and he suffered a nervous breakdown. Before too long, he found himself bordering on homelessness on the streets of Los Angeles. Thanks to support from fellow veterans, Estenzo is back on his feet but still struggles with a system that has undermined his faith in the US military (IVAW website & W.S. testimony).

Adrianne Kinne served as an Arabic linguist in Iraq. In her decade of military service, Adrienne Kinne noticed a significant decline in the quality of health care provided by the VA. Prior to the Iraq War, an end-of-service physical, for example, was routine. At the end of 2003, as she completed her duty in the army reserve, Kinne was discouraged from requesting such a physical. She finished her education and landed a job at a VA hospital where she worked with a research unit examining PTSD and traumatic brain injury (TBI). Believing that the VA system should pledge to serve the needs of all returning veterans, she was shocked to hear that plans to develop a screening mechanism for traumatic brain injuries was scuttled due to lack of "resources." Kinne believes that the system lacks a commitment to preventative health care, although, she adds, the best preventive plan is to avoid sending service men and women to fight in "illegal occupations in the first place."

Adriane Kinne explained that the symptoms for TBI and PTSD can be very similar, including restlessness, confusion, irritability, and short-term memory loss. Most disturbing was the fact that the VA decided not to screen for TBI in returning vets because they lack the resources to treat the 10,000 plus who are suspected of suffering from TBI received in Iraq or Afghanistan from the explosion of an IED (improvised explosive device).

Within our military discharge and separation work at the Peace & Justice Center of Sonoma County (as of this writing we have helped 867 enlisted persons with separations), we have encountered many returning Iraq war veterans who, though showing symptoms, have never been tested for TBI. Assessments for PTSD have been routinely denied, and no tests have been administered to determine effects of exposure to DU.

Joyce and Kevin Lucey, parents of Jeffrey Lucey, who committed suicide after returning, describe the last months of his life and his unsuccessful efforts to get help from the VA.

Jeffrey was a Marine convoy driver stationed in Iraq for five months at the start of the war. After he came back, he told his girlfriend he had done immoral things. "I've seen and done enough horrible things to last a lifetime," he said to her. Jeffrey told his sister he was a murderer. He wore the dog tags of two Iraqi soldiers for whose death he felt responsible. He wore the tags to honor the two. Shortly before he killed himself, Jeffrey asked his father to take him in his lap and rock him, and his father did. After he died, his parents found a note that read, "I am truly embarrassed of the man I became and I hope you can try to remember me only as a child, when I was happy, proud, and enjoyed life." Jeffrey was twenty-three.

Eli Wright, an active duty solder at Fort Drum, was injured in the back and neck in a vehicle accident in Iraq and then injured again in the shoulder during physical training back in the United States. He had minimal care—mostly Motrin—even after he developed symptoms of TBI, such as memory loss, headaches, and dizziness. He finally got proper care at Fort Drum two days after he spoke to the media. "Soldiers are afraid to speak out, but it's most important that they start speaking out about that," he says. "It has worked for me. Don't keep it quiet. We stepped up to serve our country, and we haven't asked for a whole lot in return. But proper healthcare should be, at a bare minimum, what we're entitled to."

RACISM AND DEHUMANIZATION
OF THE IRAQI PEOPLE

Testimony included Iraqi Civilian Statements about The Cost of War in Iraq and Afghanistan, accounting house raids, abuses, degradation, and torture.

The panel of those who testified also presented filmed interviews of Iraqi civilians recounting the terror they experienced at the hands of the military occupiers during home raids often levied against the wrong homes.

Testifiers included Salim Taleb, an Iraqi taxi driver who remembered being shot at and tortured, repeatedly taken from his cab by force and threatened and degraded. Taleb also recounted a situation in which a command to stop or be shot were yelled at drivers in English. His friend had been killed in his car, he feels, because his friend had been mistaken for him and he had been driving Americans around Iraq. He made a valiant attempt, in his testimony, to humanize and familiarize those attending with the Iraqi culture of Sunni and Shi'a and the troops inability to understand the cultural difference between the two factions as well at the vast cultural difference between themselves and the Iraqi citizens.

Soldiers Beat and Dehumanized Civilians

Jeffery Smith told how his military unit beat and mocked Iraqi prisoners. A former marine, Bryan Casler, said that his colleagues urinated on food they later gave to Iraqi children.

Scott Ewing was an Army scout in Tel Afar from 2005 to 2006. He describes how treatment of civilians became progressively more brutal. Early on, soldiers sometimes broke down gates and front walls. Later, because the residents were believed to be insurgents, they ordered everyone out of a neighborhood and into camps outside the city, while American airships bombed the houses. Then soldiers searched what was left, trashing every house they entered, but the most warlike implements they found were wood saws, kitchen knives, and old pistol belts. In another neighborhood, they sent Kurdish militiamen to round up all the military-age men and one masked militiaman picked out fifty men whom he accused of being insurgents. They were taken away, and Ewing never found out what happened to them. "It's hard for me to believe that the Iraqis who witnessed this could possibly take seriously our version of justice and democracy," he says.

Camilo Mejia, author of *Road From Ar Ramadi*, says the abuse of Iraqis is "not the result of people waking up one morning as monsters, but it's part of . . . the military culture. They train us that way." He also says the brutality comes from being told that people are out to kill you. "You . . . remove the humanity from them to make it easier to oppress them, to brutalize them, to beat them, and in doing so, you remove the humanity from yourself because you cannot act as a human being and do all of these things." He testified about abuse of prisoners to "soften them up" for interrogation. Mejia says some memories are so horrible the mind erases them. The first time he shot someone, Mejia remembers the events before and after, but the actual killing is a blank. In another incident, soldiers killed a young father in a car with his son sitting right next to him. Mejia can't remember the expression on the boy's face or even that he was a child—other people told him that later.

Andrew Duffy enlisted as a medic in the Iowa National Guard two days after he turned seventeen. He testifies to incidents in which Iraqi detainees desperately in need of medical treatment were denied it. One died as Duffy tried to save him. "A lot of people called them 'Hajis' and didn't like them because they were detainees but to me, it was just an old man that could've been somebody's father, grandfather, uncle." He says the dislike for Iraqis stemmed from attacks on Americans. "I remember a time that I treated a marine that had his legs blown off, and he died in our care. Subsequently, about a half an hour later, I had to give a detainee pills for a headache. . . . As a medic, you need to treat these people the same. They are human beings."

Mike Prysner describes a mission he took part in which his unit forced Iraqis out of half a dozen homes, with no compensation, so the US military could use them. "One family in particular, a woman with two small girls, very elderly man, and two middle-aged men—we dragged them from their houses and threw them onto the street, and arrested the men because they refused to leave." Since he left, he has been plagued by guilt "anytime I see a mother with her children, like the one who cried hysterically and screamed that we were worse than Saddam as we forced her from her home . . . anytime I see a young girl like the one I grabbed by the arm and dragged into the street." Prysner also describes the physical abuse of a wounded prisoner, with a sandbag over his head and his hands tied behind his back. "We were told we were fighting terrorists; the real terrorist was me, and the real terrorism is this occupation."

Christopher Arendt, who served at Guantanamo Bay, Cuba, describes "how one goes about becoming a concentration camp guard." His job was to track the movements of detainees. Sometimes when he started his shift at 4:30 am, "there would be a little paper in the wall with a number on it, which represented a detainee inside an interrogation room, which was anywhere from maybe 10, 20 degrees in temperature with loud music playing. . . . Sometimes that detainee would stay there for my entire twelve to fourteen-hour shift, shackled to the floor by his hands and his feet." Arendt also describes a procedure used to punish inmates who become rowdy, which involves spraying them in the face with an extremely painful, long-lasting chemical and then sometimes beating them up. These punishments are taped by the military—he taped several himself, and he wants to show them, but he doubts the tapes will be released.

Arendt is followed by a filmed interview with an Iraqi mother named Um Ahmed, who describes a terrifying raid by American soldiers on her home. The raid turned out to be a mistake: they were after a militia member who lived next door. The film is in Arabic with English subtitles.

Domingo Rosas, an ex-Army sergeant who served in Iraq from April, 2003 to 2004, describes mistreatment of detainees at a site called Tiger

Base on the Syrian border. They were crowded into a shipping container, and part of his job was to keep them from sleeping. Later, the site was taken over and rebuilt by men from another (unnamed) government agency. One day he delivered a message there, and when he opened the door, he saw a prisoner being rolled around in the mud while water was poured over his face—a version of waterboarding.

Geoff Millard describes the widespread use of "Hajis" as a derogatory term for Iraqis, including those who worked for the Americans, and even for Pakistani workers. He heard that term used by officers all the way up to General Casey. "These things start at the top, not the bottom," he says. Millard describes a briefing he attended for a general about an incident in which a young soldier saw a vehicle driving fast toward a check point, decided it was a threat, and fired 200 rounds from his machine gun, killing a mother, father, and their two small children. The response of a colonel at the briefing: "If these f'ing Hajis learned to drive, this 's' wouldn't happen."

Dahlia Wasfi was born in the US to an American-Jewish mother and an Iraqi-Muslim father. She lived in Iraq as a small child but returned to the US at age five. She has made two trips to Iraq since the invasion. Wafsi supports immediate withdrawal of American forces and maintains a website, www.LiberateThis.com. Wafsi says the inspiration for her activism on Iraq was Rachel Corey, who was killed by an Israeli bulldozer when she tried to stop the demolition of a Palestinian house. Wafsi says anti-Arab and anti-Muslim prejudice keeps many Americans from paying attention to the terrible toll of the war on Iraqis and to the ethnic cleansing waged against Palestinians.

BREAKDOWN IN THE RULES OF ENGAGEMENT

Michael Leduc served in the Marines during "Operation Venom Fury," the attack on Fallujah. Before the attack, the battalion's legal counsel told them the strict rules of engagement under which they had previously operated would not apply to this assault. They could call in artillery or air strikes on a building if they just felt unsure about what they might find: called "reconnaissance by fire." People with weapons, cell phones, binoculars—or even people with white flags if they did anything but approach slowly and obey orders—should all be killed. "I joined the military . . . to do something good to improve the whole human situation," he says. "And I felt good about myself a few times. [But] for the most part, I was just doing what I had to do . . . whether it was breaking the rules or following them, doing what I thought was right or what I knew was wrong."

Bryan Casler served in the Marines in Iraq and Afghanistan. He speaks of soldiers' disrespect for the people of those countries. One incident in particular taught him how differently he himself felt about Iraqis and Americans: He was in an ambulance rushing to pick up a badly wounded soldier, when he suddenly realized from the soldier's uniform that this was an American. "This was the first time that I was affected in such a way: I was excited about what we were doing, and then a second later, I was terrified." He says the lack of a clear mission led to brutality: "The mission just becomes to come home alive." Marines are trained to kill in battle, he says, and "it absolutely becomes that all you have is hammers and everything you find is nails, and you're gonna crush every nail. And we're crushing the Iraqi people."

One particular incident stands out in Clifton Hicks's (Army) mind. "There was a tall apartment complex, the only spot from where people could see over our perimeter," he recalls. "There would be laundry hanging off the balconies, and people hanging out on the roof for fresh air. The place was full of kids and families. On rare occasions, a fighter would get atop the building and shoot at our passing vehicles. They never really hit anybody. We just knew to be careful when we were over by that part of the wall, and nobody did shit about it until one day a lieutenant colonel was driving down and they shot at his vehicle and he got scared. So he jumped through a bunch of hoops and cut through some red tape and got a C-130 to come out the next night and all but leveled the place. Earlier that evening when I was returning from a patrol the apartment had been packed full of people."

Looking back on his time in Iraq, Hicks reflected on a hopeless situation. "You go out on your first mission and all the Iraqis think you're a loser, they ignore you, or flip you off, or draw their finger across their throat, yelling obscenities," he says. "Even though some were nice to us, you quickly lose any trust in them, and you lump them all together. The only way you can stay safe is to assume that outside the wire everybody wants to kill you. You don't want to be there. And it comes down to, 'Well fuck, I hate being here and I can't go home.' . . . So I wake up every fucking day and I think, 'The only reason I'm here is because you fucking people are forcing me to be here. I hate you fucking people, and you hate me, and that's just how it is.' And once you get to that place, it's over."

Former US Marine Corps machine gunner John Michael Turner leaned over the microphone, his voice choking with emotion, the words barely forcing themselves out, the tears barely held back.

"There's a term 'Once a Marine, always a Marine,'" he said, ripping off his medals and throwing them to the ground. "But there's also the expression 'Eat the apple, f*@ the Corps, I don't work for you no more." In the hearing hall in Silver Spring, John Turner's words were met with a standing ovation and screams of support. His angst and pain were shared by many present.

Like the other veterans assembled, Turner spoke openly about what he saw and did during his tours in Iraq. "April 18, 2006 was the date of my first confirmed kill," he said. "He was innocent, I called him the fat man. He was walking back to his house and I killed him in front of his father and friend. My first shot made him scream and look into my eyes, so I looked at my friend and said, 'Well, I can't let that happen,' and shot him again. After my first kill I was congratulated."

NOT JUST BAD APPLES

When he was done speaking, Turner received a standing ovation from the crowd of Iraq, Afghanistan, Vietnam, and Gulf War veterans. The ovation went on for over two minutes. John Turner is a member of the Paper Project: a group of Iraq Veterans who have cut their uniforms into tiny pieces and mixed and turned their uniforms in to hand made paper in order to help "turn pain into art" in order to help themselves deal with their post traumatic stress.

Iraq Veterans Against the War hoped the hearings would show to the world that well-publicized incidents of US brutality, including the Abu Ghraib prison scandal and the massacre of an entire family of Iraqis in the town of Haditha, are not isolated incidents perpetrated by "a few bad apples," as many politicians and military leaders have claimed. They are part of a pattern, the organizers said, of "an increasingly bloody occupation."

TESTIMONY OF JASON WASHBURN ON THE
DETERIORATION OF THE RULES OF ENGAGEMENT

Corporal Jason Washburn, former Marine was deployed for three tours in Iraq, including the invasion. Over the course of his service, Washburn was stationed in some of the most dangerous areas of Iraq: Najaf, Sadr City, and Anbar Province. A squad in his unit was responsible for the massacre of twenty-six civilians in Haditha in November 2005.

Washburn told the gathering his commanders encouraged lawless behavior. "We were encouraged to bring 'drop weapons' or shovels, in case we accidentally shot a civilian, we could drop the weapon on the body and pretend they were an insurgent," he said.

"By the third tour, if they were carrying a shovel or bag, we could shoot them. So we carried these tools and weapons in our vehicles, so we could toss them on civilians when we shot them. This was commonly encouraged."

Washburn related a story about the invasion of Haditha in which there was no identification of human targets. There were no rules governing the amount of force; the command "light her up" was used to kill a woman who they later found was only trying to bring them food. After Bush declared "Mission Accomplished," Jason stated, the hand-to-hand violence only escalated. When he inquired with his command what they were supposed to do, the response was, "What do you think we want? Go fuck them up!" Jason Washburn's unit was ordered to shoot anyone digging near the side of the road because they might be planting a bomb. At one point, Washburn's commander called the unit together to praise Marines for accurate shooting, his pride apparently undiminished by the fact that one of the victims was not an insurgent, but the local mayor.

Marine Corps Rifleman Vincent Emanuele was deployed to an Iraqi village, near the border with Syria, in August 2004. During his eight months there, he witnessed and participated in the aimless shooting at Iraqi vehicles; the random firing of rifles and mortars into the village rather than at specific targets; the physical abuse of Iraqi prisoners and the driving of prisoners out into the desert where they were abandoned; and the disrespectful handling of the Iraqi dead. And in his testimony, Rifleman Vincent Emanuel repeatedly said: "These were not isolated incidents."

As the casualties grew in Sergio Kochergin's platoon, the rules of engagement eroded. After seeing their friends blown up, "We were angry," he says, "we just wanted to do our job and come back." At one point, that meant that an Iraqi carrying a heavy bag and a shovel was at risk of being shot. Within months, Kochergin says that the rules of engagement were left entirely up to him and his fellow soldiers. "I want to apologize to all the people in Iraq," said a badly shaken Sergio Kochergin.

In Iraq, the rules of engagement are being loosely defined and broadly enforced at the expense of the Iraqi people, says Jason Lemieux. "Anyone who tells you different is either a liar or a fool." When he got to Baghdad, he says he was explicitly instructed by his commanders that he could shoot anyone who made him uncomfortable and refused to move when he ordered them to do so. "Better them than us," was the prevailing philosophy, he says, and everyone on the street was considered an enemy combatant who could be killed.

MEAGER MEDIA COVERAGE

The moving, often tearful personal testimonies were broadcast in their entirety through IVAW's website, the satellite station Free Speech TV, and Pacifica Radio, but they mostly went ignored by the mainstream media. All across the country families of enlisted people were tuning into alternative media to hear the truth denied them by major media.

These grassroots outlets reached a much larger audience than even the organizers expected. IVAW's website received more than 30,000 unique views every day during Winter Soldier. Warcomeshome.org, a site edited for Pacifica Radio, received hits from internet users in over 110 countries and responses from veterans, active duty service members and their families. The progressive print and online media also paid attention: articles ran in *In These Times, The Nation, AlterNet, Common Ground* and Big Noise.

Winter soldier also received some play in the military press, with favorable stories published in Stars and Stripes and the Military Times chain of newsweeklies. The IVAW has posted media coverage of the hearings on its site.

Instead, mainstream media outlets continued to convey stories produced by embedded journalists citing the administration's lies of progress in Iraq, supposedly thanks to the so-called "surge."

DIVIDE TO CONQUER: GENDER AND SEXUALITY IN THE MILITARY

Twenty-three-year-old Lars Ekstrom is a former Lance Corporal in the United States Marine Corps. While he was in Iraq, his commanding officer pulled a gun on a female member of his unit and asked her where he could find sexual gratification.

Lars gave a compelling account of being hazed both physically and psychologically by his command. Lars was forced to do repeated pushups while being kicked in his ribs from either side. At one point in his testimony, he leaned forward into the microphone and said. "Mr. President, your job is to defend the constitution."

After his testimony, I went in search of Lars to thank him for his statements, which were obviously difficult and traumatic to recount. He explained to me that his handshake felt weak because his body had been so severely abused by other Marines that his muscles were "mush." Lars is slowly recovering, his efforts to end the occupation of Iraq as a member of IVAW and draw attention to the abuses of Marine command give Lars hope for lasting change.

Abby Hiser spent eight years in the Wisconsin National Guard and was honorably discharged as a sergeant in 2007. She describes a string of her own experiences that show woman in the military still face prejudice and obstacles to advancement. These incidents include groping by a male soldier during a training exercise and barriers put in the way of her promotion. When she finally overcame those barriers, her authority as an officer was challenged.

Joe Wheeler, a former Sonoma County student and husband and father, landed in Kuwait at the beginning of the war when the Iraqis were firing Scud missiles. Wheeler states, "The American soldiers thought the missiles might contain poison gas, so they were terrified every time air raid sirens went off. Once, a female soldier who was taking a shower when the sirens sounded was raped by a male soldier." Wheeler testified at the hearings about the disparity between his respect for love for his wife and his newborn daughter and the treatment of women in the military. Wheeler says the fear of chemicals brought out the worst in people.

Margaret Stevens was a medic in the New Jersey National Guard on 9/11, and knew she was likely to be deployed to a war or occupation. She says women who are raped in the military are pressured not to try to document the crime. Is bad treatment of women inevitable as long as women serve in the military? "I don't think so," she says. "I think it's only in the context of these genocidal wars . . . where already the reason you're fighting is not a good reason."

Jeff Key was a reservist who did not plan to tell anyone he was gay, but "once you're in a fighting hole with someone who's sharing the deep contents of their soul and willing to take a bullet for you and you for them, to manufacture some bogus life is ridiculous and I would not spit in their face by doing so." He adds, "All my buddies were straight. They stood by me in war, they knew who I was . . . they stood by me in my wedding, and they . . . put themselves at risk to speak out for queer serving." When he came back, he says, "I knew I could not be a party to this occupation . . . so I went on CNN and came out of the closet . . . and made them throw me out." He believes the war machine is sustained by homophobia and the belief that real men have no feelings of compassion while women are emotional and weak. "Good men will . . . do horrible things to prove that they are not gay," he says.

Patty McCann served in Iraq with the Illinois National Guard. In her unit, she says, rank was used to coerce women into sexual relationships. She relates two instances of harassment and says women are urged not to report such incidents because reporting them would do great harm to the perpetrator.

Rafay Siddiqui, a Marine veteran of Iraq, says that in the military, "you're not a man until you've taken advantage of a woman." Impressionable eighteen and nineteen-year-old young men come into the service, see "everyone doing it, so they themselves have to do it too because they want to fit in." He testifies about his experiences not in Iraq but in Djibouti, Africa on an earlier deployment. Young girls, trying to escape poverty, came to Djibouti and ended up working as prostitutes for Marines and for French legionnaires who were also stationed there.

Wendy Barranco was trained as a combat medic. At her request, a surgeon let her work in the operating room, but then he wanted sexual favors in return. She explains why she never reported him: he was an important person, so "all I kept thinking was, 'If I speak out, it's going to be my word against him, and I'm just an E4, . . . so who are they going to believe? Are they going to get rid of the guy that's making all the decisions and saving lives, or me?" She says many women soldiers don't report abuse because of similar power relationships and because "you're looked at as a snitch." She says the military's harassment training is useless because it ignores these daily realities.

Tanya Austin speaks about the case of a Coast Guard woman who was raped by a shipmate. She filed a complaint, providing a confession letter written by the rapist. But the Coast Guard told her she would be discharged because surviving rape made her ineligible for worldwide deployment. She launched a nine-month battle to keep her job and change the policy. She tells her story at stopmilitaryrape.org, where there is also more information about rape and abuse in the military.

Moderator Jennifer Hogg and several panel members add closing comments. Panelist Jeff Key had said earlier that the deeply rooted association of men with strength and women with weakness is at the core of the war machine. He notes that one of the women panelists cried as she spoke and said, "I hate to be the girl on this panel!" Key says that demonstrates once again the power of the stereotype that "to shed a tear makes you a girl and that's somehow essentially weak." Wendy Barranco, the testifier he was referring to, says she did not want to fit the image that many people have of the abused victim: "They look at us and they're like, 'Oh, so you're the broken one, huh?'"

THE BREAKDOWN OF THE MILITARY/STOP LOSS

Many kept in the military beyond their contract dates consider themselves to be prisoners of war as well. Stop Loss was enacted by Congress in order to keep soldiers and Marines in the service involuntarily until the military sees fit to let the members leave. Kristofer Goldsmith always wanted to be a soldier. Kris was nineteen years old when he deployed to Sadr City in Baghdad, One of the most treacherous neighborhoods in Iraq. For Kris, his experiences in Sadr City were a wake up call. The ideals that drove him to become a soldier were compromised, when taking pictures of exhumed bodies, the realization that his traumatizing work would not be used to identify bodies, but instead would travel up the chain of command to be used as trophies for "kills" alarmed him to his core.

One day, Kris almost shot a six-year-old boy. His experiences in Iraq had so badly shaken him that he began drinking heavily upon his return home. Kris reported that treatment for PTSD was discouraged when he and fellow soldiers were told the their careers would be ruined were they to seek treatment for mental illness. The military continues to stigmatize the symptoms and deny treatment for those whose stress symptoms the service creates. Kris was stop-lossed with the surge. He attempted suicide the day before he was supposed to redeploy to Iraq. After spending a week in the hospital, he was discharged with a misconduct citation: his serious offense was attempting suicide. The service discouraged and denied the necessary assessment and treatment that Kris needed to keep him from further deterioration and prevent his suicide attempt.

CONCLUSION

Although the Winter Soldier hearings were not attended by mainstream media or Congress they created enough of a stir that the testimonies did result in the scheduling of Whistleblower Tribunals before the Out of Iraq Caucus on May 14, 2008. These were sponsored and attended by members of congress during their historic debates on the continuation of funding for the Occupation of Iraq.

According to Fairness And Accuracy In Reporting (FAIR), "Despite being noted in the *New York Times'* Paris-based *International Herald Tribune* (March 13, 2008), Winter Soldier has yet to be mentioned in the *New York Times* itself. No major US newspaper has covered the hearings except as a story of local interest; the few stories major US newspapers have published on the event have focused on the participation of local vets *(Boston Globe*, March 16, 2008; *Boston Herald*, March 16, 2008; *Newsday*, March 16, 2008, *Buffalo News*, March 16, 2008)."

The Internet is the new tool of resistance. YouTube videos are being made and sent home that relate the undeniable truth of the debacle accounted in the Winter Soldier testimonies.

Camilo Mejia is an Iraq War veteran, GI resister, and Chairman of the Board of IVAW and author of R*oad from Ar Ramadi: The Private Rebellion of Staff Sergeant Mejia*. At the hearings Camilo had requested that all Vietnam veterans, VVAW members, and original Winter Soldier attendees to stand as IVAW gave them a rousing ovation. "It is because of the strength of these men and women that we stand here today as Iraq Veterans Against the War. We are the new Winter Soldiers."

George Orwell wrote, "In times of universal deceit, telling the truth becomes an act of rebellion." We are truth speakers and rebels. IVAW members have been interrogated by the FBI, incarcerated for being conscientious objectors, incarcerated for standing up against military rape, and labeled troublemakers by the leadership of the military and this country. Because we have dared to follow our conscience and embrace humanity, we have been called too many names to list here. We refuse to be silenced by the government and corporate media. We heard heartbreaking testimony that weekend, but we have also heard and seen these things firsthand in Iraq and Afghanistan. Until we eradicate homophobia, sexism, and racism in the military, we will not be fully united as a military and as a nation. IVAW will not rest until we reach the three goals of our three points of unity: withdrawal of American troops from Iraq, reparations for the Iraqi people, and full benefits for the veterans when they return home.

Alternative-Independent Media willing to cover the Winter Soldier Hearings:

Interviews with fifty Iraq vets in a comprehensive investigation into the effects of the occupation on Iraqi civilians, *The Nation,* June 2007.

"Winter Soldier: Iraq & Afghanistan—Eyewitness Accounts of the Occupations," Live Broadcast *Pacifica Radio,* March 14-16, 2008, http://warcomeshome.org/ wintersoldier2008.

Aaron Glantz, "US Soldiers 'Testify' About War Crimes," OneWorld.net, March 19, 2008, http://www.commondreams.org/archive/2008/03/19/7763/.

"Why Are Winter Soldiers Not News?" FAIR, March 19, 2008, http://www.fair.org/index.php?page=3318.

Chris Hedges and Laila Al-Arian, "The Other War: Iraq Vets Bear Witness," *The Nation,* July 30, 2007, http://www.thenation.com/doc/20070730/hedges

---

ELIZABETH STINSON is director of the Sonoma County Peace and Justice Center.

CHAPTER 13

The Pentagon's Child Recruiting Strategy

by Gary Evans, MD

The human family consists, for the most part, of wonderfully ordinary people who work hard to care for themselves and their children. However, there are a few people who aspire to positions of power, and then work to use their authority to manipulate and control all the others.

This nation's teenage children are currently being tracked, targeted, and sometimes captured by a globally dominant military-industrial-media complex under orders of an exceptionally callous neoconservative group now in control of the US government. The people in power today systematically use armed services recruiters—motivated by rank and bonus—as the agents of control and manipulation of US youth.

Parents of teens and preteens are seldom aware of how their children are at increasing risk of being systematically targeted, manipulated into recruiter offices, and psychological remodeled for use within the war machine. Military planners, hungry for new recruits, commission psychological research, and carefully read neuropsychiatric literature as it pertains to adolescent behavior. They then apply that research information to their recruitment efforts that focus on the vulnerability of the teenage mind.

As the 9/11-related wars continue and as the numbers of dead and disabled young men and women climb, civilian doubts over the purpose and direction of the conflict has evolved and grown. As a result, convincing new potential recruits to enlist has become an increasingly difficult task. The Pentagon addresses this recruitment problem by spending thousands of millions of our tax dollars on programs designed to deceive, seduce, and to capture our youth. Military recruiters have been granted full access to our children at home, at school, and wherever else they can be tracked. The Pentagon has invaded our movies, our televisions, and our minds, and has invited our children to play violent, and damaging video games while feeding them emotionally charged materials designed to manipulate and reformat them into replacement soldiers.

A BRIEF AND RECENT HISTORY OF
US MILITARY RECRUITMENT

Ending the Draft

The Vietnam War was fought by a generation of young men whose teen experiences were distorted by a persistent and disruptive force—conscription. That constant threat helped fire the tremendous social unrest that attended those war years. As the war came to its painful end, Pentagon planners moved to eliminate future reliance on draftees. The recommendation was tendered and Congress agreed to end the draft, replacing it with an all-volunteer armed services system.

Building and maintaining an all-volunteer military during peacetime worked reasonably well. The process during war however, has proven to be problematic. After years of war and violent occupation in Afghanistan and Iraq, public perception of military life has gradually soured. And, as civilian jobs—albeit low paying for many—continue to be available, the recruiting process has become increasingly difficult. The Pentagon has responded by offering, or giving the appearance of offering, a set of incentives to potential enlistees. Bait has since included cash and promises (frequently unfulfilled) of job training, educational funding, and future medical care.

Teenagers Increasingly Targeted

After recent Pentagon research revealed that the desire and intention to enlist is highest among younger recruits (six in ten current US soldiers entered the military as teenagers),[1] a level of subtlety, or rather subterfuge, has been employed to guide teens toward recruiter offices. As one example of the many available: the US Army sponsors a website labeled "eCybermission." It offers "web-based science, math, and technology competition" for eleven-, twelve-, and thirteen-year-olds, and the services of online uniformed Army personnel "CyberGuides."[2]

Since 2002 the Pentagon has developed a massive teen database gleaned from sources, including records obtained via the No Child Left Behind Act. That information is filed in the Department of Defense's Joint Advertising and Marketing Research & Studies system (JAMRS)—a giant Pentagon-run, privately subcontracted (Equifax) database containing contact and identification data on over 30 million sixteen to twenty-five year-olds.[3]

Plummeting Numbers/Plummeting Standards

Despite recent reports of an increasing rate of suicides among US troops,[4] news reports of "stop-loss" troop recycling, and declining troop moral, the Pentagon's recent recruiting and retention report for 2007[5] implies success. The facts underlying the statistics offered, however, tell a different story: "The number of wavers granted to Army recruits with criminal backgrounds [125,000] has grown about 65 percent in the past three years,"[6] and the percentage of minimally qualified recruits has quadrupled since 2002.[7]

Former representative Martin T. Meechen, as chairman of the House Armed Services Subcommittee on Investigations and Oversight says, "The data is crystal clear; our armed forces are under incredible strain, and the only way that they can fill their recent quotas is by lowering their standards."[8]

Recruitment Funding

Pentagon spending on recruitment has increased dramatically over the past few years, approaching $4 billion by 2003.[9] As of 2006, there were over 22,000 recruiters nationwide,[10] charged with signing up between 180,000 and 200,000 new active duty recruits, and approximately 120,000 new reservists per year.[11] In 2000, the US House of Representatives determined that $6,400 was being spent to sign up each marine,[12] and by 2005, the military spent approximately $16,000 in total promotional costs to enlist each new recruit.[13]

Despite the enormous sums spent attempting to maintain an all-volunteer military during these times of growing antiwar sentiment, the armed forces have been unable to meet new recruit sign-up quotas. There is always a way, however, and here the balance sheets have been righted by dropping ballast, also known as "standards," and by implementing military contract fine-print: *Executive Order #12728, dated 8/22/90 referring US Code, Title 10, section 12305 and Title 3, section 301,* better known as "stop-loss," which allows troops to be returned to battlefields again by delaying their removal from active duty *indefinitely.* In this way, military statisticians have forced the claim that recruitment quotas are being fulfilled.[14]

Targeting the Adolescent Brain

Adolescence has long been recognized as a time when impulsive and risk-taking behaviors increase. As adolescence gives way to adulthood, learning to gauge risk with greater precision gradually proceeds. Modern neuroscience tools, including Magnetic Resonance Imaging (MRI) and Positron Emission Tomography (PET) scanning techniques have now shown that adolescent stereotypic behavior is based on a phase of structural brain development.[15]

In a recent study,[16] multiple high-tech scans were collated over time, and were combined with serial assessments of neuro-developmental function. It was discovered that the adolescent brain exists as a structurally and functionally distinct entity from that found earlier in childhood, or later in adulthood. The adolescent brain develops structurally enlarged, but functionally immature prefrontal and limbic grey matter areas. Those structural features appear to result in a change in balance between limbic reward and prefrontal higher executive assessment functions, and helps to explain typical adolescent behaviors of increased novelty and sensation, or thrill-seeking on the one hand, and limited consequence analysis on the other. By the early twenties, as the structurally enlarged areas decrease to typically adult volumes, brain function settles into adult patterns. These changes are accompanied by recognized adult thought processes and behaviors.

It is during adolescence, when changes in brain structure and function result in the characteristic behaviors of that age, that teens are actively recruited toward and into the military. The techniques employed by military recruiters directly targets the unique functional brain development characteristics of the adolescent; that targeting is undoubtedly purposeful.[17]

HIGH SCHOOLS AS "MARKETS"

"No Child Left Behind"—Section 9528

The Bush administration wrote and signed into law the No Child Left Behind Act, on January 8, 2002,[18] with subsequent reauthorization in 2007.[19] As is now widely known, included in the 670 pages of that voluminous act—within section 9528—is a provision enabling military recruiters to access high school students' records, and to access the students themselves as they attend high-school campuses throughout the country. Students and/or their parents are offered the choice to "opt out" of this demand, but they must actively do so, requiring of course, that they are first informed of this option. As will later be documented, this is often not the case. If school districts otherwise fail to provide military recruiters with the required information and access, millions of dollars in federal funding for that district can be cut.

Military recruiter manuals then provide guidance on how to maximize the effect of the law on targeted adolescents. Here are a few examples of advice given to recruiters from the School Recruiting Program [SRP] Handbook:[20]

> Section 1-4 c: "The objective of the SRP is to assist recruiters with programs and services so they can effectively penetrate the school market. The goal is school ownership that can only lead to a greater number of Army enlistments. Recruiters must first establish rapport in the schools. This is a basic step in the sales process and a prerequisite to an effective school program. Maintaining this rapport and establishing a good working relationship is next. Once educators are convinced recruiters have their students' best interests in mind the SRP can be effectively implemented."

> Section 2-4: "Some influential students such as the student president or the captain of the football team may not enlist; however, they can and will provide you with referrals who will enlist."

> Section 5-1-f-4: "Don't forget the administrative staff. . . .Have something to give them (pen, calendar, cup, donuts, etc.) and always remember secretary's week, with a card or flowers."

Using computers fed with socioeconomic census data, past recruiting numbers, and other demographic information, recruiters target specific schools where students are less likely to go on to college and are more likely to sign up with the military.[21] Then, school yearbooks, newspapers, and any other pertinent local informational sources are scrutinized, allowing recruiters to simulate familiarity and interest in a few of the more popular kids on campus. As those kids are approached and befriended, others are attracted to the social bait and, seeking approval, gather around.

Once a student swims anywhere near the hook, recruiter anglers use every trick available. Students are phoned and written to without end, and are offered visions of a virtual cornucopia of money, education, training, and adventure.[22] All responses are, of course, tracked.[23]

ASVAB: "REALIZE YOUR STRENGTHS. REALIZE YOUR DREAMS."

The Armed Services Vocational Aptitude Battery (ASVAB)[24] is a three-hour test offered to, and taken by, nearly 1 million high school students every year. It is placed before them ostensibly as a helping hand—as a way to explore their career potentials, and to guide them toward appropriate life choices. The offer and the test are scams.

Here is what the military tells the parents of teenage students in this confidence game:

> The ASVAB Career Exploration Program includes eight individual tests covering verbal and math skills, mechanical knowledge, electronics, and several other areas. It also produces three Career Exploration Scores for Verbal Skills, Math Skills, and Science and Technical Skills. These three scores serve as one of several pieces of information about your child that can aid in the exploration of a wide variety of career options.[25]

Recruiters, on the other hand, understand the ASVAB recruitment tool quite well. An excerpt from the Commander, Navy Recruiting Command, Policy and Programs Division, 2002—Recruiting Manual reads, "The ASVAB is used by the Armed Forces for recruiting purposes. . . . The ASVAB's ability for determining civilian job skills has not yet been proven."[26]

Because the ASVAB is exempt from the provisions of the Family Educational Rights and Privacy Act of 1974, students are given the test and information acquired is released to the military without parental consent.[27] Furthermore, military recruiters are free, at the option of school administrators, to contact test takers—even if the student, or their parents opted out of Section 9528 of the No Child Left Behind

Act.[28] Exam information is then forwarded to the JAMRS database for further analysis.[29]

THE JAMRS DATABASE

In 2002, the Pentagon joined forces with the corporate database industry and began gathering, organizing and analyzing personal information on the military's "market" of teens and their families. The JAMRS database now includes the records of over 30 million US sixteen- to twenty-five-year-olds.[30]

As families soon discovered they were unable to control the records collected on them, an ACLU lawsuit was brought against Secretary of Defense Donald Rumsfeld, Deputy Under Secretary of Defense David Chu, and JAMRS Program Manager Matt Boehmer in April 2006.[31] It was settled a few months later, and became effective January 2007, specifying that families have the power to opt out of the database.[32] To date, as both the database and the option to opt out of it is known to only a handful of families, opt-in remains the rule.

A Department of Defense survey taken November 2004, found that "only 25 percent of parents would recommend military service to their children, down from 42 percent in August 2003."[33] The Pentagon responded with a media campaign featuring faux-parents and their faux-children discussing enlistment in a positive light.[34] In addition, the Pentagon tasked JAMRS with studying "influencers"—parents, teachers, clergy, and the like—in the hope of minimizing and/or neutralizing their interference.[35]

JROTC

The Junior Reserve Officers' Training Corps (JROTC) system was created through the National Defense Act of 1916. It offers high schools federal subsidies in the form of funding, equipment, and supplies,[36] which appear to be a good deal for cash-strapped school districts. In fact, this too good to be true deal turns out to be—just that. After a short time, schools discover they have ended up on the red side of the balance sheet—paying out more than they receive. Hidden costs include additional insurance coverage, new facilities construction and maintenance, a portion of JROTC instructors' salaries, benefits, taxes, etc. In short, school districts and the children they support are ripped-off by the program.37

In exchange for the faux-benefits offered, school districts must allow retired military personnel with or without teaching credentials to act as classroom instructors, and they must allow instructors to offer students courses of training authorized by the military, as opposed to local school boards. Reading and study materials used by the program tend to stress a military approach to social and political change, and some materials have been found to include racist versions of history.38

JROTC courses are now offered in over 3,000 high schools as of June 2003,39 and bend the minds of over 500,000 teenage children toward the military.40 Former United States Secretary of Defense William Cohen described the JROTC program as "one of the best recruitment programs we could have."41 And, true enough, 40 percent of those entering the program go on to enlist.42

THINGS RECRUITS AND RECRUITERS PROMISE

Recruits and the Military Contract

A promise is a promise, unless it is offered by a military recruiter. After a recruit is promised the moon, they are asked to sign on the dotted line, most often missing the fine print:

> "Laws and regulations that govern military personnel may change without notice to me. Such changes may affect my status, pay, allowances, benefits, and responsibilities as a member of the Armed Forces REGARDLESS of the provisions of this enlistment/reenlistment document."43

In other words, recruits may be promised specific training and assignments, lofty jobs, or anything at all. The only contract made—despite any oral or written promise—is that the recruit will serve under the Uniform Code of Military Justice (UCMJ)44 rather than under civilian Constitutional law until full and final discharge is *allowed* (sans stop-loss). Any other statements, assurances, or promises—written or otherwise, do not apply.

THE MIRAGE OF JOBS AND COLLEGE FUNDING

Congress and the Department of Defense have long understood that as civilian jobs and educational opportunities decline, the military option becomes more attractive to potential recruits. Military recruiters—and a vast expanse of advertisement copy—hammer the idea home that joining the military and serving it for a few years will open to an oasis of educational and job opportunities. The oasis is a mirage.

A typical recruitment advertisement reads: "Join the Army and earn up to $70,000 for college."[45] The truth is, nearly all enlistees join the Montgomery GI Bill on entering the military, but only one in twenty qualify for the higher Army College Fund or Navy College Fund benefits.[46] In fact 30 percent of those joining the program receive nothing from it,[47] and the rest, nearly always receive only a fraction of the benefits promised.[48]

There are conditions:

➤ In order to be allowed entry into any of the college fund programs, recruits must first pay $100 per month for the first twelve months of service. That $1,200 is fully nonrefundable.[49]

➤ A full honorable discharge from the military is required.[50] One in four fail to achieve that condition.[51]

➤ For those who do achieve full honorable discharges, the payout is tricky: it is made over a total of no more than thirty-six months of educational expenditure (nine month academic year x four years = thirty-six months). If, as is typical, a veteran is unable to take full course loads over each of those thirty-six months, the payout is less, and will still be terminated after a total of thirty-six months in any case. So, for example, if a war-traumatized veteran is able to maintain only a one-half coursework load, the total payout would be—at a maximum—only one-half of that originally promised. Most veterans (56 percent) using the Montgomery GI Bill begin by attending community colleges or vocational schools spread out over time, and therefore receive only a fraction of the maximum promised for full-time, full coursework study.[52]

➤ The cost of education has continually increased while educational benefits have increased less rapidly. As benefits lag further and further behind the inflation curve, the value of the original promise is equally degraded with time.[53]

In summary, recruits rarely collect on the military's "big print" promise to provide significant educational funding.

RECRUITMENT TOOLBOX: MOVIES, TOYS, TV, AND COMPUTER GAMES

Blackhawk Helicopters on High School Campuses

As US families pushed back against the slogans "Be All You Can Be," and "An Army of One," and as potential new recruits increasingly said "no" to joining up, military planners moved new people into command chairs, ramped up their efforts, crafted new slogans, and basically pulled out the stops.54 Fully camo'ed military recruiters now land Blackhawk helicopter warships on elementary, middle, and high school campuses around the country, and issue promises of fun, excitement, and glory to the overwhelmed kids.

The US Army, in a well-funded effort to recruit children, has decked out seven "Cinema Vans" with multiple slide projectors, viewing screens, and rock-climbing walls. Another eighteen-wheeler, the "Army Adventure Van," features a helicopter simulator, an M-1 tank simulator, and an M-16 machine-gun simulator, allowing high school kids to practice and to visualize cutting enemies to pieces. Other vehicles include a "Nuclear Power Van," an "America's Sea Power Van," etc. Together, these propaganda shows on eighteen wheels visit nearly 400,000 of America's children each year.56

"'The vans zero in on our target market, and that's in high schools,' explained Fred Zinchiak, Public Affairs Specialist in the Sacramento Army Recruiting Battalion."57

The targeted markets—this nation's teenagers—are offered a vision of military life as being sexy and exciting. The reality of post-traumatic stress disorder, major depression, and traumatic brain injury suffered by over 1/3 of a million troops returning from the current wars in Iraq and Afghanistan58 is ignored.

Recruitment via Television

As of March 2008, over 11,000 schools have contracted with Channel One, an organization which promises to provide schools with free television equipment and wiring in exchange for a mandatory daily viewing of the programs produced, edited, and broadcast by them.

The twelve-minute programs, aired daily, are interspersed with two minutes of "corporate sponsorship" messages, half of which are paid for by US taxpayers care of the Department of Defense, and in the form of military recruitment pitches to the captive children who are required to watch.[59]

From the Channel One Network website: "Nearly 30 percent of all American teens are in classrooms that show Channel One News." In other words, over 6 million middle and high school students are presently forced to receive daily military recruiter pitches during classroom time.[60]

Recruitment via Hollywood Movies

"We may think that the content of American movies is free from government interference, but in fact, the Pentagon has been telling filmmakers what to say—and what not to say—for decades. It's Hollywood's dirtiest little secret."[61]

The Pentagon has had a cozy relationship with the entertainment industry for many years, providing open door base access, material, and consultation to movie studios . . . for a price.[62]

It is now widely known that the Pentagon has influenced film producers and studios for years—trading access to military resources for censorship rights. Under authority of the Office of the Assistant Secretary of Defense for Public Affairs, the Pentagon's film liaison office trades script changes—acceptable to the brass—with access to otherwise impossibly expensive military material, locations, and expertise. In the end, we the taxpayers pay for our own propagandizing. Recent movies that were given a "hand" by the Pentagon include *Stripes, Black Hawk Down, Pearl Harbor, Top Gun, The Great Santini, The Right Stuff, Apollo 13,* and many others.[63] From David Robb's book *Operation Hollywood*: "The Pentagon is quite candid about why it provides this assistance to Hollywood. According to the army's own handbook, *A Producer's Guide to U.S. Army Cooperation with the Entertainment Industry,* this collaboration must 'aid in the recruiting and retention of personnel.'"[64]

Recruitment via Video Gaming

The Pentagon has vigorously supported development of PC war game software after discovering their use as both recruitment and as military training vehicles. Take, for example, the Microsoft Xbox game *Close Combat: First to Fight*—created by and for the military, but soon ported directly to "T" for Teens.[65]

Another "success" story, in terms of the number of teens and young adults participating, is the US Army's video game project *America's Army*, accessed by several million "players" as of 2007.[66] *America's Army* is a highly graphic, fast paced and graphically violent battle simulation for youthful players. The army states that the game is for growing adults, but it is freely available on the Internet without age restriction and is widely distributed to children.[67]

It has been argued that *America's Army* is blatant government propaganda pitched to those who are least able to understand the effects of exposure to its various subtle and not-so-subtle messages.[68]

VIOLENT VIDEO/VIDEO GAMING IS HARMFUL TO CHILDREN

Despite the overwhelming raft of data documenting ill effects in children and adolescents exposed to violent video and video games, the military services continue to support delivery of those images and experiences to children, seen only as potential future recruits.[69]

From the Committee on Public Education of the American Academy of Pediatrics:

> The American Academy of Pediatrics recognizes exposure to violence in media, including television, movies, music, and video games as a significant risk to the health of children and adolescents. Extensive research evidence indicates that media violence can contribute to aggressive behavior, desensitization to violence, nightmares, and fear of being harmed. Pediatricians should assess their patients' level of media exposure and intervene on media-related health risks. Pediatricians and other child health care providers can advocate for a safer media environment for children by encouraging media literacy, more

thoughtful and proactive use of media by children and their parents, more responsible portrayal of violence by media producers, and more useful and effective media ratings.[70]

From the American Academy of Child and Adolescent Psychiatry:

> Studies of children exposed to violence have shown that they can become: "immune" or numb to the horror of violence, imitate the violence they see, and show more aggressive behavior with greater exposure to violence. Some children accept violence as a way to handle problems. Studies have also shown that the more realistic and repeated the exposure to violence, the greater the impact on children. In addition, children with emotional, behavioral and learning problems may be more influenced by violent images.
>
> Youth who exposed themselves to greater amounts of video game violence saw the world as a more hostile place, were more hostile themselves, got into arguments with teachers more frequently, were more likely to be involved in physical fights, and performed more poorly in school. Video game violence exposure was a significant predictor of physical fights even when respondent sex, hostility level, and weekly amount of game play were statistically controlled."[71]

Summary of the Evidence

Exposure to violent video, whether in the form of video games, television, or theater movies is linked to, and causal of, increases in aggressive cognition, affect and behavior.[72]

Students, Parents, Schools, and Communities Respond

Here is a small sampling of student, parent, school, and community responses to predatory military recruiters and the tactics they employ:

Vallejo, California (2008): The Vallejo School Board voted to end the practice of providing military recruiters with complete and unrestricted access to student information. District spokesman Jason Hodge: "This action brings the school district into compliance with the 'No Child Left Behind Act' which requires parents and students be given the option to 'opt-out' of having military recruiters gain access to their personal information."73

Berkeley, California (2008): The Berkeley City Council passed a resolution that initially stated Marine recruiters were "uninvited and unwelcome intruders." The council later issued a clarification, stating that the recruiting center retains the legal right to exist, but telegraphed to citizens that vigorous protesting of the center's existence is also a protected right.74

Seattle, Washington (2005): The Garfield High School PTA voted to adopt a resolution stating in part: "public schools are not a place for military recruiters."75

National PTA (2005): The National PTA issued a petition stating, "National PTA seeks to increase awareness and community sensitivity about the collection and dissemination of information regarding students and believes that such records should respect the rights to privacy and be relevant to a child's education.

National PTA will continue to support legislation and policies [that] would change current law by providing for an 'opt-in' policy where interested students and families can instead choose to request contact from military recruiters. Parents and students deserve to know who has their information, and parents should be involved in the important decision to enlist in military service."76

Lindale, Georgia (2006): Two seventeen year-old Pepperell High School students confronted recruiters, the school board, and the school's administration, who had insisted students were compelled under law to take the ASVAB military (recruiting tool) test. As the result of their ad-hoc plan to distribute anti-ASVAB flyers to their fellow students and despite the argumentative efforts of local recruiters, an estimated two-thirds of the eligible students present refused to be "tested."77

CONCLUSION

Military recruiters have been given legal authority to openly recruit adolescents on high school campuses, and tacit authority to recruit both adolescents and younger children through more subtle means. Techniques employed include those that are known to be harmful to children, including repeated exposure to violent games and images. Recruiters rely on the immature status of their prey to capture them with false promises, and subterfuge. Military recruitment of children must be understood for what it is: predatory.

The highest calling of any society is to protect its young from harm. Our society is failing to heed this call.

With many thanks to Rick Jahnkow, Project on Youth and Non-Military Opportunities.

GARY EVANS, MD, is a practicing pediatrician and activist in Sonoma County, California. He maintains a website, www.ringnebula.com, dedicated to peaceful activism.

For More Information

American Friends Service Committee: Youth & Militarism, http://www.afsc.org/youthmil/default.htm

Code Pink: Women for Peace, http://www.codepink4peace.org/article.php?id=3911

Committee Opposed to Militarism and the Draft, http://www.comdsd.org/

National Network Opposing Militarism In Our Schools, http://www.nnomy.org/joomla/index.php

Project on Youth and Non-Military Opportunities, http://www.projectyano.org/

Opt-Out Forms

No Child Left Behind Act (NCLB):
English: http://themmob.org//lmca/lmca_forms/Opt_Out_Form_Schools.pdf
Spanish: http://themmob.org//lmca/lmca_forms/lmca-e.pdf

The Joint Advertising and Marketing Research & Studies (JAMRS) Database

Note: Opt-Out requests will be honored for ten years. However, because opt-out screening is based, in part, on the current address of the individual, any change in address will require the submission of a new opt-out request with the new address.

English: http://themmob.org//lmca/lmca_forms/JAMRS_OPT_OUT.pdf
Spanish: http://themmob.org//lmca/lmca_forms/lmca-pentagon-espanol.pdf

Notes

1. Population Representation in the Military Services, Fiscal Year 2004, Table A-1, http://www.defenselink.mil/prhome/poprep2004/download/2004report.pdf; America's Child

Soldier Problem," *In These Times*, May 17, 2007, http://www.inthesetimes .com/article/3199/americas_child_soldier_problem/; "Pentagon's Teen Recruiting Methods Would Make Tobacco Companies Proud," Alternet, http://www.alternet.org/story/51889/.

2. See the US Army's e-Cybermission website, http://www.ecybermission.com/base_public.cfm?url =38500C5F40530E011C27501A1D4A564C.

3. See DOD's Joint Advertising Market Research & Studies database website, www.jamrs.org.

4. "'Epidemic' of military suicides investigated," *The Seattle Times*, November 17, 2007, http://seattletimes.nwsource.com/html/localnews/2004019358_aliciacol17.html.

5. "DoD Announces Recruiting and Retention Numbers for FY2007," US Department of Defense, News Release No. 1202-07, October 10, 2007,http://www.defenselink.mil/releases/ release.aspx?releaseid=11398.

6. "Army Giving More Waivers in Recruiting," *New York Times*, February 14, 2007, http://www.nytimes.com/2007/02/14/us/14military.html.

7. "Recruiters struggle to find an Army," *Seattle Times*, November 12, 2007, http://seattletimes.nwsource.com/html/nationworld/2004008540_recruit12.html.

8. "Army Giving More Waivers in Recruiting," *New York Times*, February 14, 2007, http://www.nytimes.com/2007/02/14/us/14military.html.

9. "Military Recruiting: DOD Needs to Establish Objectives and Measures to Better Evaluate Advertising's Effectiveness;" GAO 03-1005, http://www.gao.gov/new.items/d031005.pdf.

10. "Military Recruiting: DOD and Services Need Better Data to Enhance Visibility over Recruiter Irregularities;" GAO 06-0846, August 2006, http://www.gao.gov/new.items/d06846.pdf.

11. Ibid.

12. Hearings On National Defense Authorization Act for Fiscal Year 2001—H.R. 4205 and Oversight of Previously Authorized Programs Before the Committee On Armed Services—House of Representatives, 106 Congress, 2nd Session, Full Committee Hearings on Authorization and Oversight; Feb. 10, 2000: http://commdocs.house.gov/committees/security/ has041000.000/has041000_of.htm

13. "Army Recruiters Take Show On Road," CBS News, March 16, 2005, http://www.cbsnews.com/stories/2005/03/16/eveningnews/printable681055.shtml.

14. "Military Personnel: Preliminary Observations on Recruiting and Retention Issues within the U.S. Armed Forces," GAO 05-419t, March 16, 2005, http://www.gao.gov/new.items/ d05419t.pdf.

15. Jay N. Giedd, "The Teen Brain: Insights from Neuroimaging," *Journal of Adolescent Health*, Volume 42, Issue 4, April 2008; Elizabeth R. McAnarney "Adolescent Brain Development: Forging New Links?" *Journal of Adolescent Health*, Volume 42, Issue 4, April 2008; "In Vivo Evidence for Post-Adolescent Brain Maturation in Frontal and Striatal Regions," *Nature Neuroscience*, Volume 2, 859–861, 1999, http://www.nature.com/neuro/journal/v2/n10/full/nn1099_859.html.

16. Giedd, "The Teen Brain."

17. Paul R. Sackett and Anne S., "Evaluating Military Advertising and Recruiting: Theory and Methodology," Committee on the Youth Population and Military Recruitment, Phase II, p. 25, http://www.nap.edu/openbook.php?record_id=10867; "Attitudes, Aptitudes, and Aspirations of American Youth: Implications for Military Recruitment," http://books.nap.edu/openbook.php?record_id=10478&page=R1.

18. See NCLB of 2001, signed January 8, 2002, (Contained in § 9528 of the ESEA (20 U.S.C. § 7908), as amended by the No Child Left Behind Act of 2001 (P.L. No. 107-110), and in ten U.S.C. § 503, as amended by 544 of the National Defense Authorization Act for Fiscal Year 2002 (P.L. No. 107-107), http://www.ed.gov/policy/elsec/leg/esea02/107-110.pdf.

19. See NCLB Reauthorization 2007, http://www.ed.gov/nclb/overview/intro/reauth/index.html.

20. United States Army Recruiting Command, USAREC Pamphlet 350-13, 2004, http://www.nodraftnoway.org/public_html/USAREC%20Pam%20350-13%202004090l.pdf.

21. "Military Recruits by High School, Zip Code, Community, State," National Priorities Project Bulletin, November 1, 2005, http://www.uslaboragainstwar.org/article.php?id=9492; Pentagon Creating Student Database, *Washington Post*, June 23, 2005, http://www.washingtonpost.com/wp-dyn/content/article/2005/06/22/AR2005062202305.html.

22. "Army Offers $40K Recruiting Bonus to H.S. Grads," NPR, February 5, 2008,

http://www.npr.org/templates/story/story.php?storyId=18710386; "Earn Money For College," US Navy, http://www.navy.com/benefits/education/earnmoney/; David Solnit and Aimee Allison, *Army of None* (New York: Seven Stories Press, 2007).

23. "Modeling the Individual Enlistment Decision: Final Study Report," US Army Research Institute for the Behavioral and Social Sciences, June 1999, http://stinet.dtic.mil/oai/oai?verb=getRecord&metadataPrefix=html&identifier=ADA364946.

24. See the ASVAB Program, http://www.asvabprogram.com/.

25. "Parent Fact Sheet," ASVAB, http://www.asvabprogram.com/downloads/ASVAB_factsheet-parents.pdf.

26. Navy Recruiting Manual 1130.8F, p. 2-59, http://usmilitary.about.com/od/navyregs/p/usmilitary.about.com/library/pdf/navrecruit.pdf.

27. ASVAB Counselor Manual, November 2005, p. 13, http://www.asvabprogram.com/downloads/asvab_counselor_manual.pdf.

28. Ibid.

29. See DOD's Joint Advertising Market Research & Studies database website, www.jamrs.org.

30. Ibid.

31. See ACLU Complaint/Lawsuit regarding JAMRS, http://www.nyclu.org/files/hanson_v_rumsfeld_complaint_042406.pdf.

32. "DOD's Answer to ACLU's Revised JAMRS Plan," January 9, 2007, http://www.nyclu.org/files/jamrs_revised_rules_notice_0109007.pdf.

33. "Growing Problem for Military Recruiters: Parents," *New York Times*, June 3, 2005, http://www.nytimes.com/2005/06/03/nyregion/03recruit.html?oref=login.

34. "Army, Marine recruiters shift focus to wary parents," *USA Today*, April 4, 2005, http://www.usatoday.com/news/washington/2005-04-04-recruiters-parents_x.htm.

35. See DoD's Joint Advertising Market Research & Studies database website, www.jamrs.org.

36. "Making Soldiers in the Public Schools," American Friends Service Committee, 1995, http://www.afsc.org/youthmil/militarism-in-schools/msitps.pdf; David Goodman, "Recruiting the Class of 2005," *Mother Jones*, January/February 2002, http://motherjones.com/news/feature/2002/01/rotc.html.

37. Philip Clark, "Trading Books for Soldiers: The True Cost of JROTC," American Friends Service Committee, 2000, http://web.archive.org/web/20000816192857/www.afsc.org/youthmil/html/issues/schools/jrotcost.htm.

38. "Making Soldiers in the Public Schools"; Goodman, "Recruiting the Class of 2005."

39. "Feeding the military machine: JROTC expansion and inner-city academies mark recruiting incursion into U.S. public school classrooms, critics say"; Mar. 28, 2003, National Catholic Reporter: http://findarticles.com/p/articles/mi_m1141/is_21_39/ai_99849547

40. Philip Clark, "Trading Books for Soldiers: The True Cost of JROTC," American Friends Service Committee, 2000, http://web.archive.org/web/20000816192857/www.afsc.org/youthmil/html/issues/schools/jrotcost.htm.

41. Ibid.

42. Goodman, "Recruiting the Class of 2005."

43. See Enlistment Contract, DD FORM 4/3, October 2007, page 2, section C. 9(b), www.dtic.mil/whs/directives/infomgt/forms/eforms/dd0004.pdf.

44. See Uniform Code of Military Justice Legislative History, http://www.loc.gov/rr/frd/Military_Law/UCMJ_LHP.html.

45. Solnit and Allison, *Army of None*.

46. "Joining the Military is Hazardous to Your Education," Objector.org, http://www.objector.org/before-you-enlist/gi-bill.html.

47. Terry Howell, "Lawmakers Urge GI Bill Extension," Military.com, May 9, 2007, http://www.military.com/NewsContent/0,13319,135109,00.html.

48. Marla Jo Fisher, "Why aren't military vets going to college?" *Orange County Register*, March 10, 2008, http://www.ocregister.com/news/veterans-college-state-1995807-people-military.

49. Howell, "Lawmakers Urge GI Bill Extension"; see US Dept. of Veterans Affairs, Montgomergy GI Bill -CH30 Pamphlet, http://www.gibill.va.gov/pamphlets/CH30/CH30_Pamphlet_General.htm; for the entire program, see US Dept. of Veterans Affairs, GI Bill Website: http://www.gibill.va.gov/GI_Bill_Info/benefits.htm.

50. Ibid.

51. Solnit and Allison, *Army of None.*

52. "GI Bill falling short of college tuition costs," *Boston Globe*, February 10, 2008, http://www.boston.com/news/nation/washington/articles/2008/02/10/gi_bill_falling_short_of _college_tuition_costs/.

53. Ibid.

54. Solnit and Allison, *Army of None.*

55. "Hanna grad flies Blackhawk to school," *Sonoma Index-Tribune*, March 20, 2008, http://www.sonomanews.com/articles/2008/03/21/news/doc47df124d179b9525933769.txt; "Black Hawk touches down at schools," *Press Democrat*, March 15, 2008, http://www1.pressdemocrat.com/article/20080315/NEWS/803150397/1033/NEWS&template=k art.

56. "Mobile Recruiting 2001," Objector.org, http://www.objector.org/awol/mobile.html.

57. Ibid.

58. "One In Five Iraq and Afghanistan Veterans Suffer from PTSD or Major Depression," RAND Corporation News Release, April 17, 2008, http://rand.org/news/press/2008/04/17/.

59. Solnit and Allison, *Army of None.*

60. "Why Go to College, When You Can Be Cannon Fodder?" Counterpunch, February 17, 2005, http://www.counterpunch.org/whitehurst02172005.html; see "Fast Facts," Channel One News website, http://www.channelonenetwork.com/corporate/fast_facts.html; see also "FAQS," Channel One News website, http://www.channelonenetwork.com/corporate/faqs.html.

61. David Robb, "Operation Hollywood: How the Pentagon Shapes and Censors the Movies," *Mother Jones*, 2004, http://www.motherjones.com/news/qa/2004/09/09_403.html.

62. "The Pentagon Goes Hollywood," *Time Magazine*, November 24, 1986, http://www.time.com/time/magazine/article/0,9171,962933,00.html.

63. Ibid.; Nick Turse, *The Complex* (New York: Henry Holt, 2008), 115-117.

64. Robb, "Operation Hollywood."

65. Turse, *The Complex.*

66. "Gamers Downloading America's Army," January 12, 2007, http://www.voanews.com/english/archive/2007-01/2007-01-12-voa35.cfm.

67. See the US Army's "Official Army Game" website: http://www.americasarmy.com/.

68. Joan Ryan, "Army's War Game Recruits Kids," *San Francisco Chronicle*, September 24, 2004.

69. Turse, *The Complex.*

70. "Media Violence," American Academy of Pediatrics Policy Statement, Volume 108, Number 5, November 2001, p.1222-1226, http://aappolicy.aappublications.org/cgi/content/full/pediatrics ;108/5/1222.

71. "Children and Video Games: Playing with Violence," American Academy of Child and Adolescent Psychiatry, Facts for Families: No. 91, http://www.aacap.org/cs/root/facts _for_families/children_and_video_games_playing_with_violence; see also No. 13, "Children and TV Violence," http://www.aacap.org/cs/root/facts_for_families/children_and_tv_violence.

72. "An update on the effects of playing violent video games," *Journal of Adolescence*, Volume 27: 2004, p. 113-122; Paul J. Lynch, Douglas A. Gentile, Abbie A. Olson, and Tara M., "The Effects of Violent Video Game Habits on Adolescent Aggressive Attitudes and Behaviors," Presentation for the Biennial meeting of the Society for Research in Child Development, Minneapolis, MN, April 19-22, 2001; B.J. Bushman and R. Huesmann, "Short term and long term effects of violent media on aggression in children and adults," *Archives of Pediatrics and Adolescent Medicine*, Volume 160: 2006, p. 348-352; S.H. Chaffee, "Television and adolescent aggressiveness," G.A. Comstock and E.A. Rubinstein, eds., "Television and social behavior: a technical report to the Surgeon General's Scientific Advisory Committee on Television and Social Behavior," DHEW Publication No. HSM 72-9058 (Washington, DC: U.S. Government Printing Office, 1972), p. 1-34; B.E. Sheese and W.G. Graziano, "Deciding to defect: the effects of video game violence on cooperative behavior," *Psychological Science*, Volume 16: 2005, p. 354-357; D.A. Gentile, P.J. Lynch, J.R. Linder, and D.A. Walsh, "The effects of violent video game habits on adolescent hostility, aggressive behaviors, and school performance," *Journal of Adolescence*, Volume 27: 2004, p. 5-22; E. Uhlmann and J. Swanson, "Exposure to violent video games increases automatic aggressiveness," *Journal of Adolescence*, Volume 27:2004, p. 41-52.

73. "Vallejo School District Votes To Shut Out Military Recruiters," NBC.com, March 20, 2008, http://www.nbc11.com/newsarchive/15655946/detail.html.

74. "The Military vs. Berkeley," *Newsweek*, February 13, 2008, http://www.newsweek.com/id/110911.

75. "Rift Over Recruiting At Public High School," *Christian Science Monitor*, May 18, 2005, http://www.csmonitor.com/2005/0518/p02s01-ussc.html.

76. "Military Recruitment in Schools," National PTA, August 2, 2005, www.pta.org/documents/military.pdf.

77. "Teens Frustrate Military Recruiter's ASVAB Scam," Antiwar.com, November 24, 2006, http://www.antiwar.com/orig/horton.php?articleid=10055.

Deconstructing Deceit
9/11, the Media, and Myth Information

by Mickey S. Huff and Paul W. Rea

> They say goldfish have no memory
> I guess their lives are much like mine
> and the little plastic castle
> is a surprise every time
> and it's hard to say if they're happy
> but they don't seem much to mind.
> —Ani DiFranco, *Little Plastic Castles*

For the past eight years, American culture has experienced an outburst of media-driven mythmaking. Corporate mainstream media organizations, the pundits they sponsor, and politicians from both major parties have formed a new contextual chorus singing the same refrain: "On September 11th, 2001, everything changed." From cable TV to AM radio, from the blogosphere to the townhall meeting, Americans are repeatedly told "this is a post-9/11 world."

Although there is some truth to this platitude of pivotal change, independently minded citizens may also wonder whether such mass media messages have become self-fulfilling prophecies. This provides an interesting point of debate about what has or has not changed in America since 9/11.

This chapter concerns itself with the ongoing phenomena of media mythmaking and how, like many Americans surmised just after 9/11, everything has not changed.[1] Corporate mainstream media have resurrected powerful myths from America's past to shape public perception in the present. Through the prism of 9/11, one can see how the corporate mass media are in fact doing more mythmaking than news reporting. Here, the authors will examine central historic American myths the corporate media and even much of the alternative independent media have extended into the post-9/11 era. This analysis looks at how media mythmaking surrounding the events of 9/11, exploiting the strong emotions these events aroused, has prevented a dispassionate inquiry of its causes or of those responsible.

TELLING ONLY THE OFFICIAL STORY: AN ACT OF CENSORSHIP

Both the corporate and independent media have typically not approached the events of 9/11 with open inquiry. With very few exceptions, the corporate mainstream media and their independent alternatives have dismissed critical 9/11 questions as "conspiratorial" or "unpatriotic." Even the left press, including the *Nation, In These Times, Mother Jones,* and the *Progressive,* among others, have repeatedly demonstrated resistance, even hostility, to free inquiry into the attacks. Perhaps some muckraking progressives have forgotten the words of one of their own icons, American anarchist and feminist Emma Goldman, who aptly remarked, "The most unpardonable sin in society is independence of thought." Like their mainstream corporate counterparts, journalists in the independent press have often highlighted eccentric personalities and extreme statements rather than focus on the troubling evidence skeptics have brought forth. This practice institutionalizes acts of self-censorship based upon America's historical mythology, which will be discussed later in this article.[2]

Traditional American mythology was used to exalt the official story of 9/11, a story that has become the only story. New York University historian Tony Judt recently lamented that today's discourse centers almost exclusively on "official accounts as officially rendered and received."[3] Nowhere is this truer than with the case of 9/11. The mainstream corporate media and even the progressive press have repeatedly endorsed the government-sponsored official story formalized in the *9/11 Commission Report.* This narrative tells us that nineteen Islamic extremists conspired and outwitted the best-defended country in the world. Because government agencies ignored the many pre-warnings, these terrorists were able to catch American defenders by surprise, hijack four airliners, and ram three of them into targets symbolic of American economic and military might.[4]

But is this the full and true story? Are there other narratives that square better with the evidence? Are significant details being ignored?

These are not questions that the American news media have encouraged the public to ask. Resistance from the news media, both corporate and independent, has effectively prevented adequate reportage, fact-based discussions, and in-depth analyses of 9/11. This paradoxical suppression has made the full story of 9/11 a recurring concern in the publications of Project Censored.5

In fact, some pundits have actively attacked those who have challenged the official story of 9/11, as if they were blasphemers, and continue to rely upon strong religious overtones in defense of American mythology and government-endorsed interpretations of the events of 9/11. MSNBC's Tucker Carlson exemplified this tendency during an interview with 9/11 scholar and theologian Dr. David Ray Griffin. On the program, Carlson attacked the professor for challenging the official narrative of 9/11. As soon as Griffin claimed he rejected the government's explanation for the events of 9/11, before he had any chance to explain his views, Carlson interrupted and attacked, ". . . it is wrong, blasphemous, and sinful for you to suggest, imply, or help other people come to the conclusion that the US government killed 3,000 of its own citizens because it didn't."6 In this case, as in many others, the interviewer attacked even the prospect of discussion concerning alternative ideas about 9/11 before they began, thus framing the rest of the interview and reinforcing the official myths of 9/11.

Here we arrive at a crucial corollary: media mythmaking discourages pluralistic perspectives on reality, and thus also amounts to a form of censorship.

A CULTURE DEEPLY ROOTED IN ITS MYTHS

Myths which are believed in tend to become true. —George Orwell

Even before it became a country, America relied heavily on cultural mythology to provide a sense of meaning and purpose. This was evident in the belief, expressed by several early colonial leaders, that America and the New World were "virgin lands," places free of the historical taints left behind in Europe. Early Puritan leader John Winthrop stated that America "shall be as a city on a hill," to be looked upon and revered as the new promised land.7

As their needs changed, Americans told themselves new stories. To create a new republic, Americans needed defining beliefs in their own uniqueness and needed to generate a sense of national mission. By the nineteenth century, this constellation of ideals came to dominate the minds of most Americans under the rubric of Manifest Destiny, a term coined by nineteenth-century journalist and media mythmaker, John O'Sullivan. These included that 1) America is both exceptional and triumphant in all endeavors; 2) America, divinely inspired, is destined become the worldwide beacon for democracy; and 3) the new republic would act militarily only in defense of its national interests.[8]

Intellectuals, politicians, journalists, pundits, and radio/TV/Internet personalities have long reinforced these mythic motifs. They have become part of America's historical grand narrative. However, there exist alternatives more grounded in the historical record that often contradict the official narratives. These should be explored.

THE AFTERMATH OF 9/11: A FRENZY OF MEDIA MYTHMAKING

In times of psychological trauma, societies tend to revert to their myths. After 9/11, many distraught Americans looked to their traditional mythology for personal meaning and national purpose; no one in America wanted to appear unpatriotic. Always attuned to popular moods and trends, politicians also framed subsequent events in familiar terms of traditional myths. In turn, the media, echoing powerful political forces, resurrected the myths of national purpose and loyalty, moral exceptionalism, and triumph over adversity, to make sense of recent events.

Leading the way for others in the media, *CBS News* anchor Dan Rather proclaimed, "I'm going to do my job as a journalist, but at the same time I will give them [the Bush administration] the benefit of the doubt, whenever possible in this kind of crisis, emergency situation. Not because I am concerned about any [public] backlash. I'm not. But because I want to be a patriotic American without apology."[9] Rather later regretted such a stance, but at the time, this reinforced the power of blind nationalism in a time of crisis. Most in the corporate press mimicked this sycophancy, relinquishing their role as watchdogs and becoming mere lapdogs to those in power.

President George W. Bush continued this trajectory of nationalist mythology after the 9/11 attacks by claiming that the world had changed and was now divided into binary forces of good and evil. People and nations around the globe had to choose a side: they were either with us or against us. In this vein, "enemies" were not just abroad, or "over there" like in the two previous world wars, but were also domestic, possibly including American citizens themselves.

Not long after 9/11, Bill Maher, host of ABC's *Politically Incorrect*, responded to a statement by President Bush claiming that the 9/11 terrorists were cowards. Maher quipped, "We have been the cowards. Lobbing cruise missiles from two thousand miles away. That's cowardly. Staying in the airplane when it hits the building. Say what you want about it. Not cowardly."[10] Shortly thereafter, Maher lost his show at ABC. In response to Maher, White House spokesperson Ari Fleischer warned that in a post-9/11 world, Americans needed to "watch what they say."[11]

Such McCarthyism demonstrated the consequences of straying from the nationalist narrative.[12] Ironically, journalists should have been the ones leading national policy debate after 9/11, all the while including pluralistic viewpoints. But, like Dan Rather, many became stenographers for those in power, marginalizing and even demonizing critical perspectives along the way.

RESURRECTING TRADITIONAL AMERICAN MYTHS

Just days after 9/11, Bush revived the enshrined myths of the Wild West and frontier days to normalize the War on Terror. Bush resorted to false dilemmas such as "you are either with us or against us," and "this is a battle of good and evil," in addition to notions of vigilante justice, employing phrases like "Wanted: Dead or Alive" and "I say, bring it on," to express national security concerns and foreign policies. Few in the media exposed the president's simplistic, emotionally charged, even macho posturing.

Bush's Wild West allusions further allowed the administration to substitute al Qaeda terrorists for previously demonized Native Americans, outlaws, and other stereotyped villains, including Osama bin Laden. Bin Laden not only lacked any connection to Iraq, according to the FBI, he was not a suspect in the crimes of 9/11 due to lack of evidence. Still, a $25 million reward for bin Laden in connection with

9/11 was offered by the Rewards for Justice Program, administered by the US Department of State, a non-investigatory body. This contradicts the FBI's position on the matter.[13]

Furthermore, this mythical path of Wild West justice paved the way to later justifications for preemptive wars, torture, and seeing the Geneva Conventions as "quaint."[14] Again, the mainstream media did not question this path, rather, they heralded it as necessary in a post-9/11 world.[15] America hurtled headlong into the abstract War on Terror while watching a Western melodrama in the rear-view mirror.

SUPPRESSION, DISTORTION, AND DENIAL BASED ON COLLECTIVE HISTORICAL AMNESIA

Another factor that has blocked discussion of the events of 9/11 is the overt denial that a supposedly democratically elected government could have played a role in the attacks. Right or wrong, this denial has largely precluded analyses of the attacks beyond the official conspiracy theory pointing to government unawareness or incompetence exploited by nineteen al Qaeda jihadists, as well as the "blowback" theory pointing to the resentments generated by decades of misguided US foreign policy. Except among liberals, the latter view is still unpopular. This became apparent in the recent media-driven outrage over the "America has blood on its hands" remark, attributed to James Wright, former reverand of Democratic presidential candidate Barack Obama, when interviewed on Bill Moyers's PBS program.[16]

Other interpretations of 9/11 events have rarely received fair and open treatment in the American press. These alternative hypotheses suggest possible involvement by elements within the American government: letting the attacks happen on purpose to enable a war, or making the attacks happen on purpose to enable a war. A better knowledge of relevant history might have helped both journalists and the public to consider these additional possibilities in a broader context. Looking to American history, one can see the 9/11 attacks in a pattern of contrived provocations.[17]

HISTORICAL PRECEDENTS FOR UNOFFICIAL ALTERNATIVE INTERPRETATIONS

Who controls the past controls the future. Who controls the present controls the past. —George Orwell

Historical precedents can operate as counternarratives to national myths. When looked at inclusively, they can be a great teacher. Mainstream corporate media have largely excluded historical context of the type that might generate critical inquiry surrounding the tragic events of 9/11 and the War on Terror. It is as if the facts surrounding certain important historical events have virtually been written *out* of history. A walk down this "memory hole lane" can be an antidote to another kind of censorship, the sin of omission, which otherwise provides quite useful information.

One may find stunning the following chronology of US foreign policy events, especially given that it is based on historical facts. Given this pattern of provocations, pretexts, and false-flag operations, the alternative hypotheses about 9/11 fit the pattern of government deception, while the standard mythic narrative becomes the anomaly. While this does not prove anything outright about 9/11, it should at least pave the way for—rather than be an obstruction to—open inquiry by the media.[18] Observe:

1846: US maneuvers along the Mexican border are calculated to spark a war between the US and Mexico, resulting in the American-Mexican War. President James K. Polk was directly implicated in the affair, of provoking a war with Mexico on contested territory that garnered all of what is now the American Southwest. These actions were widely supported by what was known as the Southern Slave Power Conspiracy.[19]

1898: The Spanish-American War began after an accidental explosion took place on the *USS Maine* as it was moored in the Havana Harbor. Though the Spanish attempted to avert war, major US news outlets, with the Hearst papers taking the lead, claimed that Spain had attacked a US warship despite a lack of evidence. Waving the bloody shirt, the "yellow" press popularized a well-known battle cry: "Remember the Maine and to Hell with Spain!" In the war that ensued, the US seized not only Cuba, but also the other Spanish colonies of Puerto Rico and the Philippines.[20]

1915: At the outset of World War I, other "trigger incidents" occurred. Among the most well known was the sinking of the British luxury liner *Lusitania*, which served as a pretext, this time for entry into WWI. Though the US government was aware that the liner would be secretly carrying munitions in its hold, it did little to alert the public. The stow-away munitions included shells and cartridges intended for English forces fighting the Germans. When a German U-boat sank the great liner, 1195 passengers and crew perished. As public outrage in response to the German atrocity mounted, and as propaganda efforts ensued, President Woodrow Wilson brought the US into World War I by 1917.[21]

1941: The alleged sneak attack at Pearl Harbor is one of the most powerful mythic tales in US history, a historic event that has been used as propaganda to manipulate public opinion to this day. For Americans, the trauma that launched World War II was the Japanese attack on Pearl Harbor. While it was and has long since been billed as a sneak attack, ample evidence shows, most recently by historian Robert Stinnett in *Day of Deceit*, that the event was in fact provoked by the US government and allowed to happen in order to manipulate public opinion, thus leading to war. This became America's mythical Day of Infamy. Now enshrined in the American psyche, the Pearl Harbor myth strongly reinforces the idea that America only attacks when attacked. Regardless, the facts show that the Pearl Harbor example is another in a long line of deceptive events used to marshal public support for wars throughout American history.[22]

Utilizing the power of the Pearl Harbor myth, the neoconservative Project for a New American Century used this historical analogy in the fall of 2000, in a document called *Rebuilding America's Defenses*. In it, they hypothesized what might be necessary to justify a radical shift in US foreign policy. The authors stated that a transformation in US policy promoting a projecting force would be difficult, as ". . . the process of transformation, even if it brings revolutionary change, is likely to be a long one, absent some catastrophic and catalyzing event—like a new Pearl Harbor."[23] The Bush administration, along with the corporate press, used the events of 9/11 to revive the myth that America doesn't strike first and only fights when attacked, and then only to spread and preserve liberty at home and abroad. Pearl Harbor was the historical glue that held the 9/11 official narrative together without much analysis by journalists.[24]

1964: The Gulf of Tonkin "Incident" sparked mass escalation of the Vietnam War. To ready a reluctant public for war, American planners executed several raids along the North Vietnamese coast but became frustrated when American ships took no return fire. President Lyndon B. Johnson, Defense Secretary Robert McNamara, and other top officials concluded that some flashpoint, some pretext beyond just "stopping communism," would be needed to arouse public outrage. If there was no attack, then one must be contrived.[25]

The "response" took the form of purported North Vietnamese torpedo-boat attacks on two US destroyers. In August 1964, the first of these ships was supposedly attacked by North Vietnamese torpedo boats.[26] Two days later, the news media announced that the North Vietnamese had attacked a second American ship. Although the Pentagon insisted that its warships frightened off the attackers, officers on the destroyers later revealed that "our destroyers were just shooting at phantom targets—there were no PT boats there."[27]

Nevertheless, within days Congress passed the Tonkin Gulf Resolution, based on events that did not happen, plunging the United States into a disastrous "police action" that lasted for a decade, killed 3 million people, and disgraced the United States.[28]

Observations

These historical examples should be recounted by those in the media reporting on relevant matters in the present. Instead, important events that counter official American mythology are often ignored, a trend that was formalized in the early twentieth century.

The advent of World War I catapulted the new science of propaganda to the forefront of government operations. President Woodrow Wilson established the first official propaganda system, placing public relations wizard George Creel in charge of the Committee on Public Information. The role of the CPI was to selectively inform the public to a desired end. The program was a success. With the help of Edward Bernays, an early proponent of propaganda and nephew of Sigmund

Freud, the government developed new ways to persuade a pacifistic American public into "The War to End all Wars" and "The War to make the World Safe for Democracy." In his 1928 classic, *Propaganda*, Bernays said, "The conscious and intelligent manipulation of the organized habits and opinions of the masses is an important element in democratic society. Those who manipulate this unseen mechanism of society constitute an invisible government which is the true ruling power of our country."29

This chapter will further deconstruct the denials and deceptions of the official grand narrative of 9/11 and analyze the role of the media in popularizing them in the public mind.

INSTANT MYTHMAKING ON 9/11

I. Immediate Construction of an Official Narrative

The great enemy of the truth is very often not the lie, deliberate, contrived and dishonest, but the myth—persistent, persuasive and unrealistic. —John F. Kennedy

On September 11, 2001, government officials and media outlets began to construct an official account with unprecedented dispatch. Even before the attacks were over, the counterterrorism division of the Federal Bureau of Investigation (FBI) was telling National Security Advisor Richard Clarke it was al Qaeda operatives who had attacked the World Trade Center. This account was adapted and amplified in the days, weeks, and months following the attacks.30

On the one hand, top officials were claiming that these were sneak attacks and that they were caught completely off guard. Yet by 11 a.m. on 9/11, the FBI started releasing the names, nationalities, and photos of the nineteen suspected hijackers. Before the smoke and dust settled, media mythmakers were ready to supply instant meaning, relying heavily on traditional mythology and popular history.

But if the federal establishment knew so little as to be taken completely by surprise, how could they so rapidly come up with an exact list of those responsible? Had federal agencies been keeping close watch on these al Qaeda operatives? Adding to the contradictions, the accuracy of this roster proved suspect. In the weeks immediately following the attacks, several news outlets, including the British Broadcasting Corporation (BBC), reported that individuals on the FBI's list were still alive.[31] Those reports had to raise logical doubts about the validity of the official story, which may be one reason why they received scant media coverage in the US.

II. News Networks Lead 9/11 Mythmaking

History is the present. That's why every generation writes it anew. But what most people think of as history is its end product, myth.
—E. L. Doctorow

If the rapidity of these initial identifications was amazing, the instant involvement of the news media was equally so. Reporting by major TV networks in the initial hours contributed immensely to instant mythmaking; in retrospect, though, it has also stirred serious questions.

Just two hours after the Towers came down, Senator Orrin Hatch (R-Utah), of the Senate Intelligence Committee, implicated bin Laden in the events of 9/11, even though few facts pointed to his involvement then or later.[32] Through media mythmaking, bin Laden became the ready-made, chief suspect of the 9/11 attacks, despite his denial of involvement. The FBI later dropped him from the Most Wanted list, citing lack of evidence.[33]

But, if these were surprise attacks, then how, on the very day of the attacks, could the government and some corporate media outlets have known who was responsible? For example, CNN, at four o'clock in the afternoon on 9/11, blamed bin Laden "based on new and specific information developed since the attacks."[34] Corporate media and the federal government were peering through the smoke of the day with amazing clarity, foreshadowing future policy, perhaps generating another self-fulfilling prophesy in the ensuing War on Terror. President Bush wrote in his diary the night of the attacks, "The Pearl Harbor of the twenty-first century took place today. . . . We think it's Osama bin Laden."[35]

After the destruction of the Twin Towers, FOX News cut to a "man on the street," an eyewitness who foreshadowed what would later become the official story born at Ground Zero. FOX News interviewed the man, who somehow explained, ". . . I witness[ed] both Towers collapse, one first and then the second, mostly due to structural failure because the fire was just too intense."[36] This, too, seems odd. In a state of near shock, this man speculated on the cause of the catastrophe, foreshadowing what later became the official view. Alternative narratives were offered that first day and afterwards, but were crowded out by this tale born on the street, which would later become the official narrative of the *9/11 Commission Report.*

Alternative Narratives: Suppression of First Responder Testimonies

Instead of simply interviewing a passerby, the news media might have interviewed first responders for insight into what might have brought down the buildings. When news teams interviewed first responders, they typically focused on their accounts of heroism or the horror of their experiences. Almost without exception, news coverage did not report the vast number of first-responder testimonials about explosions before and during the fall of the Towers.

Possibly anticipating the importance of their onsite, eyewitness observations, some first responders made a tape of their testimonials. On this tape, dozens of firefighters spoke of hearing explosions, particularly "boom, boom, boom" sounds just as the Towers began to come down. In 2002, similar reports emerged in interviews with firefighters. Firefighter Thomas Turilli recalled that it "sounded like bombs going off, like boom, boom, boom, like seven or eight, and then just a huge wind gust just came and my officer just actually took all of us and threw us down on the ground and kind of just jumped on top of us, laid on top of us."[37] This was only one of literally dozens of similar first-responders testimonials, all of them speaking of explosions.

Right after the attacks, the City of New York impounded the firefighters' tape and the Fire Department forbade anyone to discuss its contents because, it claimed, the tape might later become evidence in court trials. This suppression of evidence continued under mayors Rudy Giuliani and Michael Bloomberg. Only three years later, after ongoing pressure from the families of victims and a suit by the *New York Times*, would the city finally release the taped oral histories.[38]

Because of the way the buildings disintegrated and dropped, other observers also suspected that the Towers had not simply "collapsed." In fact, *CBS News* anchor Dan Rather reported on 9/11 that the collapse was "reminiscent of . . . when a building was deliberately destroyed by well-placed dynamite to knock it down." *ABC News with Peter Jennings* also pointed out this resemblance. Since 9/11, however, no one in the corporate media has ever made such a comparison again.39

III. Premature Reports on WTC Building 7

Odd journalistic practices also surrounded the fall of a third World Trade Center skyscraper, World Trade Center Building 7 (WTC-7). That CNN's breaking story about the "collapse" of WTC-7 aired a half hour before it happened, and BBC's coverage, twenty-six minutes before it came down, should have generated considerable media buzz at the time, but they were immediately forgotten.40

Since no plane had hit this forty-seven-story, steel-framed skyscraper, and since its fires were far smaller than those in the Towers, why would anyone anticipate its disintegration and collapse? Once again, an unbelievably early journalistic report anticipated the official story. Thus media mythmakers offered what later became the official narrative prior to the event and then expanded it in the days and months following.41 How likely is it, though, that two networks would make the *same* mistake while covering the *same* event? Here we have instances in which the timing of news reports either seems highly improbable or is completely incredible. Regardless of one's interpretation, why has this issue not been explored by the mainstream media in the US? Very recently, the London-based *Financial Times* published one of the most detailed pieces on WTC-7 in the corporate press to date. Otherwise, few in that genre have covered this controversial story.42

In the context of narrative myth building, this is something that should be questioned and debated within the media. Virtually no one in the American mainstream media and only a few people in the independent press have investigated these stories. This malpractice of the corporate mainstream media alone merits investigation.

IV. The Last Moments of Flight 93: Old Myths Find New Applications

Not all the myths contextualizing 9/11 came from the past. The calamity of a homeland attack called for new myths to be developed and allowed the opinion-formation industry to exploit this cultural vulnerability. Not only did corporate media fail to adequately explain these tragic events, but they generated mythic tales in their stead (e.g. the popular TV film *Flight 93*).

Best known of these myths is that of the heroic passengers on Flight 93, who, by revolting against their captors, prevented another strike on Washington, DC. In so doing, the passengers not only provided a model of how Americans could fight back, but they launched the first counterattack in the War on Terror. While few would deny that rising up against captors on an airplane is heroic, assuming that this action necessarily prevented another "hit" on the nation's capital requires other assumptions, such as that multi-trillion dollar US air defenses would somehow continue to fail. To believe the myth of Flight 93, one also has to ignore significant amounts of forensic evidence, including fragments of the plane found fully eight miles from its crash site.[43]

Networks Script Story of Unselfish Heroism

All myths need heroes. In the case of Flight 93, several possible heroes were identified by networks through alleged cell phone calls. Although there is ongoing controversy about whether or not calls could be placed by cell phones at that time, this detail is immaterial to the construction of the myth of Flight 93.[44]

Whether the calls actually went through or not, the "Let's Roll" flight, as it came to be known, occasioned an unprecedented outburst of instant media mythmaking. Over the next few days, well over a dozen people reported receiving calls from loved ones—mostly calls to new widows whose spouses had gone down with Flight 93 when it crashed near Shanksville, Pennsylvania. Poignant stories told by these survivors of the victims entered a public consciousness already engulfed with pathos and anxiety.

Looking for sensational human-interest stories, the mainstream networks immediately focused on the life-and-death heroism aboard United Flight 93.[45] In the complete absence of empirical proof, the major networks became involved in scripting stories they apparently intended to tell and later sell. Although passengers' calls to loved ones had not been verified, the corporate news media jumped on the story. Several networks rushed the story on the air, devoting enormous amounts of time to survivors' relatives who had reportedly received calls, and thus indelibly imprinted a story of heroic sacrifice. Given the need for both affirmation and emotional identification with the bereaved spouses, these shows achieved sensational ratings. Software salesman Todd Beamer's enigmatic last words, overheard by an Airfone operator, have become legendary: "You ready? OK. Let's roll." As most of us recall, the passenger revolt reportedly began in response to this battle cry.[46]

Few viewers seemed to care that Todd Beamer never spoke to his wife, but rather talked for fifteen minutes with GTE Airfone/Verizon operator Lisa Jefferson. Ms. Jefferson promised to call Todd's wife Lisa if he didn't make it home. However, Jefferson failed to follow GTE company protocol: she did not record the emergency call from Todd Beamer. Therefore the networks had no way to verify the call.[47] Once the call went public, media outlets deluged Lisa Beamer with invitations: over the next year or so, she granted over two hundred interviews. CNN's Larry King provided a platform from which Beamer could advocate the Bush administration's $7 billion victim-compensation plan.[48] Again, rather than report in the context of a possibly unknowable reality, corporate media presented the heroic myth without disclaimers.

Further traumatizing the public, this came at a time when the country was still reeling in shock from the horrific images of the falling Twin Towers. It wasn't just that the images of the falling Towers ran hundreds of times on primetime TV, it was also that these images were so hauntingly suggestive. Ever attuned to the power of metaphor, linguist and cognitive psychologist George Lakoff has pointed out that many Americans saw the disintegration of the Towers much as they perceived the fall of the people who jumped from them: as the "falling bodies" of themselves and their compatriots. Even more graphically, Lakoff remarked, "the image of the plane going into [the] South Tower was for me an image of a bullet going through someone's head, the flames pouring from the other side like blood spurting out. It was an assassination."[49] This further buttressed the myth of the official story: that on 9/11, freedom itself, personified in the Towers, was attacked.

Many observers have also pointed out that, in the popular mind, the Towers were symbols of American capitalism and global interventionism. This was why al Qaeda "mastermind" Khalid Shaikh Mohammed claimed they were repeatedly selected as targets.[50] An interesting counter myth in corporate media can be seen in a book by

Time magazine's Mitch Frank, in which he claims the Towers were global symbols of peace, and the evildoers, as Bush called the terrorists, were attacking not only American freedom, but the concept of peace itself. The latter myth would become a powerful justification for the War on Terror.[51]

As though planned in accord with Naomi Klein's book *Shock Doctrine*, the alarming images of 9/11 prepared the public for new myths which undergirded new policies—the War on Terror, Homeland Security, and the USA PATRIOT ACT—policies that were unthinkable before the psychic cataclysm of 9/11.[52]

The Need for an Affirmative Tale of Heroism

In this time of national trauma and humiliation, another account with immense appeal began to emerge. It told of a passenger revolt that, after several minutes of struggle, either took back the cockpit and/or caused the hijackers to lose control of the plane.[53] This cockpit-takeover story told Americans that heroic passengers not only fought back, but prevented another attack on Washington. Even before the last plane went down, the first battle in the War on Terror began.

But this was not just a feel-good, patriotic myth; it also distracted and crowded out another story, one with more sinister implications. On 9/11 and in the days that followed, military sources reported a shoot-down in Pennsylvania, and considerable forensic evidence pointed to one.[54] A variety of sources, from local news media to top Pentagon officials, initially reported that Flight 93 was shot down, only to drop or change their stories soon afterward.[55] The Pentagon's initial accounts of Flight 93 disclosed that F-16 fighters were tracking the troubled flight, and some military accounts even indicated that an F-16 shot it down.[56] However, evidence for a shoot-down was far from what the public wanted to hear. Again, regardless of what one concludes about the fate of Flight 93, the corporate media focus was on tales of heroism and American might, not the forensics on the ground.

Ongoing Media Reinforcement of the Flight 93 Myth

Whatever the truth about the final moments of Flight 93, they were highly charged, dramatic material with mass appeal. Four movie reenactments soon followed: *Let's Roll: The Story of Flight 93* (2002), *The Flight That Fought Back* (2005), *Flight 93: The Movie* (2006), and *United*

93 (2006).57 The potential for suspense, conflict, heroism, and human interest was enormous.

REWRITING HISTORY, REVISING THE MYTH THROUGH FILM

The fifth anniversary of the 9/11 tragedy provides an example of how a quasi-historical account can both reinforce and/or revise an earlier account. A docudrama can also shape public perceptions, in this case shifting blame for the catastrophe onto the Clinton administration—and, by extension, onto the Democrats, despite the fact that the events of 9/11 happened under Republican watch. The result, baldly stated, was pseudo-history as partisan propaganda. An ABC/Disney docudrama, *The Path To 9/11*, generated controversy behind the scenes. Promoted by full-page advertisements that depicted dark eyes peering through a slash in the American flag, this TV special occasioned a big flap. It was co-produced by former Commission Chairman Thomas Kean, who apparently was still eager both to promote the final version of an official story he'd helped to write, and to place more blame on the Clinton administration than it had received in the Commission's *Report*. Thus one could argue the docudrama's content was determined by politicos with partisan axes to grind.58

SHOCK JOCKS DISCOVER POP HISTORY

Conservative talk radio hosts discovered popular history after the ABC/Disney docudrama aired. They spotlighted what US intelligence agencies had known and what the White House hadn't done about al Qaeda—though only during the *Clinton* years.59 Republican spokespersons and shock jocks spoke as though reading from the same study guide. Suddenly the pundits were discussing significant issues that the 9/11 Commission hadn't covered and that they had never before faulted anybody for failing to address. Rush Limbaugh started citing al Qaeda's Bojinka Plots of 1994 as evidence that it was Clinton's administration, not Bush's, who could have stopped the 9/11 attacks. The timing and shift of this selective historical focus by some radio personalities is noteworthy in the context of mythic narrative construction.

As the mythmaking, myth revision, and myth reinforcement continues, so does the search for a story that makes more sense. Although the myths persist, they now face increasing logical analysis. While the mainstream corporate media and even many in the progressive press perpetuate historic myths, many Americans are calling for a fact-based narrative; a Zogby International poll taken in 2007 showed that 51 percent of Americans wanted President Bush and Vice President Dick Cheney to be further investigated and scrutinized about the events of 9/11, and that 67 percent wanted the 9/11 Commission investigated for ignoring altogether the collapse of WTC-7. This suggests that many Americans, despite the bombardment of media mythologizing, are still curious about what might have actually happened on 9/11.[60]

HEROES AND VICTIMS

In a time of doubt, vulnerability and fear, mythologizing the heroism and victimization did make many Americans feel better about themselves and their compatriots. Enemies were identified and wagons were circled, imparting the impression that everyone was "standing tall together," otherwise expressed as "united we stand." Yet fixating on heroes and victims also had other effects: it reinforced a simplistic notion of uncomplicated goodness, intensifying a sense that the US was merely a blameless victim—that its foreign policy bore no responsibility for its being targeted. In addition, media preoccupations with heroes and victims tended to distract from other more complex, more unsettling, less uplifting dimensions of the catastrophe.

Media mythmakers have succeeded thus far in preventing a national discussion on the crucial matters of 9/11. The power of myth to suppress the quest for truth can be great. However, the movement to understand these events and offer counternarratives is growing as part of a larger Truth Emergency movement. As University of California–Berkeley Professor Emeritus Peter Dale Scott recently remarked, "In short, we are in an ongoing state of emergency whose exact limits are unknown, on the basis of a controversial deep event—9/11—that is still largely a mystery."[61]

DRAWING CONCLUSIONS

A popular government without popular information or the means
of acquiring it, is but a prologue to a farce or a tragedy or perhaps both.
Knowledge will forever govern ignorance, and a people who mean
to be their own governors, must arm themselves with the power
knowledge gives. —James Madison

Two conclusions emerge from this examination of media mythmaking and the varied narratives, official and alternative, surrounding 9/11: 1) corporate and even alternative media outlets draw selectively on a mythic past to shape the present, and 2) the US has not yet undertaken a serious inquiry into the role played by major media institutions and government in obscuring the actual events of 9/11.

Given how much the shock and trauma of 9/11 have been used to justify major policy changes over the past eight years, one would imagine that a serious and transparent investigation of such an important event would have been completed years ago. In light of the known contradictory facts, it is apparent that the 9/11 Commission was largely an exercise in the refinement and enshrinement of an official myth, not a probing inquiry into the who, what, when, and why of those tragic events. Could we imagine that individuals, beyond the dead suicide bombers, might actually be held accountable?[62]

In a democratic society, it is essential that the people can become well informed through a free press so as to make government accessible, accountable, and thus legitimate. Unfortunately, examining 9/11 and the pattern of historical precedents, one can see how these American ideals have been subverted. The media have continually failed to perform their constitutionally protected objective—to accurately inform the public and act as the true fourth estate.

Alternative narratives to mythic history that have been overlooked, actively ignored, or censored offer many paths to knowledge and can aid in understanding the present. Media mythmakers and their political allies continue to project their grand narrative of the world, with perceptions anchored in fear, xenophobia, and unaccountability, rather than report or reflect a complex, chaotic, frightening reality, and thus present only one acceptable analysis. Even at a time when Internet alternatives are increasingly available, this is hardly the role of a free press in a democratic society.

As Americans, we owe it to ourselves to insist on open and honest inquiry unattached to conclusions, unswayed by ideologies, and unafraid of what the truth may be. While we deserve a media that will lead by example, we may, as never before, find ways to "be the media."[63] A key step toward achieving this end is to understand how dominant media myths crowd out alternative historical and factual perspectives that the public desperately needs to consider. Through analyzing media mythmaking, we can forge a clearer path to a more genuine, pluralistic reality.

MICKEY S. HUFF is an assistant professor of history at Diablo Valley College, an adjunct lecturer in sociology at Sonoma State University, and a longtime associate of Project Censored. He teaches courses in US history, critical thinking, and sociology of media. He blogs at http://mythinfo.blogspot.com. PAUL W. REA, PHD, a broad-spectrum humanities professor, has taught classes exploring political issues. These include "Politics of the Nuclear Age" and "Science, Technology, and Human Values" at St. Mary's College in California. In 2004, he published *Still Seeking the Truth About 9/11*, and is now completing a much-expanded book, *Mounting Evidence: Why We Need a Serious Investigation of 9/11*.

Notes

(Note: All websites were accessed between June 10 and June -15, 2008. Look for an expanded, updated, and more detailed version of this chapter at http://www.projectcensored.org).

1. Radford, Benjamin. *Media Mythmakers: How Journalists, Activists, and Advertisers Mislead Us,* 2003. Remarked Radford, " . . . in the wake of the September 11 attacks, when the conventional wisdom espoused by the news media was that Americans had been changed forever . . . only weeks later, 90% of Americans who were polled said that their lives had never really changed, or had already returned to normal. The news media had assumed, wrongly, that all Americans were changed forever." Online at http://www.mediamythmakers.com/cgi-bin/mediamythmakers.cgi.
2. Phillips, Peter. *Censored 2008*, New York: Seven Stories Press, 2007. pp. 233–251. Chapter 7 in the book, entitled, "Left Progressive Media Inside the Propaganda Model" examines how and why progressive media mirror corporate coverage of certain controversial issues like 9/11 and election fraud among others. Or see http://www.projectcensored.org/articles/story/left-progressive-media-inside-the-propaganda-model/.
3. Rose, Charlie. PBS, June 6, 2008. Online at http://www.charlierose.com/home.
4. The website of the 9/11 Commission, http://911commission.gov.
5. See *Censored 2003*, Chapter 1, Story #4 and all of Chapter 2; *Censored 2005*, Chapter 1, Story #9; *Censored 2006*, all of Chapter 4 entitled "Unanswered Questions of 9/11" or see http://www.projectcensored.org/articles/story/unanswered-questions-of-9-11-july-2005/; *Cen-*

sored 2007, Chapter 1, Story #18; *Censored 2008*, Chapter 1, Story #16, Chapter 2 updates p. 139, and Chapter 7, pp. 233–251.

6. Carlson, Tucker. MSNBC, August 9, 2006, Interview with Dr. David Ray Griffin, quote at 1:40 into the clip. Available at http://www.youtube.com/watch?v=AxKW3EqbfRE&mode =related&search.

7. Winthrop, John. *City Upon a Hill*. 1630. Archived at http://www.mtholyoke.edu/acad/ intrel/winthrop.htm.

8. McCrisken, Trevor B., *Exceptionalism: Manifest Destiny, Encyclopedia of American Foreign Policy*, Vol. 2. New York: Charles Scribner's Sons, 2002. p. 68. Journalist John O'Sullivan stated, "And that claim is by the right of our manifest destiny to overspread and to possess the whole of the continent which Providence has given us for the development of the great experiment of liberty and federated self-government entrusted to us." *New York Morning News*, December 27, 1845. These formative myths of origin have been well examined in standard scholarship, such as Henry Nash Smith's *Virgin Land: The American West as Symbol and Myth* and Perry Miller's *The New England Mind*, among many other standard historical texts.

9. Rather, Dan. CNN, September 22, 2001. For an entire listing of post 9/11 interviews from Rather, see: http://www.cooperativeresearch.org/entity.jsp?entity=dan_rather For further reading and the direct quote, see Artz, Lee, and Kamalipour, Yahya R. *Bring 'Em On: Media and Politics in the Iraq War*, New York: Rowman and Littlefield, 2005. p. 69.

10. Maher, Bill. *Politically Incorrect*. See the story online at http://thebigstory.org/ov/ov-politicallyin-correct.html.

11. Fleisher, Ari. White House spokesperson, September, 26, 2001. Online at http://www.whitehouse.gov/news/releases/2001/09/20010926-5.html.

12. Though not the focus here, other examples of attacks on those who questioned the War on Terror and the official accounting of 9/11 included the firing of Professor Ward Churchill at the University of Colorado, Boulder, and the corporate media blacklisting of the country group, the Dixie Chicks. On Ward Churchill see: http://wardchurchill.net/. For the Dixie Chicks blacklisting and many others see: http://www.thirdworldtraveler.com/McCarthyism/Dixie _Chicking.html. On the recurrence of McCarthyism post-9/11, see Matthew Rothchild's "McCarthy Watch" at http://www.progressive.org/list/mccarthy.

13. Phillips, *Censored 2008*. Chapter 1, Story #16, p. 93. For more on the contradiction between the FBI and State Department, see http://www.rewardsforjustice.net/index.cfm?page =Bin_Laden&language=english

14. American Progress. Online at http://www.americanprogress.org/issues/kfiles/b79532.html.

15. This thesis is explored at length in the documentary film *Hijacking Catastrophe: 9/11, Fear, and the Selling of the American Empire*, Media Education Foundation, 2004. Online at http://www.mediaed.org/videos/CommercialismPoliticsAndMedia/Hijacking_Catastrophe and http://freedocumentaries.org.

16. Moyers, Bill. *Bill Moyers' Journal*. PBS. April 25, 2008. http://www.pbs .org/moyers/journal/04252008/watch.html.

17. Petras, James. "Provocations as Pretexts for Imperial War: From Pearl Harbor to 9/11," Centre for Research on Globalisation, online at http://www.globalresearch.ca/ index.php?context=va&aid=9063. Petras has a detailed accounting of historical precedents for 9/11 focusing heavily on Pearl Harbor. Additionally, author Mickey Huff has remarked on this topic at his blog and in several national radio interviews available at http://mythinfo.blogspot.com/2007/09/manifest-tyranny-propaganda-grand.html and http://mythinfo.blogspot.com/2007/08/911-and-weaponization-of-information-in.html. Further, considering 9/11 research, among the most thorough online sites dedicated to alternative theories of 9/11 are researcher James Hoffman's http://911research.wtc7.net/ and the Scholars for 9/11 Truth and Justice with Dr. Steven Jones at http://stj911.org/.

18. For a brief overview of this, see Griffin, David Ray. *Christian Faith and the Truth Behind 9/11*, Louisville: John Knox Press, 2006. pp. 3–15.

19. Foner, Eric. *Give Me Liberty: An American History, Volume 1, Seagull Edition*. New York: W.W. Norton and Company, 2006. pp. 402–405; and Zinn, Howard. *A People's History of the United States*. Abridged teaching ed. New York:New Press, 2003. pp. 113–124.

20. Kinzer, Stephen. *Overthrow: America's Century of Regime Change from Hawaii to Iraq*. New York: Henry Holt and Company, 2006, pp. 31–55. Also see, Zinn, *A People's History of the United States*, pp. 219–232.

21. Foner, Eric. *Give Me Liberty, Volume 2, Seagull Edition*. New York: W.W. Norton and Company, 2006. pp. 629–632. Also see , Zinn, *A People's History*, pp. 263–274.

22. Stinnett, Robert. *Day of Deceit: The Truth About FDR and Pearl Harbor*. New York: Touchstone, 2000. pp. 1–5. Petras, James. "Provocations as Pretexts for Imperial War: From Pearl Harbor to 9/11," Centre for Research on Globalisation, online at http://www.globalresearch.ca/index.php?context=va&aid=9063.

   Robert Stinnett demonstrated that President Roosevelt provoked war with Japan. Deliberately following a program of harassment and embargo against Japan developed by Lt. Commander Arthur H. McCollum, head of the Far East desk of the Office of Naval Intelligence, FDR ensured that the Japan would attack the US. In the run-up to the attack, explains sociologist/historian James Petras, FDR ordered "eight specific measures which amounted to acts of war, including an economic embargo of Japan, the shipment of arms to Japan's adversaries, the prevention of Tokyo from securing strategic raw materials essential for its economy, and the denial of port access, thus provoking a military confrontation." Also see, Thomas, William. *Days of Deception: Ground Zero and Beyond*. Carson City, Nev.: Bridger House, 2006. Chapter 1. Citations in Thomas are not as good as Stinnett, but the first chapter is of worth on this topic.

23. Project for the New American Century. *Rebuilding America's Defenses*. Washington, D.C., September, 2000. pp.50–51. Also, see Griffin, David Ray. *The New Pearl Harbor: Disturbing Questions about the Bush Administration and 9/11*. Northampton: Olive Branch Press, 2004. p. xi. Note: The Project for the New American Century website was closed down in spring of 2008. See http://www.blacklistednews.com/view.asp?ID=6647 for details.

24. See aforementioned works by Stinnett and Griffin for more on this. It should also be noted, PBS documentarian Ken Burns went on to make a film in 2007, simply called "The War" about WWII that further elevated the sneak attack myth to new heights, perhaps subconsciously to remind Americans that the War on Terror, like WWII, was a just war. For more analysis on this, see author Mickey Huff's blog piece, "Myth America: The War, 9/11, and the Propaganda of Grand Historical Narratives." October 1, 2007. Online at http://mythinfo.blogspot.com/2007/10/myth-america-war-911-and-propaganda-of.html.

25. Petras, online at www.globalresearch.ca/index.php?context=va&aid=9063.

26. US Naval Historical Center USS Maddox (DD-731), 1944–1972, "Actions in the Gulf of Tonkin," August 1964.

27. Hallin, Daniel C. The "Uncensored War": The Media and Vietnam. Berkeley, Ca.: University of California Press, 1989. pp. 16–17.

28. Hanyok, Robert J., "His NSC study on Tonkin Gulf Deception The History Network," online at http://hnn.us/roundup/entries/17620.html, and Shane, Scott, "Vietnam War Intelligence 'Deliberately Skewed,' Secret Study Says," *New York Times*, December 2, 2005. Online at http://www.commondreams.org/headlines05/1202-06.htm, and Agence France Presse, "Report Reveals Vietnam War Hoaxes, Faked Attacks," January 9, 2008. Online at http://www.commondreams.org/archive/2008/01/09/6264/.

29. Bernays, Edward. *Propaganda*. New York: H. Liveright, 1928. Quote taken from IG Publishing reissue, 2005. p. 37.

30. Clarke, Richard. *Against All Enemies: Inside America's War on Terror*. New York: The New Press, 2004. pp. 2, 13–14.

31. Thompson, Paul. *The Terror Timeline*, New York: Regan Books, 2004. pp. 496–98.

32. Thompson, *The Terror Timeline*, pp. 462–63.

33. Phillips, *Censored 2008*, Chapter 1, Story #16, p. 93.

34. Thompson, *The Terror Timeline*, p. 465.

35. Thompson, *The Terror Timeline*, pp. 462–468. Bush was quoted in Thompson from the *Washington Post*, January 27, 2002. For a detailed look of network news activity on the day of 9/11, see http://cnparm.home.texas.net/911/911/911b.htm.

36. The Fox interview was archived and shown in the film *911 Mysteries* available at http://video.google.com/videosearch?client=safari&rls=en-us&q=911%20mysteries&ie=UTF-8&oe=UTF-8&um=1&sa=N&tab=wv# and at http://freedocumentaries.org/film.php?id=147.

Note that one does not have to agree with the premise of the film to observe and analyze the role of the corporate media on 9/11.

37. World Trade Center Talk Force Interview. Firefighter Thomas Turilli. January 17, 2002. Available online at http://graphics8.nytimes.com/packages/pdf/nyregion/20050812_WTC _GRAPHIC/9110501.PDF. For more extensive coverage on first responders see MacQueen, Graeme. "118 Witnesses: The Firefighters' Testimony to Explosions in the Twin Towers." *The Journal of 9/11 Studies.* II August, 2006. pp. 37–56. Available online at http://www.journalof911studies.com/articles/Article_5_118Witnesses_WorldTradeCenter.pdf.

38. Faludi, Susan. *Terror Dream: Fear and Fantasy in Post-9/11 America.* New York: Metropolitan Books, 2007. p. 67. Chapter 3 in this work, "The Cowboys of Yesterday" is of particular interest here as well.

39. See a collection of Dan Rather's statements archived at the Cooperative Research History Commons available at http://www.cooperativeresearch.org/entity.jsp?entity=dan_rather. See the Rather clip in context at http://www.youtube.com/watch?v=Nvx904dAwoo and the Peter Jennings clip in context at http://www.archive.org/details/abc200109110954-1036. Further, see the online slide presentation of architect Richard Gage of www.AE911Truth.org which shows the clips as part of a larger presentation, and includes more first responder testimony left out of corporate media coverage, at http://www.ae911truth.net/ppt_web/slideshow.php?i=263&lores=1.

40. For footage of CNN see http://www.youtube.com/watch?v=N1LetB0z8_0 and for the BBC see http://www.youtube.com/watch?v=C7SwOT29gbc. See further documentation at researcher James Hoffman's site at http://www.wtc7.net/foreknowledge.html.

41. When questioned about the premature coverage, Richard Porter, Head of News at BBC World, offered an equally bizarre explanation: the reporter, he claimed, "doesn't remember minute-by-minute what she said . . . and what was being told to her by colleagues in London. . . ." See www.bbc.co.uk/blogs/theeditors/2007/02/part_of_the_conspiracy.html. Even if it were true, all this seems irrelevant. Porter's statement skirts the obvious questions: If honest mistakes were made, the BBC could simply issue a correction. Instead, the network not only withheld a transcript of its faulty report, but its video footage was pulled from Google Video and YouTube. Even more remarkably, BBC would claim that all of its archives on 9/11 had disappeared because of a "cock-up"! See www.bbc.co.uk/blogs/theeditors/2007/02/part_of_the_conspiracy.html.

42. Barber, Peter. "The Truth is Out There." *The Financial Times.* June 7, 2008. Available at http://www.ft.com/cms/s/0/8d66e778-3128-11dd-ab22-000077b07658.html?nclick_check=1. The original print version displayed remarkably objective accounts about the WTC-7 controversy, atypical in the corporate media. It should also be noted that the *911 Commission Report* did not mention WTC-7 once in its 571 pages.

43. Erdley, Debra. "Crash Debris Found 8 Miles Away." *The Pittsburgh Tribune-Review.* September 14, 2001. Available at http://www.pittsburghlive.com/x/pittsburghtrib/s_12967.html and researcher James Hoffman's http://911research.wtc7.net/planes/attack/flight93sitc.html.

44. O'Brien, Tim. "Wife of Solicitor General Alerted Him of Hijacking from Plane," CNN, September 11, 2001.

45. For more on sensationalism in the corporate news see "Junk Food News and News Abuse," Phillips, *Censored 2008.* Chapter 3.

46. *The 9/11 Commission Report.* New York: Norton, 2004, pp. 12–13.

47. For more detail and background, see Faludi, *Terror Dream,* pp. 46–64.

48. Morgan, Rowland. *Flight 93 Revealed: What Really Happened on the 9/11 Let's Roll Flight.* New York: Carol and Graf, 2006. p. 19.

49. Lakoff, George. *Don't Think of an Elephant! Know Your Values and Frame the Debate.* White River Junction, VT.: Chelsea Green, 2004. p. 53. Also, consider the thoughts of Baudrillard, Jean. *The Spirit of Terrorism.* New York: Verso, 2002. Within the work, see "Requiem for the Twin Towers" for more philosophical and metaphorical ideas about the 9/11 attacks.

50. Coll, Steve. *The Bin Ladens: An Arabian Family in an American Century.* New York: Penguin, 2008, pp. 508–509.

51. Frank, Mitch. *Understanding September 11th: Answering Questions about the Attacks on America.* New York: Turtleback Books and Demco Media, 2002. p.16. This book was aimed at adolescent audiences, possibly illustrating the interest of the corporate press and publishing industry in introducing the official story of 9/11 to youth in an institutionalized educational setting.

52. Klein, Naomi. "The Rise of Disaster Capitalism." *The Nation*, May 2, 2005. Also by the Klein, see *The Shock Doctrine: The Rise of Disaster Capitalism*. New York: Metropolitan Books, 2007. Online at http://www.naomiklein.org/shock-doctrine.

53. *The 9/11 Commission Report*, p. 45.

54. Griffin, *The New Pearl Harbor*, pp. 51–53.

55. Morgan *Flight 93 Revealed*, pp. 31–36, 43–45.

56. *News Hour with Jim Lehrer*. PBS. September 14, 2001. Online at http://www.pbs.org/newshour/search_results.html?q=9-14-01&x=0&y=0. For more independent press coverage of this controversial event and fact based alternative interpretations outside the official narrative, see researcher James Hoffman's http://911research.wtc7.net/planes/attack/flight93.html#course and Christopher Bollyn's http://www.americanfreepress.net/html/flight_93.html.

57. Morgan, *Flight 93 Revealed*, pp. 134–146.

58. *News Hour with Jim Lehrer*. PBS. September 13, 2006. Also, see Yen, Hope. "Book: 9/11 Commission Executive Director Had Closer White House Ties Than Publicly Disclosed." Associated Press. Archived at http://www.commondreams.org/archive/2008/02/04/6826/. See further material and links to articles about this at researcher James Hoffman's http://911research.wtc7.net/post911/commission/index.html.

59. *News Hour with Jim Lehrer*. PBS. September 13, 2006. Online at http://www.pbs.org/newshour/.

60. See the Zogby poll results at http://www.zogby.com/news/ReadNews.dbm?ID=1354

61. Scott quoted in Hamburg, Dan and Seiler, Lewis. "State of Emergency: The US in the Final Six Months of the George W. Bush Administration" online at http://www.commondreams.org/archive/2008/06/13/9596/. For more details on the Truth Emergency Movement, see http://truthemergency.us. Also, see Chapter 11 in this volume, Phillips, *Censored 2009*.

62. This seems to be more the case in other countries, like Japan. (See Phillips, *Censored 2009*, Chapter 1, Story #24 in this volume for details.) Also, major problems with the 9/11 Commission have been the demonstrated in the notable scholarship of Griffin, David Ray. *The 9/11 Commission Report: Omissions and Distortions*. Northampton: Olive Branch Press, 2005. For an analysis of global power structure, this following study looks at "who wins, who decides, and who facilitates action inside the most powerful military-industrial complex in the world." See Phillips, Peter, "The Global Dominance Group: 9/11 Pre-Warnings & Election Irregularities in Context" online at http://s31076.gridserver.com/assets-managed/pdf/Global_Dominance_Group.pdf.

63. See Dave Mathison's *Be the Media* at http://www.bethemedia.org/.

CHAPTER 15

Thirty-Three Years of US Military Domination and Economic Deception

by Nelson Calderon

For thirty-two years, Project Censored has been publishing the news stories the corporate media has failed to cover. This chapter will address Project Censored's three-decade coverage of Latin American news. The stories document how the US has continued in the tradition of colonialism, seeking to dominate, exploit, and control the economic wealth of the Americas. The stories cover slavery, corporate agriculture, war crimes, mistreatment of indigenous peoples, chemical contamination, political prisoners, exploitive trade agreements, deforestation, multiple failed and successful military coupes, harassment of immigrants, and manipulation of elections.

Since the first visit from Europe, White America has exploited Native Americans of all nations. For centuries, the Americas have been dominated by slavery, thievery, and rape in all forms. The United States in the past century has taken a chapter from the colonial history of the Portuguese, Spanish, and British in an accelerated neocolonial form for Central and South America.

Now the US seeks to bring forced trade agreements and isolate those countries, besides Cuba, that resist neocolonial intrusions. The continuing struggle for natural resources and control of indigenous food has resulted in a broadening of resistance in many Central and South American countries. New left-leaning political parties have emerged to challenge the neoliberal mandates orchestrated by the US at the World Bank and the International Monetary Fund. Latin nations have come together to resist private corporate penetration of their economies. In reaction, President Bush is ramping up efforts to get congressional approval of free trade agreements (FTAs) already negotiated with Colombia, Panama, and South Korea (Lafranchi, 2008), as well as launching a new US naval fleet in the region.

CORPORATIONS GONE WILD:
FREE TRADE IN THE RAINFOREST

In 1979, Project Censored covered a story entitled "The Corporate Crime of the Century." *Mother Jones* magazine revealed that the United States had been dumping pesticides in Mexico and using unsafe disposal practices. This was one of our first exposures of the "profit at any human cost" attitude of many corporations in the US towards Latin America.

In 1980, the practice of cash cropping became prevalent in Mexico and Brazil. This was the deliberate US-encouraged economic policy of converting the countries to agriculture-exporting economies at the cost of reducing food self-sufficiency. Brazil's former staple protein was the black bean, but so much land became dedicated to soybeans as an export cash crop that the country eventually was required to import black beans. The same thing happened with corn in Mexico after the US, Mexico, and Canada entered the North American Free Trade Agreement (NAFTA) in the mid-1990s. These policies have left many of the poorest citizens unable to afford the necessary protein for normal human growth, therefore increasing malnutrition and hunger throughout the region.

Multinational companies have been misappropriating resources, creating a backlash of problems for Latin America. The downfall of self-sufficient economies is a cycle that is difficult to stop. Latin countries begin to realize that once a country has become a food importer it is at the mercy and control of powerful external forces. This imbalance of power makes if far easier for corporations to take over mineral and other natural resources.

By the mid-1990s, Georgia-Pacific, Alcoa, Amoco, Arco, Chevron, Exxon Mobil, Occidental Petroleum, Texaco, and the World Bank were all busy looting resources from the rainforests and natural regions of Central and South America. The process of pulling the resources has contaminated the water and polluted huge areas.

Cuba is the one country that for fifty years has successfully resisted corporate control. Cuba has established itself as the most sustainable economy and the number one organic farming country in the world. Cuba's success has shown that there are alternatives to dependency on multinational corporations.

FTAs are the multinationals' way of creating different laws to disrupt social order. Once order has been disrupted, it can flood markets with food and cheaper ways of getting food, essentially making modest farmers obsolete. The FTA market has made many companies rich by giving them a virtual monopoly, as small-scale farmers cannot compete with agribusiness and flee to the cities to find work to feed their families.

Free trade agreements also have continued to take jobs from the US. In March 2007, polls showed a 46 percent American disapproval rate for free trade agreements on the grounds that it is hurting the country and allowing multinational corporations to consistently get richer (Carlsen, 2007). FTAs have become the breeding ground for many of the problems that have occurred in Latin America. Insidiously, corporations have pilfered the rights to patents on seed stock of indigenous agricultural necessities, such as corn. The undermining of Mexico's staple crop has made campesinos go hungry and lose much of their land.

FTAs have flooded the market with food from multinationals, such as Con Agra. NAFTA destroyed farming communities and allowed multinationals to come in and flood the market with corn from the US. Mexicans have been coming to the United States because of the resulting inflation and hunger. Tortilla prices have risen more than 500 percent between 1993 and 2000 (Global Exchange, 2008). Three years before NAFTA was implemented, migration to the United States had dropped by 18 percent. After eight years of NAFTA, the migrant population grew by 61 percent (Global Exchange, 2008).

In 1998, Mattel cut US jobs to open toy factories in Mexico. Mattel had everything to gain because they could give Mexicans less pay and no benefits, and make them work more hours; FTAs have proven time and time again that Latin America gets the short end of the stick. FTAs continue to create problems in Latin countries because they create a ready atmosphere for corporations to invade and flood the markets, allowing the trade agreements to act as a tool for extraction of resources, cheap labor.

Labor and farm groups have protested the FTA in Panama. "For months the agreement was held up by sovereignty issues surrounding the US demand to adopt looser US meat inspection standards. . . . Panamanians also object to the projected influx of US construction firms as the $5.2 billion canal expansion begins . . ." (Carlsen, 2007). The Salvadorian Supreme Court acknowledged a dispute that the Central American Free Trade Agreement (CAFTA) has been the culprit of unjust competition and tariff infringement. CAFTA was also disputed in Costa Rica where acceptance is still pending implementation.

Free Trade Agreements and Environmental Corruption Chronologically Documented by Project Censored

1979
The Corporate Crime of the Century: The mass media have yet to explore and expose the international tragedy of dumping of pesticides in Mexico . . . it is a widespread practice which endangers the health, lives, and environment of millions of people.

1980
Something is Rotten in the Global Supermarket: Multinational corporations increased their profits, taking advantage of cheap labor resources abroad. But peasant farmers were displaced and forced off their lands.

The Circle of Poison: Investigative reporters have discovered that 50 to 70 percent of the chemicals are used not to grow food for the hungry but on luxury crops like coffee and bananas destined for the US and Europe.

1993
Black Gold Conquistadors Invade Ecuador Amazon Drilling: Texaco Petroleum Co. drilled the first oil well in Amazon territory in 1969. Today oil drilling occurs in 10 percent of Ecuador's 32 million acres of the upper Amazon Basin. The destruction left behind by Texaco, and now continued by PetroEcuador, was so great that the Amsterdam-based International Water Tribunal morally condemned the two companies for spoiling Amazon water systems.

1994
Public Input and Congressional Oversight Locked Out of NAFTA: The North American Free Trade Agreement between the US, Canada, and Mexico cited as perhaps one of the most important international trade policies in history, was created in what one member of Congress called "fifteen months of the most secretive trade negotiations I've ever monitored."

Tropical Rainforests—More Endangered Than Ever Before?: Companies negotiated with governments for the rights to pull lots of resources out of the Amazon forests.

1996
The Broken Promises of NAFTA: NAFTA's own members are blatantly breaking the coalition's grand promises. Many of the firms that only a short time ago were extolling the benefits of NAFTA for US workers and communities—have cut jobs, moved plants to Mexico, or continued to violate labor rights and environmental regulations in Mexico.

1997
Dark Alliance—Tuna, Free Trade, and Cocaine: With the help of NAFTA and tuna boat drug smuggling, Mexico has become one of the most important countries of legal trade and illegal drug trafficking across the US border. And the free trade agreements will continue to be a boon for the world's drug smuggling cartels because of the relaxed inspection of commercial cross-border traffic between Mexico and the US. In addition, liberalized international banking rules have made it easier to launder billions in drug revenues.

1999
Secret International Trade Agreement Undermines the Sovereignty of Nations: The apparent goal of the latest international trade negotiations is to safeguard multinational corporate investments by eliminating democratic regulatory control by nation-states and local governments. The Multilateral Agreement on Investment (MAI) plans to set in place a vast series of protections for foreign investment at the cost of national sovereignty.

2001
Cuba Leads the World in Organic Farming: Cuba has developed one of the most efficient organic agriculture systems in the world, and organic farmers from other countries are visiting the island to learn the methods.

US Using Dangerous Fungus to Eradicate Coca Plants in Columbia: The United States plans to deploy, or may have already deployed, new biological weapons for the war on drugs that seriously threaten both humans and the environment.

2003

NAFTA Destroys Farming Communities in US and Abroad: NAFTA and IMF are responsible for the impoverishment and loss of many small farms in Mexico and Haiti. NAFTA is also causing the economic destruction of rural farming communities in the United States and Canada. The resulting loss of rural employment has created a landslide of socioeconomic and environmental consequences that are worsening with the continued dismantling and deregulation of trade barriers.

NAFTA Overrides Public Protection Laws of Countries: Certain investor protections in NAFTA are giving business investors new power over sovereign nations and providing an expansive new definition of property rights.

2004

Plan Puebla-Panama and the FTAA: The Free Trade Area of the Americas (FTAA) is a trade agreement intended to spread NAFTA's trade rules to an additional thirty-one Latin American nations by 2005. Working in conjunction with FTAA is Plan Puebla-Panama (PPP) a multi-billion dollar development plan in progress that would turn southern Mexico and all of Central America into a colossal free trade zone, competing in the worldwide race to drain wages, working conditions, environmental protection, and human rights.

2005

Brazil Holds Back in FTAA Talks, But Provides Little Comfort for the Poor: The US has reacted swiftly by making bilateral agreements with individual Central and South American countries and threatening to restrict their access to US markets if they refuse to cooperate. In many cases, these poorer countries have no choice but to agree to the very strict and unfair agreements that the United States demands.

2006

US Plans For Hemispheric Integration to Include Canada: The US and Canada have been sharing national information since the creation of NORAD (North American Aerospace Defense Command) in 1958. This bi-national agreement to provide aerospace warning and control for North America is scheduled to expire in May 2006. In preparation for the renewal of this contract, the US and Canadian commanders are proposing to expand the integration of the two countries, including cooperation in the "Star Wars" program, cross-national integration of military command structures, immigration, law enforcement, intelligence-gathering, and sharing under the new title of NORTHCOM, US Northern Command.

2007

Destruction of Rainforests Worst Ever: New developments in satellite imaging technology reveal that the Amazon rainforest is being destroyed twice as quickly as previously estimated due to the surreptitious practice of selective logging.

Gold Mining Threatens Ancient Andean Glacers; Barrick Gold's Pascua Lama Project represents one of the largest foreign investments in Chile in recent years, totaling $1.5 billion. However, some 70,000 downstream farmers, backed by international environmental organizations and activists around the world waged a campaign against the proposed mine.

2008

Frenzy of Increasingly Destructive Trade Agreements: The Oxfam report, "Signing Away the Future," reveals that the US and the European Union are vigorously pursuing increasingly destructive regional and bilateral trade and investment agreements outside the auspices of the WTO. These agreements are requiring enormous irreversible concessions from developing countries, while offering almost nothing in return.

North Invades Mexico: The number of North Americans living in Mexico has soared from 200,000 to 1 million (one-quarter of all US expatriates) in the past decade. With more than 70 million American baby-boomers expected to retire in the next two decades, experts predict "a tidal wave" of migration to warmer—and cheaper climates.

MILITARY MIGHT FOR COKE AND BAUXITE

When communities or freedom fighters try to get involved in elections or protests, somehow they end up missing. This is a common phenomenon that goes on in Latin America. In 1997, the Zapatistas from Chiapas lost communal lands because the Mexican government priva-

372 | CENSORED 2009

tized the land. It is the same guise they have been using since the eighties. The Mexican Army Airborne Special Forces (GAFE) were killing Zapatismos because Mexican communal land was at stake. The indigenous people had been farming these lands for centuries.

The war on drugs has been one of the best tools to suppress the Mexican indigenous people. The US is training the Mexican military as part of an antidrug program, but the forces also are repressing indigenous resistance movements.

The US is giving more monetary support to Colombia's "war on drugs" than ever before. In 2003, "Plan Colombia" was the facade the US used to give $7.5 billion in counter-narcotics initiatives. The same thing that happened to the Zapatistas happened to the people of Colombia. "Since January 2001, Colombian aircrafts have been spraying toxic herbicides over Colombian fields in order to kill opium poppy and coca plants. These sprayings are killing food crops that indigenous Colombians depend on for survival, as well as harming their health. The sprayings have killed fish, livestock, and have contaminated water supplies" (Project Censored, 2003).

The continued US militarization of Colombia has been the main system of oppression. The US's policies support murder, with over 30,000 people killed in Colombia. The right-wing paramilitary forces that were trained in the US run School of the Americas were guilty of torture and murder. The facts are stated clearly: the US has had the most devastating influence in terms of military training in Latin America.

This year's number four story, "Is the US Restarting Dirty Wars in Latin America?" covers the new wave of military training. The US has sent the Fourth Fleet to Caribbean and South American Waters. This fleet was last used during World War II against Nazi submarines.

Pointing the big guns at Latin America is a strategic move for the US to counter the left-leaning governments in Venezuela, Ecuador, Bolivia, and Paraguay. Lugo, Morales, Corellas, and Chávez have begun to unite Latin America to end hunger, poverty, and death. Their policies fly in the face of US non-colonial ambitions in Latin America.

Now, Latin America is collectively seeking to show the US that they are a force to be reckoned with. The US decision to reassemble the Fourth Fleet was announced the first week of April. This move was vigorously condemned by Latin American leaders at the Rio Group meeting held in the Dominican Republic's capital (Castro, 2008).

Members of the Fourth Fleet include the George H. W. Bush, a new commissioned ship that has supreme fire power and sophisticated nuclear weapons, as well as the newest aircraft carrier, the *USS Gerald Ford*. This vessel will have stealth technology that cannot be detected by radar and cutting edge weaponry. The Latin countries have become well aware of the Fourth Fleet, but only time will tell what impact it will have on US and Latin American relations.

Castro has been continually ostracized by the United States, and Hugo Chávez has been named by many conservative think tanks as the next Fidel. Chávez has brought back the Marxist idea of living equally. He wants to bring power and wealth to his country and share it with the poor. He has nationalized the oil in Venezuela and he is working to get his country out of debt. Hugo Chávez has been a progressive president for the majority of the people in Venezuela, but according to US media he is a murderer, a rebel leader, a communist, and a dictator.

US oil interests became evident when a 2002 coup attempt against Chávez was orchestrated by the US. The CIA helped with the attempted takeover, along with a Special Forces lieutenant colonel from Fort Bragg (School of the Americas). They placed Pedro Carmona (one of Bush's business partners) as acting president. But the people rebelled and within two days Chávez had retaken his place as president of Venezuela. Chávez prevailed because the masses would not allow foreign interest to dominate.

Militarization and Imperialism Chronologically Documented by Project Censored

1979
There's Still Much More to the 'CIA in Chile' Story: According to secret portions of a Senate report, several members of the current Chilean government worked directly for the CIA in the campaign to overthrow Salvadore Allende.

1981
Reagan's Propaganda on Central America: There is considerable evidence that the Reagan administration has tried to mislead the American public with inaccurate propaganda. While the administration tries to manipulate public opinion into believing we are witnessing a massive Communist takeover of our neighbors to the South, others suggest that

the real issue is a civil war between military-supported wealthy landowners and poor peasants. Much of the material, which has appeared in small investigative publications, tends to support the latter contention.

1983

Israel: Merchant of Death in Central America: Israel, now the fifth biggest exporter of arms in the world, was the largest supplier of weapons to Latin America.

Peter Fox and Central America: Peter Fox's journalistic ethics were called into question after his report of the US military's involvement in Central America. The article resulted in numerous media outlets labeling Fox as a "liar."

The Grenada Invasion—A Classic Case of Censorship: The US invasion of Grenada provided a case study of governmental censorship, which misinformed or denied information to the American public before, during, and after the invasion.

1984

Nicaragua: Fair Elections Versus Unfair Press: Contrary to US media prediction and popular belief, the November 4, 1984 Nicaraguan national election was not rigged by the ruling Sandinistas nor were they the rubber-stamp of Soviet Communism.

CIA and the Death Squads: Twenty Years of Immortality, Ten Years of Illegality: While President Ronald Reagan publicly condemned the Salvadoran Death Squads, a paramilitary apparatus responsible for the deaths of thousands of Salvadoran leftists and peasants, the CIA continues to train, support, and provide intelligence to forces directly involved in Death Squad activity.

1985

Fierce Aerial War in Central America Unreported in US Press: President Jose Duarte boasts about the decline in Death Squad killings, while the people of El Salvador experience the most intense saturation bombing ever conducted in the Americas.

Nicaraguan Contra Aid and the International Court of Justice: President Reagan was pressuring Congress for $100 million of aid to be sent to the contras—his "freedom fighter" colleagues—in Nicaragua.

1986

Pro Contra Media Coverage—Paid For By the CIA—According to Edgar Chamorro, former head of the contra communications office, "approximately fifteen Honduran journalists and broadcasters were on the CIA payroll and our influence was thereby extended to every major Honduran newspaper and television station."

United States Senator Instigates Argentine Coup and Blood Bath: FBI documents and testimony by US diplomatic staff, exposed in 1986, have implicated US Senator Jesse Helms (R-NC) in the 1976 Argentinean military coup.

1987

The United States of America and Its Contra Drug Connection: Testimony by convicted drug smugglers as well as private citizens for CBC's "West 57th Street" program provided a startling picture of large-scale drug trafficking under the auspices of the US government/contra supply network.

The United States of America: International Outlaw: The International Court of Justice, in a 12–3 decision, held that US support of the contras was illegal. A further decision, 14–1, held the US mining of Nicaragua's harbors and distribution of a CIA assassination manual also violated international law.

Congressional Conflict of Interest: Company Man Probes Contras: The integrity of the congressional panel investigation into the Iran-Contra scandal was seriously compromised by the appointment of Thomas Polgar as an investigator. The appointment also illuminates why CIA involvement in drug trafficking and the La Penca bombing were not explored during the televised hearings.

1988

Oliver North & Co. Banned From Costa Rica: In July of 1989, Oliver North and other major contra-gate figures were barred from Costa Rica. The order was issued by none other than Oscar Arias Sanchez, president of Costa Rica and winner of the 1987 Nobel Peace Prize. President Arias was acting on recommendations from a Costa Rican congressional commission investigating drug trafficking. The commission concluded that the contra re-supply network in Costa Rica, which North coordinated from the White House, doubled as a drug smuggling operation.

US Refuses to Abide By International Court of Justice: The US faces the possibility of a multi-billion dollar damage award as a result of its involvement in the contra war in Nicaragua.

New Tribes Mission Hunts Down Last of Paraguayan Indians: The invasion of religious radicals is accompanied by a religious crusade that has resulted in numerous Native Americans becoming "born again" and losing their roots in their old traditions.

1990

The Chemical Industry and its Cocaine Connection: American industry openly and legally collaborated with South America's cocaine cartels, supplying the chemicals needed to turn coca leaves into cocaine.

National Media Ignoring CIA Misdeeds: Unfortunately, the investigative journalism successes of the Watergate era seem like a distant memory when compared with today's media coverage. Currently our national news media, in particular network television, have shown little interest in a number of scandals involving the CIA, resulting in an uninformed audience.

2004

Bush Administration Behind Failed Military Coup in Venezuela: During attempted Venezuelan coup, US military was stationed at the Colombia-Venezuela border to provide support, and to evacuate US citizens if there were problems. According to intelligence analyst Wayne Madsen, the CIA actively organized the coup. "The CIA provided Special Operations Group personnel, headed by a lieutenant colonel on loan from the US Special Operations Command at Fort Bragg, North Carolina, to help organize the coup against Chavez," he said.

2006

US Uses South American Military Bases to Expand Control of the Region: The US has a military base in Manta, Ecuador, which is one of three US military bases located in Latin America. According to Miguel Moran, head of Movimiento Tohalli, a group which opposes the Manta military base, "Manta is part of a broader US imperialist strategy aimed at exploiting the continent's natural resources, suppressing popular movements, and ultimately invading neighboring Colombia."

2007
Ecuador and Mexico Defy Use on International Criminal Court: On June 22, 2005 Ecuador's president Alfredo Palacios vocalized emphatic refusal to sign a Bilateral Investment Agreement (also known as an Article 98 agreement to the Rome Statute of the ICC) in spite of Washington's threat to withhold $70 million a year in military aid.

US Military in Paraguay Threatens Region: Five hundred US troops arrived in Paraguay with planes, weapons, and ammunition in July 2005, shortly after the Paraguayan Senate granted US troops immunity from national and International Criminal Court (ICC) jurisdiction. Neighboring countries and human rights organizations are concerned that the massive air base at Mariscal Estigarribia, Paraguay is potential real estate for the US military.

2008
Mexico's Stolen Election: Overwhelming evidence reveals massive fraud in the 2006 Mexican presidential election between "president-elect" Felipe Calderón of the conservative PAN party and Andrés Manuel López Obrador of the more liberal PRD. In an election riddled with "arithmetic mistakes," a partial recount uncovered evidence of abundant stuffing and stealing of ballots that favored the PAN victory.

HUMAN RIGHTS ON THE MARGIN: JUST OVER OUR BORDERS

The US has turned Mexico upside down. The borders have become slums and are basically inhabitable. The US has been beefing up military presence on the borders and water and food contamination has been prevalent, especially since NAFTA. The US Department of Homeland Security has created many obstacles for both sides.

Many people have suffered on the border because of maquiladoras, prostitution, and slavery. The maquiladora controversy has been kept very secretive. Women go off to work a twelve-hour day in unkempt, dark, and usually contaminated areas. They are most likely sewing or assembling a product in a duty-free tax shelter. The young women who work there have been targeted for rape and even murder. There are hundreds of women missing to this date who had been working in a maquiladora.

Those not fortunate enough to be working in the factories are often working the streets; the sex industry has explodedUS-Mexican border. Institutional corruption is rampant, as police and government officials are profiting from the exploitation. The sex industry in Mexico is one based on a system of slavery. Organized crime groups promise women from all over the world that they will work in Hollywood and make it as famous actresses. They also lure Latin children with gifts, money, and false promises. They usually give them a high dose of heroin or methamphetamine to keep them calm and transportable.

Mexico is one of the biggest child transfer sites for sex, smut, and other abuse. The police and border patrol take bribes in exchange for their feigned ignorance.

Throughout the years the US has taken advantage of immigrants from all countries, but Latin populations have been particularly targeted. The roundups and detention camps harass the immigrant population. Mexico has lost 900,000 rural jobs and 700,000 industrial jobs in the past five years, forcing people to flee to the US, where they are treated as criminals.

Human Rights Issues, Chronologically Documented by Project Censored

1977

"Illegal Aliens": Most employers benefit from undocumented immigrants in that they can demand more work for less compensation. Employers can also utilize the threat of notifying the border patrol in order to keep employees working under extreme conditions.

1980

Distorted Reports of the El Salvador Crisis: Through willful misinformation or ignorance the major US media has contributed to a misguided foreign policy that threatens to embroil Americans in another Vietnam War.

1982

The Real Story of Central America: The American public has been misinformed about social unrest in Central America. New evidence suggests that the Reagan administration was funding multiple wars in Central America in order to extend US control.

1984
Worst Radiation Spill in North America Still Spreading: Two hundred Mexicans citizens are slowly dying from Cobalt-60 contamination, an incident that has been under-reported, so that most Americans are unaware of the situation.

1986
Criticizing the President's Policies Can Be Dangerous: Political opponents of the Reagan administration's Central America policies have been the targets of mysterious break-ins, IRS audits, FBI questioning, and physical surveillance leading many to feel unsure about their freedom to safely express dissent.

Salvadoran Media Advertise Death Lists: Ronald Reagan castigates Nicaragua for compromising freedom of the press tenets. The oligarchy-owned mass media in El Salvador are subverted to the whim and caprice of the El Salvadoran government, resulting in the publication of "Death Lists."

1987
Torture in El Salvador: The Censored Report From Mariona Prison: The report was compiled by five imprisoned members of the Human Rights Commission of El Salvador (CDHES). The report documents the "routine" and "systematic" use of at least forty methods of torture on political prisoners held in the Mariona prison.

US Sends Bullets to Starving Children: The US military and economic aid to Honduras jumped from $31 to $282 million in one year, the largest increase was in military aid since the 1979 level. In exchange, Honduras agreed to become a base for some 15,000 Nicaraguan "contras."

The Tragedy of Grenada Since October 25, 1983: The media permitted Reagan to cite Grenada as an American success story by not questioning his decleration. Though the US media has allowed this fallacy, the people of Grenada aren't buying Reagan's spin on the tragedy.

Puerto Rico: The Revolution At Our Doorstep: The UN committee on decolonization voted to ask (for the 11th time) the US to immediately remove itself from Puerto Rico and to recognize the Puerto Ricans' right for independence.

1988

The US Presence That Is Killing Central America: The roots of Central America's present environmental crisis can be traced to decades of development policies that have favored production for export over production for local needs, with the support of multilateral development banks, US government, private banks, and multinational firms.

US/Mexican Plants Turning Border Into A Toxic Wasteland: A US/Mexican presidential agreement was reached which required US owned plants along the Mexican border to return waste products to the US for disposal. The agreement is routinely violated by the maquiladora plants.

What's Happening in Guatemala?: Human rights atrocities have been occurring in Guatemala for at least thirty years, since the CIA overthrew the democratic Arbenz government in the late 1950s.

Abusing Women Is Routine At Border: Hispanic women attempting to enter the country as undocumented workers routinely suffer abuse, ranging from blackmail to battery and rape. Due to their status as illegal immigrants they are not in a position to report the crimes, and the pattern of abuse continues unchecked.

1989

Guatemalan Blood On US Hands: US military involvement in Guatemala includes the sale of 16,000 rifles to the Guatemalan army, training of Guatemalan paratroopers, and teaching parachute and jungle survival tactics. The increased cooperation with the Guatemalan military inevitably puts a stamp of tacit US approval on ongoing military oppression.

1990

What Really Happened To Panama Is A Different Story: It now appears that the legal implication of the invasion, the Bush-Noriega relationship, and the actual post-invasion conditions in Panama have all been misrepresented to the American people. But perhaps the most fraudulent news coverage dealt with the true numbers of civilian and combat fatalities.

CIA La Penca Bombing: A Murder Indictment; No News?: Official Costa Rican judicial investigation recommended that two US citizens (John Hull and Felipe Vidal), who played prominent roles in the Iran-contra affair, be indicted for murder in connection with the La Penca bombing of 1984.

1994
Haiti: Drugs, Thugs, the CIA and the Deterrence of Democracy: The Clinton administration's silence on the Haitian drug flow has led some congressional critics, such as John Conyers (D-MI), to suggest that this silence reflects de facto support for the drug-trafficking by Haitian military and a reluctance to substantively support the democratically-elected Aristide.

Maquiladoras in Silicon Valley: The people who work on the assembly lines, making printed circuit boards and other electronic components for companies like IBM and Digital Microwave Corporation, earn about $6 per hour, have no health benefits, and routinely have to handle highly toxic substances without even the most rudimentary safety equipment, such as gloves and goggles.

Thousands of Cubans Losing Their Sight Due To Malnutrition: The US embargo is to blame for the terrifying health conditions of Cubans due to malnutrition. The embargo has already cost Cuba more than $37 billion in trade and investments, created fuel shortages that have slowed agricultural and industrial development, and now is causing tens of thousands of people to go blind from lack of proper nutritional care.

1997
Inside INS Detention Centers: Racism, Abuse, and No Accountability: The overpopulation of undocumented immigrants, those in the custody of the Department of Justice's Immigration and Naturalization Service (INS), are now being widely transferred to local jails across the country. This transferring of prisoners has not only become a means of reducing the size of immigrants in the INS's nine service processing centers, but it has also become an abusive and frequently lucrative business.

1998

Russian Plutonium Lost Over Chile and Bolivia: On November 16, 1996, Russia's Mars 96 space probe broke and burned while descending over Chile and Bolivia, scattering its remains across a 10,000 square-mile area. The probe carried about a half pound of deadly plutonium divided into four battery canisters.

Little Known Federal Law Paves the Way For National Identification Card: In September 1996, President Clinton signed the Illegal Immigration Reform and Responsibility Act of 1996. Buried on approximately page 650 was a section that creates a framework for establishing a national ID card for the American public. This legislation was slipped tough without fanfare or publicity.

Mattel Cuts US Jobs To Open Sweatshops In Other Countries: Thanks to NAFTA and the General Agreement on Tariffs and Trade (GATT), US toy factories have cut a one-time American work force of 56,000 in half and sent many of those jobs to other countries where workers lack basic rights and are employed at lower wages.

US Paper Companies Conspire To Squash Zapatistas: The passage of NAFTA has ushered in an era of unprecedented military and corporate domination over the already beleaguered indigenous citizens of Mexico. On the day NAFTA went into effect, the Zapatistas of Chiapas in Southern Mexico rose up in rebellion against the exploitation that they feared NAFTA portended. Though the initial violence did not last long, the Zapatistas have continued to resist intrusions into their communally held lands, known as *eijdos*. Inhabited by the indigenous people of Mexico, the *eijdos* have been farmed collectively for centuries.

1999

US Tax Dollars Support Death Squads In Chiapas: On December 22, 1997, in the village of Acteal, in the highlands of the Mexican state of Chiapas, forty-five indigenous men, women and children were shot as they were praying, their bodies dumped into a ravine. Elsewhere through out the state of Chiapas, unarmed indigenous women faced down armies "with fists held high in rebellion and babies slung from their shoulder." In Jalisco, more than a dozen young men were kidnapped and tortured.

2001

Silicon Valley Uses Immigrant Engineers To Keep Salaries: An existing immigration law sets a cap on the amount of HI-B visas the industry can use to hire immigrant engineers, so this year Silicon Valley electronics giants have been pushing for more HI-B workers. While HI-B status laborers boost corporate bottom lines, there is a devastating effect on the workers themselves.

Indigenous People Challenge Private Ownership and Patenting of Life: On July 25, 1999, a gathering of indigenous peoples signed a document that called for an amendment to the TRIPS agreement that would be put as a priority item on the agenda at the WTO Ministerial Conference in Seattle.

2003

US Policies In Colombia Support Mass Murder: Colombia's annual murder rate is 30,000. It is reported that around 19,000 of these murders are linked to illegal right-wing paramilitary forces. Many leaders of these paramilitary groups were once officers in the Colombian military, trained at the US Military run School of the Americas.

2004

Argentina Crisis Sparks Cooperative Growth: The citizens of Argentina are cooperatively rebuilding their country, rising above the financial devastation caused by decades of privatization and military leadership. In December 2001 the International Monetary Fund (IMF) "recipe" had gone sour destroying currency values and employment levels. The IMF recipe had used loans to prop up an overvalued peso, as well as push the multinational privatization of Argentine companies.

2005

The Destabilization of Haiti: On February 29, 2004, President Jean-Bertrand Aristide was forced into exile by the American military. While the US was forced to acknowledge the kidnapping allegations, they were quick to discredit them and deny responsibility. The circumstances underlying the current situation in Haiti, as well as the history of US involvement is being ignored by US officials and the mainstream media.

Wal-Mart Brings Inequality and Low Prices To the World: Wal-Mart's strategy of corporate takeovers in other countries has come into question. When entering a new market, the company never opens directly to the public; instead they buy into an already fully operational company and slowly take control. First, a large competitor is eliminated, then Wal-Mart gains real estate and employees, creating a massive presence in its targeted location.

2006

New Immigration Plan Favors Business Over People: A bi-partisan effort from the Federal government is emerging to close the borders with Mexico by increasing barriers that keep "illegal" immigrants from traveling to and from Mexico, and in turn creating a guest worker program with specific time limits for residency.

2008

Another Massacre In Haiti By UN Troops: Eyewitness testimony confirms indiscriminate killings by UN forces in Haiti's Cité Soleil community on December 22, 2006, reportedly as collective punishment against the community for a massive demonstration of Lavalas supporters in which about 10,000 people rallied for the return of President Aristide in clear condemnation of the foreign military occupation of their country.

Immigrant Roundups To Gain Cheap Labor For US Corporate Giants: NAFTA has flooded Mexico with cheap subsidized US agricultural products that displaced millions of Mexican farmers. Between 2000 and 2005, Mexico lost 900,000 rural jobs and 700,000 industrial jobs, resulting in deep unemployment throughout the country. Immigration Customs Enforcement (ICE) has conducted workplace and home invasions across the country in an attempt to round up "illegal" immigrants. ICE justifies these raids under the rubric of keeping our homeland safe and preventing terrorism. However the real goal of these actions is to disrupt the immigrant work force in the US and replace it with a tightly regulated non-union guest-worker program.

CONCLUSION

The history between Latin America and the US has been one dominated by the powerful. Drugs, sex, monopolistic land ownership, coups, stolen elections, and shady business practices have all been supported by military invasions, reoccupations, and continuing threats by the US.

Americans believe that the US is a diplomatic nation. But the *Censored* stories tell a different story. Perhaps we may need to take a page of Hugo Chávez and Evo Morales's playbook. These two presidents have and are creating social change in a wide variety of ways that is aimed to benefit the working people in their countries.

We like to think of ourselves as a peaceful nation, but a long history of Manifest Destiny in Latin America for US corporate power and profit belies that belief. If "we the people" were to accept diplomacy, instead of military threats and occupation, the Americas can start the healing process. Diplomacy—not military force—with Latin American countries is the answer. Oil, water, and alternative energy are going to become more essential than ever. The Americas have to work together to ensure that all peoples are getting food, water, and shelter.

NELSON CALDERON is a graduate-level research assistant with Project Censored. His parents moved to the US from Mexico and El Salvador. He will be attending University of Southern California for an MSW in the fall of 2008.

Sources

L. Carlsen, "Moratorium on Free Trade Agreements," *Foreign Policy In Focus*, June 10, 2008, http://www.fpif.org/fpiftxt/4135.

H. Lafranchi, "US Free Trade Accords Face Rocky Road," *Latin American Post*, June 9, 2008, http://www.latinamericanpost.com/index.php?mod=seccion&secc=2&conn=5246.

L. Oualalou, "US Navy Aims its Big Guns at Latin America," *San Francisco Bay View*, May 7, 2008, 1,11.

S. Shashikant, "The Politics of United States Free Trade Agreements," *Third World Resurgence*, 167, 1-12.

"Roots of migration," *Global Exchange*, June 11, 2008, http://www.globalexchange.org/countries/americas/mexico/migration.html.pf.

"Human Trafficking & Modern-day Slavery," June 6, 2008, http://gvnet.com/humantrafficking/Mexico.htm.

The Project Censored crew (SSU faculty, students, and PC staff).

Acknowledgments

by Peter Phillips

Project Censored is managed through the Department of Sociology in the School of Social Sciences at Sonoma State University. We are an investigative sociology and media analysis project dedicated to journalistic integrity and the freedom of information throughout the United States.

Sociology professor Andrew Roth has been associate director of Project Censored since 2006 and co-editor of this year's book, however he is leaving the university for a second career in direct activism and self-actualization. We will miss his involvement. In his place, Dr. Ben Frymer and Dr. Heidi LaMoreaux from Sonoma State University Liberal Studies program will step into the role of associate directors for the 2008–09 research year.

I want to personally thank those close friends and intimates who have counseled and supported me through another year of Project Censored. Most important is my wife Mary M. Lia, who as my trusted friend and life partner provides daily consulting support to Project Censored. The men in the Green Oaks Breakfast Group, Noel Byrne, Bob Butler, Bob Klose, Derrick West, Colin Godwin, Peter Tracy, and Bill Simon, are personal advisors and confidants who help with difficult decisions. A special thanks also to Carl Jensen, founder of Project Censored and director for twenty years. His continued advice and support are critical to the project. Trish Boreta and Kate Sims are Project Censored coordinators and associate administrators. Their dedication and enthusiasm are greatly appreciated.

A big thanks goes to the people at Seven Stories Press. They are not just a publishing house, but also have become close friends, who help edit our annual book in record time, and serve as advisors in the annual release process of the "Most Censored Stories." Publisher Dan Simon is dedicated to building democracy in America through knowledge and literature. He deserves full credit for assembling an excellent support crew, including: Jon Gilbert, Veronica Liu, Anna Lui, Theresa Noll, Tara Parmiter, Lars Reilly, Amy Scholder, Ruth Weiner, Crystal Yakacki, and Ashley Roberts.

Thanks also to Bill Mockler and the sales staff at Consortium Books, who will see to it that every independent bookstore, chain store, and wholesaler in the US are aware of Censored 2009. Thanks to Publishers Group Canada, our distributors up north, as well as Turnaround Publishers Services Ltd. in Great Britain and Palgrave Macmillan in Australia.

We especially thank Novi Mondi Media in Italy for translating and distributing the Censored yearbooks in Italian and for coordinating the Project Censored Italy visit in the summer of 2008.

Thank you to Cynthia McKinney, who wrote the introduction to the Censored 2009 edition. Her continuing political work for better government and human rights is dear to our hearts.

Thanks also to the authors of the most censored stories for 2009, for without their often-unsupported efforts as investigative news reporters and writers, the stories presented in Censored would not be revealed.

Our guest writers this year include Dr. Gary Evans, Elizabeth Stinson, Judith Siers-Poisson, Janine Jackson, Peter Hart, Padraig Reidy, Mickey Huff, Paul Rea, David Kubiak, Nelson Calderon, and the wonderful team at Yes! Magazine led by Sarah van Gelder.

This year's book features the cartoons of Khalil Bendib. We welcome his brilliant and satirical work to our 2009 edition.

Our national judges, some of whom have been involved with the Project for thirty-two years, are among the top experts in the country concerned with First Amendment freedoms and media principles. We are honored to have them as the final voice in ranking the top 25 Censored stories. We welcome four new national judges to our roster this year: Dr. Tom Lough, professor emeritus of sociology at Kent State University; Mr. Geoff Davidian, Milwaukee investigative journalist; Dr. Deepa Kumar, assistant professor of journalism and media studies at Rutgers University; and Dr. Oliver Boyd-Barrett, director of the school and professor of journalism and telecommunications at Bowling Green State University.

An important thanks goes to our financial supporters, including the Sonoma State University Instructionally Related Activity Fund, the School of Social Sciences at Sonoma State University, the Wallace Global Fund, Elizabeth Sherif, Lori Grace, Michael Kieschnick at Credo Mobile, Cornelia Fletcher, Mark Swedlund and Deborah Dobish, Lynn and Leonard Riepenhoff, Louise Aldrich, trustee of the Helen Callbeck estate, and especially the thousands of individuals who purchase books and send us financial gifts each year. You are our financial base, the important few who continue to give year after year to this important student-run media research project.

This year we had over one hundred faculty/community evaluators assisting with our story assessment process. These expert volunteers read and rated the nominated stories for national importance, accuracy, and credibility. In April, they participated with over 100 students in selecting the final top 25 stories for 2007–08.

Most of all, we need to recognize the Sonoma State University students in the Spring 2008 Media Censorship class and the Fall 2007 Sociology of Media class, who worked thousands of hours nominating and researching some 300 under-published news stories. Students are the principle writers of the Censored news synopses in the book each year. Additionally, over sixty students served as interns for the project, working on various teams to support public relations, web design, news story research, office support, events/fundraising, book/chapter research and writing, and broadcast production. Student education is the most important aspect of Project Censored, and we could not do this work without the dedication and effort of our student interns.

Mark Blair is the web coordinator for the Project Censored website, www.projectcensored.org.

Lastly, I want to thank our readers and supporters from all over the United States and the world. Hundreds of you nominated stories for consideration as the censored news story of the year. Thank you very much!

PROJECT CENSORED STAFF

Peter Phillips, PhD	Director
Andrew Roth, PhD	Associate Director
Carl Jensen, PhD	Director Emeritus and Project Advisor
Tricia Boreta	Coordinator/Editor
Katie Sims	Finance/Production Coordinator
Nelson Calderon	Graduate Research Assistant
Zoe Hawkins	Administrative Support
Sheila Frazier	Administrative Support

Media Freedom Foundation, 501(C)(3) nonprofit support corporation for Project Censored Board of Directors: Peter Phillips, Andrew Roth, Noel Byrne, Carl Jensen, Mary Lia, Myrna Goodman, William Simon, Alice Chan

SPRING & FALL 2007–08 INTERNS AND COMMUNITY VOLUNTEERS

David Abbott, Brett Alfoldy, Dan Anderson, Selina Anjum, Margo Baggo, John Bertucci, Dan Bluthardt, Nelson Calderon, Kat Pat Crespan, Marie Daghlian, Brian Gellman, Bill Gibbons, Susanna Gibson, Eric Good, Erica Haikara, Andrew Hobbs, Tim LeDonne, Andrea Lochtefeld, Ioana Lupu, Sarah Maddox, Marley Miller, Linda Moore, Chris Morello, Rebecca Newsome, Darcy Newton, Jennifer Ojima, April Pearce, Kaitlyn Pinson, Luke Plasse, Seamus Rafferty, Janeen Rashmawi, Elizabeth Rathbun, Rainer Rayson, Jessica Read, Gabrielle Robinson, Carmela Rocha, Michele Salvail, Alan Scher, Corey Sharp-Sabatino, Juana Som, Patricia Stengle, Angela Tejeda, Cedric Therene, Bridget Thornton, Margo Tyack, Melissa Willenborg, Tyler Wood

STUDENT RESEARCHERS IN SOCIOLOGY OF MEDIA CLASS, FALL 2007

Elizabeth Allen, Joshua Argyle, Dan Bluthardt Jr., Samantha Burchard, Eliana Chandler, Paige Corbin, Erica Elkington, Katie Ernest, Derek Harms, Andrew Hobbs, Caitlyn Ioli, Andrew Kochevar, Tim LeDonne, Andrea Lochtefeld, Christina Long, Lindsey Lucia, Sarah Maddox, Jennifer Ojima, April Pearce, Jennifer Routh, Jessie Toress, Ashley Vanmaanen, Cristina Wilson

STUDENT RESEARCHERS IN SOCIOLOGY OF MEDIA CENSORSHIP CLASS, SPRING 2008

Dan Anderson, Lauren Anderson, Chris Armanino, Dan Bluthardt Jr., Kyle Corcoran, Suha Diab, Brian Gellman, Derek Harms, Benjamin Herzfeldt, Robert Hunter, Brandon Leahy, Sarah Maddox, Christopher Navarre, Rebecca Newsome, April Pearce, Carmela Rocha, Maureen Santos, Alan Scher, Stephanie Smith, Courtney Snow, Juana Som, Danielle Stanton, Dana Vaz

PROJECT CENSORED TRAVELING TEAM: MEDIA REFORM CONFERENCE, MINNEAPOLIS, JUNE, 2008

Sarah Maddox, April Pearce, Kaitlyn Pinson, Carmela Rocha, Nelson Calderon, Andrew Hobbs, Kat Pat Crespan, Kate Sims, Mickey Huff, Ben Frymer

PROJECT CENSORED 2007-08 BROADCAST SUPPORT

John Bertucci, Michael Litle, Dora Ruhs, Paul Sarran, Tyler Wood

PROJECT CENSORED 2007-08 NATIONAL JUDGES

ROBIN ANDERSEN is an associate professor and chair of the Department of Communication and Media Studies at Fordham University, as well as the Director of Peace and Justice Studies. Her publications include *Critical Studies in Media Commercialism*.

OLIVER BOYD-BARRETT is the Director of School and a Professor of Journalism and Telecommunications at Bowling Green State University. His publications include *The International New Agencies: the Globalization of News, Media in Global Context*.

LIANE CLORFENE-CASTEN is the cofounder and president of Chicago Media Watch. She is an award-winning journalist with credits in national periodicals such as *E Magazine, The Nation, Mother Jones, Ms., Environmental Health Perspectives, In These Times,* and *Business Ethics*. She is the author of *Breast Cancer: Poisons, Profits, and Prevention*.

LENORE FOERSTEL works with Women for Mutual Security and is a facilitator of the Progressive International Media Exchange (PRIME).

GEOFF DAVIDIAN is a Milwaukee investigative journalist and editor of the *Putman Pit* online newspaper.

ROBERT HACKETT is a professor in the School of Communication at Simon Fraser University and has been Co-director of News Watch Canada since 1993. His most recent publications include *Democratizing Global Media: One World, Many Struggles* (Co-Edited With Yuezhi Zhao, 2005), And *Remaking Media: The Struggle To Democratize Public Communication* (With William K. Carroll, 2006).

CARL JENSEN is professor emeritus of Communication Studies at Sonoma State University. He is the founder and former director of Project Censored, and author of *Censored: The News That Didn't Make the News and Why* (1990–1996) and *20 Years of Censored News* (1997).

SUT JHALLY is professor of Communications and executive director of the Media Education Foundation at the University of Massachusetts.

His publications include *The Spectacle of Accumulation: Essays in Media. Culture & Politics.*

NICHOLAS JOHNSON* is a professor in the College of Law at the University of Iowa, former FCC Commissioner (1966–1973), and author of *How to Talk Back to Your Television Set.*

RHODA H. KARPATKIN is President Emeritus of Consumers Union, the non-profit publisher of *Consumer Reports.*

CHARLES L. KLOTZER is an editor and a publisher emeritus of the *St. Louis Journalism Review.*

NANCY KRANICH is a past president of the American Library Association (ALA), a Senior Research Fellow for the Free Expression Policy Project.

JUDITH KRUG is director of the Office for Intellectual Freedom at the American Library Association (ALA) and editor of the *Newsletter on Intellectual Freedom; Freedom to Read Foundation News;* and *Intellectual Freedom Action News.*

DEEPA KAMUR is an assistant professor in the Department of Journalism and Media Studies at Rutgers and the author of *Outside the Box: Corporate Media, Globalization and the UPS Strike.*

MARTIN LEE is an investigative journalist, media critic and author. He was an original founder of Fairness and Accuracy in Reporting in New York and former editor of *Extra Magazine.* He also wrote *Acid Dreams: The Complete Social History of LSD—The CIA, the Sixties and Beyond.*

DENNIS LOO is an associate professor of Sociology at California State University Polytechnic University in Pomona. He is co-editor of *Impeach the President: The Case Against Bush and Cheney,* Seven Stories press, 2006.

THOM LOUGH is professor emeritus of Sociology at Kent State University. He has been a Project Censored faculty evaluator for ten years.

WILLIAM LUTZ is a professor of English at Rutgers University, a former editor of *The Quarterly Review of Doublespeak,* and author of *The New Doublespeak: Why No One Knows What Anyone's Saying Anymore* (1966).

CYNTHIA MCKINNEY, US House of Representatives from 1993 to 2003, and from 2005 to 2007, representing Georgia's 4th Congressional District, 2008 Green Party candidate for President of the United States.

MARK CRISPIN MILLER is Professor of Media Ecology at New York University and director of the Project on Media Ownership.

BRIAN MURPHY is an associate professor of Communications Studies at Niagara University, specializing in Media Programming and Management, Investigation and Reporting, Media History and Theory and International Communication.

JACK L. NELSON,* is professor emeritus at the Graduate School of Education at Rutgers University. He is the author of sixteen books, including *Critical Issues in Education* (1996), and more than 150 articles.

NANCY SNOW is a professor at the College of Communications, California State University-Fullerton; Senior Fellow at the USC Center on Public Diplomacy; adjunct professor at University of Southern California, Annenberg School for Communication; author of *Propaganda, Inc.* (Seven Stories, 2002), *Information War* (Seven Stories, 2004), and co-editor with Yahya R. Kamalipour of *War, Media and Propaganda* (Rowman & Littlefield, 2004).

SHEILA RABB WEIDENFELD* is president of D.C. Productions, Ltd. and former press secretary to Betty Ford.

*Indicates having been a Project Censored judge since our founding in 1976

PROJECT CENSORED EDITORIAL BOARD

Carolyn Epple, Charlene Tung, Dorothy Freidel, Francisco Vazquez, Greta Vollmer, Jeanette Koshar, Mary Gomes, Michael Ezra, Myrna Goodman, Patricia Kim-Rajal, Philip Beard, Rashmi Singh, Rick Luttmann, Ronald Lopez, Stephanie Dyer, Thom Lough, Tim Wandling, Tony White, Gary Evans, Andrew Roth, Ben Frymer, Wingham Liddell, April Hurley and Karilee Shames

PROJECT CENSORED 2007–08 FACULTY, STAFF, AND COMMUNITY EVALUATORS

Bob Alpern, Community Expert on Peace and Social Justice
Melinda Barnard, PhD Communications

Philip Beard, PhD Modern Languages
Jim Berkland, PhD Geology
Stephen Bittner, PhD History
Barbara Bloom, PhD Criminal Justice Admin
Andrew Botterell, PhD Philosophy
Maureen Buckley, PhD Counseling
Elizabeth Burch, PhD Communications
Ken Burrows, PhD Journalism, SFSU
Noel Byrne, PhD Sociology
James R. Carr, PhD Geology
Yvonne Clarke, MA, University Affairs
Liz Close, PhD Nursing (Chair)
G. Dennis Cooke, PhD Zoology
Bill Crowley, PhD Geography
Victor Daniels, PhD Psychology
Laurie Dawson, PhD Labor Education
James Dean, PhD Sociology
Randall Dodgen, PhD History
Stephanie Dyer, PhD Cultural History
Carolyn Epple, PhD Anthropology
Gary Evans, MD
Michael Ezra, PhD Chemistry
Tamara Falicov, M.A. Communication Studies
Fred Fletcher, Community expert Labor
Dorothy (Dolly) Friedel, PhD Geography
Ben Frymer, PhD Sociology/Liberal Studies
Nick Geist, PhD Biology
Patricia Leigh Gibbs, PhD Sociology
Robert Girling, PhD Business Econ
Mary Gomes, PhD Psychology
Myrna Goodman, PhD Sociology
Scott Gordon, PhD Computer Science
Keith Gouveia, J.D. Political Science
Karen Grady, PhD Education
Diana Grant, PhD Criminal Justice. Admin
Bill Griggs, PhD Sociology, Eastern Oregon University
Velma Guillory-Taylor, Ed.D. American Multicultural Studies
Chad Harris, M.A. Communication Studies
Laurel Holmstrom, Academic Programs; MA (English)

Jeffrey Holtzman, PhD Environmental Sciences
Mickey Huff, MA, History/Media Studies, Diablo Valley College
Kevin Howdy, PhD Communications, DePauw University
Pat Jackson, PhD Criminal Justice Admin.
Tom Jacobson JD, Environmental Studies & Planning
Sherril Jaffe, PhD English
Paul Jess, Community Expert Environmental Law
Cheri Ketchum, PhD Communications
Amy Kittelstrom, PhD History
Patricia Kim-Rajal, PhD American Culture
Mary King MD Health
Paul Kingsley, MD
Jeanette Koshar, Nursing
John Kramer, PhD Political Science
Heidi LaMoreaux, PhD Liberal Studies
Virginia Lea, PhD Education
Benet Leigh, M.A. Communications Studies
Wingham Liddell, PhD Business. Administration
Jennifer Lillig Whiles, PhD Chemistry
Ron Lopez, PhD Latino Studies
Thom Lough, PhD Sociology
John Lund, Business & Political Issues,
Rick Luttmann, PhD Math
Robert Manning, Peace Issues
Regina Marchi, M.A. Communication Studies
Ken Marcus, PhD Criminal Justice Admin.
Perry Marker, PhD Education
Elizabeth Martinez, PhD Modern Languages
David McCuan, PhD Political Science
Eric McGuckin, PhD Liberal Studies
Robert McNamara, PhD Political Science
Josh Meisel, PhD Criminal Justice
Andy Merrifield, PhD Political Science
Jack Munsee, PhD Political Science
Ann Neel, PhD Sociology
Catherine Nelson, PhD Political Science
Leilani Nishime, PhD Ethnic Studies Department
Linda Nowak, PhD Business
Tim Ogburn, International Business

Tom Ormond, PhD Kinesiology
Wendy Ostroff, PhD Liberal Studies
Ervand M. Peterson, PhD Environmental Sciences
Jorge E. Porras, PhD Modern Languages
Robert Proctor, PhD Politcal Science
Jeffrey T. Reeder, PhD Modern Languages
Rick Robison, PhD Library
R. Thomas Rosin, PhD Anthropology
Richard Senghas, PhD Anthropology/Linguistics
Rashmi Singh, PhD American Multicultural Studies
Cindy Stearns, PhD Sociology
Greg Storino, American Airlines Pilot
Meri Storino, PhD Counseling
Elaine Sundberg, M.A. Academic Programs
Scott Suneson, M.A. Sociology/Political Science
Jessica Taft, PhD Sociology
Laxmi G. Tewari, PhD Music
Karen Thompson, PhD Business
Suzanne Toczyski, PhD Modern Languages
Carol Tremmel, M.A. Extended Education
Charlene Tung, PhD Women's Gender Studies
David Van Nuys, PhD Psychology
Francisco H. Vazquez, PhD Liberal Studies
Greta Vollmer, PhD English
Alexandra (Sascha) Von Meier, PhD Environmental Sciences
Albert Wahrhaftig, PhD Anthropology
Tim Wandling, PhD English
Tony White, PhD History
John Wingard, PhD Anthropology
Craig Winston, J.D. Criminal Justice
Richard Zimmer, PhD Liberal Studies

SONOMA STATE UNIVERSITY SUPPORTING STAFF AND OFFICES

Ruben Arminaña, President, Sonoma State University and staff
Eduardo Ochoa: Chief Academic Officer and staff
Carol Blackshire-Belay: Vice Provost Academic Affairs
Elaine Leeder: Dean of School of Sciences and staff
Erica Wilcher: Administrative Manager

Katie McCormick: Operations Analyst
Holly Sautner: Dean's Assistant
William Babula: Dean of School of Arts and Humanities
Barbara Butler and the SSU Library Staff
Paula Hammett: Social Sciences Library Resources
Jonah Raskin and Faculty in Communications Studies
Susan Kashack, Jean Wasp and staff in SSU Public Relations Office

About the Editors

Peter Phillips is a Professor Sociology at Sonoma State University and Director of Project Censored. He teaches classes in Media Censorship, Investigative Sociology, Sociology of Power, Political Sociology, and Sociology of Media. He has published eleven editions of Censored: Media Democracy in Acton from Seven Stories Press. Also from Seven Stories Press is Impeach the President: The Case Against Bush and Cheney (2006) and Project Censored Guide to Independent Media and Activism (2003).

Phillips writes op-ed pieces for independent media nationwide having published in dozens of publications newspapers and websites including: Z magazine, Free Inquiry, Counterpunch, Common Dreams, Buzzflash, Dissident Voice, Social Policy, and Briarpatch. He frequently speaks on media censorship and various socio-political issues on radio and TV talks shows including Talk of the Nation, Air America, Talk America, World Radio Network, Flashpoints, and the Jim Hightower Show.

Phillips has completed several investigative sociology research studies that are available at Projectcensored.org including: The Global Dominance Group: 9/11 Pre-Warnings & Election Irregularities in Context, A Study of Bias in the Associated Press, Practices in Health Care and Disability insurance: Deny Delay Diminish and Blame, US Electromagnetic Weapons and Human Rights, and The Left Progressive Media Inside the Propaganda Model.

Phillips earned a B.A. degree in Social Science in 1970 from Santa Clara University, and an M.A. degree in Social Science from California State University at Sacramento in 1974. He earned a second M.A. in Sociology in 1991 and a Ph.D. in Sociology in 1994. His doctoral dissertation was entitled A Relative Advantage: Sociology of the San Francisco Bohemian Club (http://libweb.sonoma.edu/regional/faculty/Phillips/bohemianindex.htm).

Phillips is a fifth generation Californian, who grew up on a family-owned farm west of the Central Valley town of Lodi. Phillips lives today in rural Sonoma County with his wife Mary Lia.

Andrew Roth, Associate Director of Project Censored, studied Sociology and Anthropology at Haverford College. He earned his M.A. (1992) and Ph.D. (1998) in Sociology at UCLA. His dissertation, "Who Makes the News: Social Identity and the Explanation of Action in the Broadcast News Interview" compared interviewing techniques in the UK and US.

Roth has published research articles on communities organizing for urban parklands (in the journal City and Community), journalists' questioning of electoral candidates (Harvard International Journal of Press/Politics), public commentary on federal tobacco control legislation (Social Studies of Science), and social interaction in broadcast news interviews (Language in Society and Media, Culture & Society).

Roth is a third generation Californian who grew up in Claremont, where his mother and father both served as teachers. He now lives in Tucson, Arizona.

How to Support Project Censored

To nominate a *Censored* story send us a copy of the article and include the name of the source publication, the date that the article appeared, and page number. For internet published news stories of which we should be aware please forward the URL to Censored@sonoma.edu. The final deadline period for nominating a Most Censored Stories of the year is March of each year.

Criteria for project censored news stories nominations

1. A censored news story is one which contains information that the general United States population has a right and need to know, but to which it has had limited access.

2. The news story is timely, on-going, and has implications for a significant number of residents in the United States.

3. The story has clearly defined concepts and is backed up with solid, verifiable documentation.

4. The news story has been publicly published, either electronically or in print, in a circulated newspaper, journal, magazine, newsletter, or similar publication from either a foreign or domestic source.

5. The news story has direct connections to and implications for people in the United States, which can include activities that U.S. citizens are engaged in abroad.

SUPPORT PROJECT CENSORED BY MAKING A
FINANCIAL GIFT

Project Censored is supported by Media Freedom Foundation 501-C-3 non-profit organization. We depend on tax-deductible donations and foundation grants to continue our work. To support our efforts for freedom of information send checks to the address below or call 707-664-2500. Visa and Mastercard accepted. Donations can be made through our website at: www.projectcensored.org.

Media Freedom Foundation
P.O. Box 571
Cotati, CA 94931
e-mail: censored@sonoma.edu

Index

Traumatic Brain Injury, 306
Trillanes, Antonio, IV, 276
truth-based news service, 286–87
truth emergency, 283
  action steps in, 286–87
  corporate news media needing, 281–82
  media consolidation and, 285–86
  media democracy activists questions from,
    293–95
  Santa Cruz conference of, 283
  survey questions in, 288–90
Truth Emergency Movement, 282, 291–92
Tsai, Michelle, 259
Tunisia, 278
Turett, Nancy, 244
Turilli, Thomas, 352
Turkey, 278
Turner, John Michael, 312
Turner, Molly, 250
"twenty-first century slavery," 51
Twin Towers, 49
2000 election, 125–26
2008 presidential candidates, 209–11
2006 election
  Global War on Terrorism and, 197–99
  habeas corpus mentions and, 198t
  MCA position in, 198t
  MCA/quotations opposing in, 199

UCMJ. See Uniform Code of Military Justice
Ulmer, Richard, 96
undervotes, 128
UNFCCC. See United Nations Framework
    Convention on Climate Change
Uniform Code of Military Justice (UCMJ), 328
United Kingdom, 278
United Nations forces, 150–51
United Nations Framework Convention on
    Climate Change (UNFCCC), 89–90
United Nations Refugee Agency, 21
United States (US), 36
  African command center of, 133
  Bailey killed in, 278
  as best entertained/least informed society,
    281–82
  Canada allowing troops of, 28–29
  contractors, 143–44
  drug trafficking in, 375
  embassy, 138–40
  energy innovations in, 180–81
  energy security and, 27
  food aid program of, 105–6
  FTAs forced by, 365–67
  grassroots movements in, 185–86
  guestworker program in, 50–52
  imperialism in, 285–86
  Latin America military strategy of, 33
  Latin America's history with, 384–85
  marijuana arrests record in, 99–100

Mexico interest of, 26
Mexico invaded by, 317
Mexico's border fence with, 118–19
Middle East operations threatened of, 38
Navy's Fourth Fleet of, 36–37
9/11 explanation of, 112
Palestine gas field profits blocked by, 120
security interpretation of, 26
Supreme Court election interference in,
    129
terrorism combatted by, 40–41
as world's nuclear waste dump, 81
United States Marshals Service (USMS), 142
Universal Declaration on the Rights of
    Indigenous Peoples, 88
UN World Food Program, 106
US. See United States
USA PATRIOT Act, 66, 356
US government
  Blackwater Inc. expense to, 144
  domestic police agencies under control of,
    140–41
  El Salvador's destruction by, 68–69
  individual liberties v., 200
US military
  breakdown/stop loss of, 302–4, 317–18,
    323
  crude racism from, 59
  detainee abuse by, 65
  gender/sexuality issues of, 315–17
  in Iraq, 185
  Iraqi home raids by, 21
  in Latin America, 371–73
  martial law and, 131–32
  recruitment history of, 322–23
  recruitment techniques of, 323–35
  soldier brutality of, 312–13
USMS. See United States Marshals Service
US Northern Command (NORTHCOM), 28
Uzbekistan, 278

Venezuela, 279, 376
Ventura, Hector Antonio, 69, 71
veteran healthcare crisis, 305–7
Vick, Michael, 171–72
Vidal, Gore, 127
video games, 332–33
video news releases (VNRs), 182, 255
Vijayan, Sabulal, 53
"Violent Islamist Extremism, the Internet,
    and the Homegrown Terrorism Threat,"
    45, 47
Violent Radicalization and Homegrown
    Terrorism Prevention Act, 17, 40,
    43–49, 157
Vioxx, 240
VNRs. See video news releases
vulture funds, 149–50